AF531078

TEN SERIES / *106* PHOTOGRAPHS

Matthew SLEETH

aperture

01

WOMEN IN UNIFORM
Tokyo, 2004

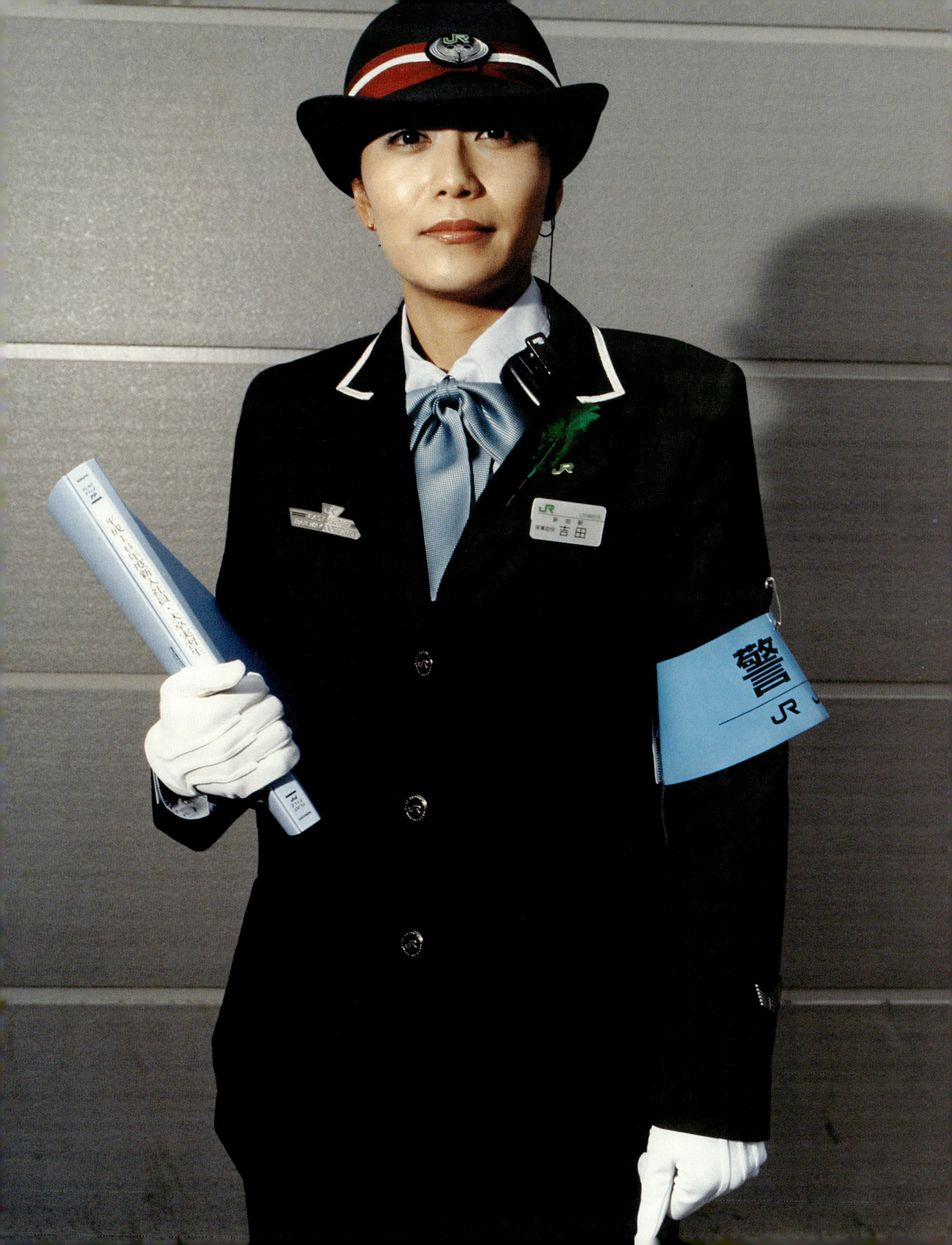
JR
吉田
警
JR

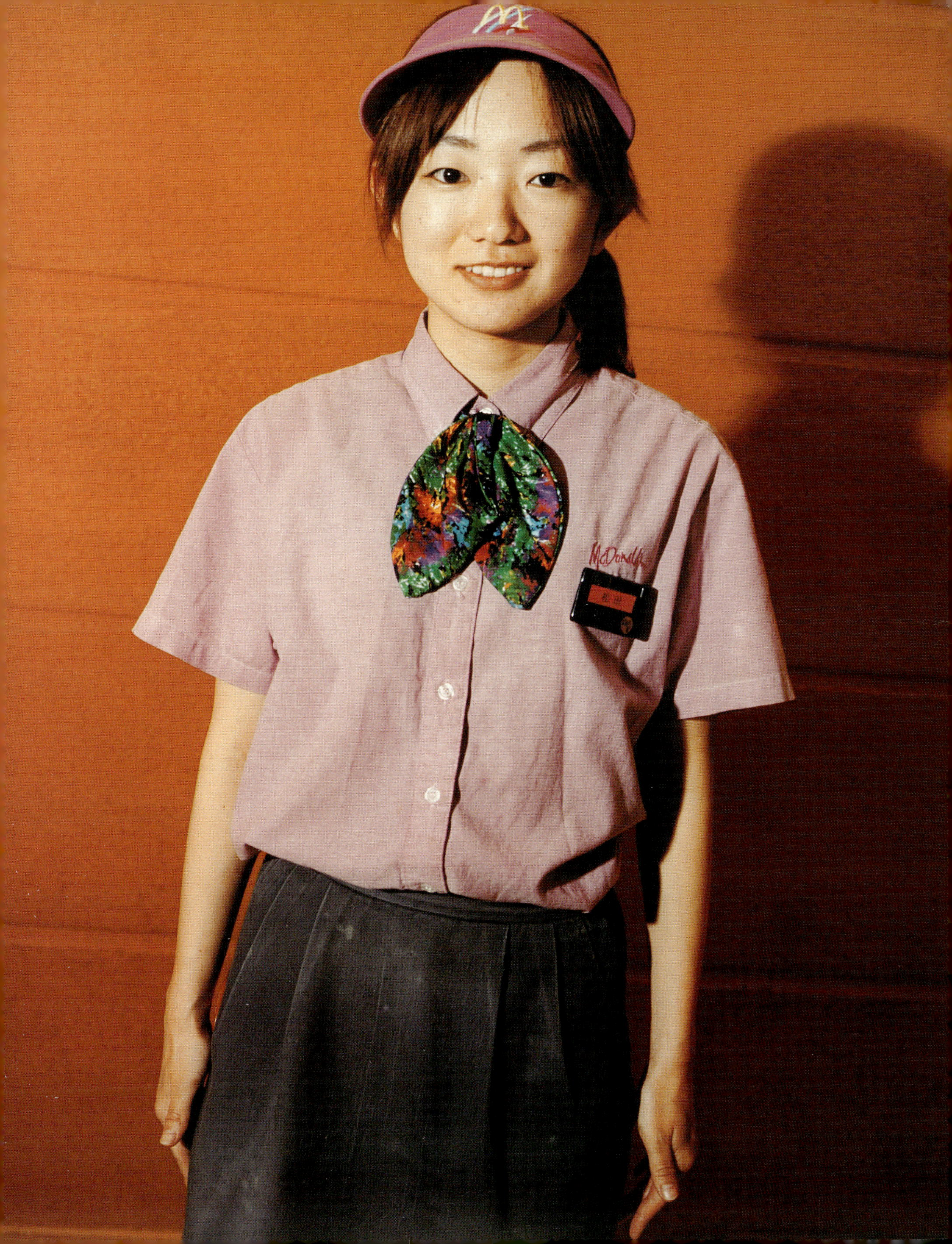

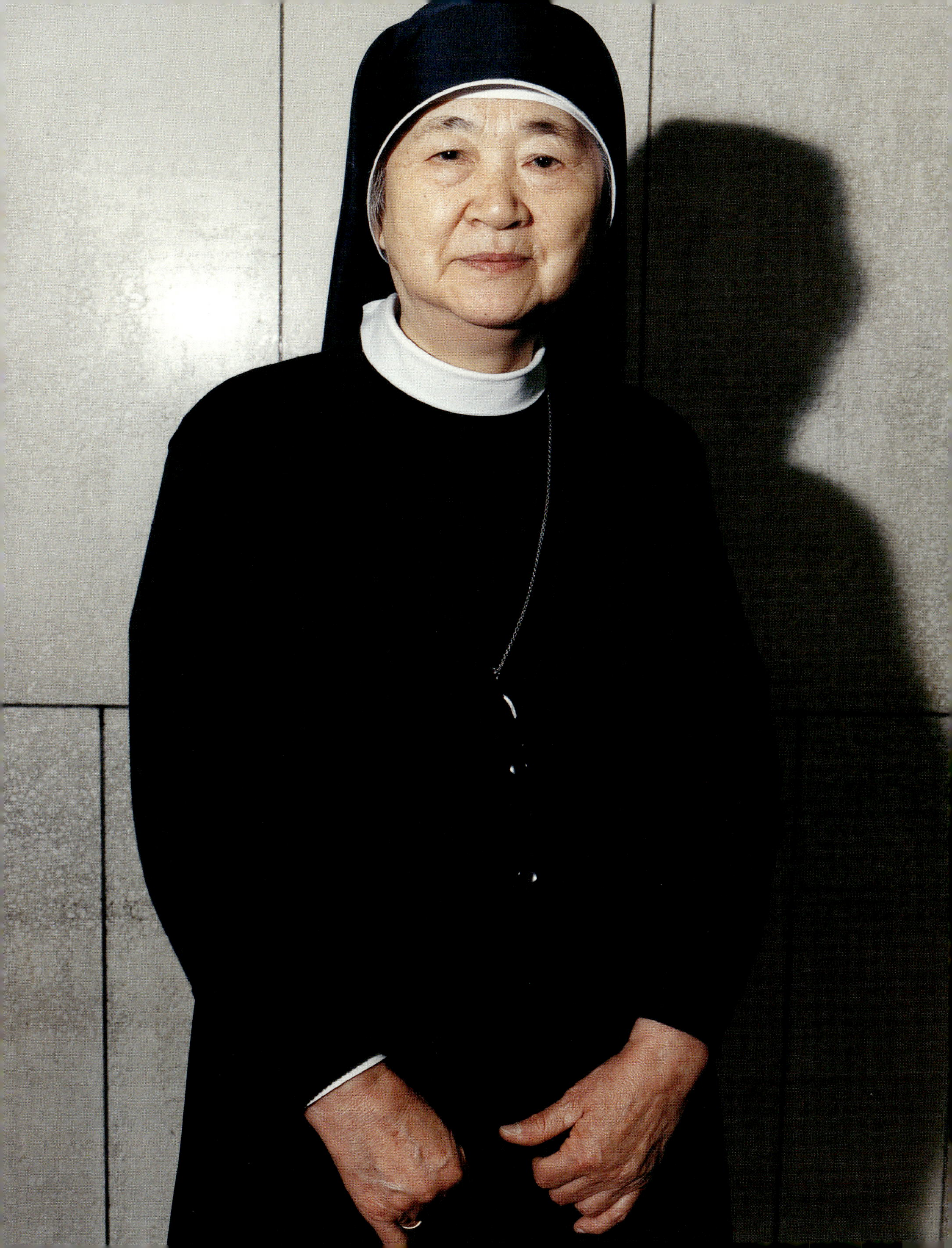

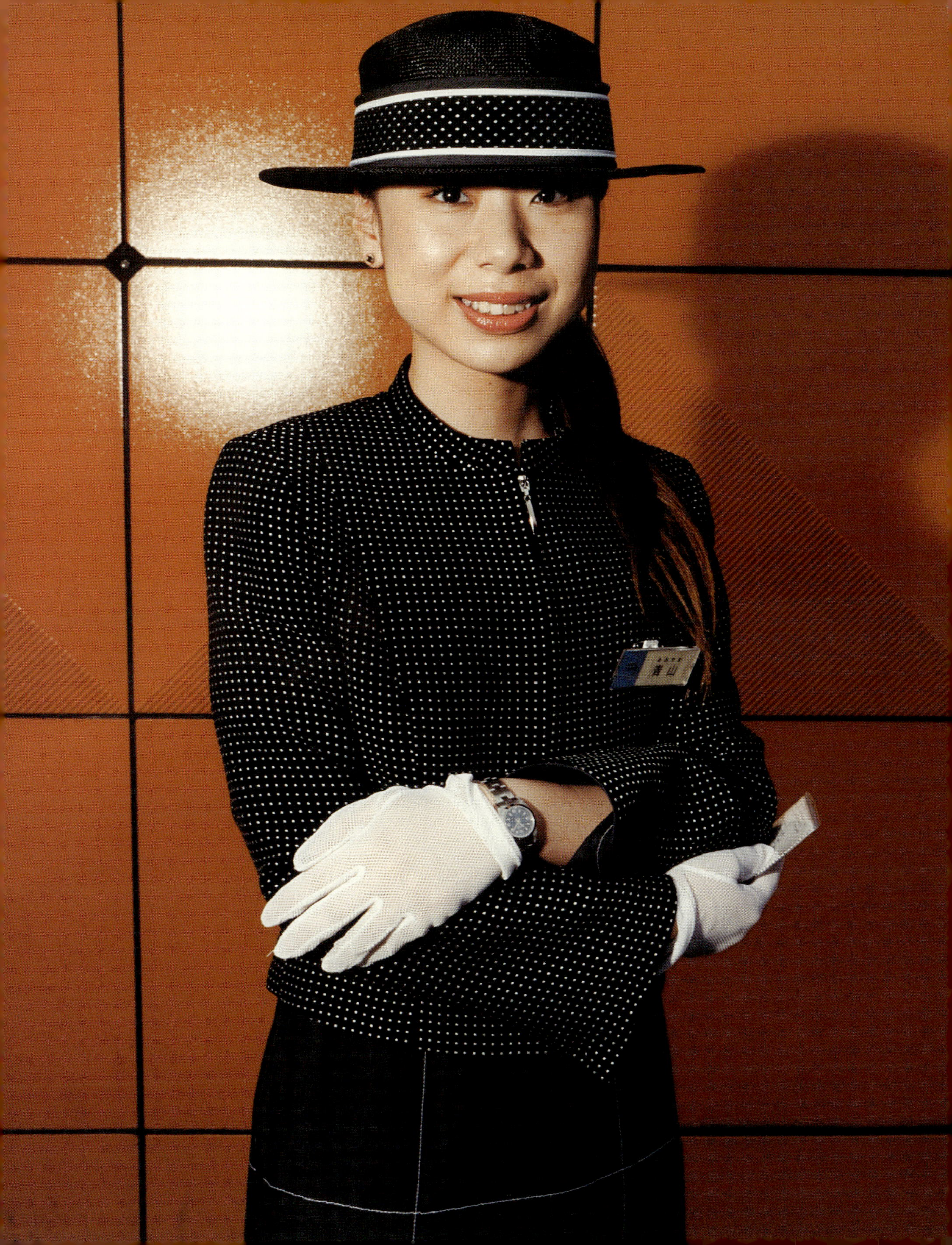
青山

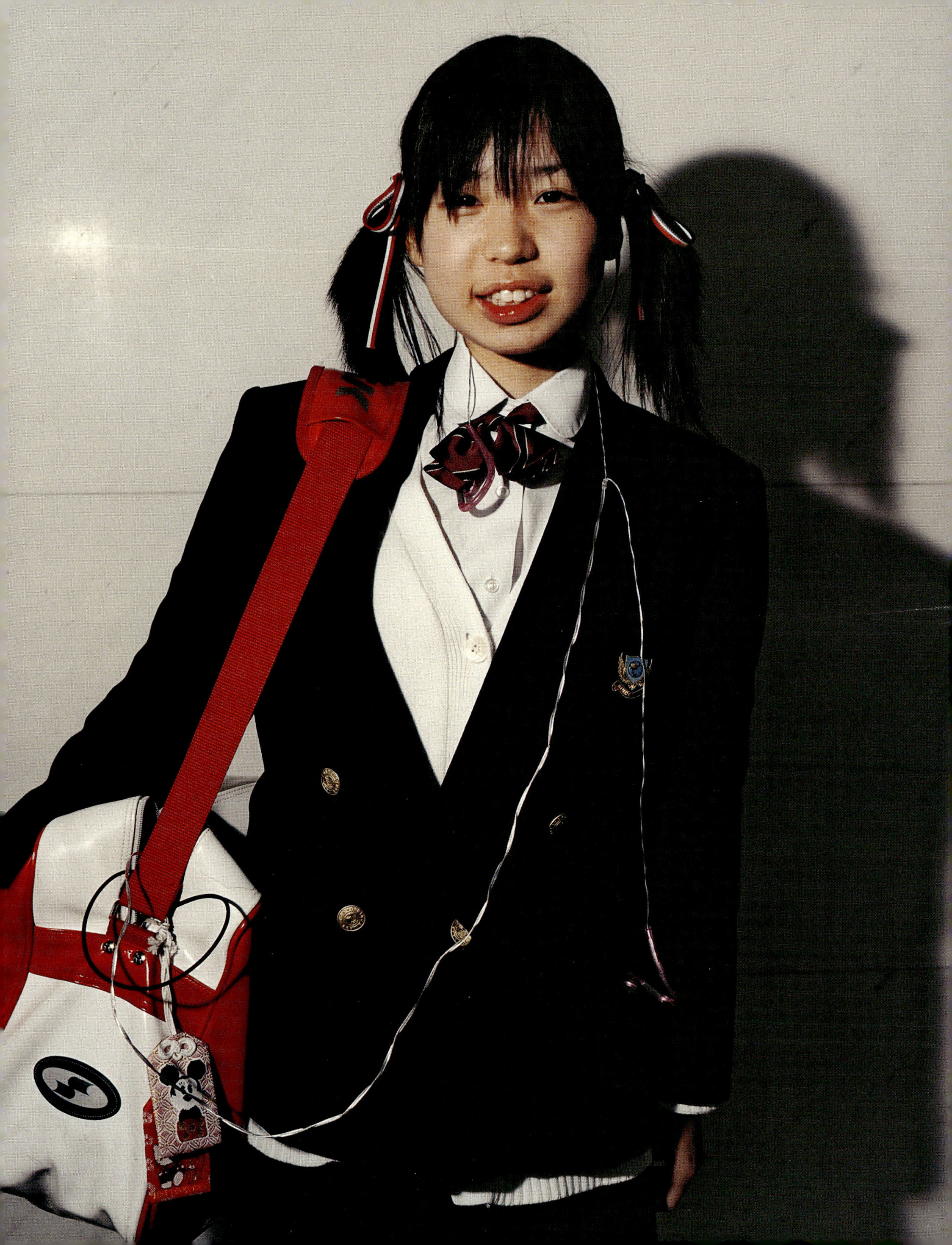

02

RED CHINA

Beijing, 2003

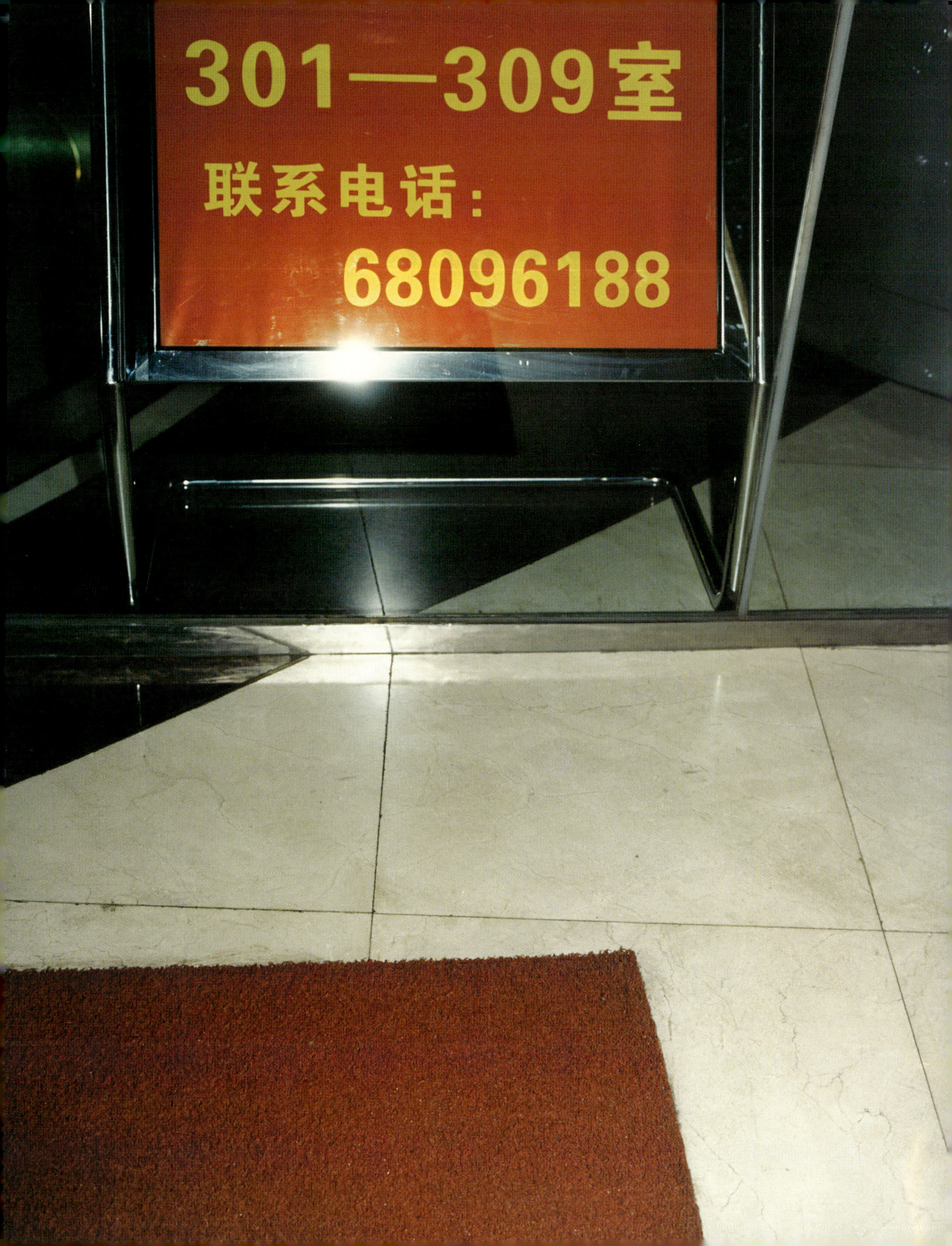
301—309室
联系电话：
68096188

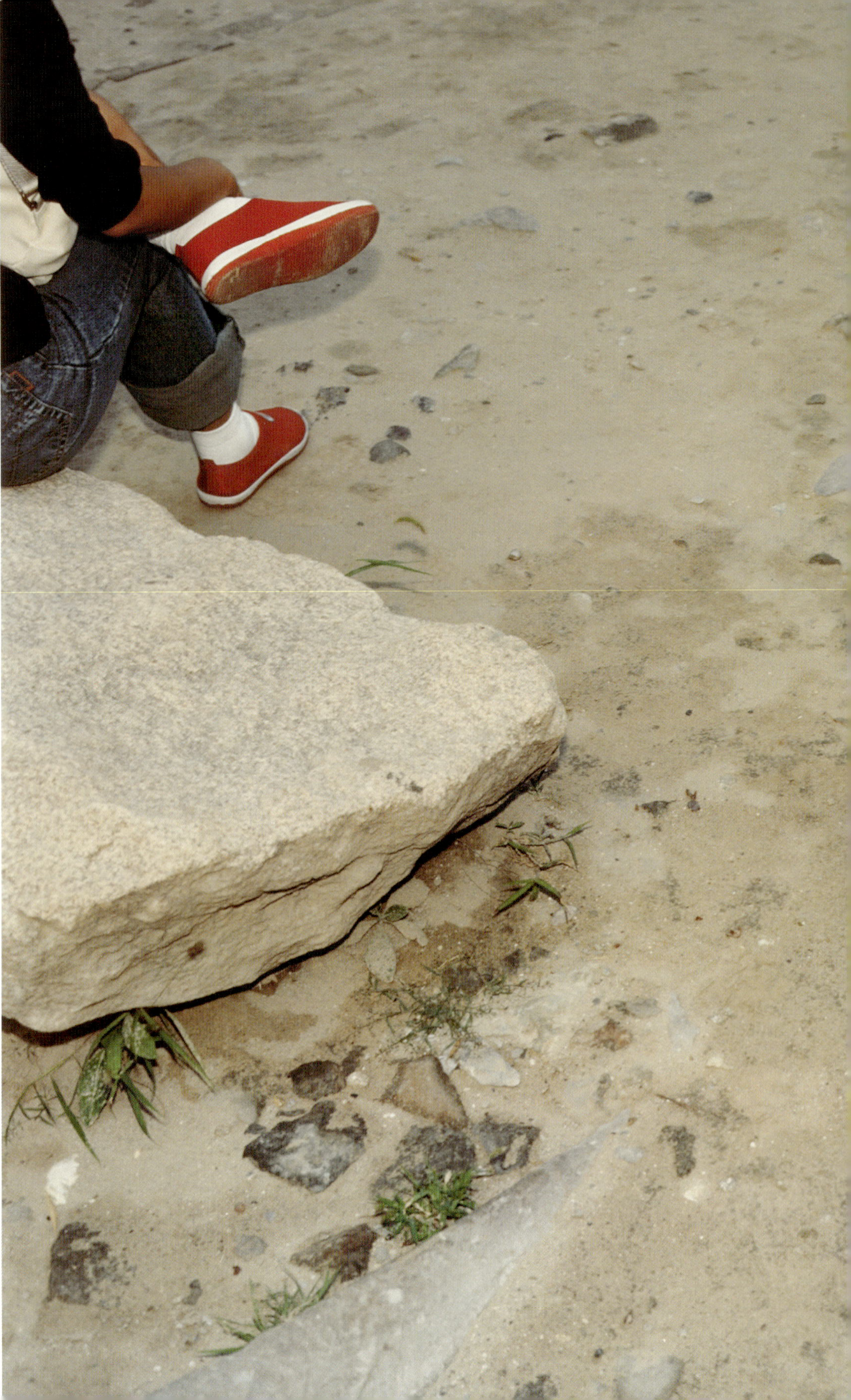

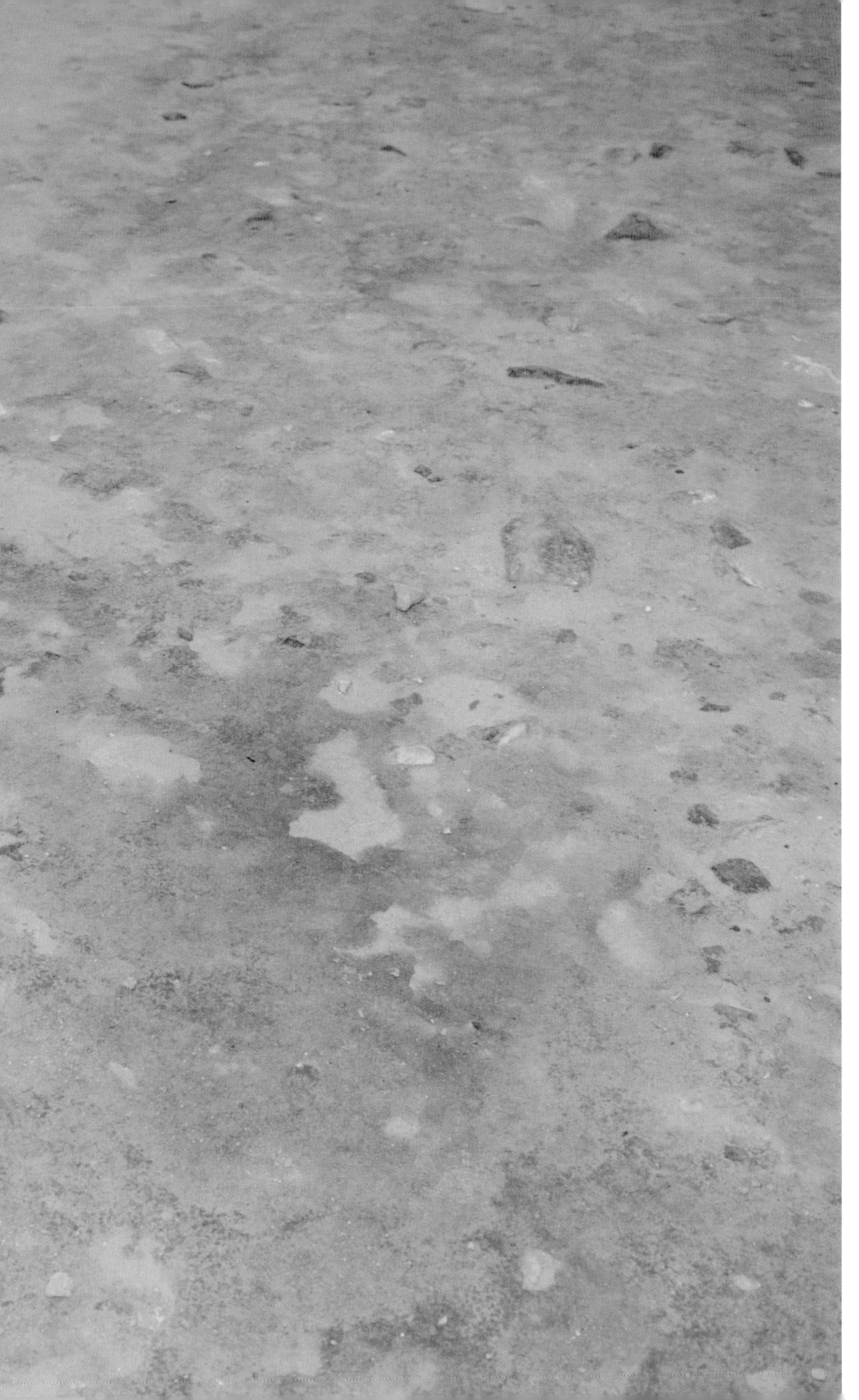

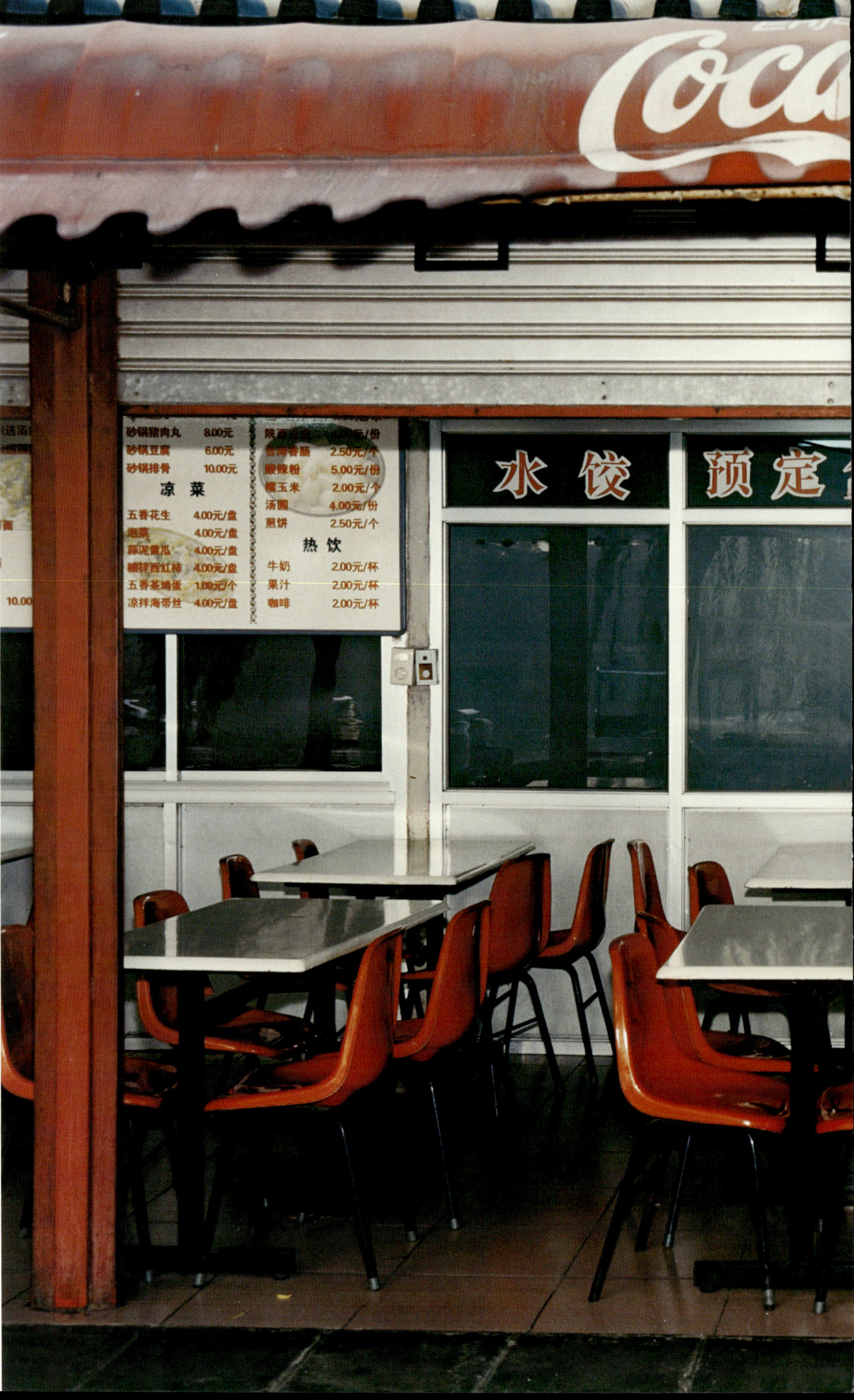

Coca
砂锅猪肉丸 8.00元
砂锅豆腐 6.00元
砂锅排骨 10.00元
凉 菜
五香花生 4.00元/盘
泡菜 4.00元/盘
蒜泥黄瓜 4.00元/盘
糖拌西红柿 4.00元/盘
五香茶鸡蛋 1.00元/个
凉拌海带丝 4.00元/盘
台湾香肠 2.50元/个
酸辣粉 5.00元/份
糯玉米 2.00元/个
汤圆 4.00元/份
煎饼 2.50元/个
热 饮
牛奶 2.00元/杯
果汁 2.00元/杯
咖啡 2.00元/杯
水饺
预定

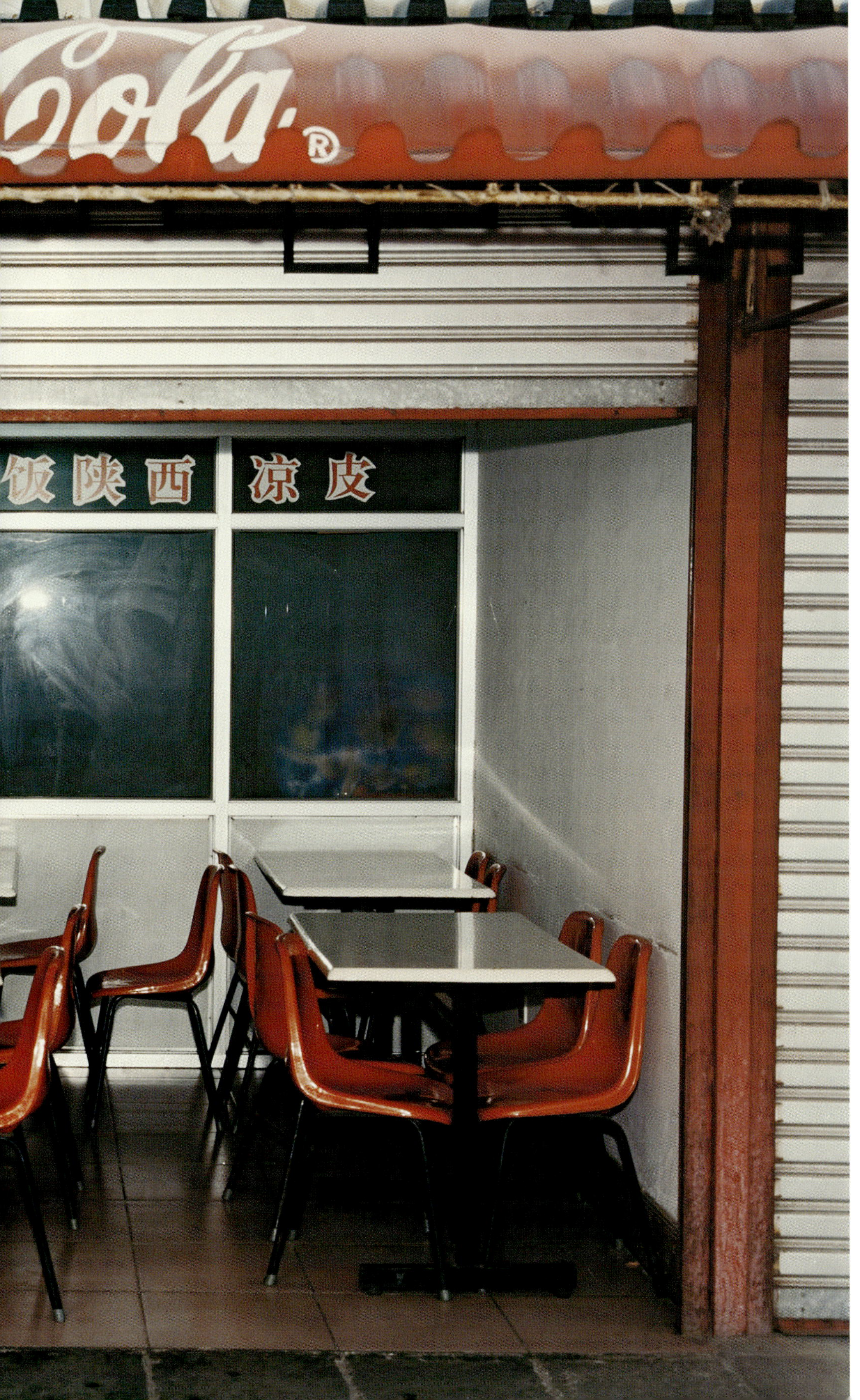
Cola®
饭陕西
凉皮

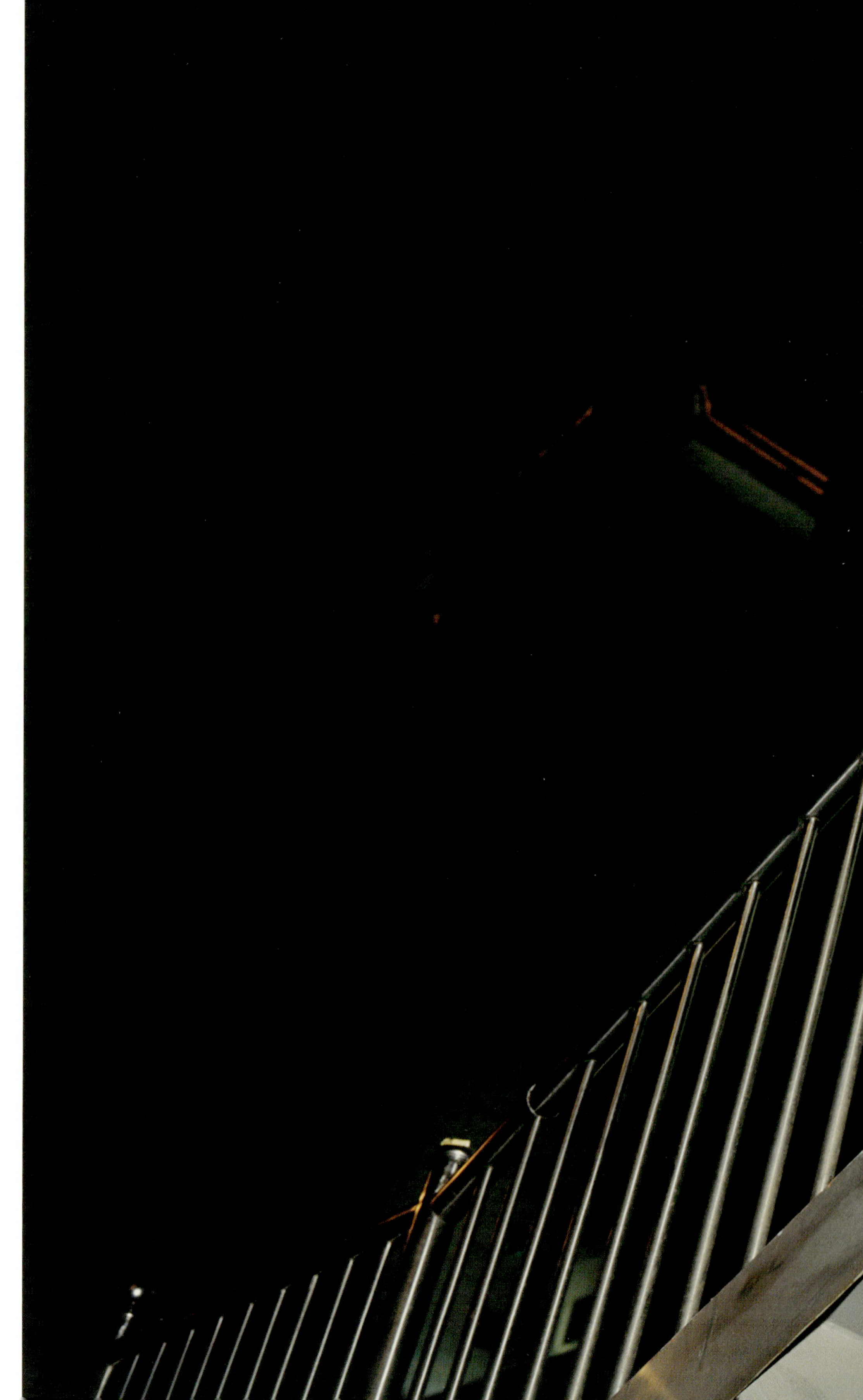

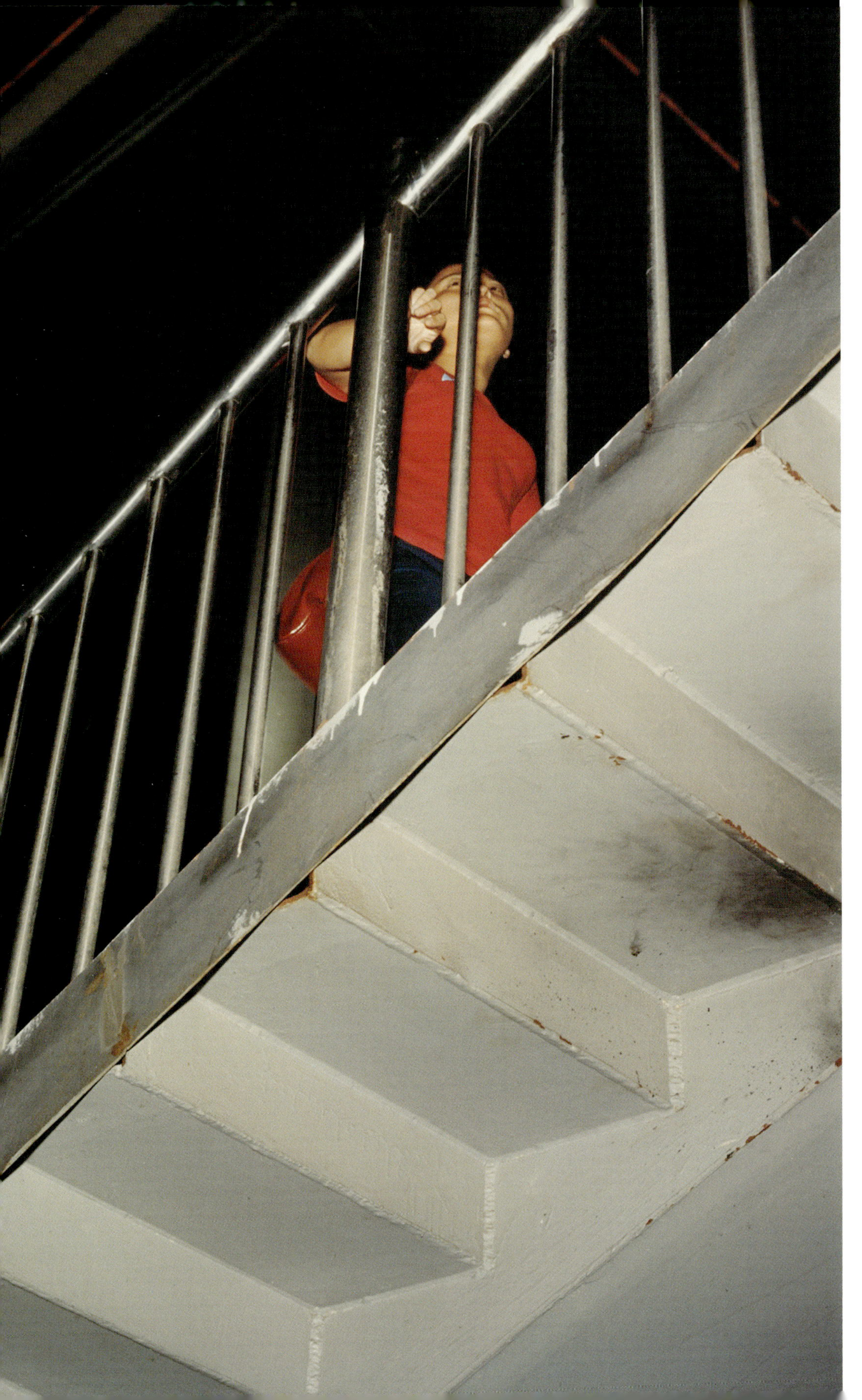

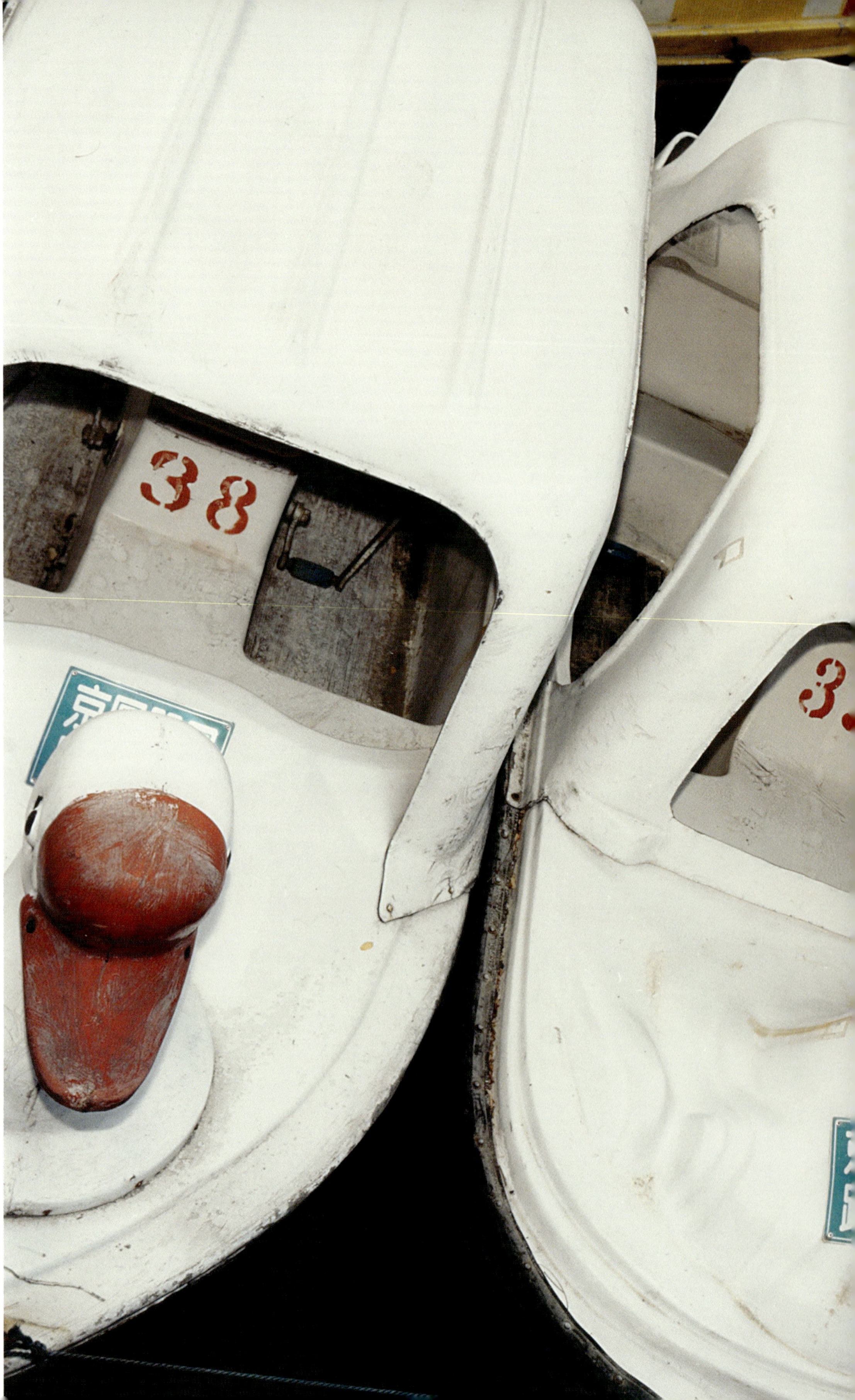
38

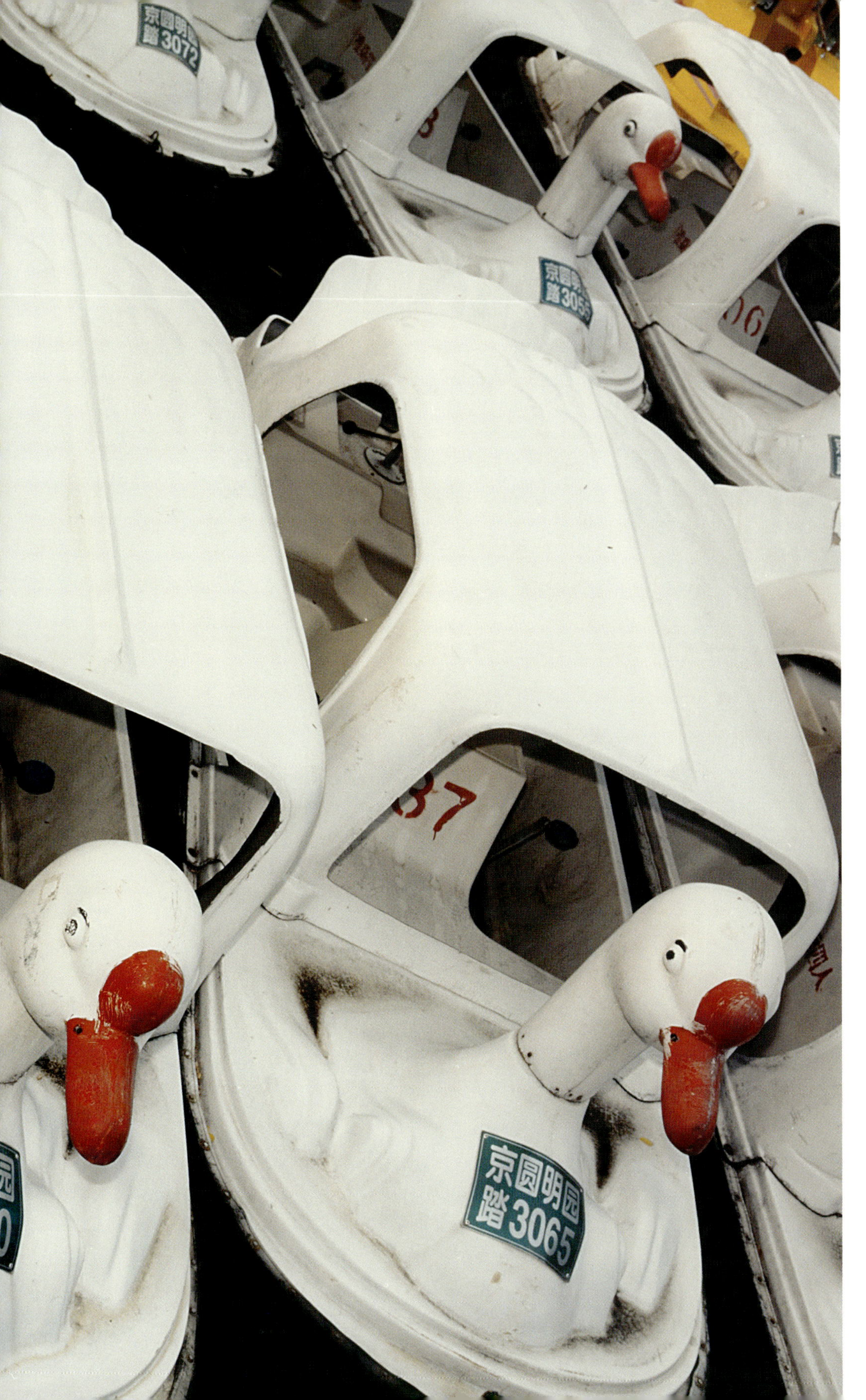
京圆明园
踏3065

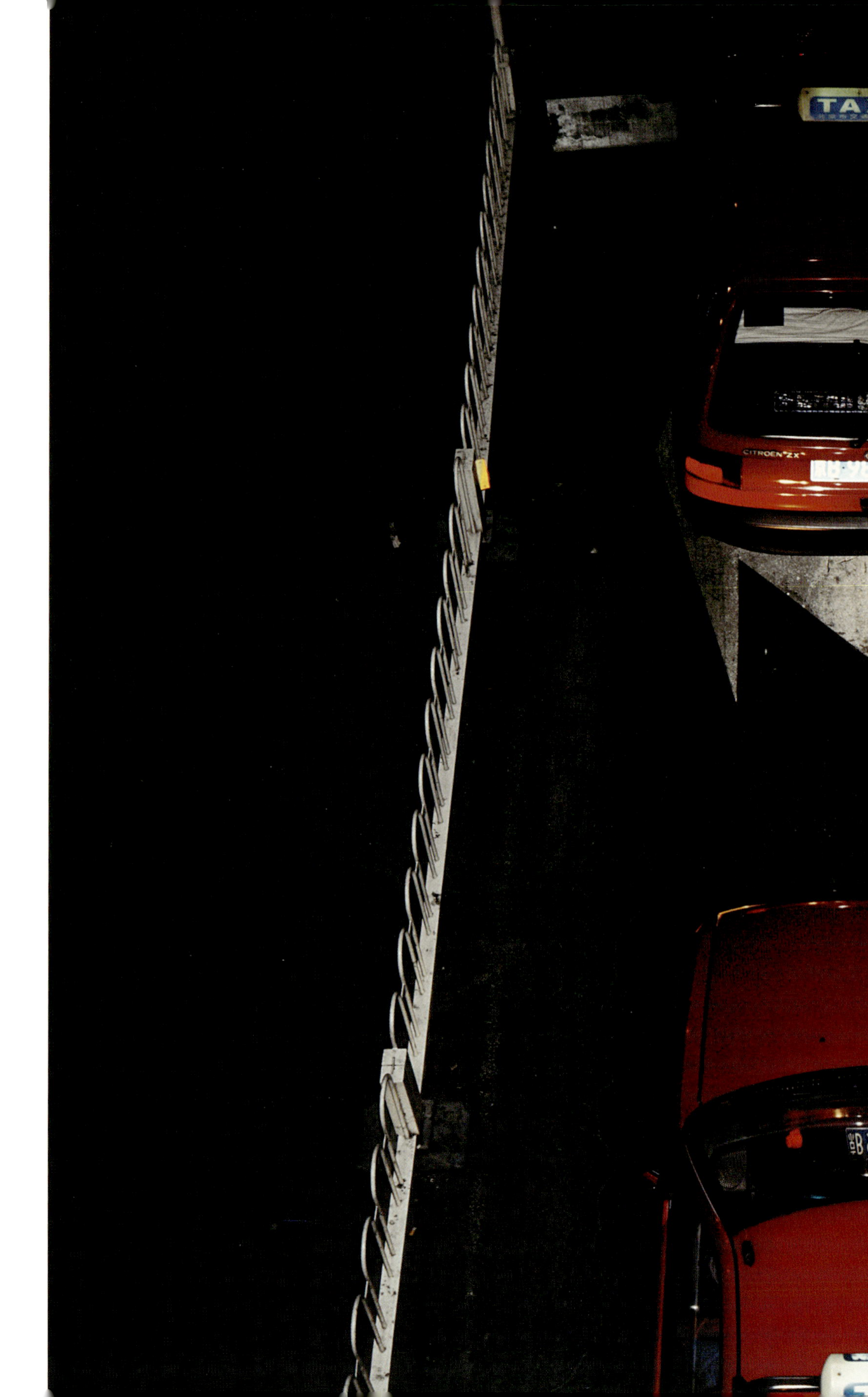
CITROEN "ZX"

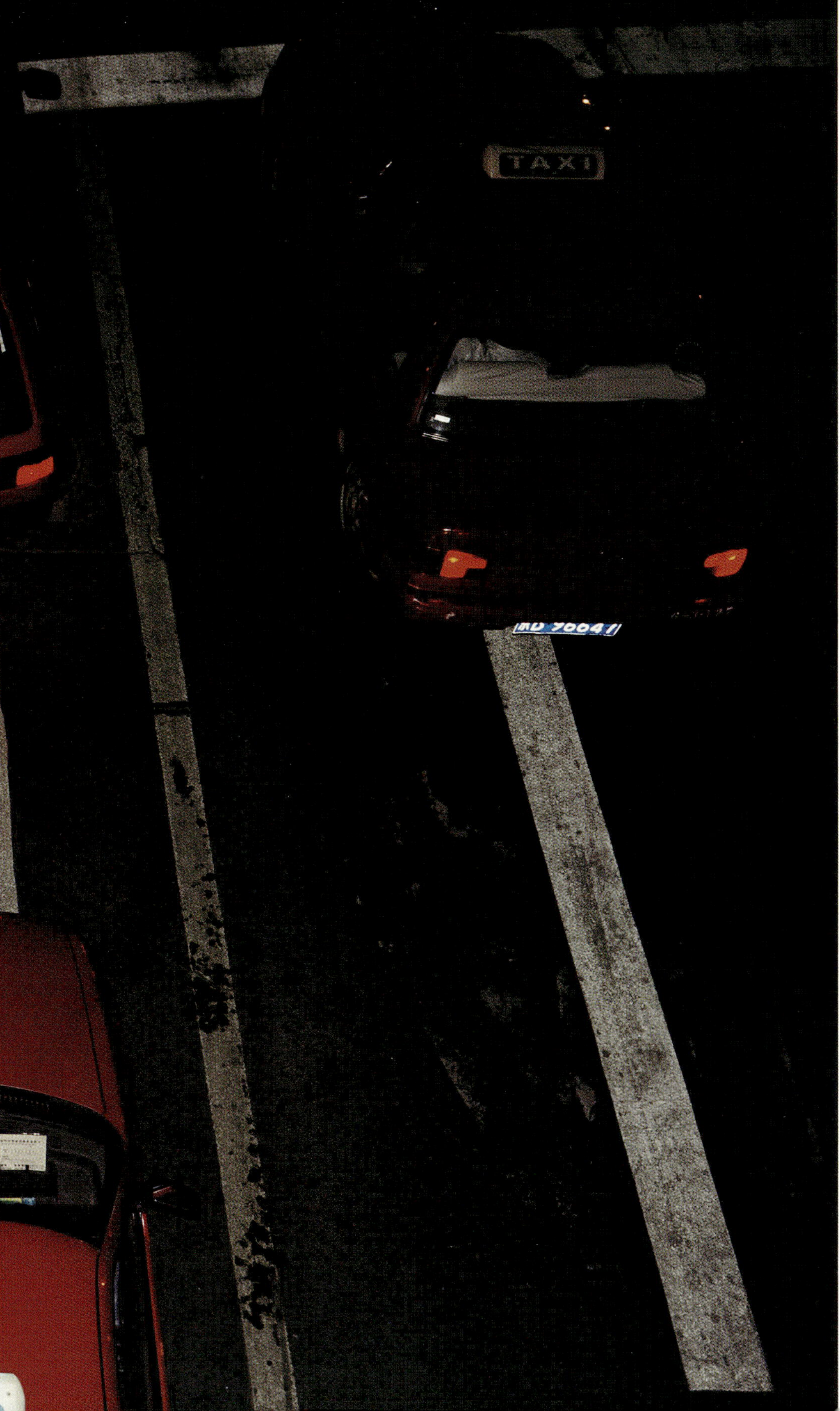
TAXI

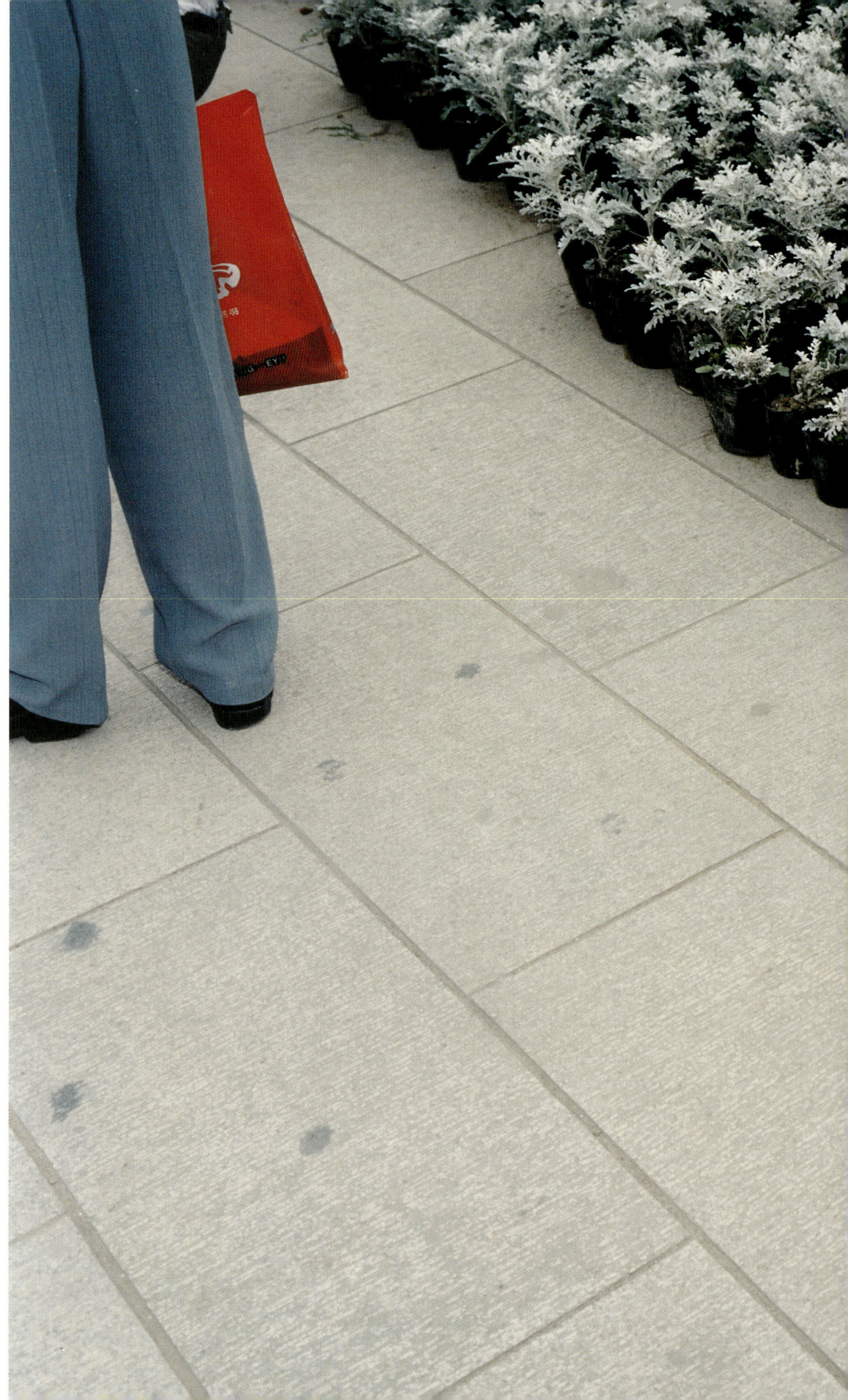

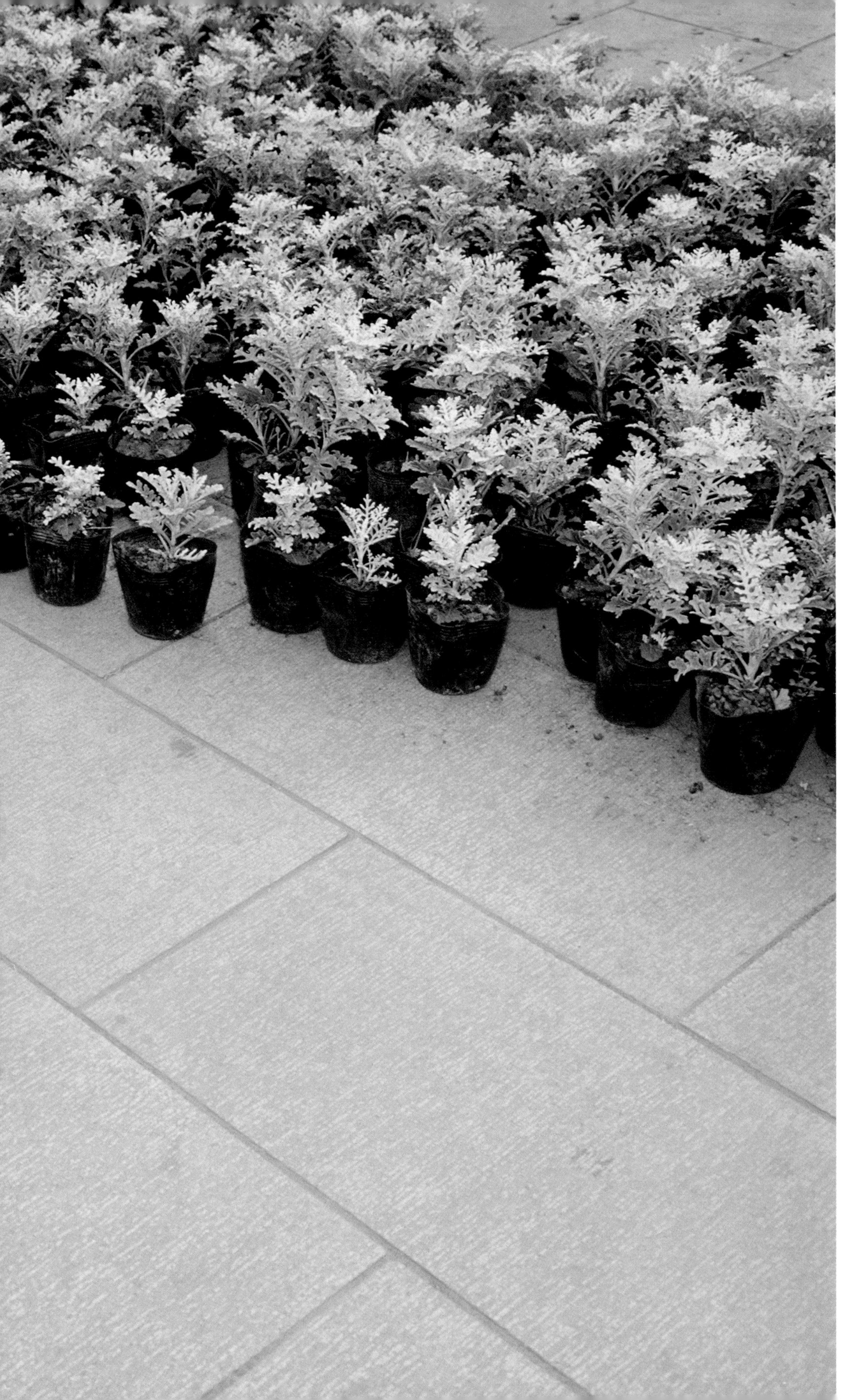

03

ABANDONED UMBRELLAS

Tokyo, 2004

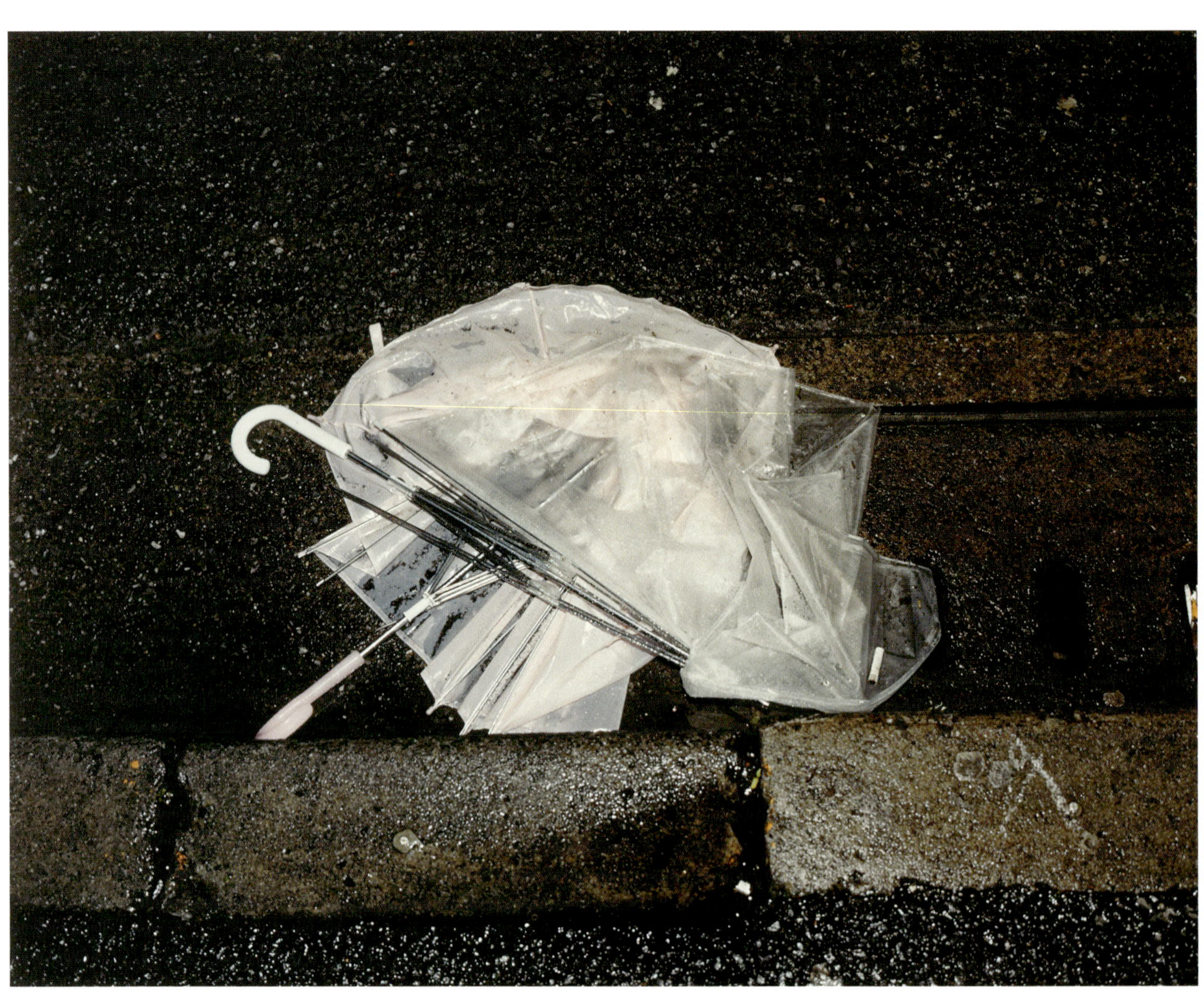

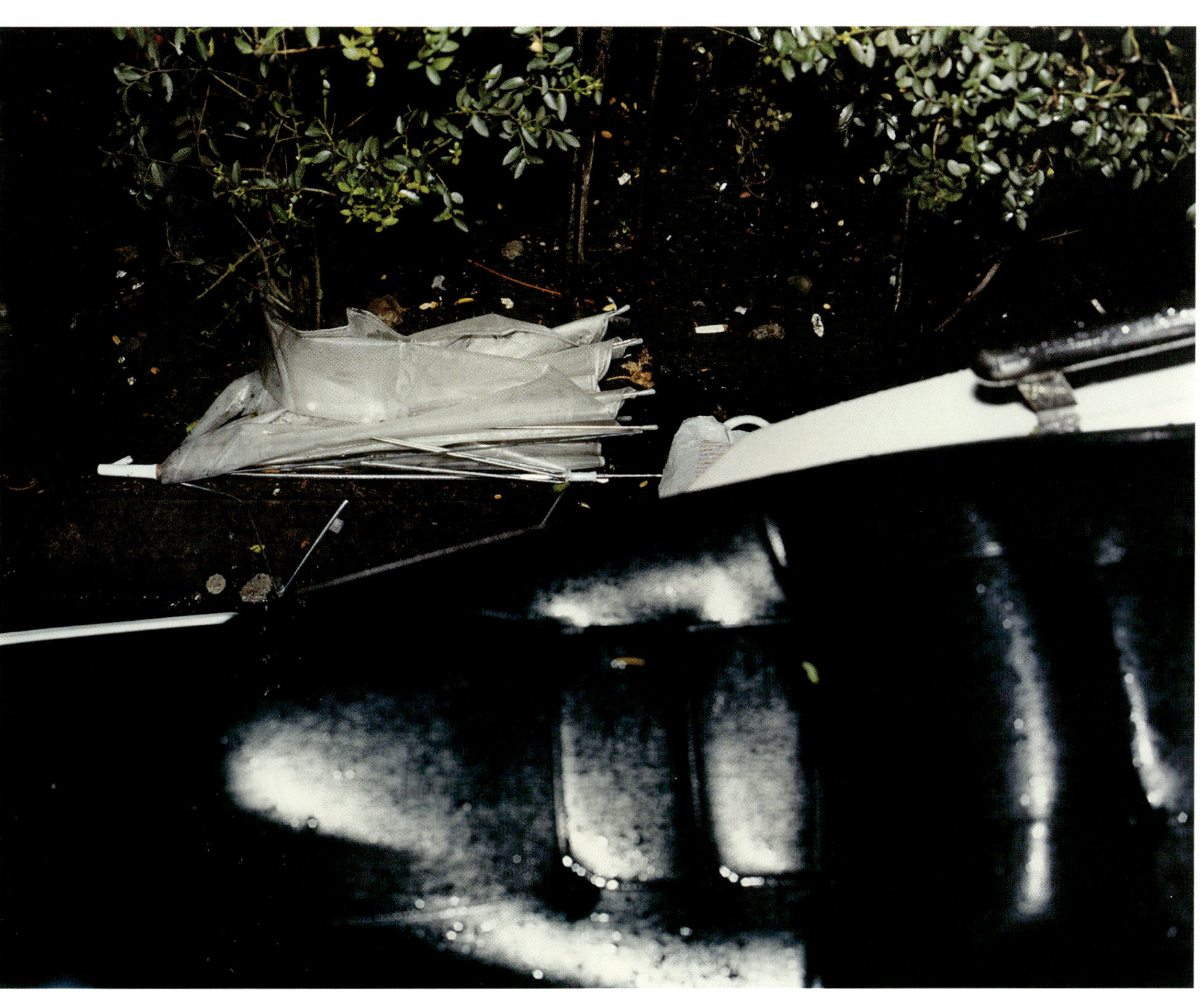

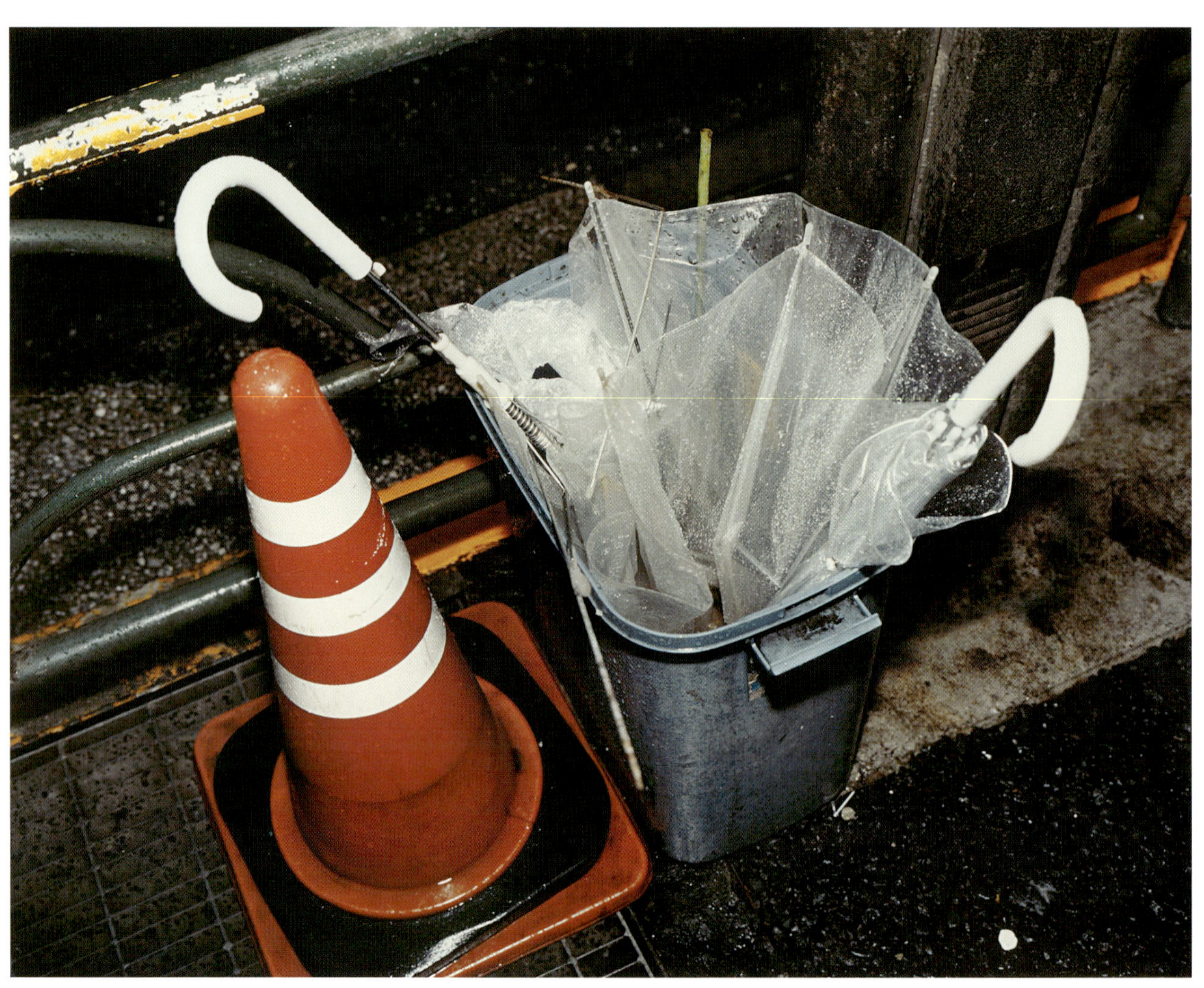

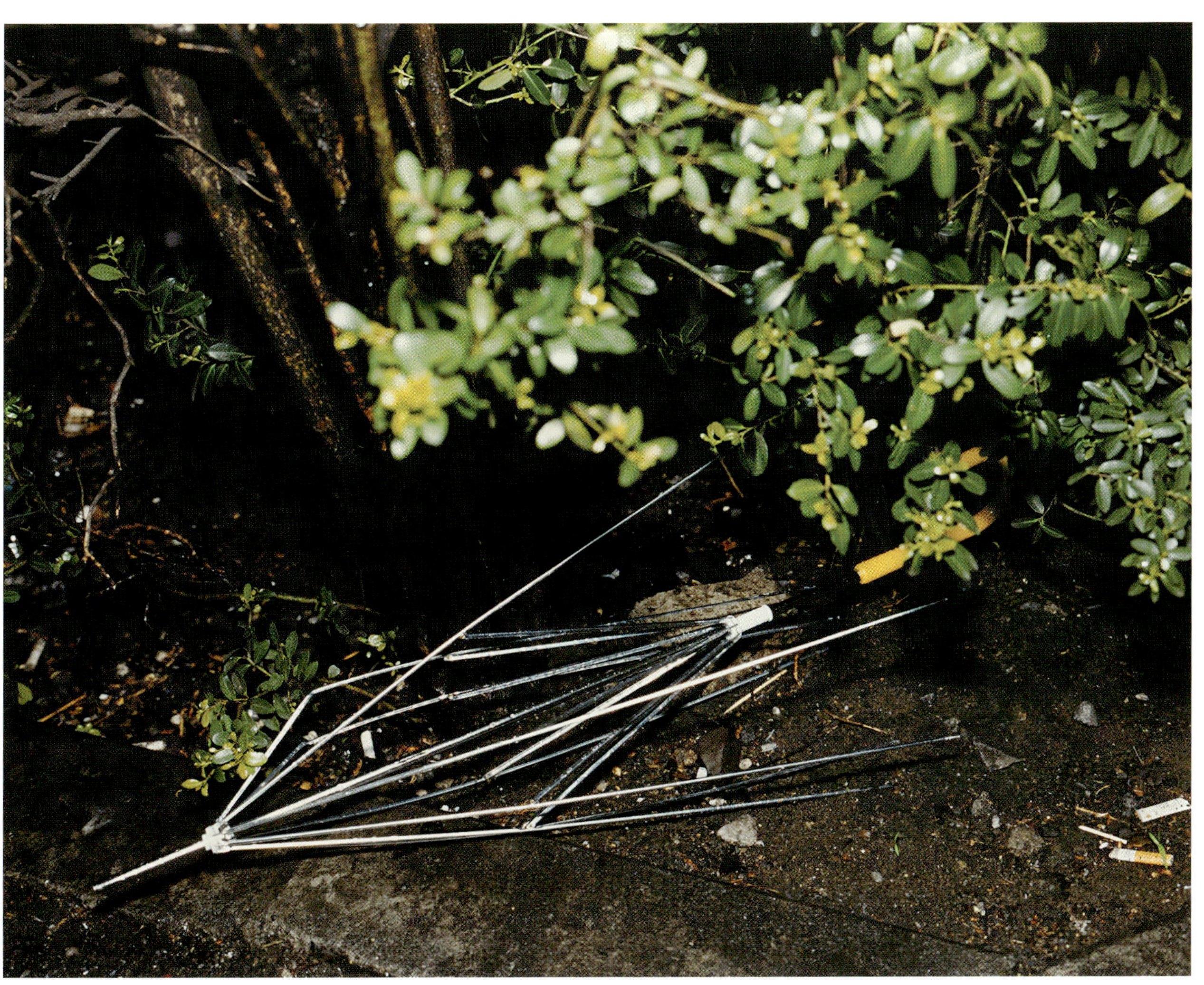

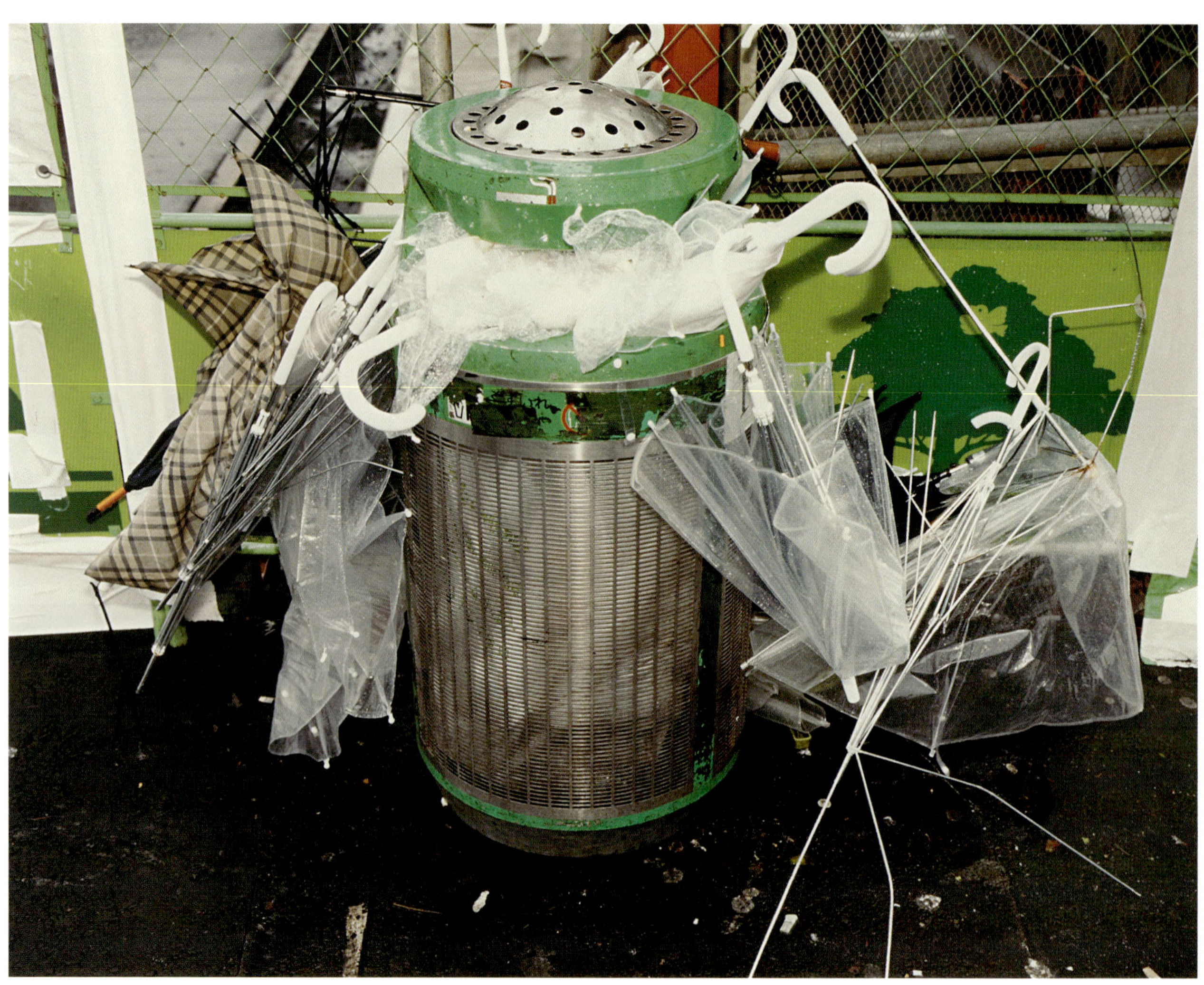

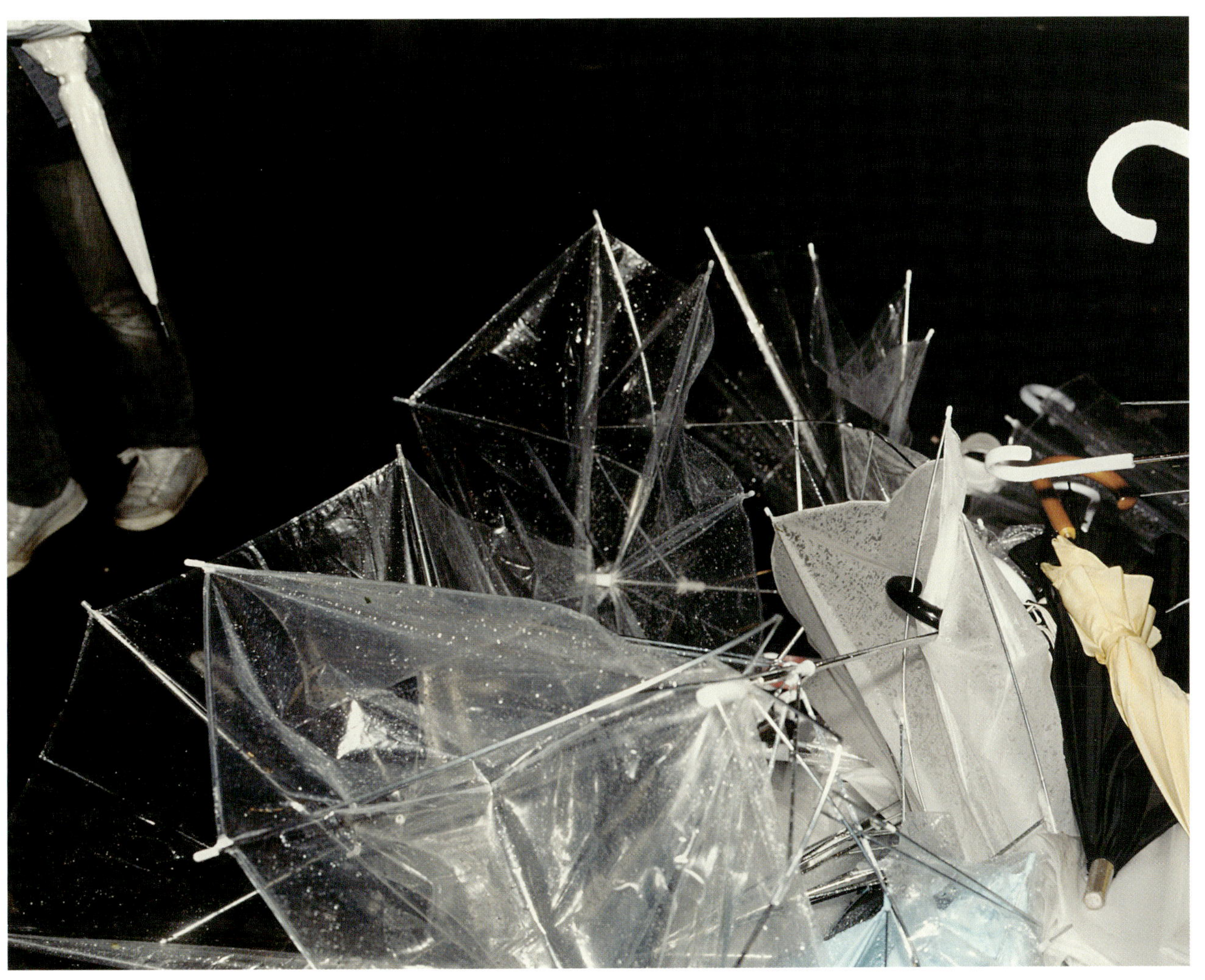

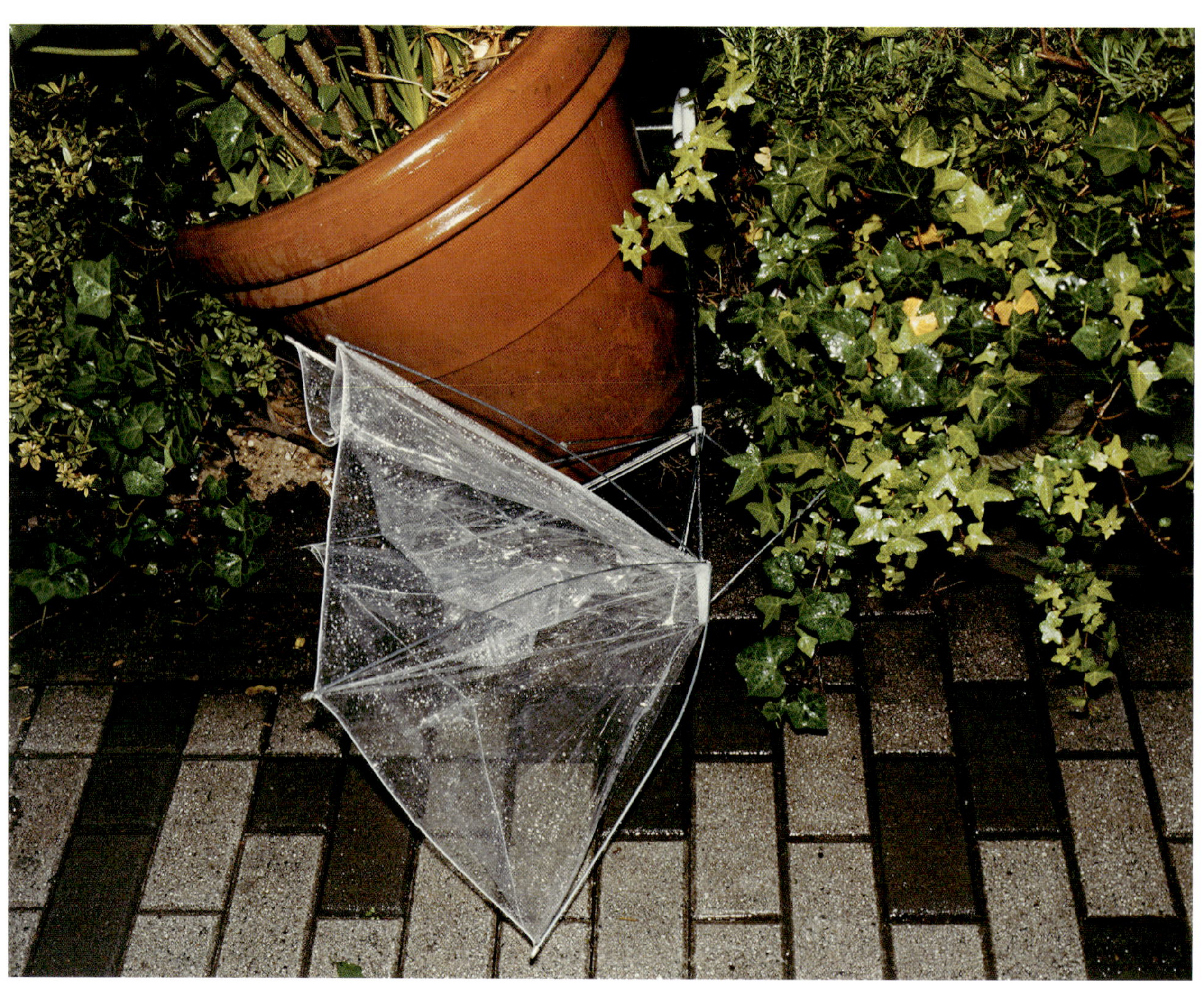

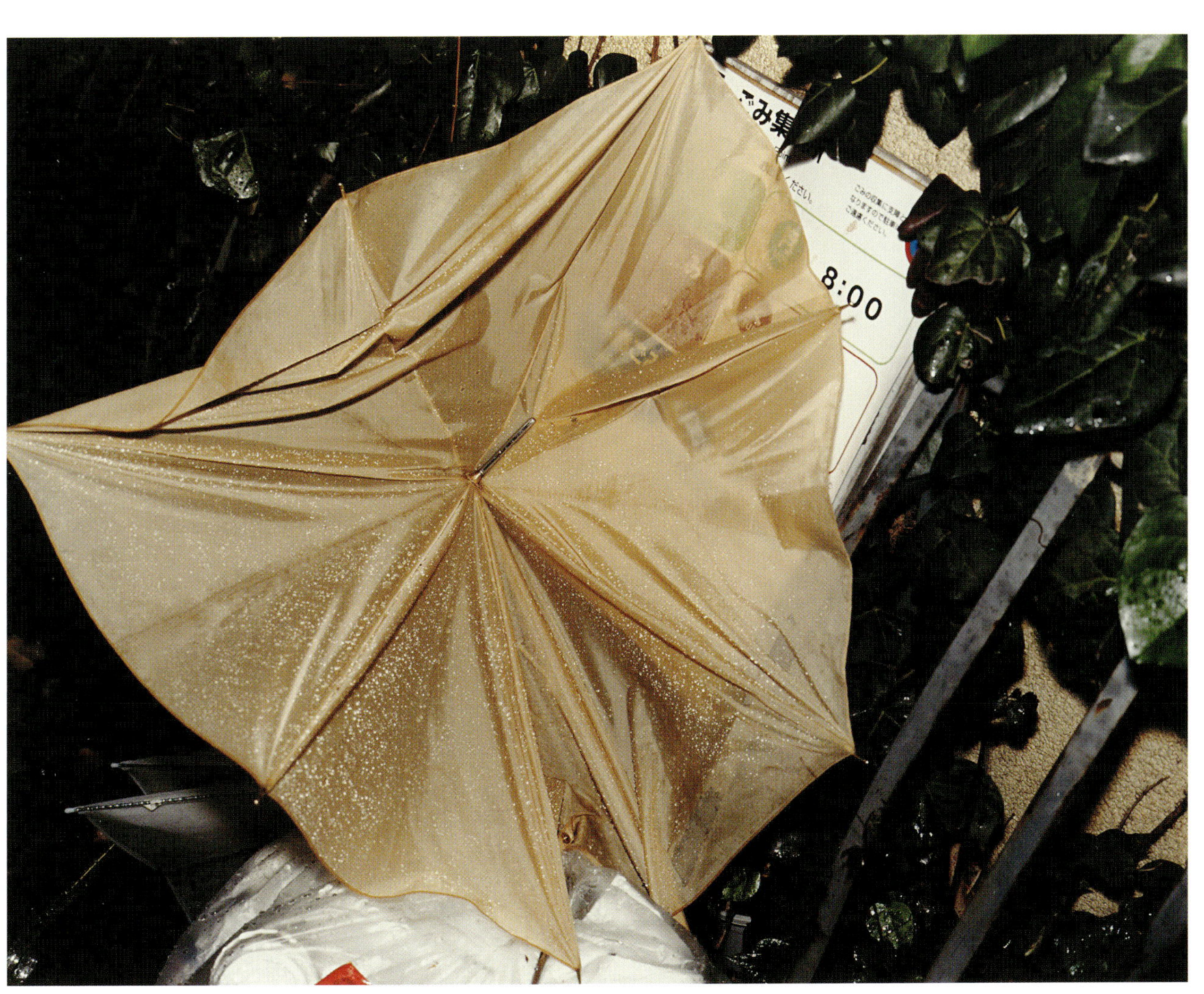
ごみ集
ださい。
8:00

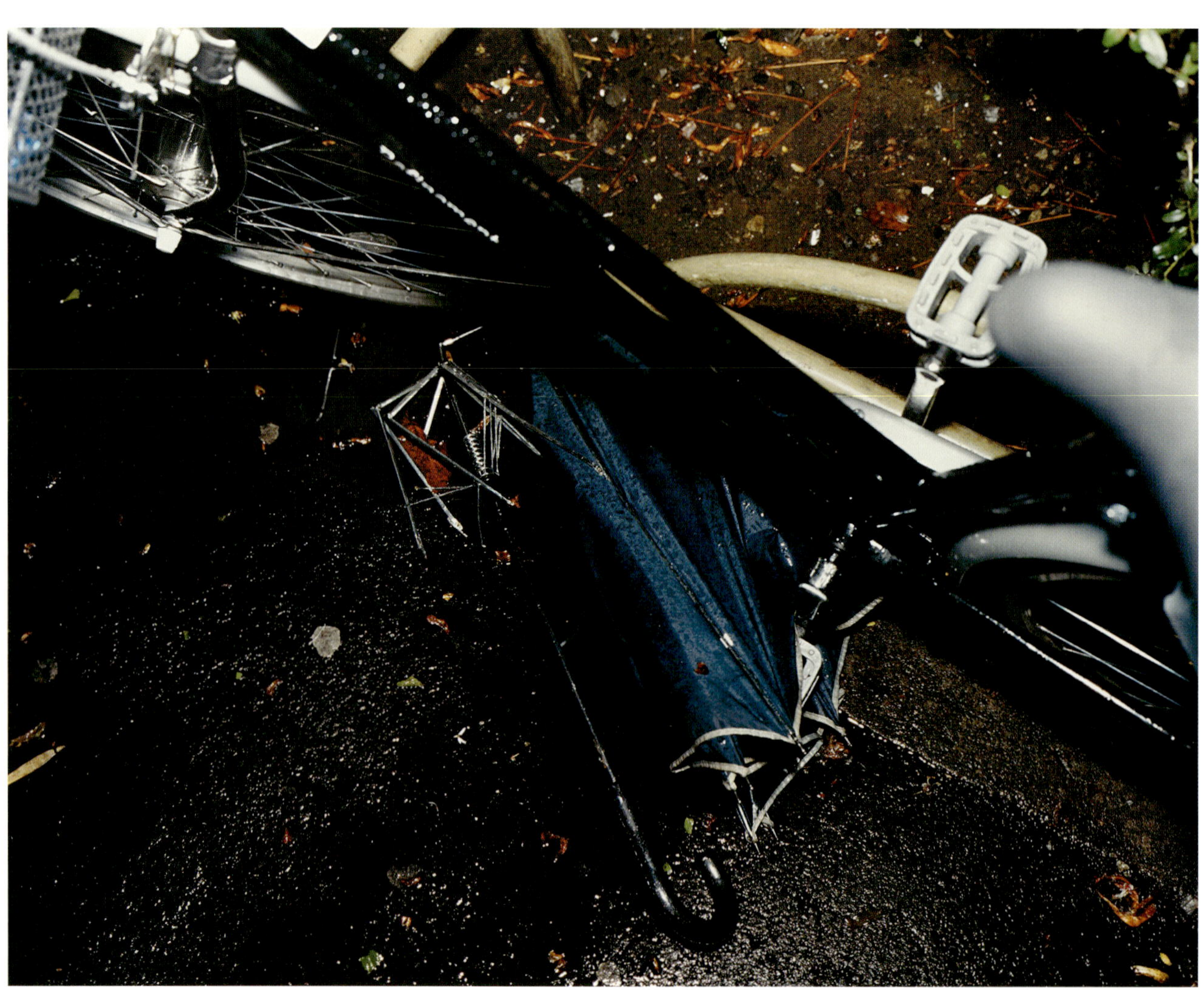

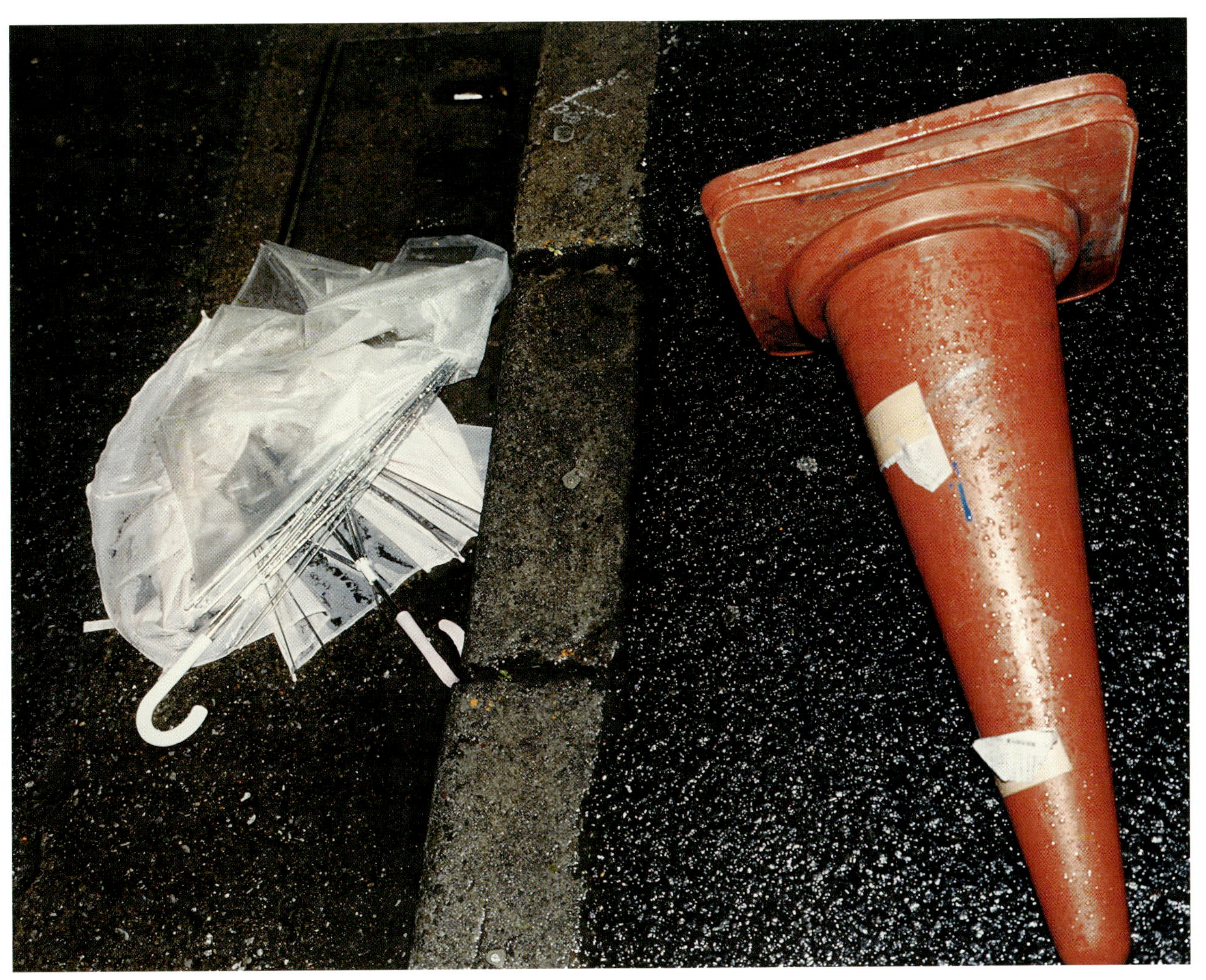

04

12 VIEWS OF MOUNT FUJI
Japan, 2004–06

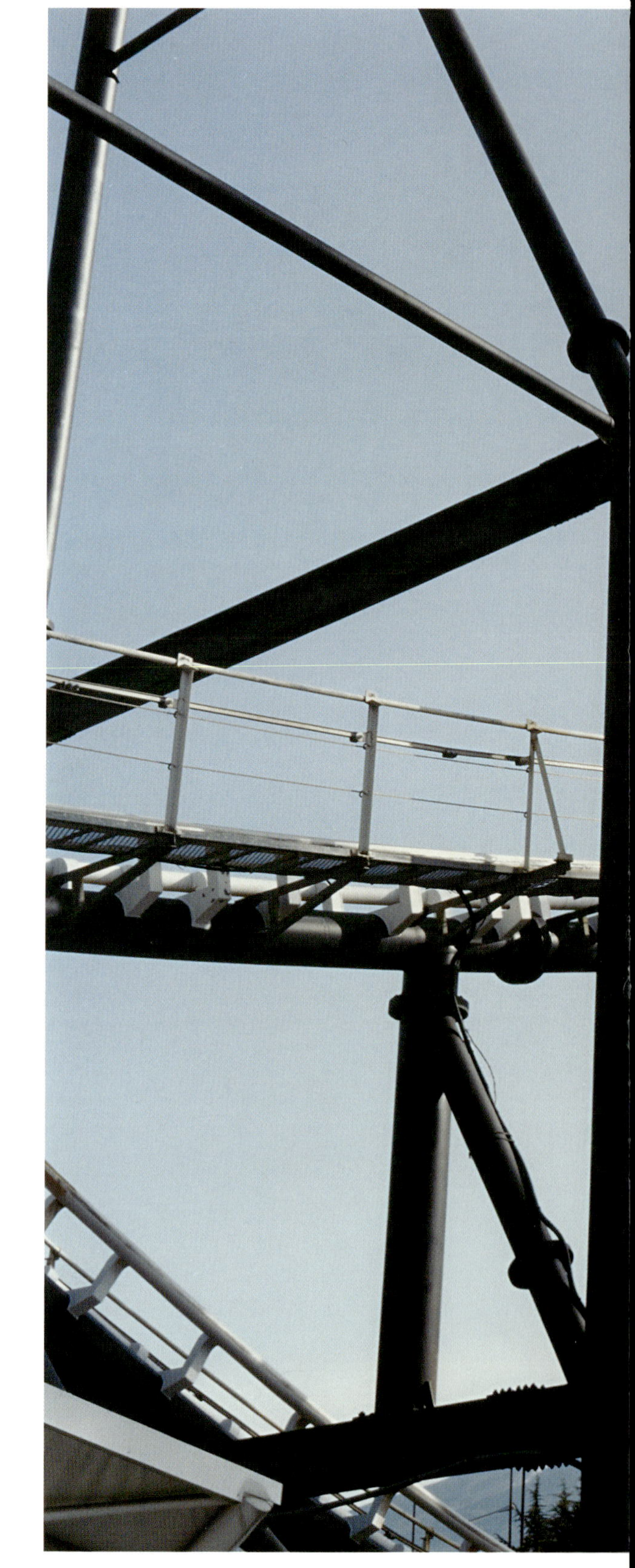

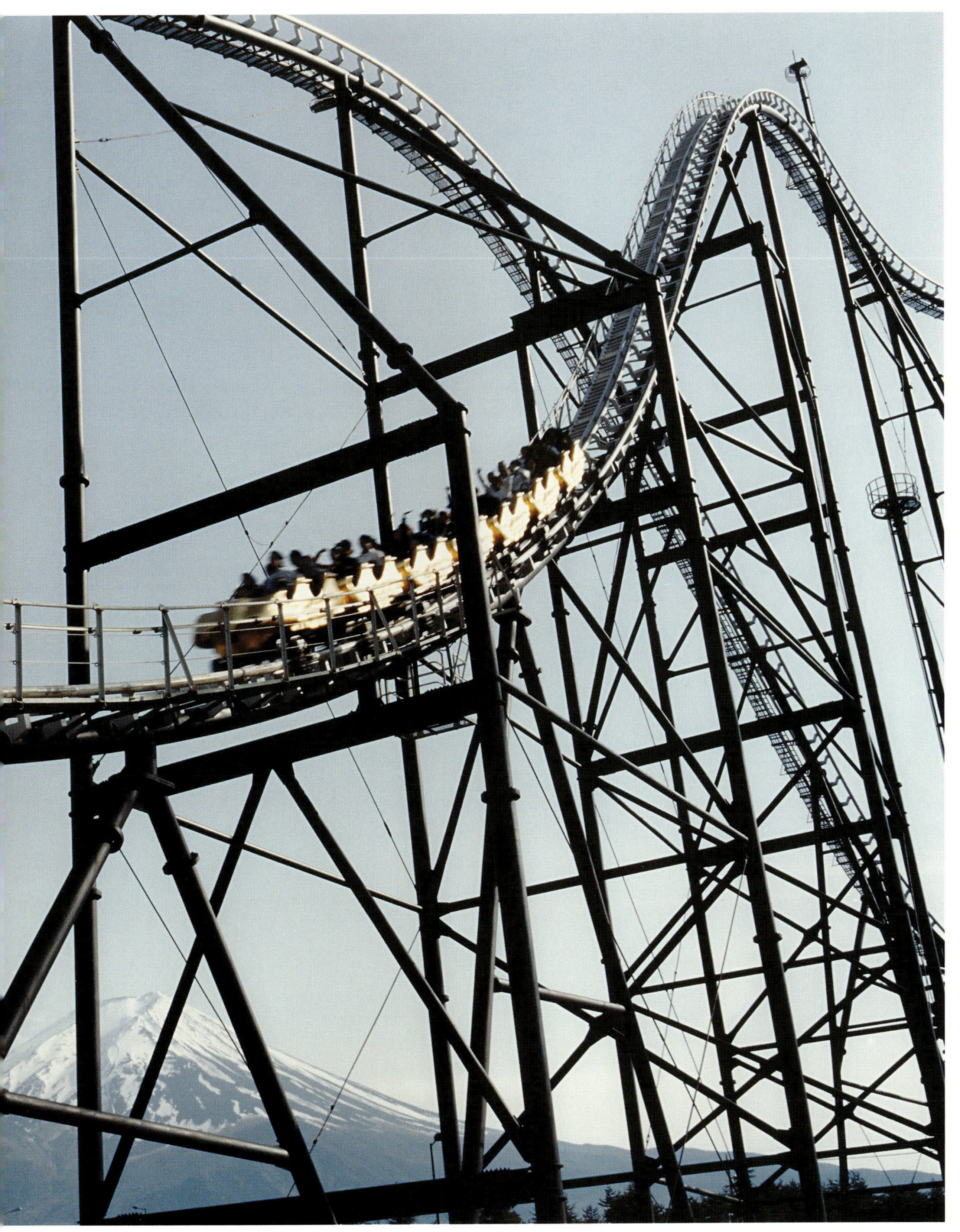

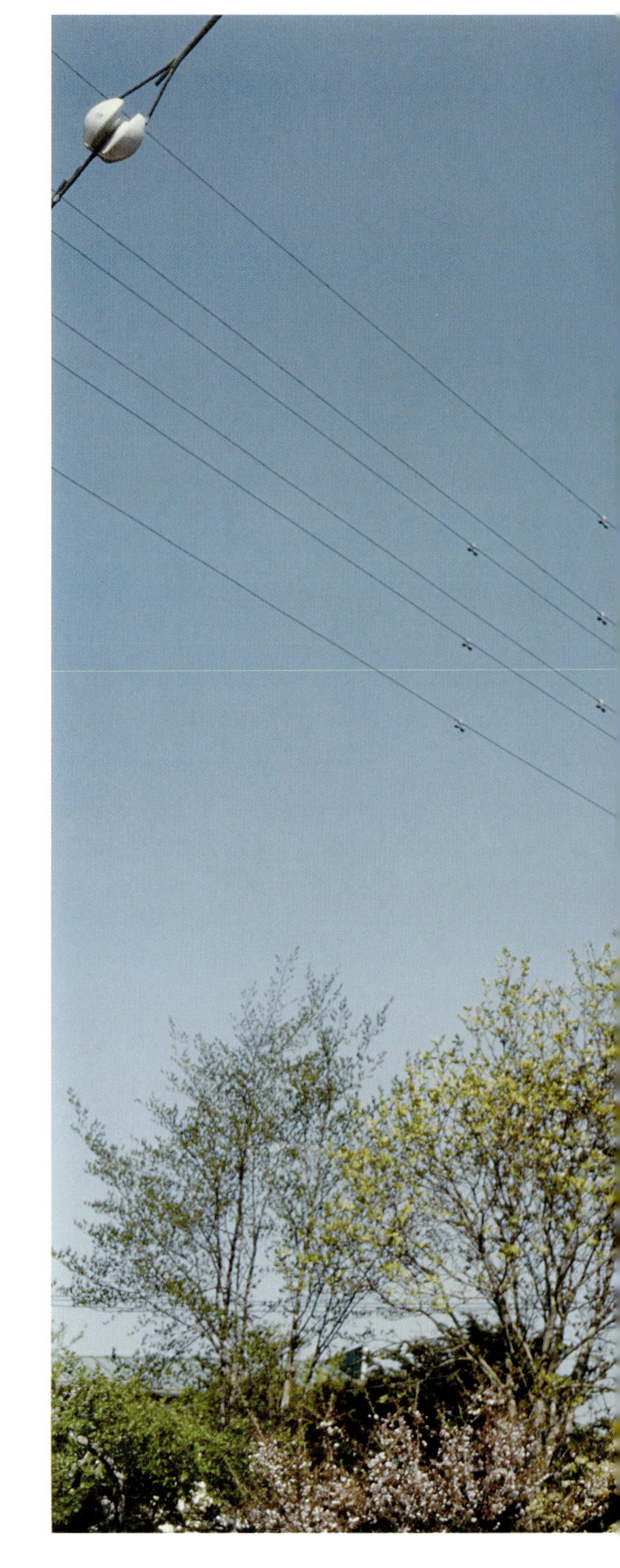

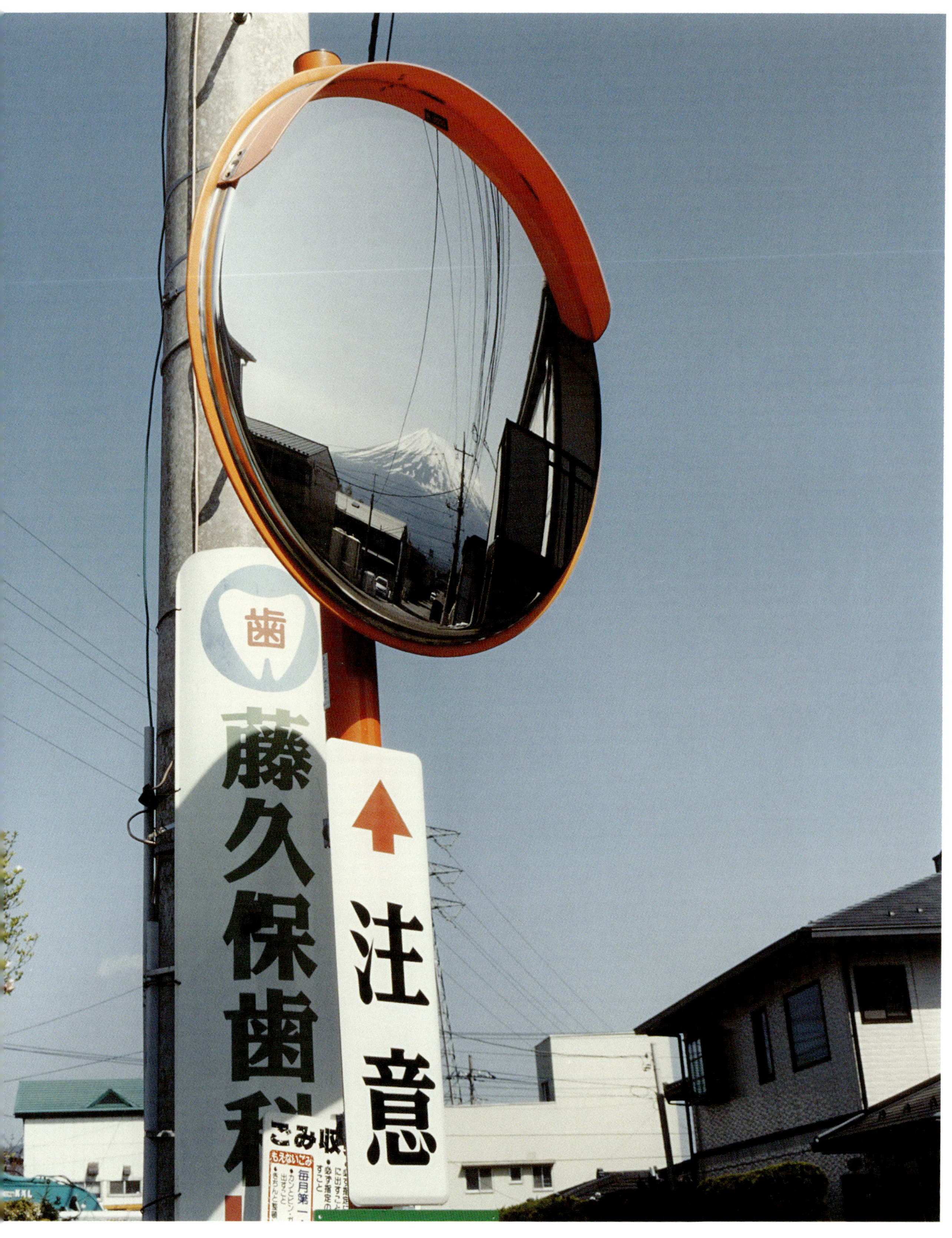
歯
藤久保歯
注意
もえないごみ

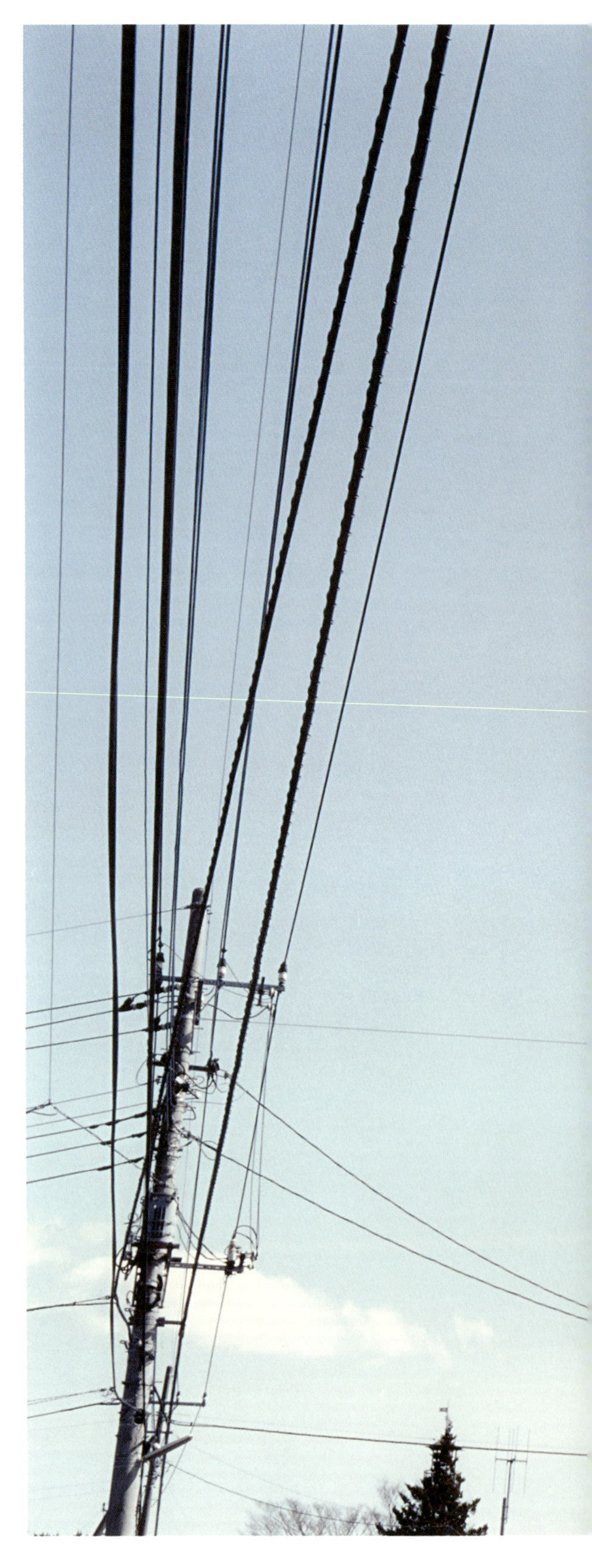

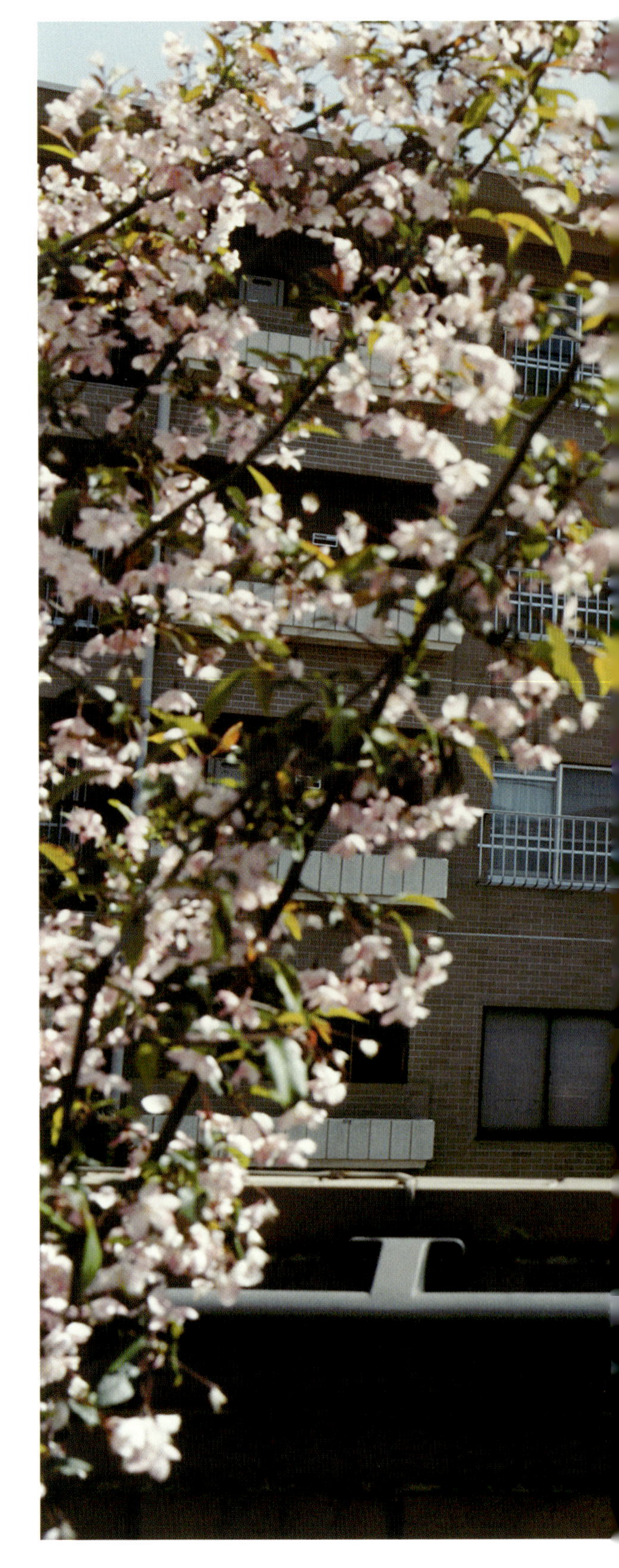

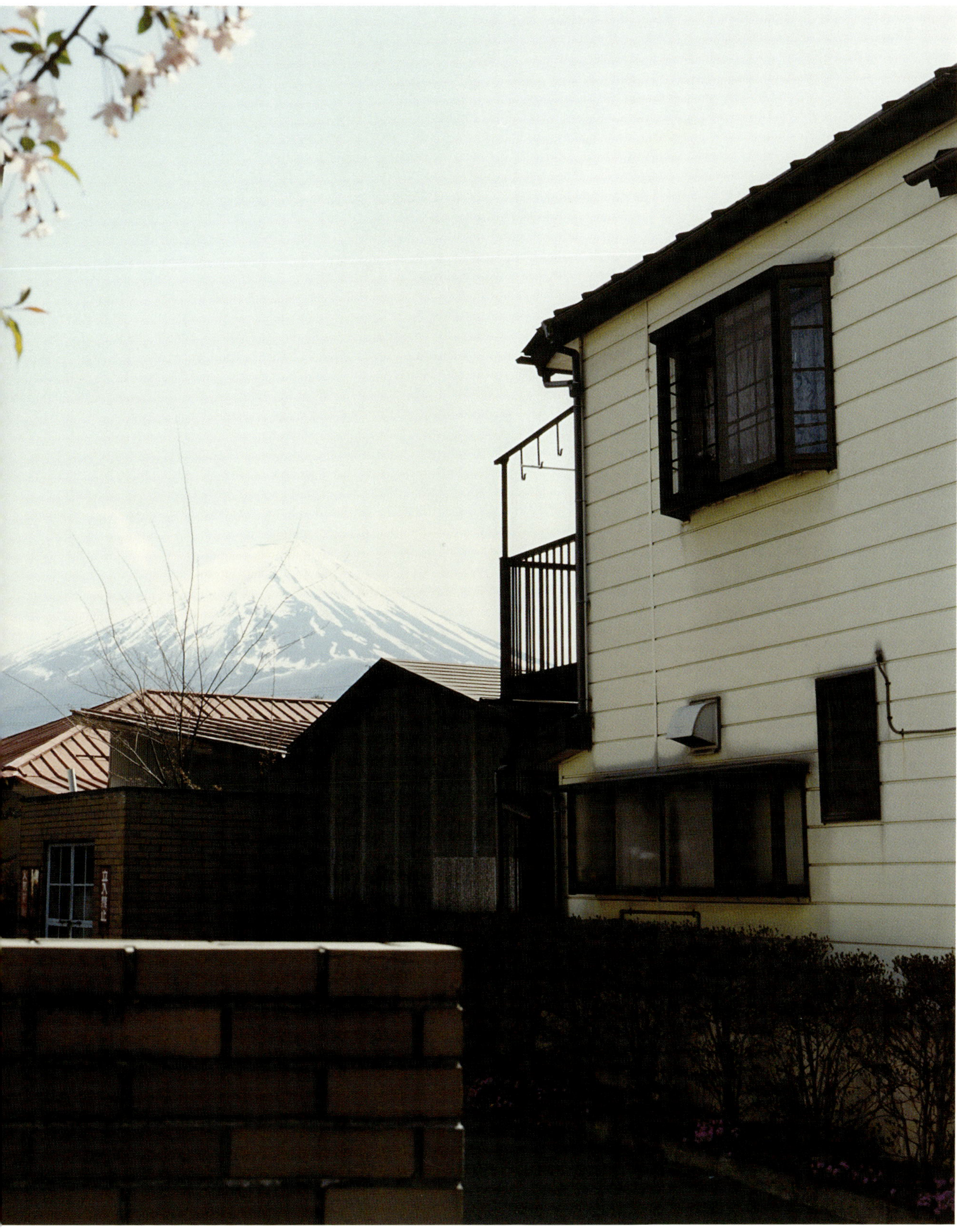

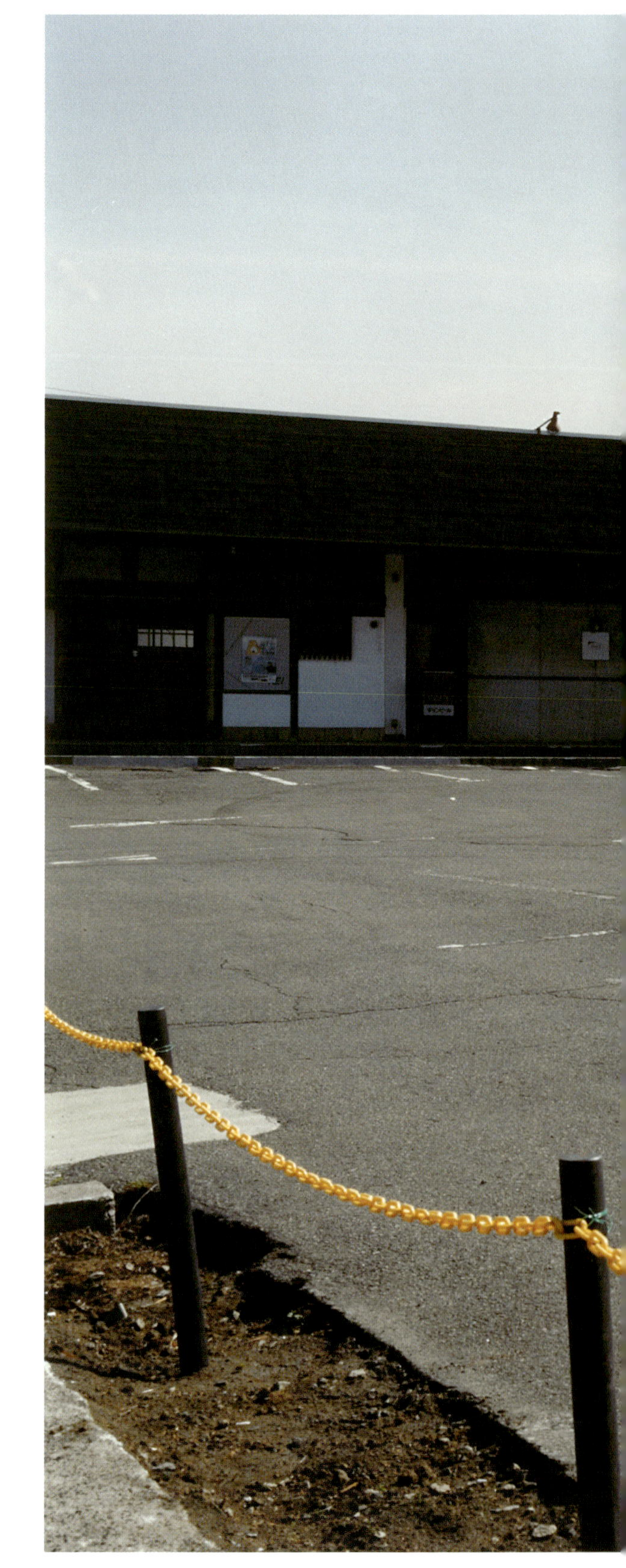

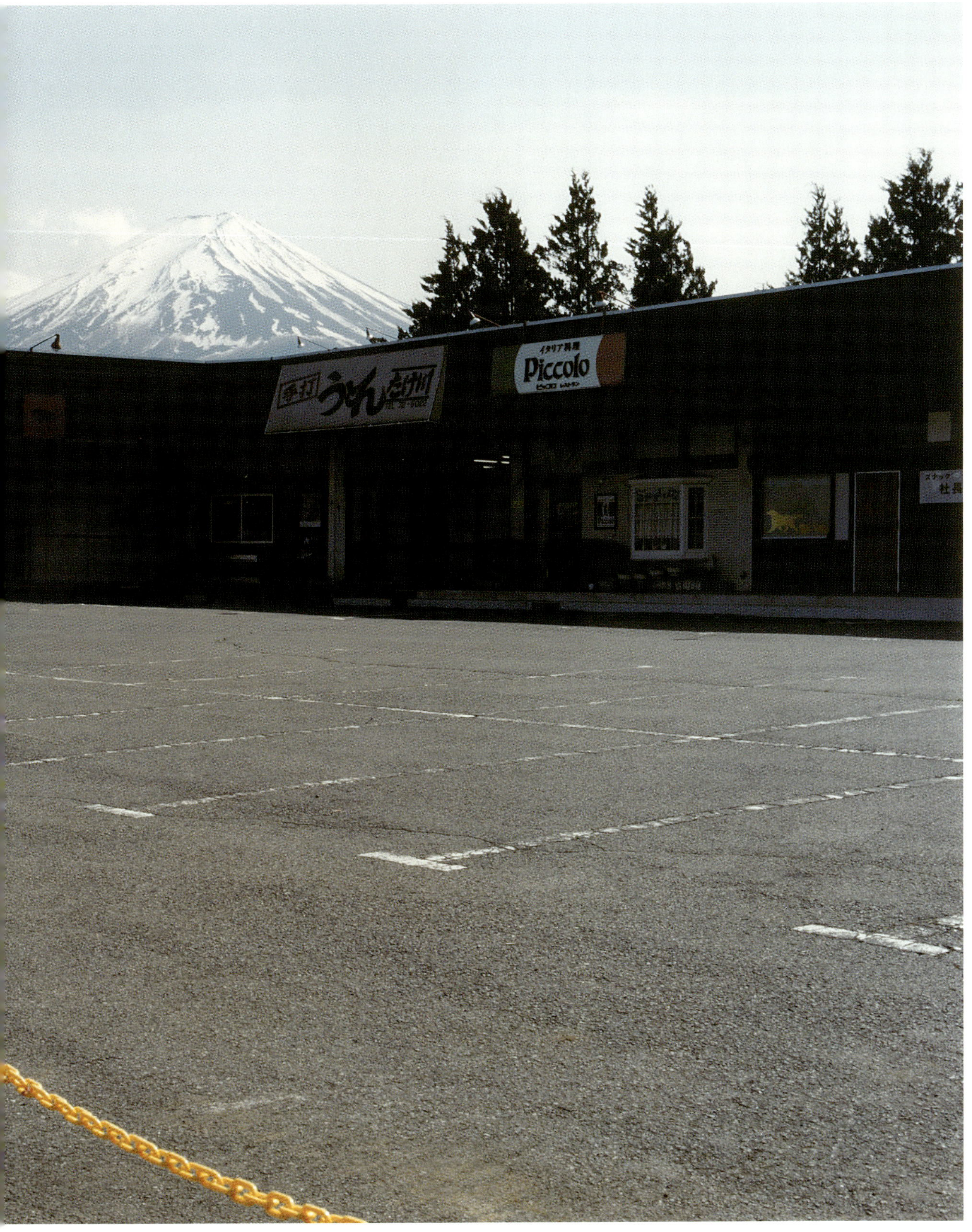

手打
うどん たけ川
イタリア料理
Piccolo
ピッコロ レストラン
スナック
社長

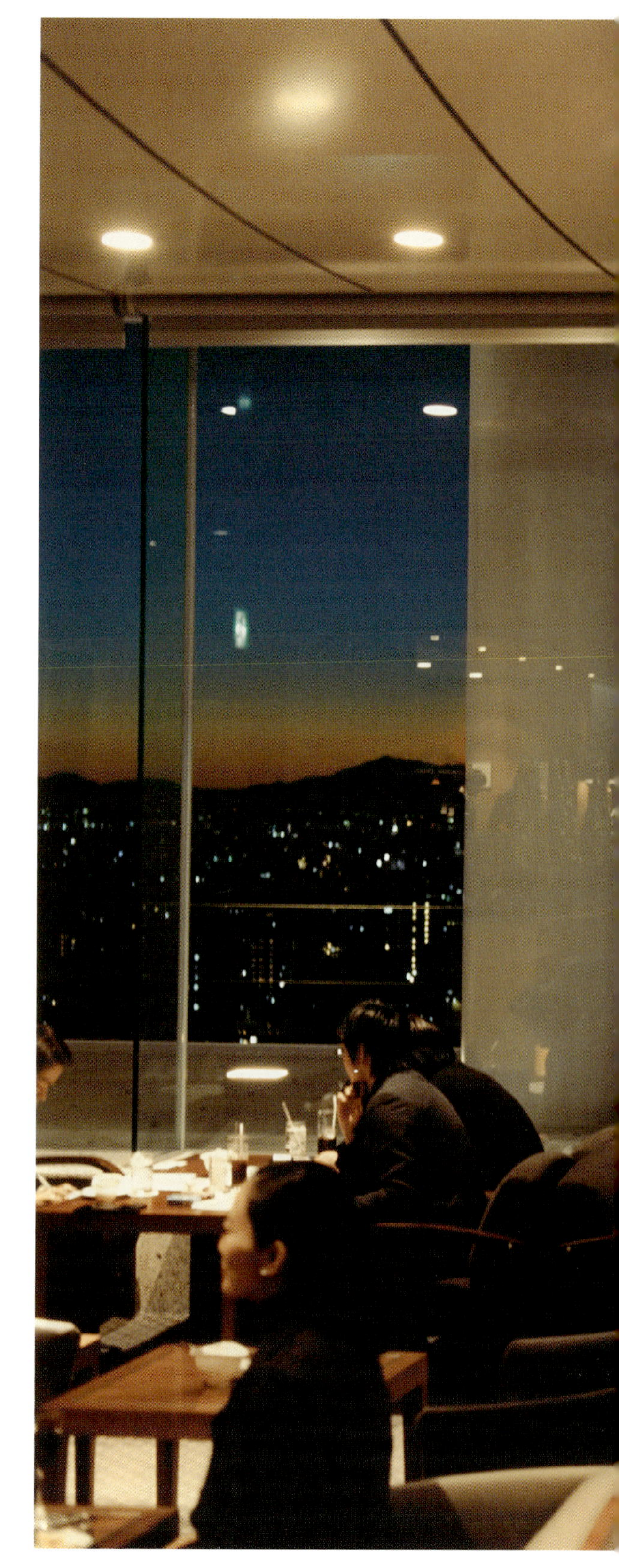

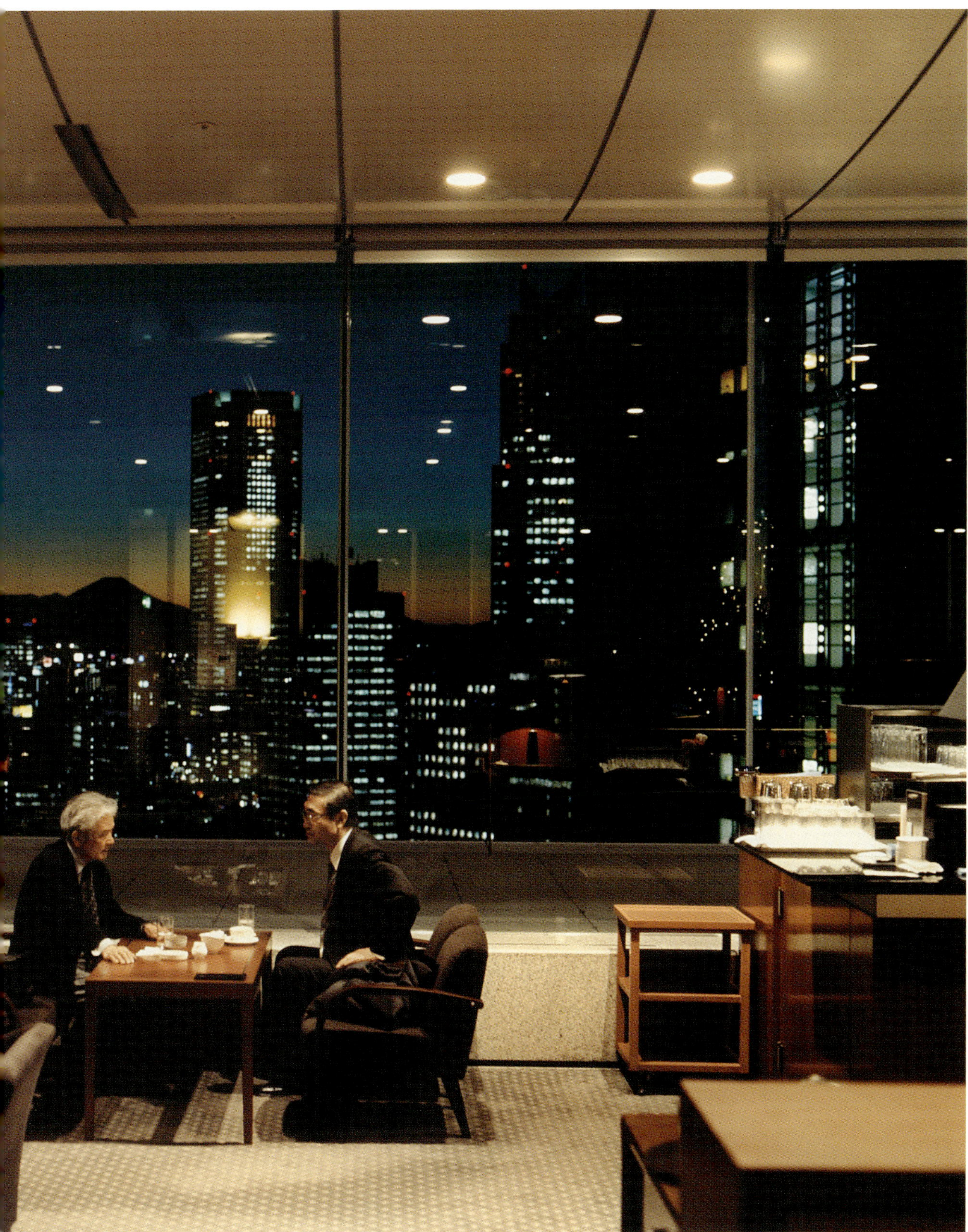

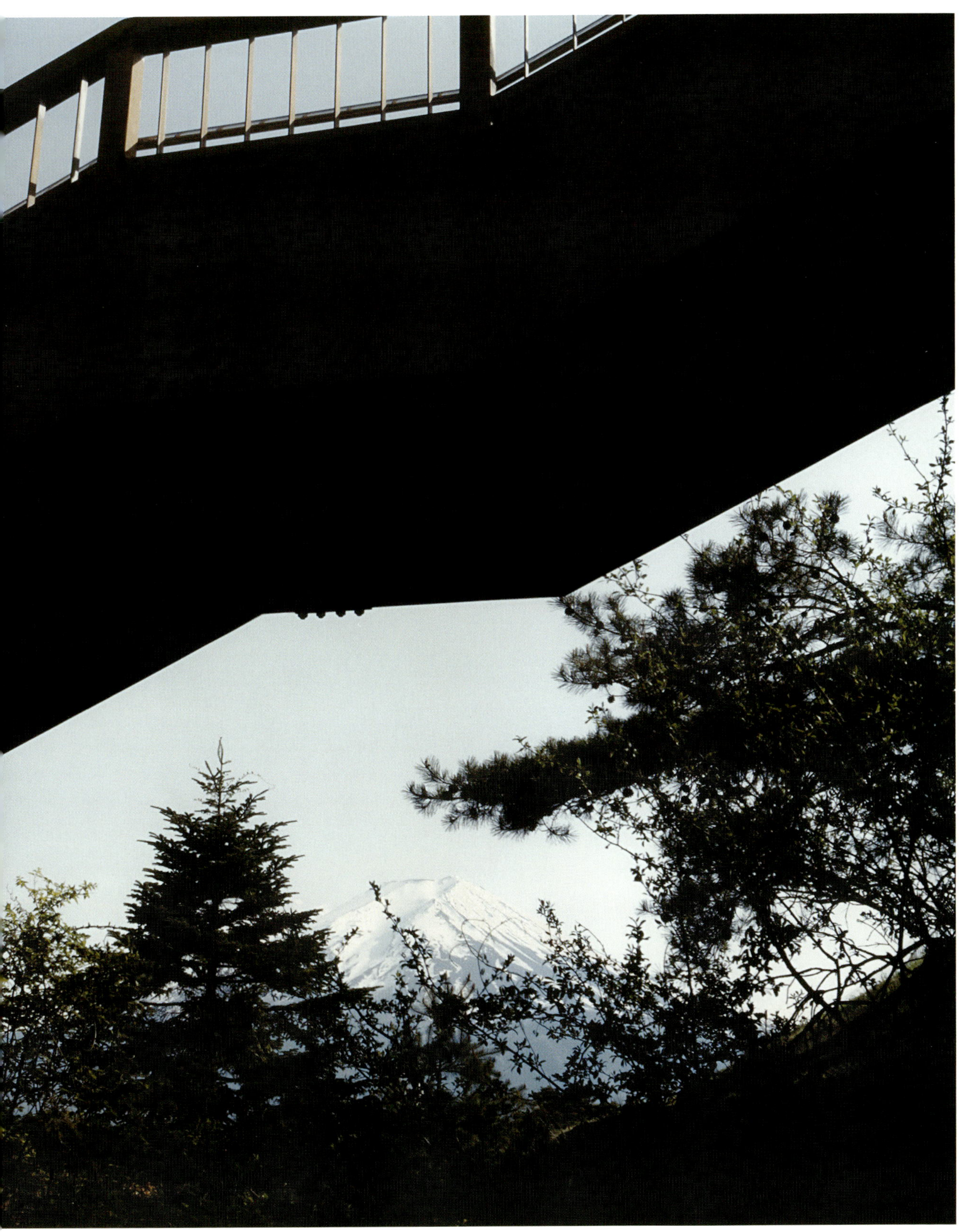

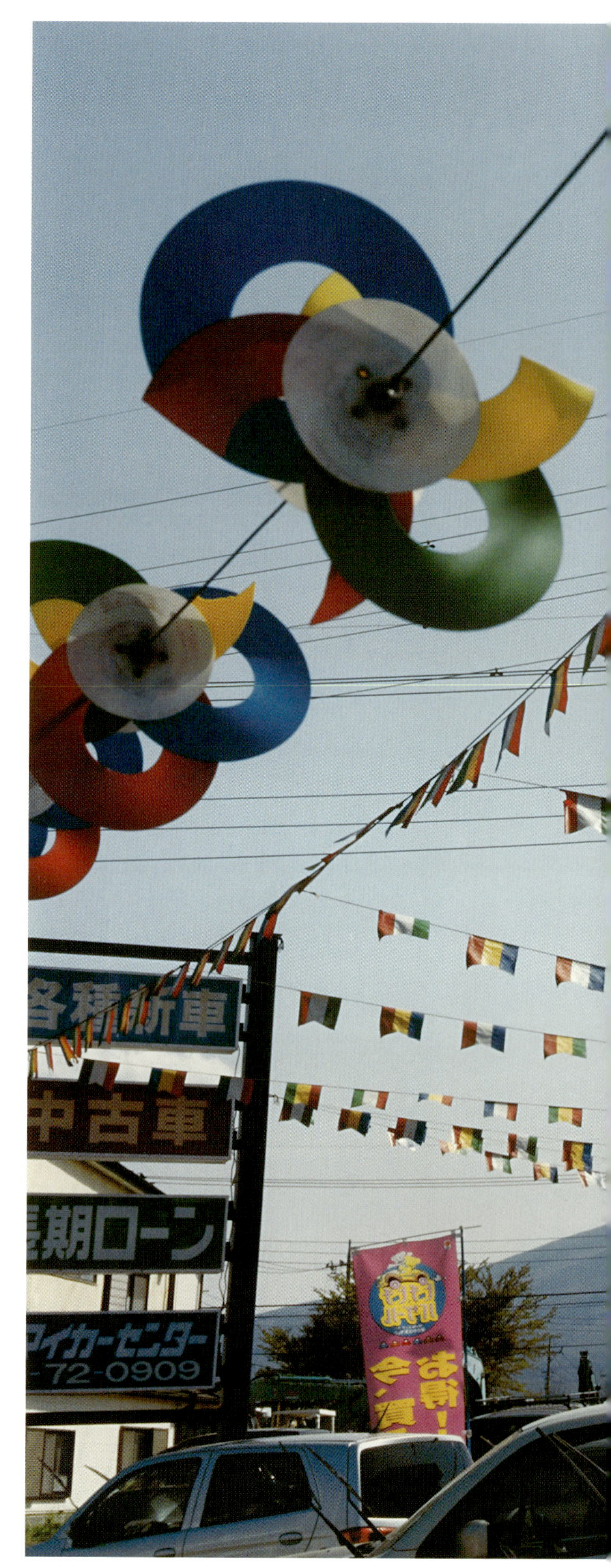
各種新車
中古車
期ローン
イカーセンター
72-0909
お得！
今、

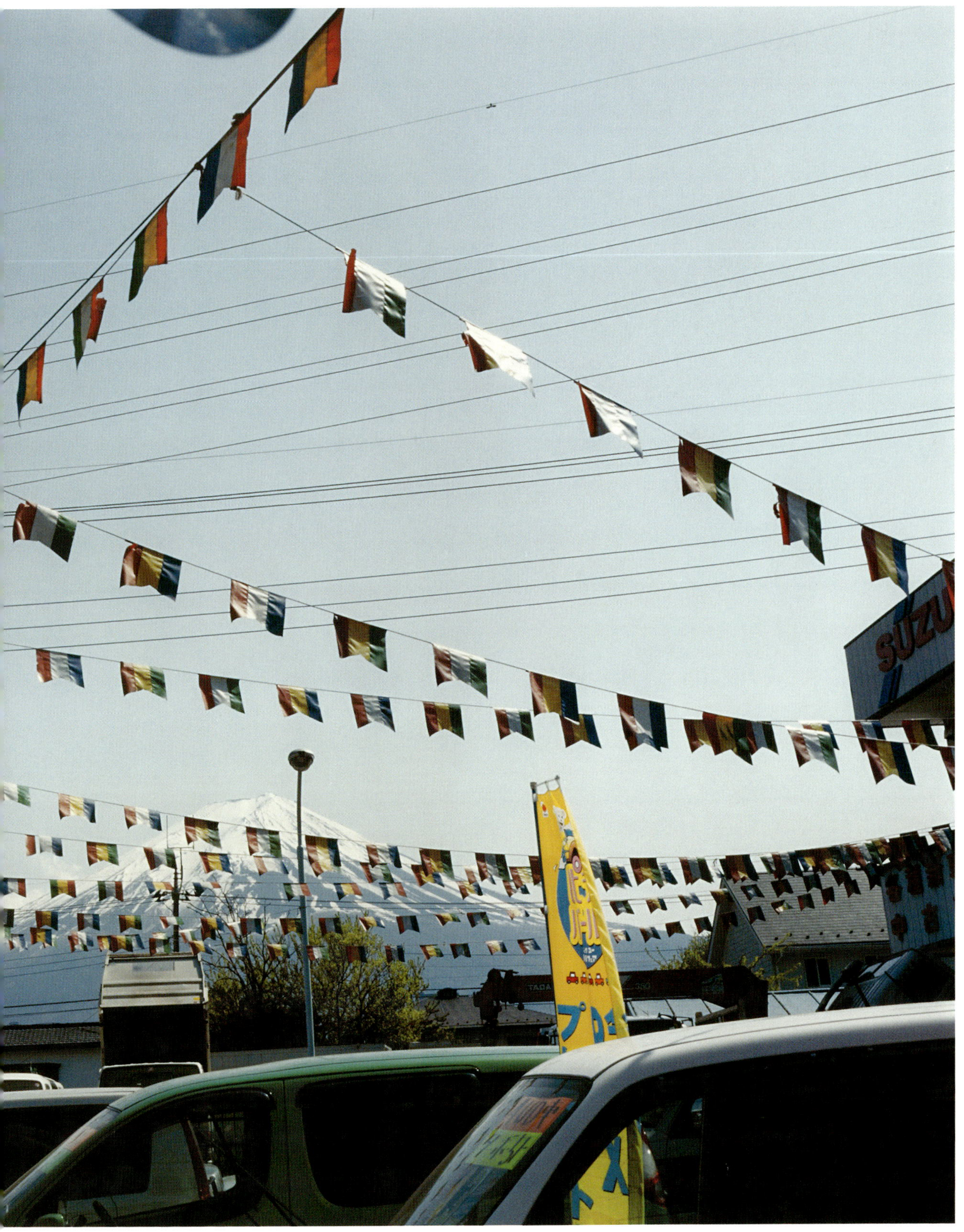

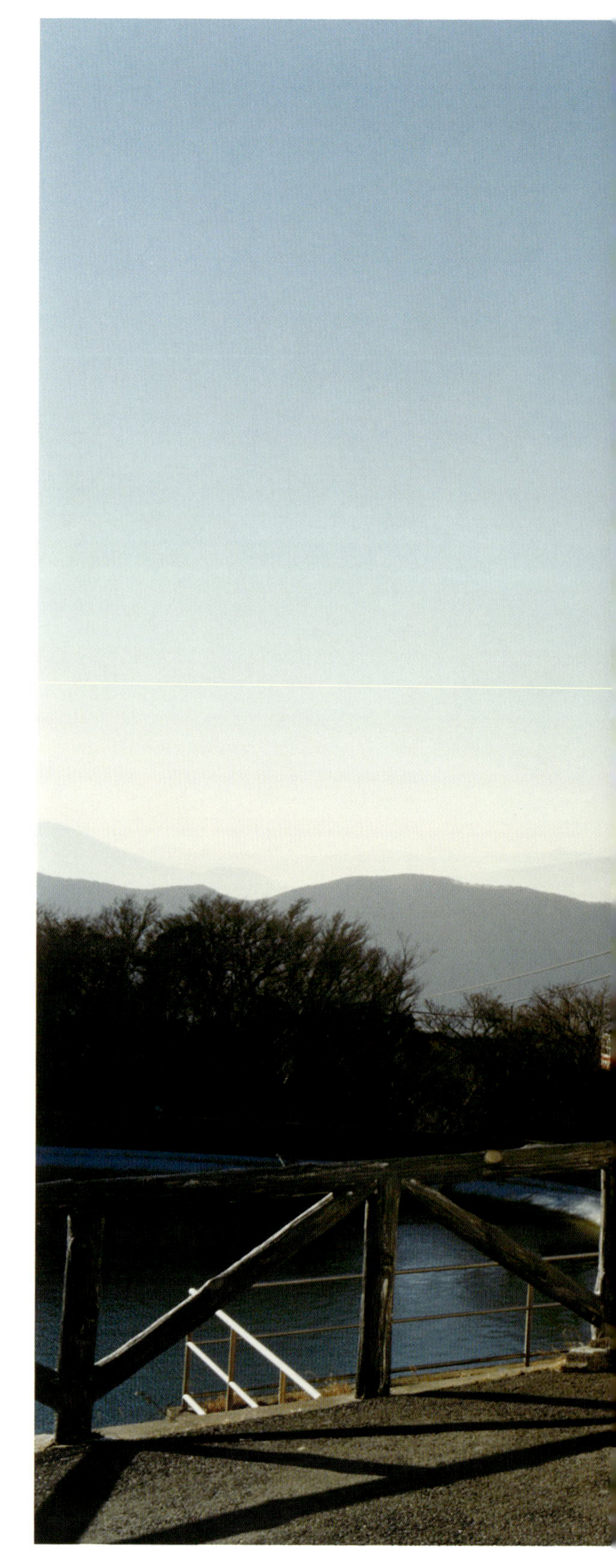

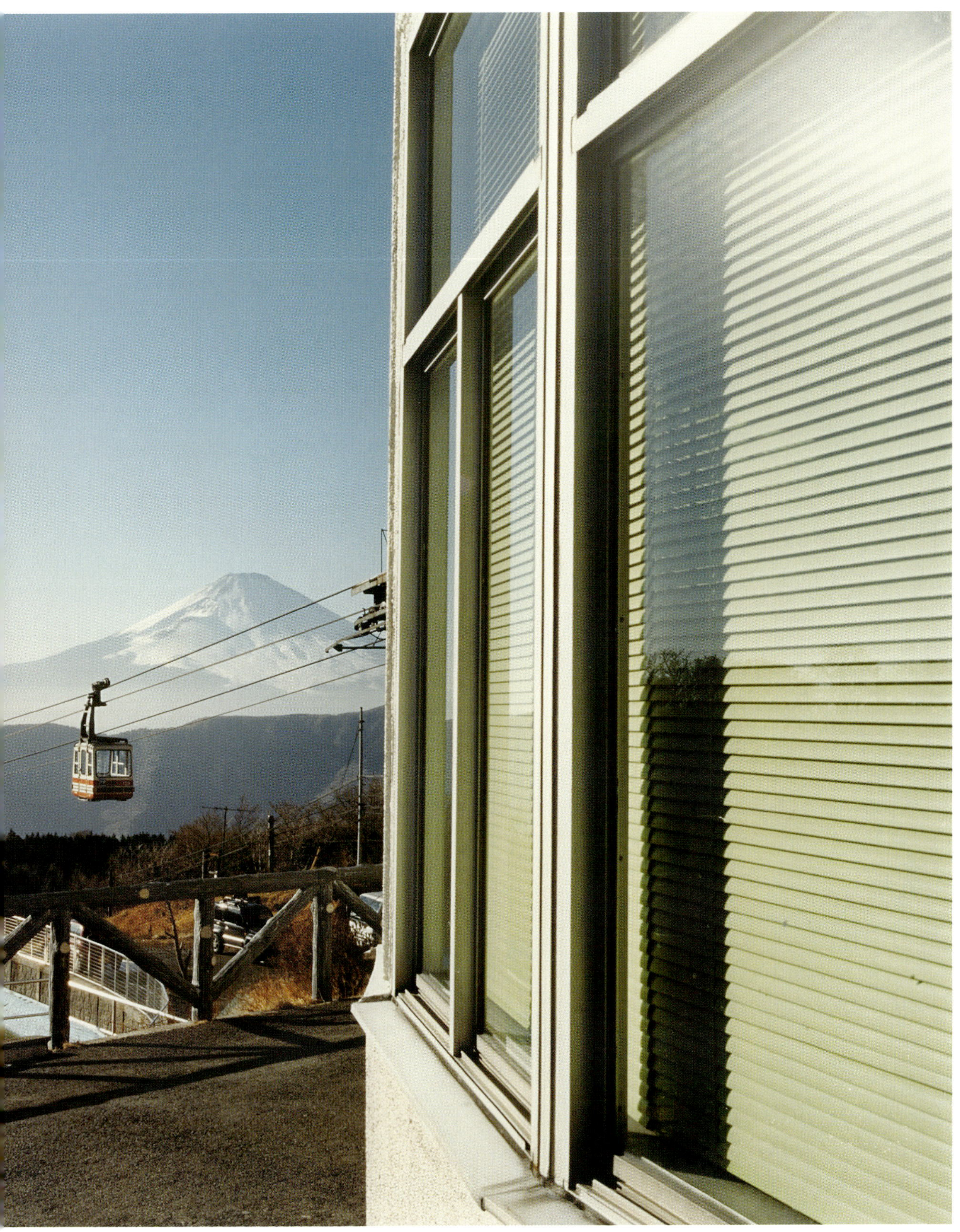

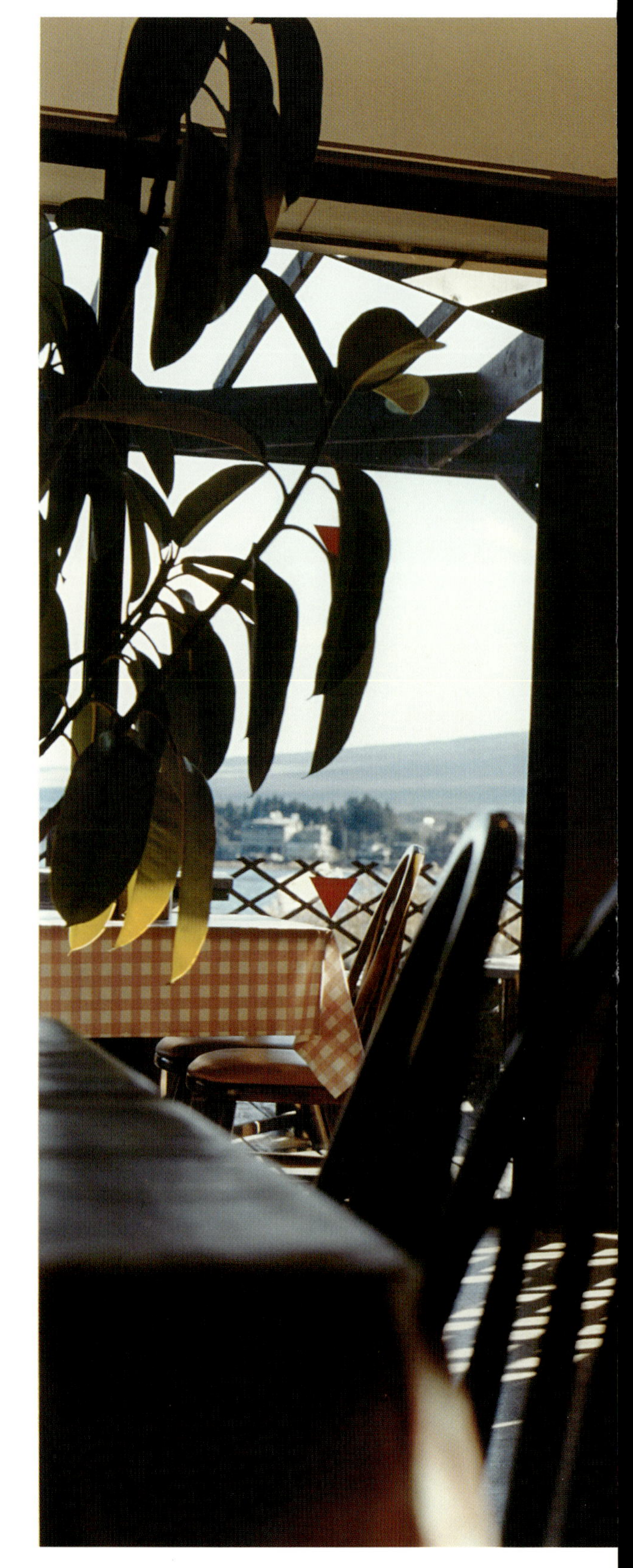

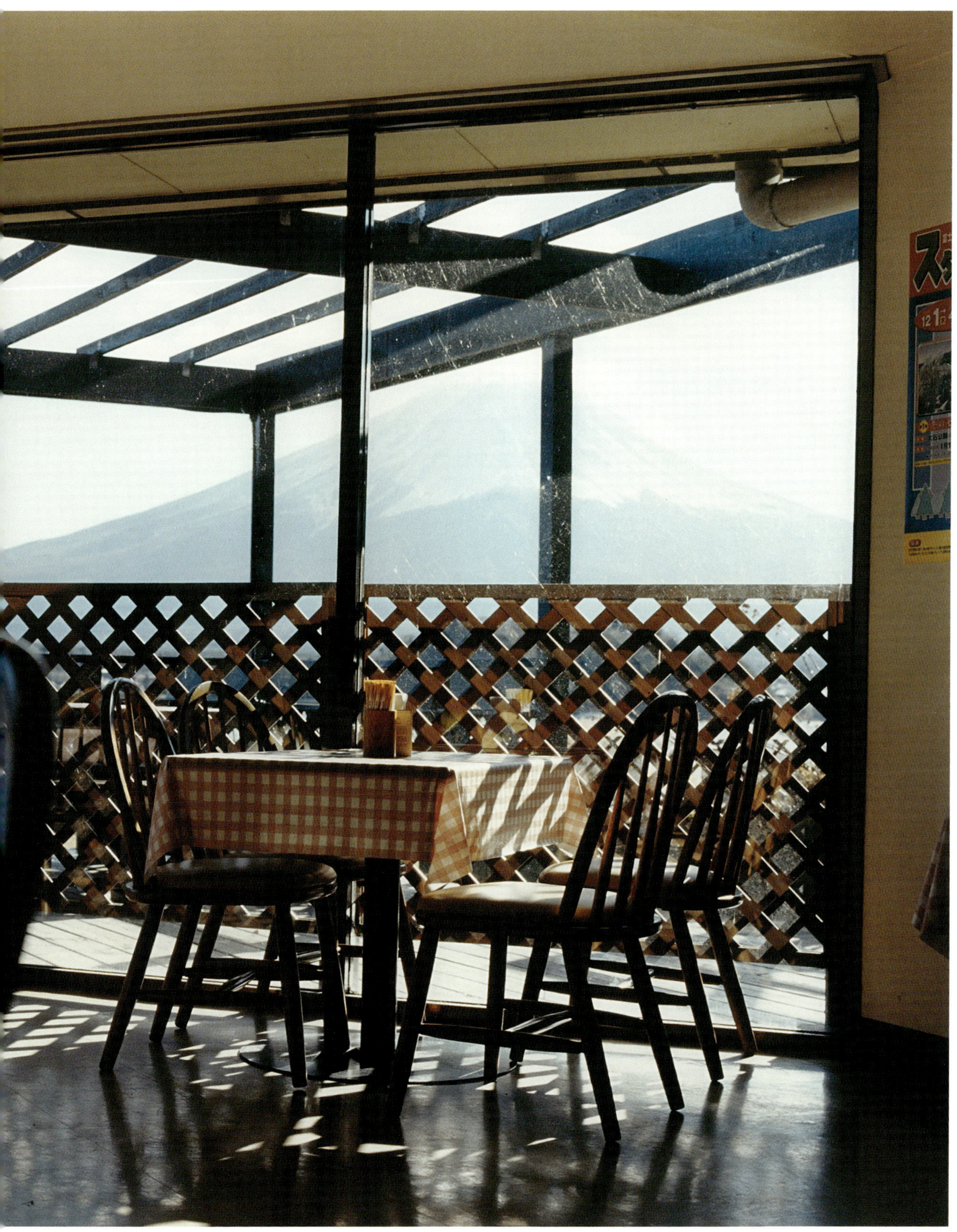

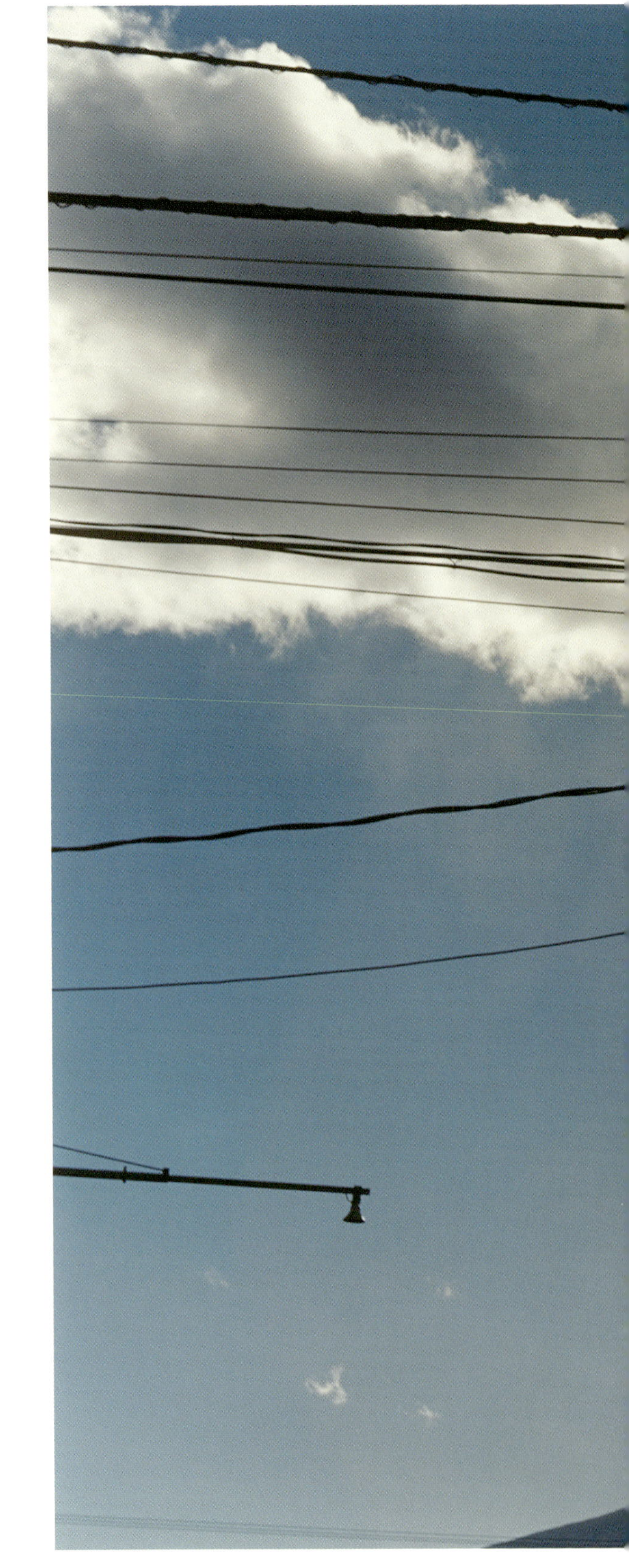

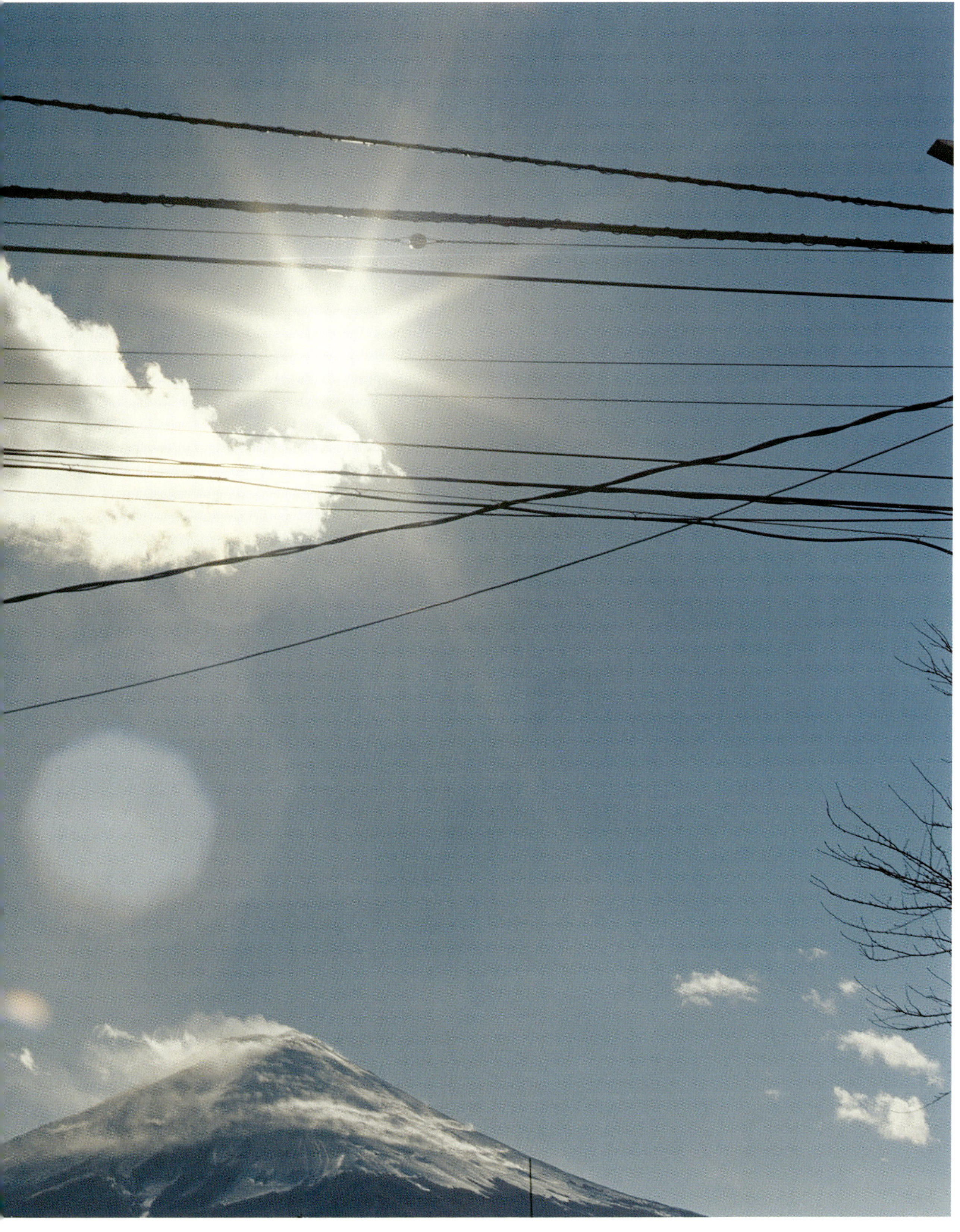

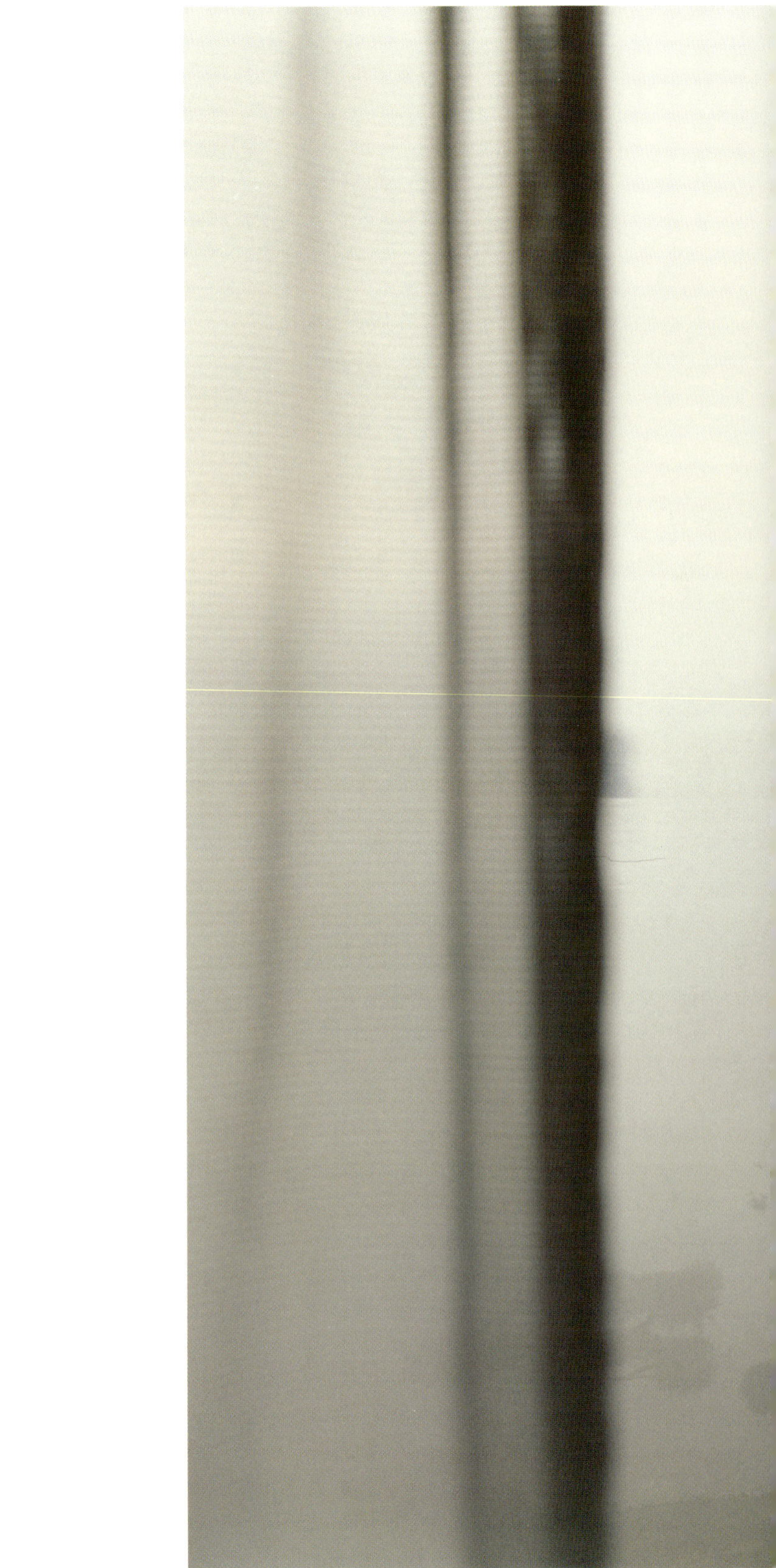

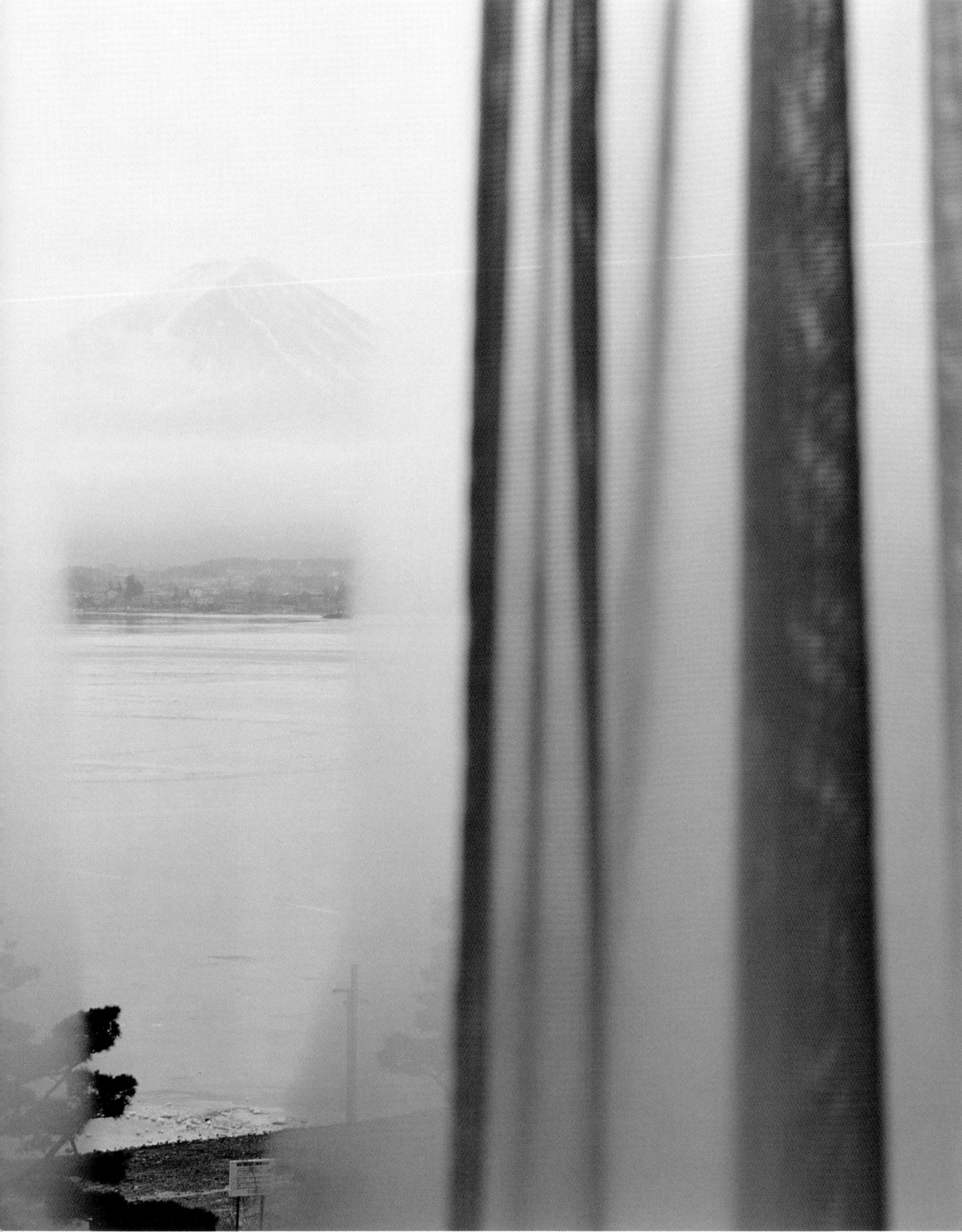

05

LA JOCONDE
Paris, 2005

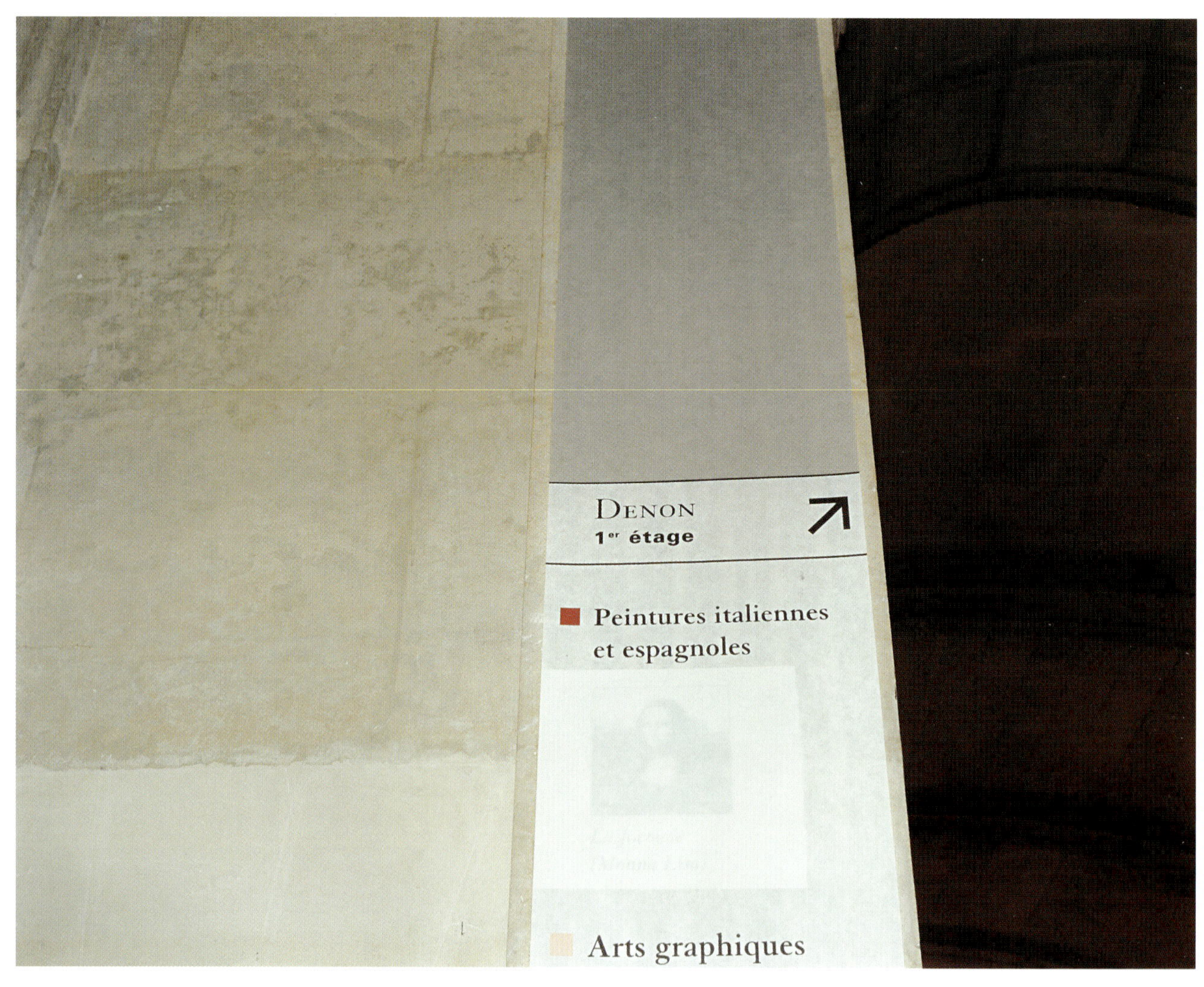
DENON
1er étage
Peintures italiennes
et espagnoles
Arts graphiques

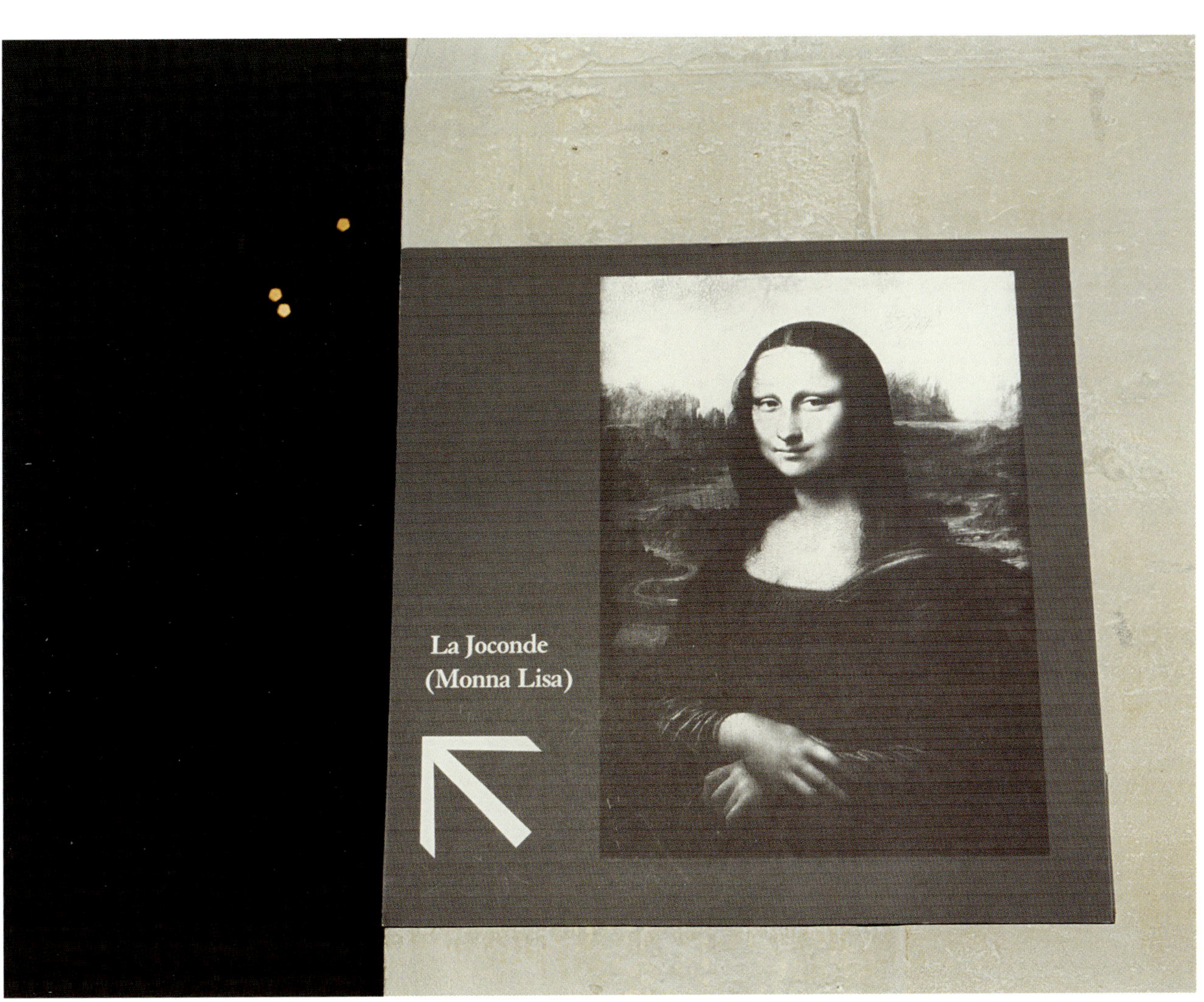
La Joconde
(Monna Lisa)

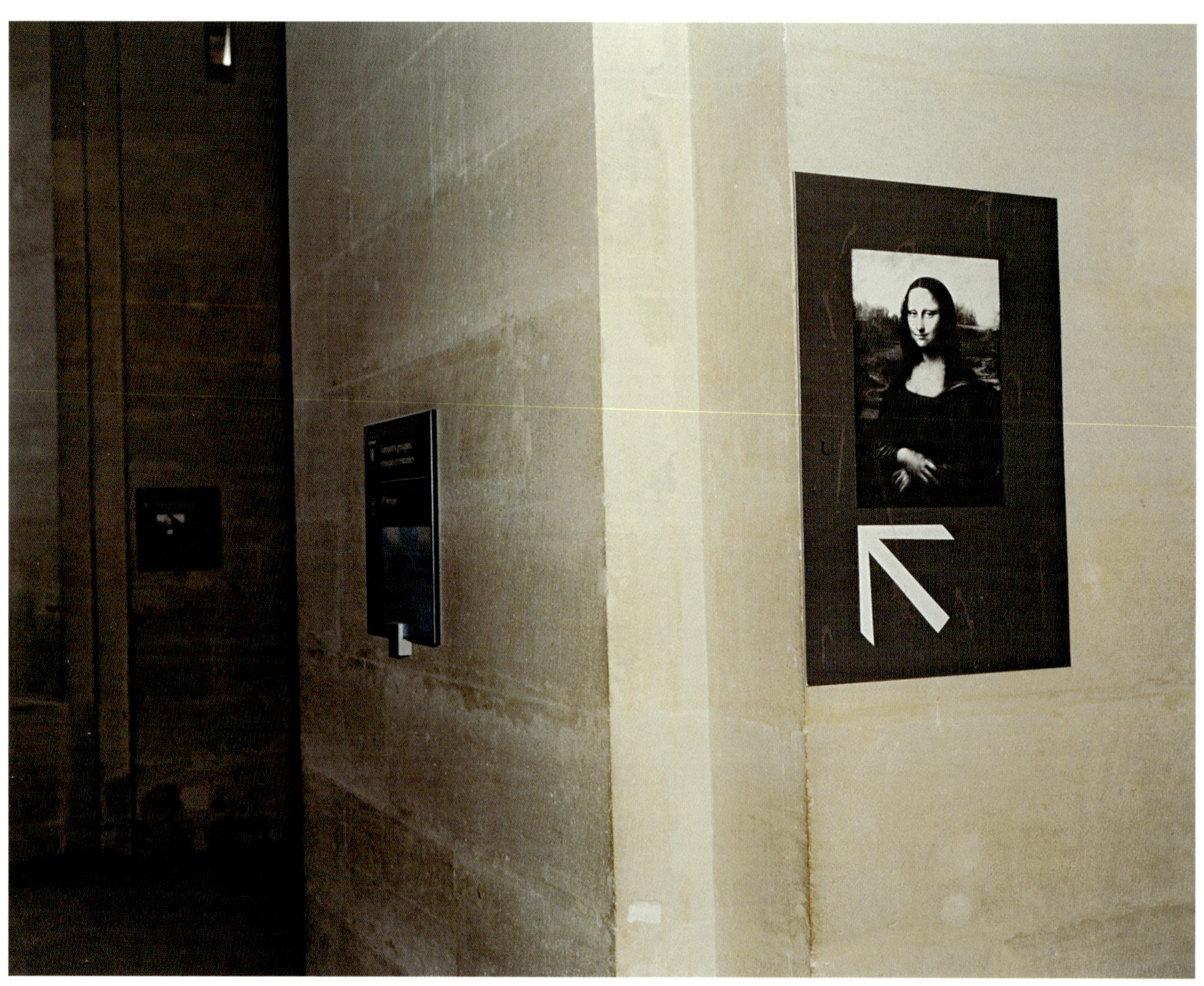

Peintures italiennes
La Joconde (Monna Lisa)

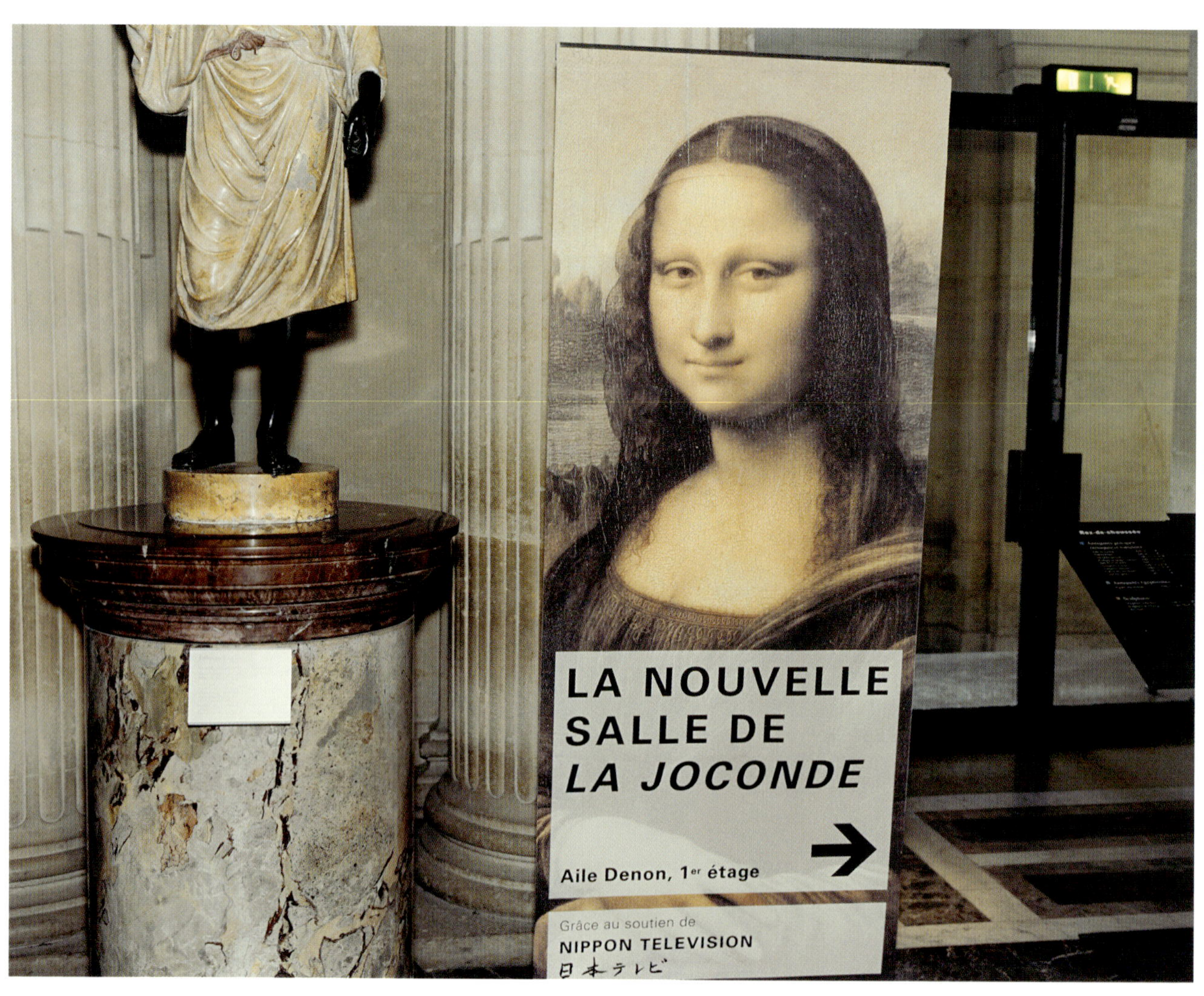
LA NOUVELLE
SALLE DE
LA JOCONDE
Aile Denon, 1er étage
Grâce au soutien de
NIPPON TELEVISION
日本テレビ

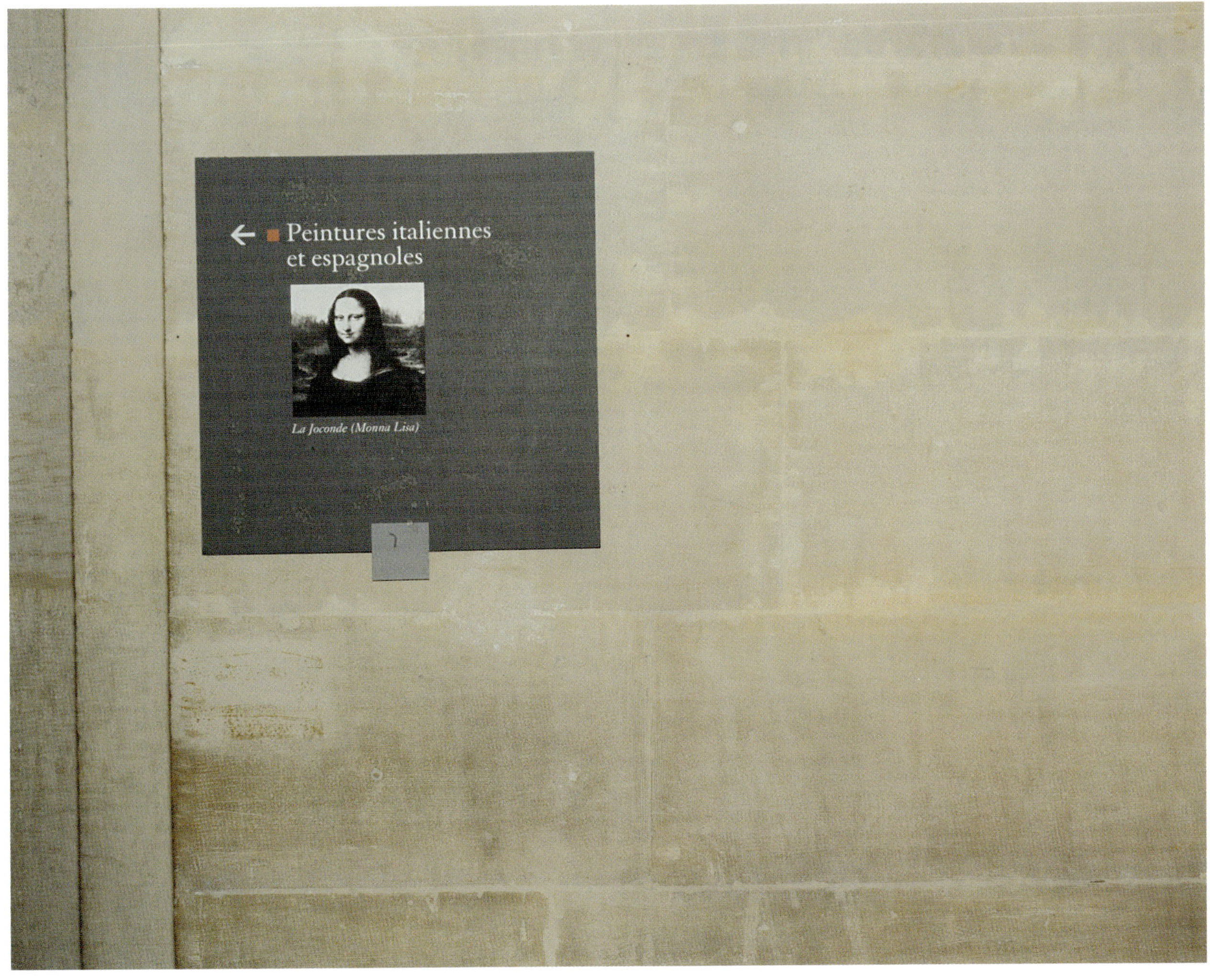
Peintures italiennes
et espagnoles
La Joconde (Monna Lisa)

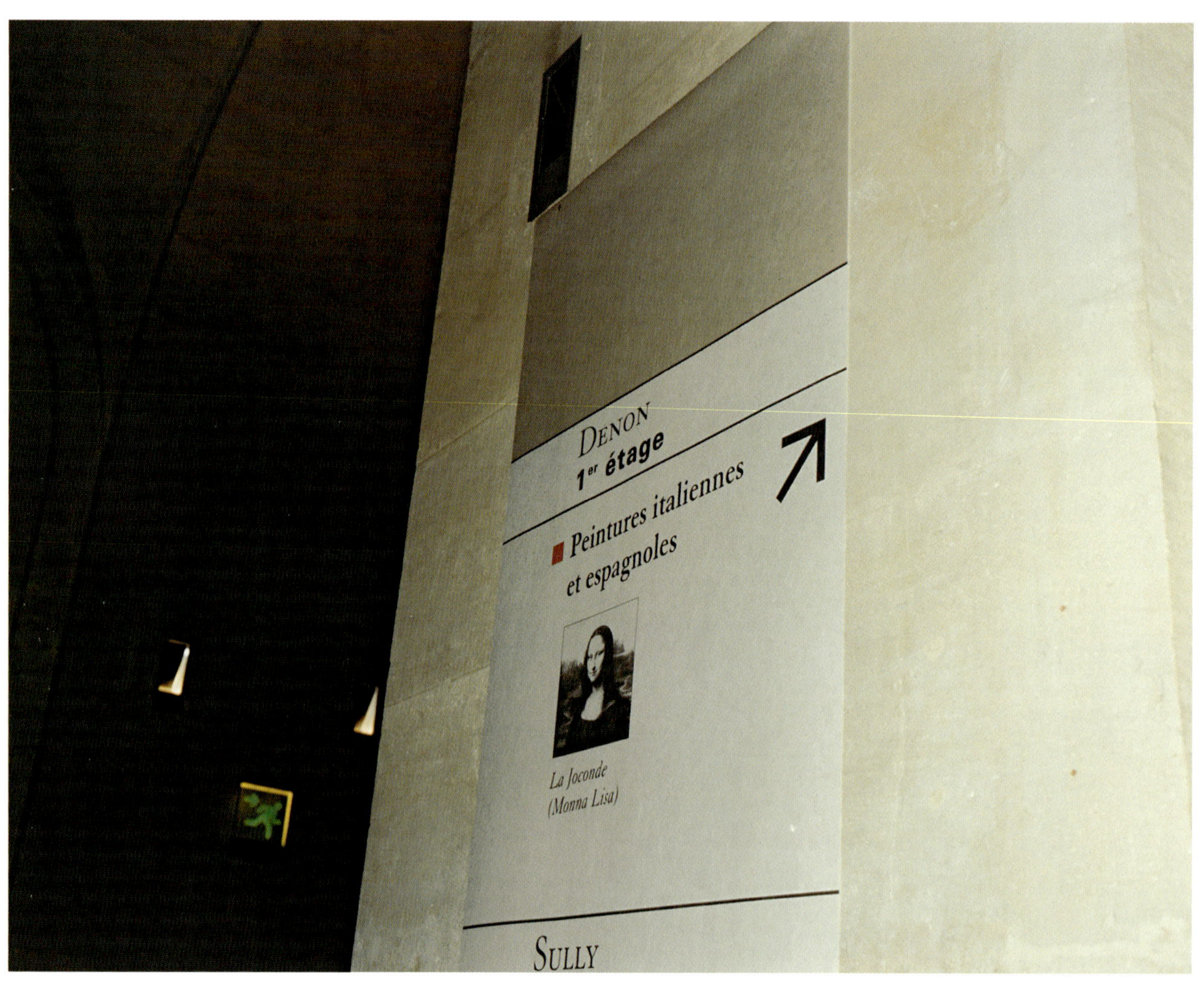
DENON
1er étage
Peintures italiennes
et espagnoles
La Joconde
(Monna Lisa)
SULLY

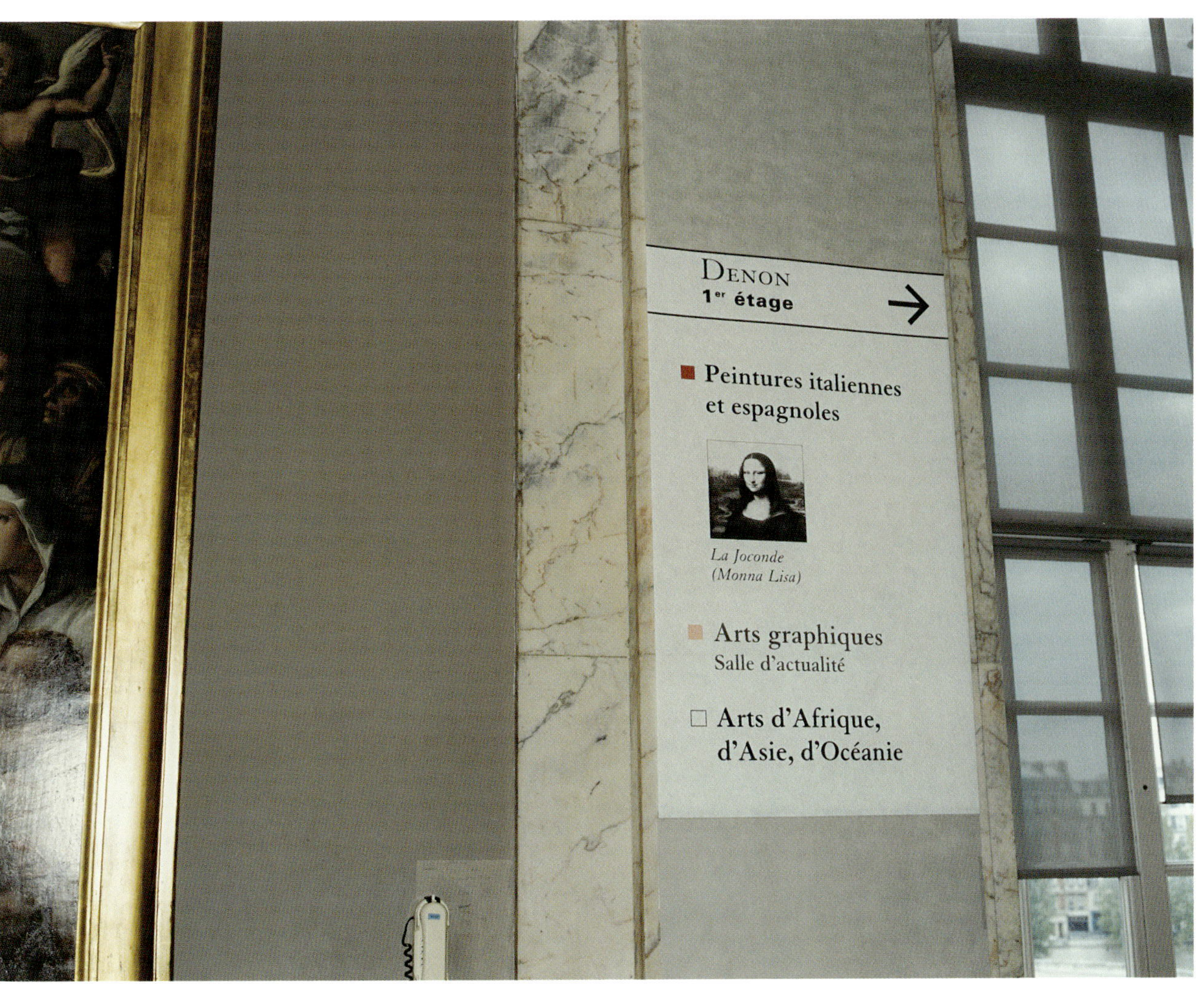
DENON
1er étage
Peintures italiennes
et espagnoles
La Joconde
(Monna Lisa)
Arts graphiques
Salle d'actualité
Arts d'Afrique,
d'Asie, d'Océanie

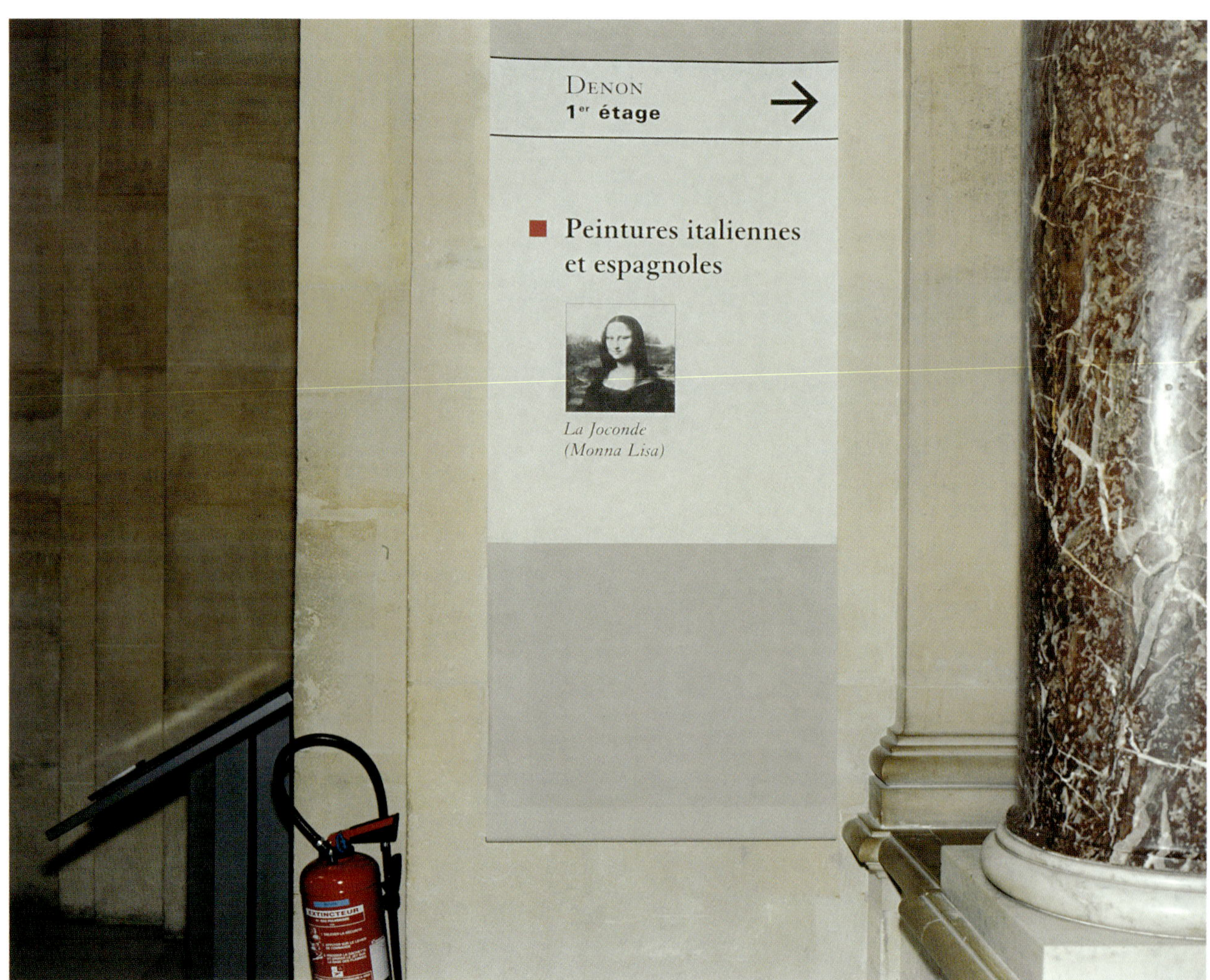
DENON
1er étage
Peintures italiennes
et espagnoles
La Joconde
(Monna Lisa)
EXTINCTEUR

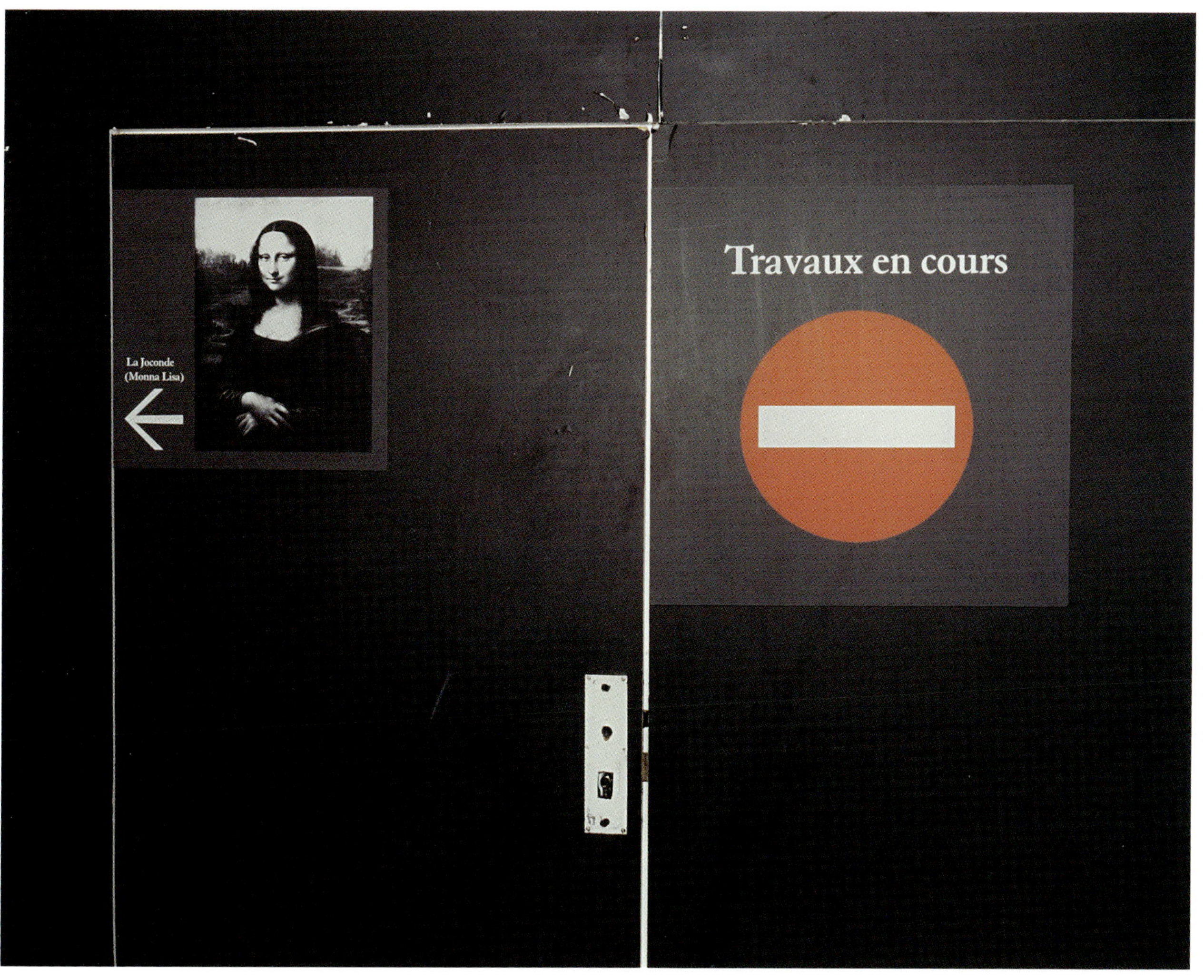
La Joconde
(Monna Lisa)
Travaux en cours

PICTURED
2004–06

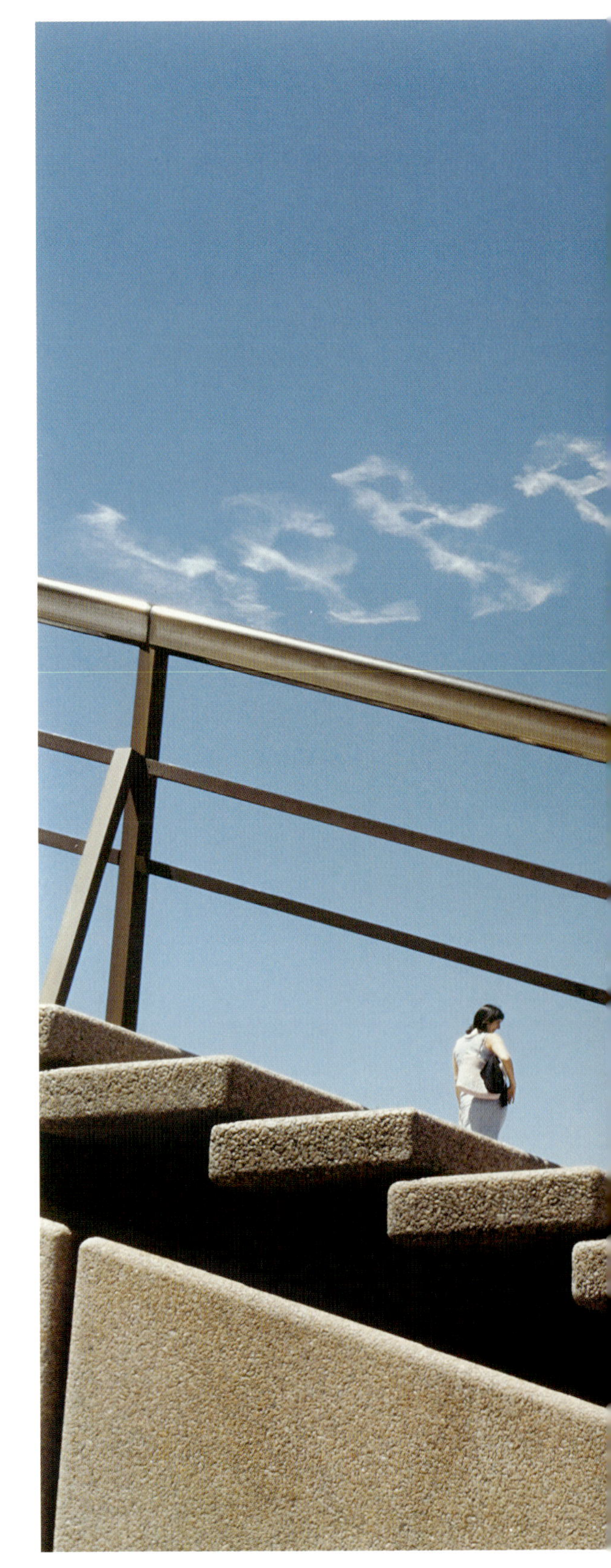

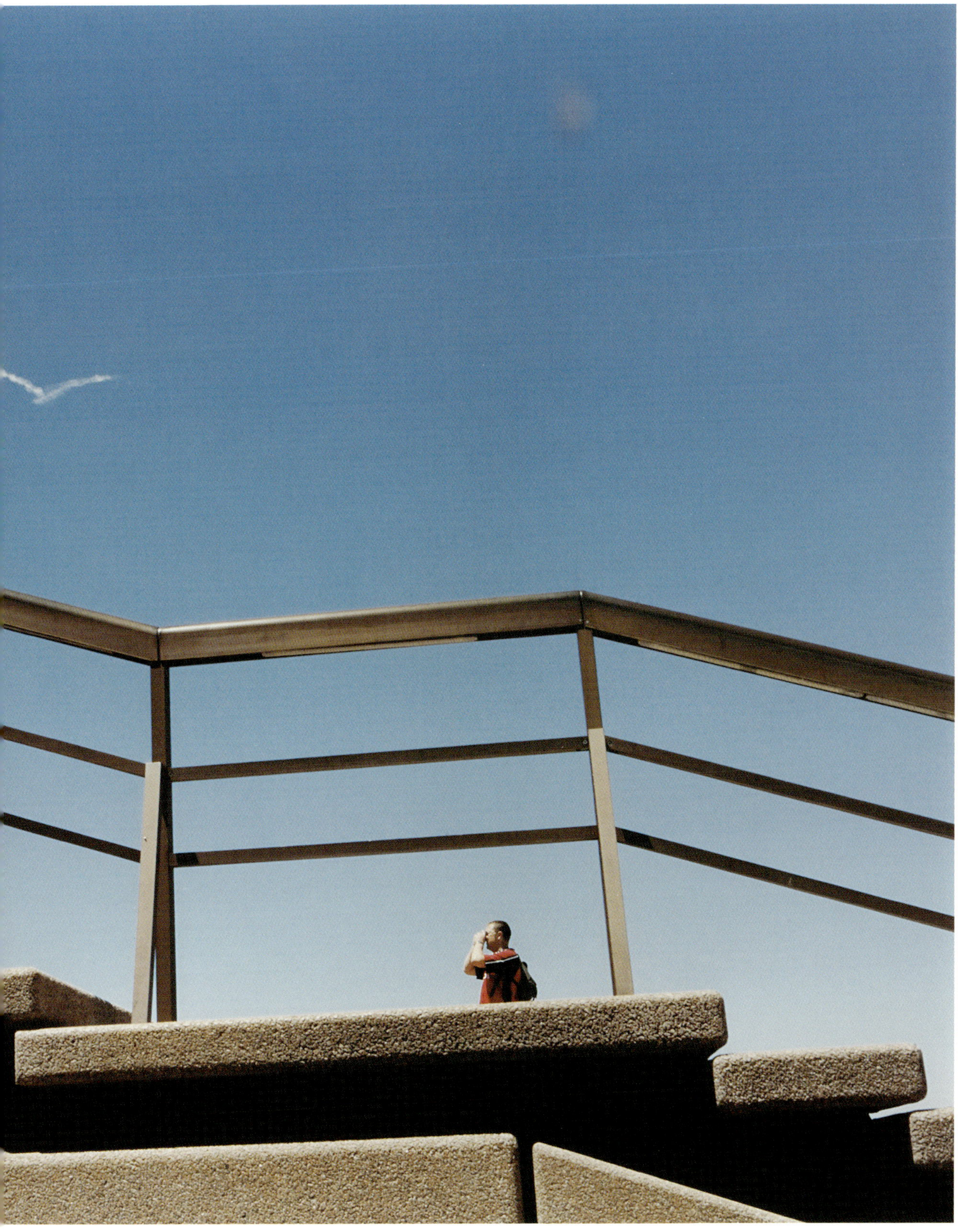

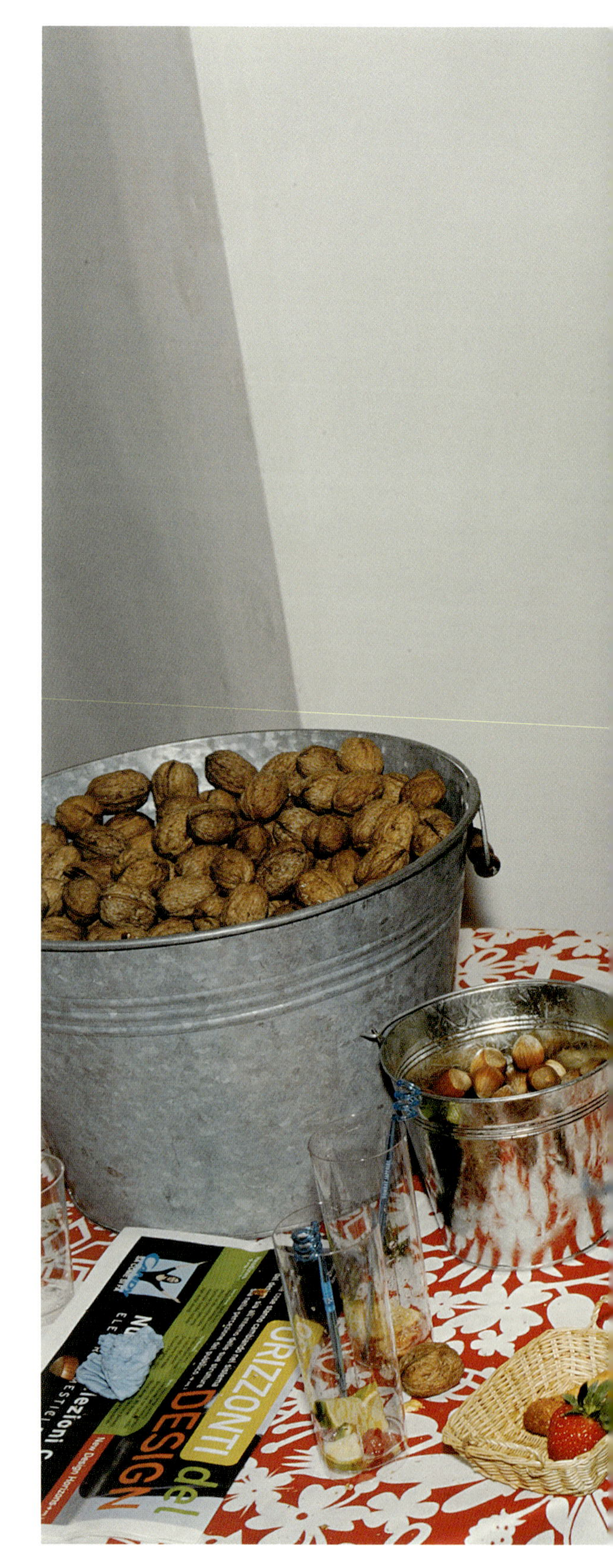
del
DESIGN

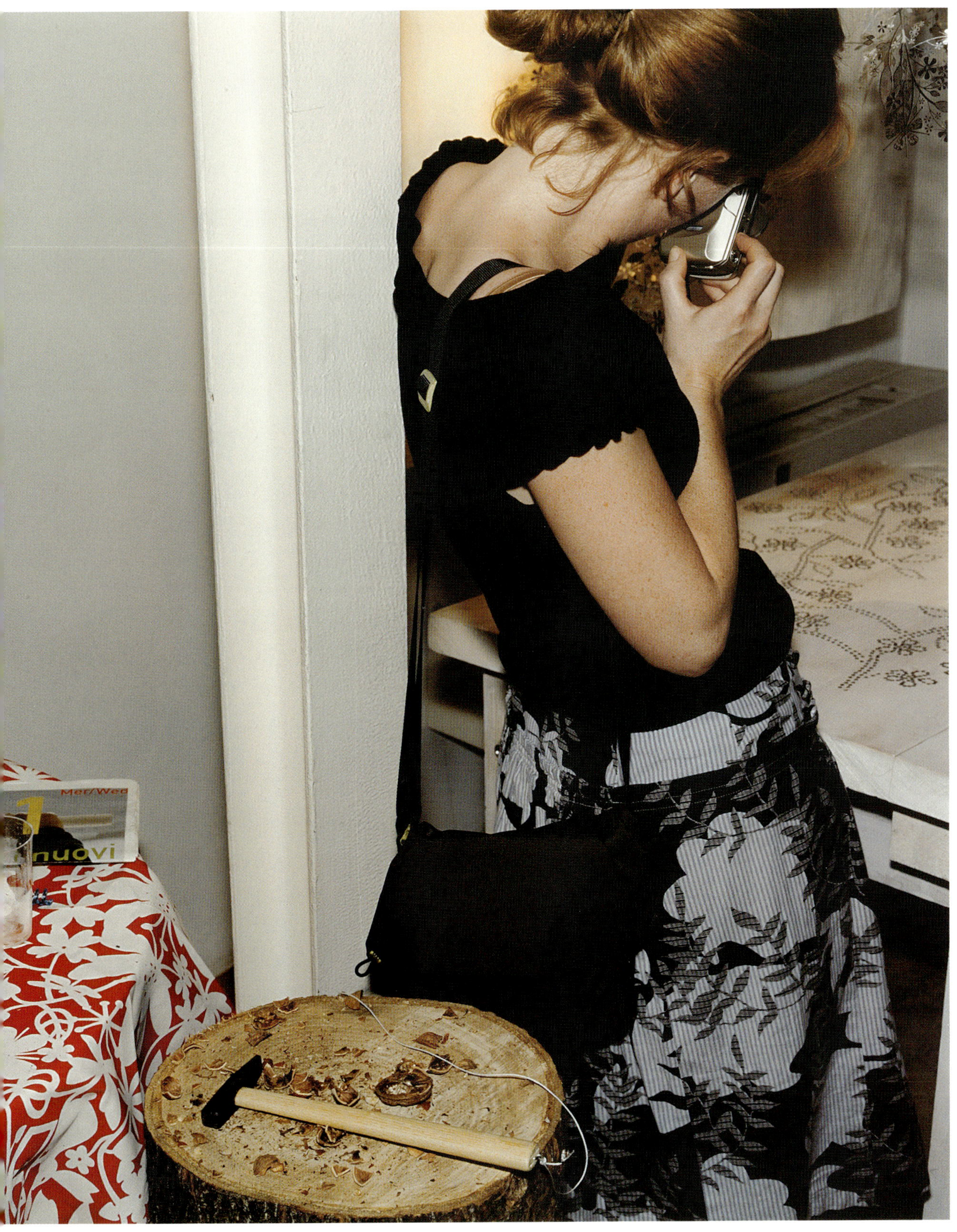
Mer/Wed
1
nuovi

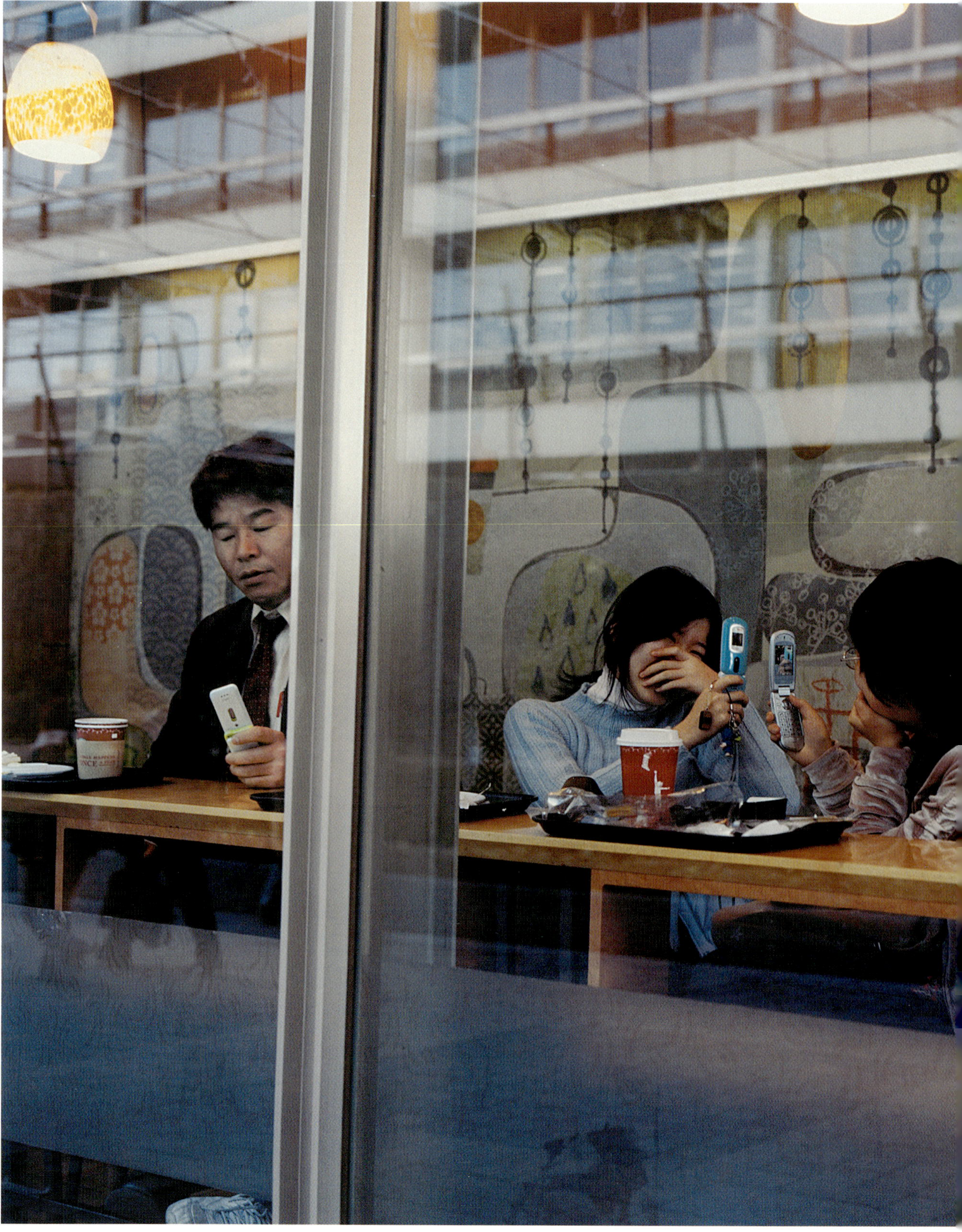

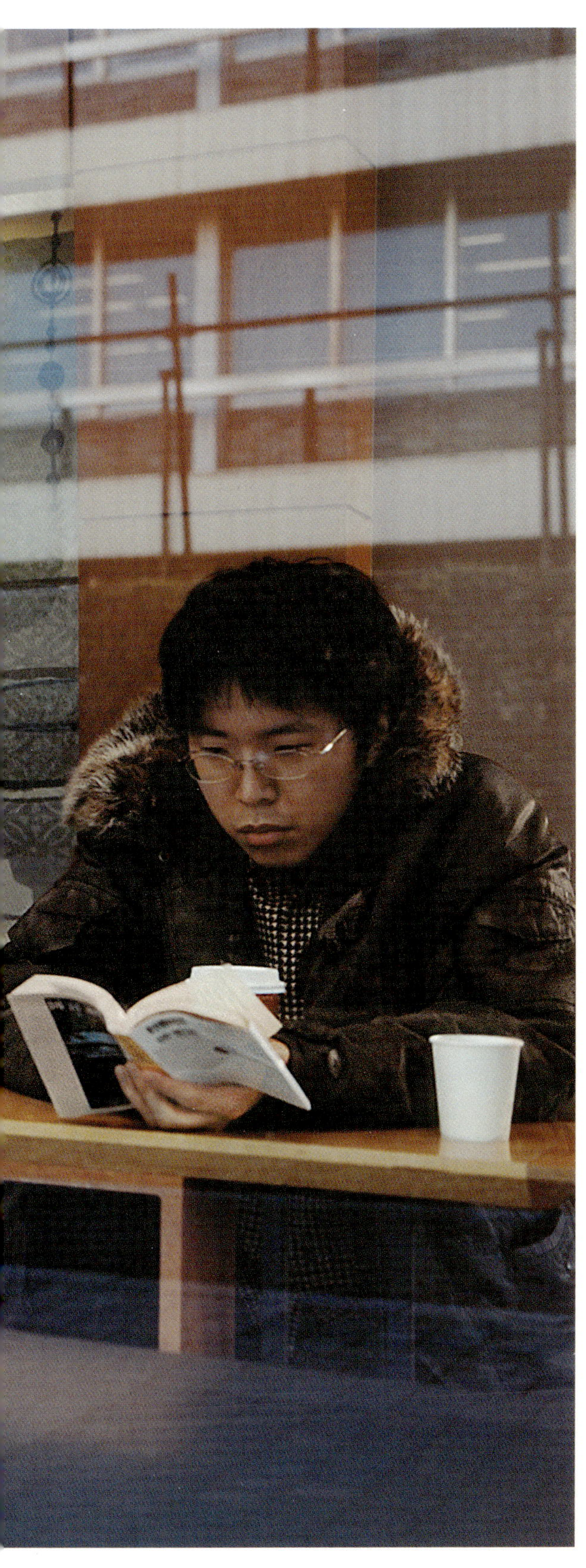

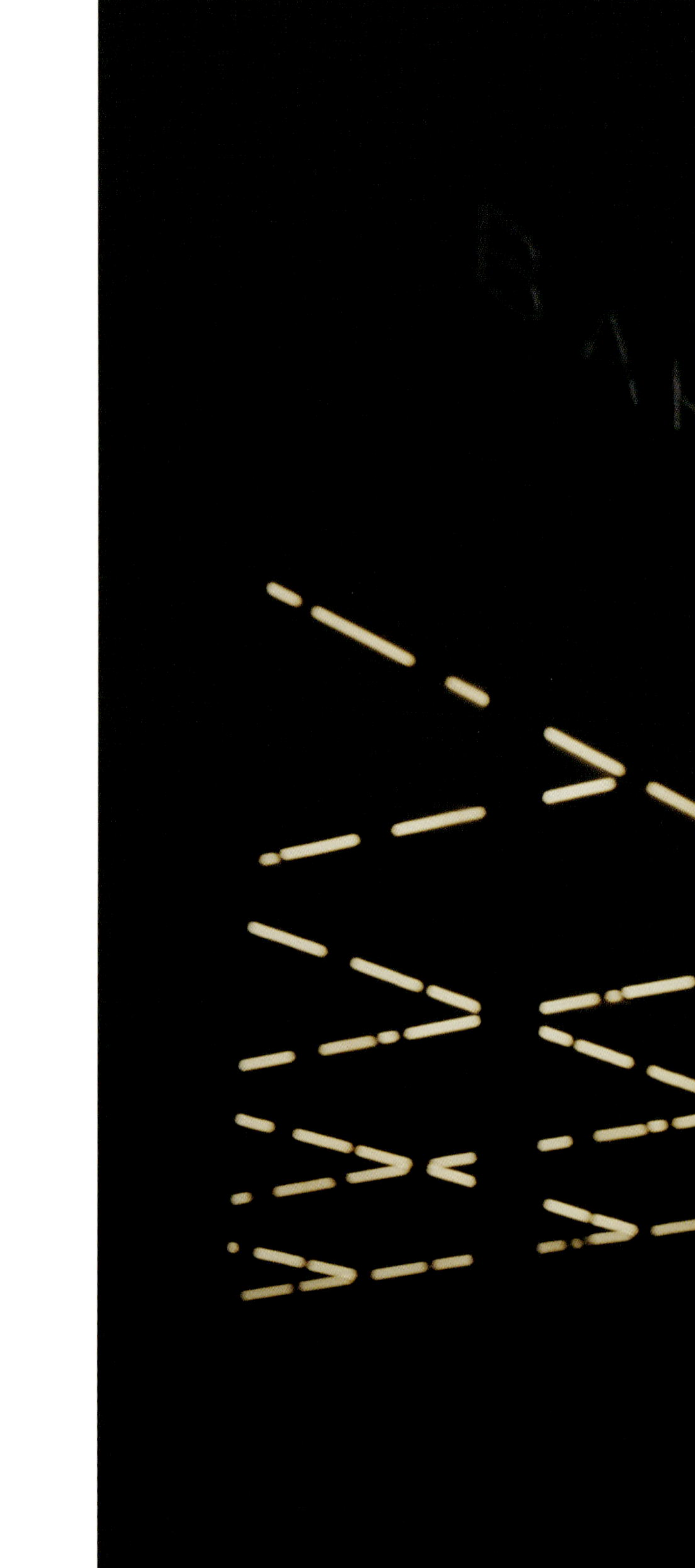

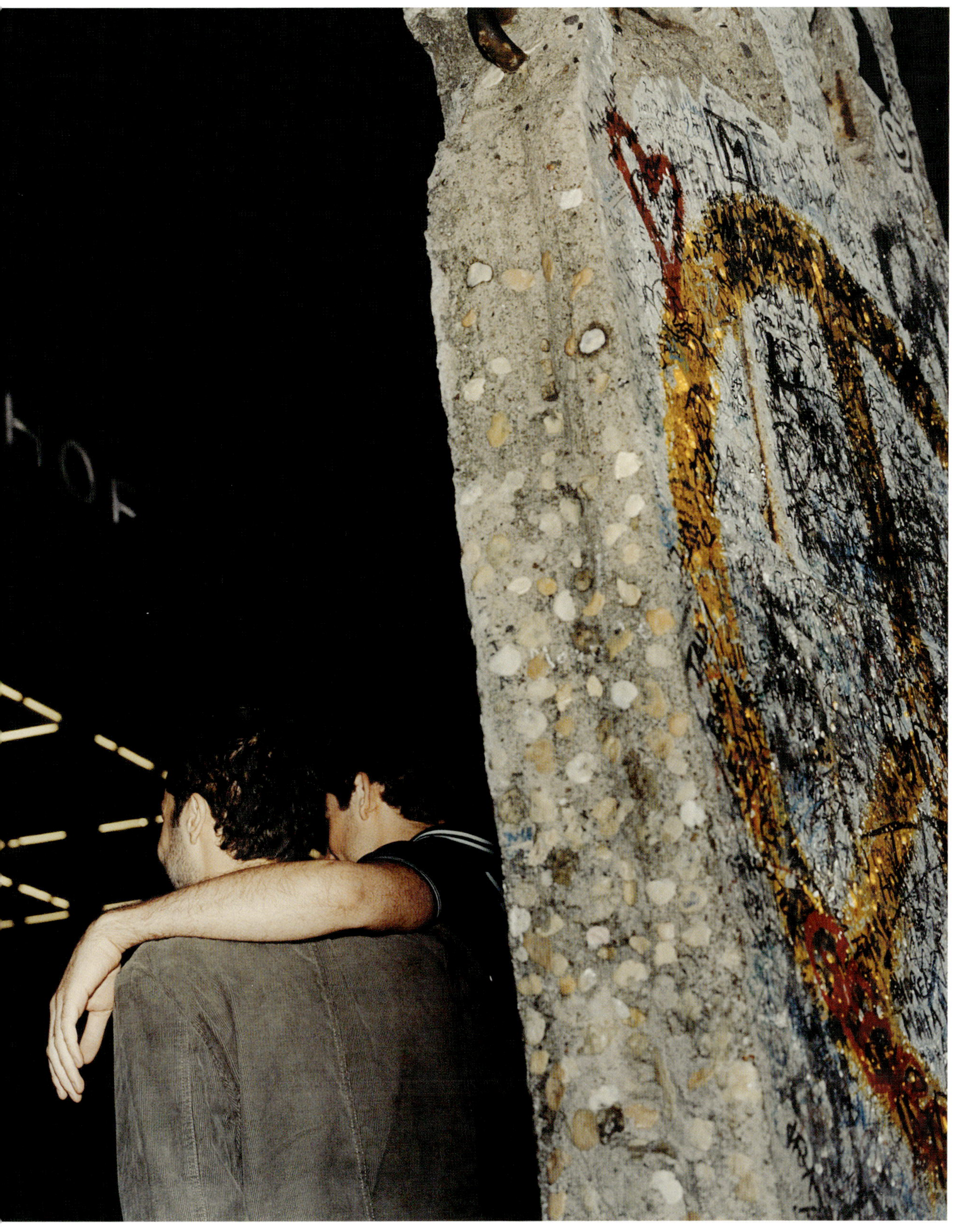

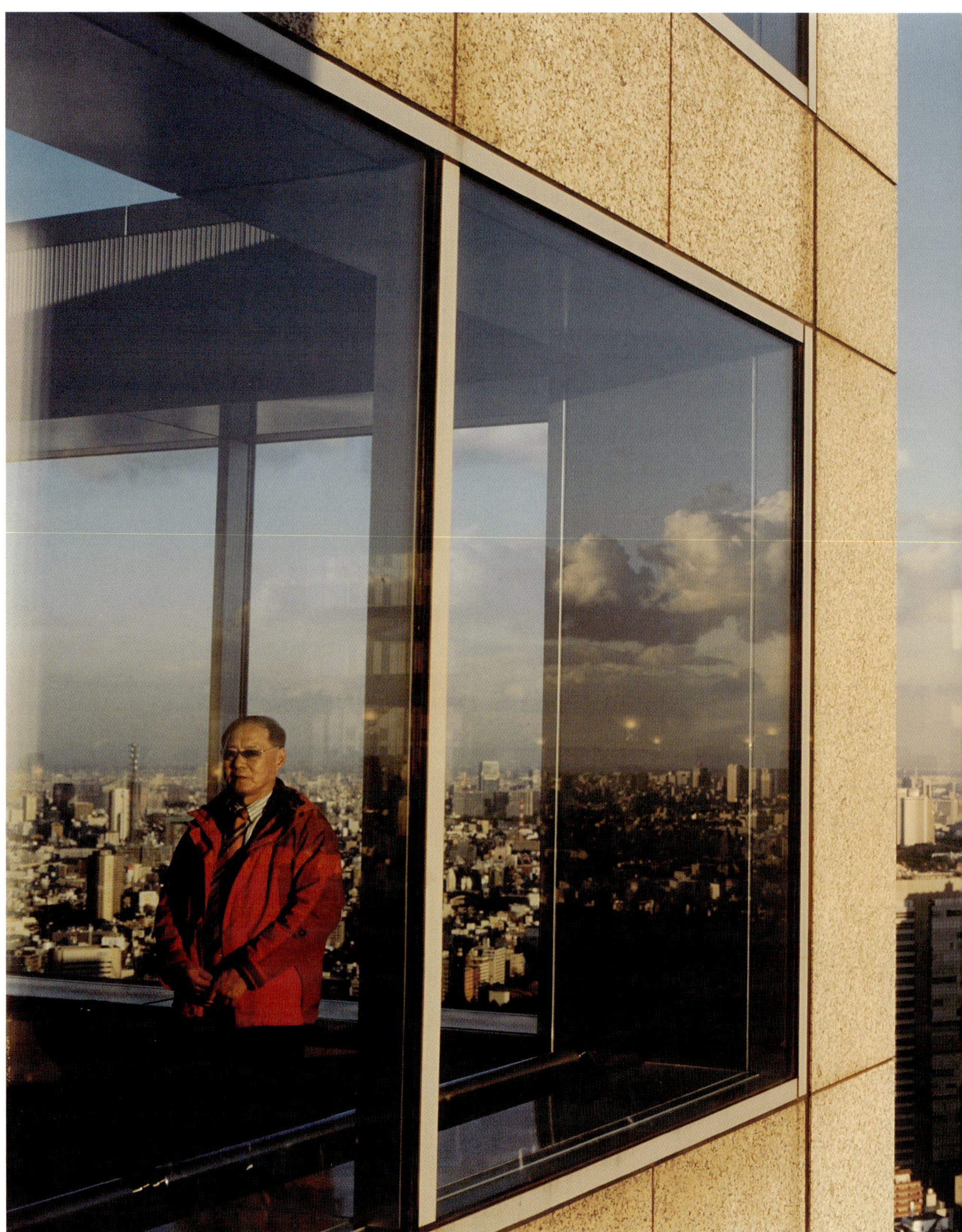

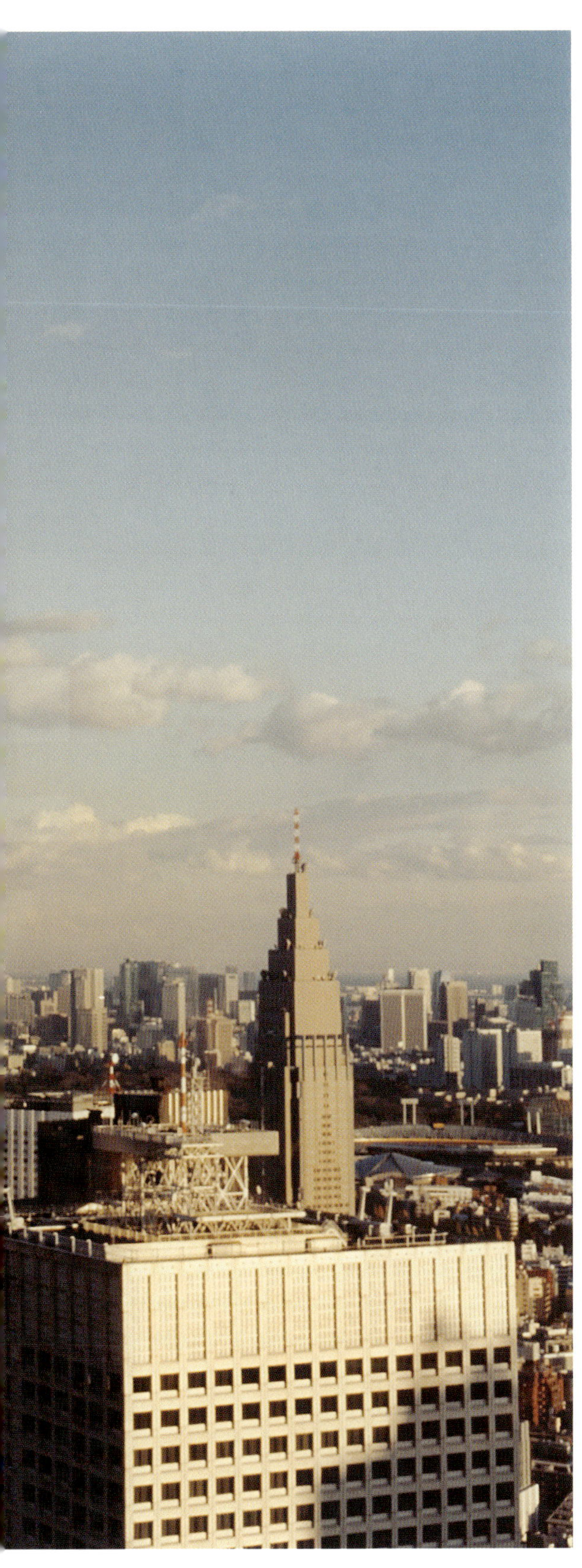

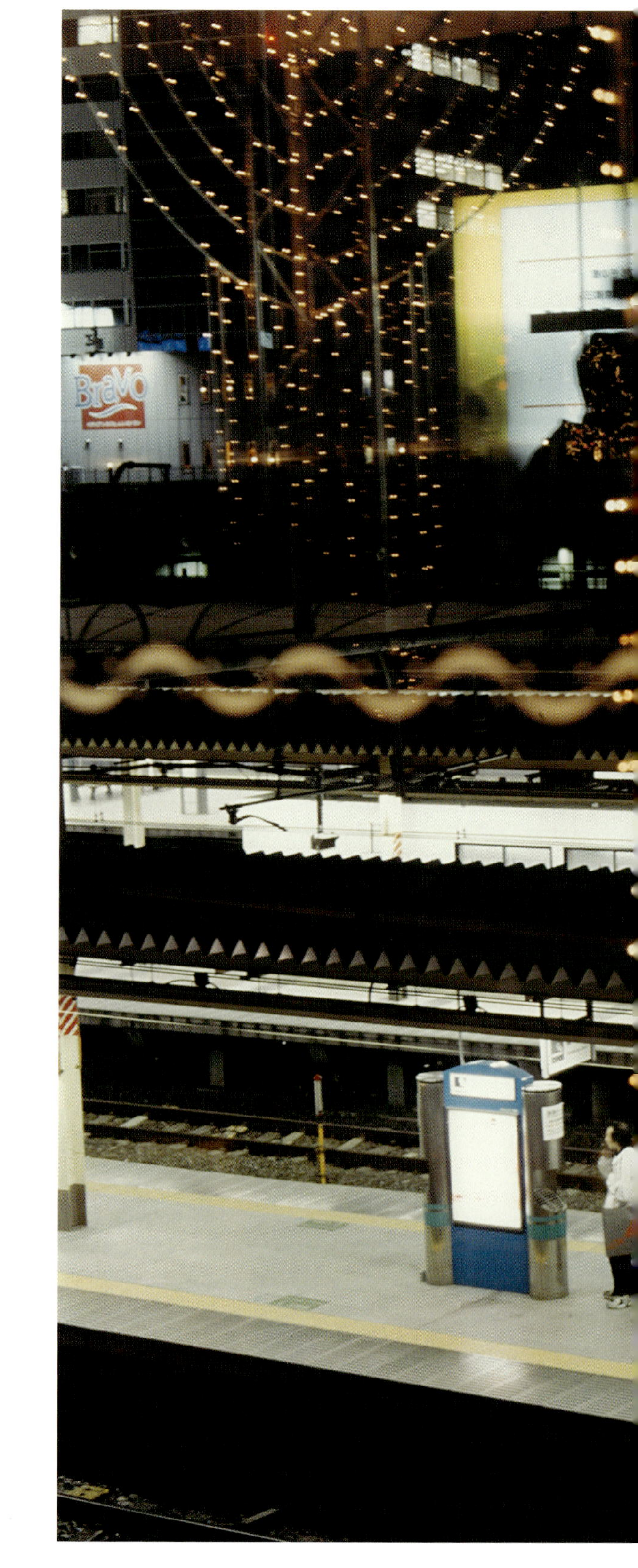
BraVo

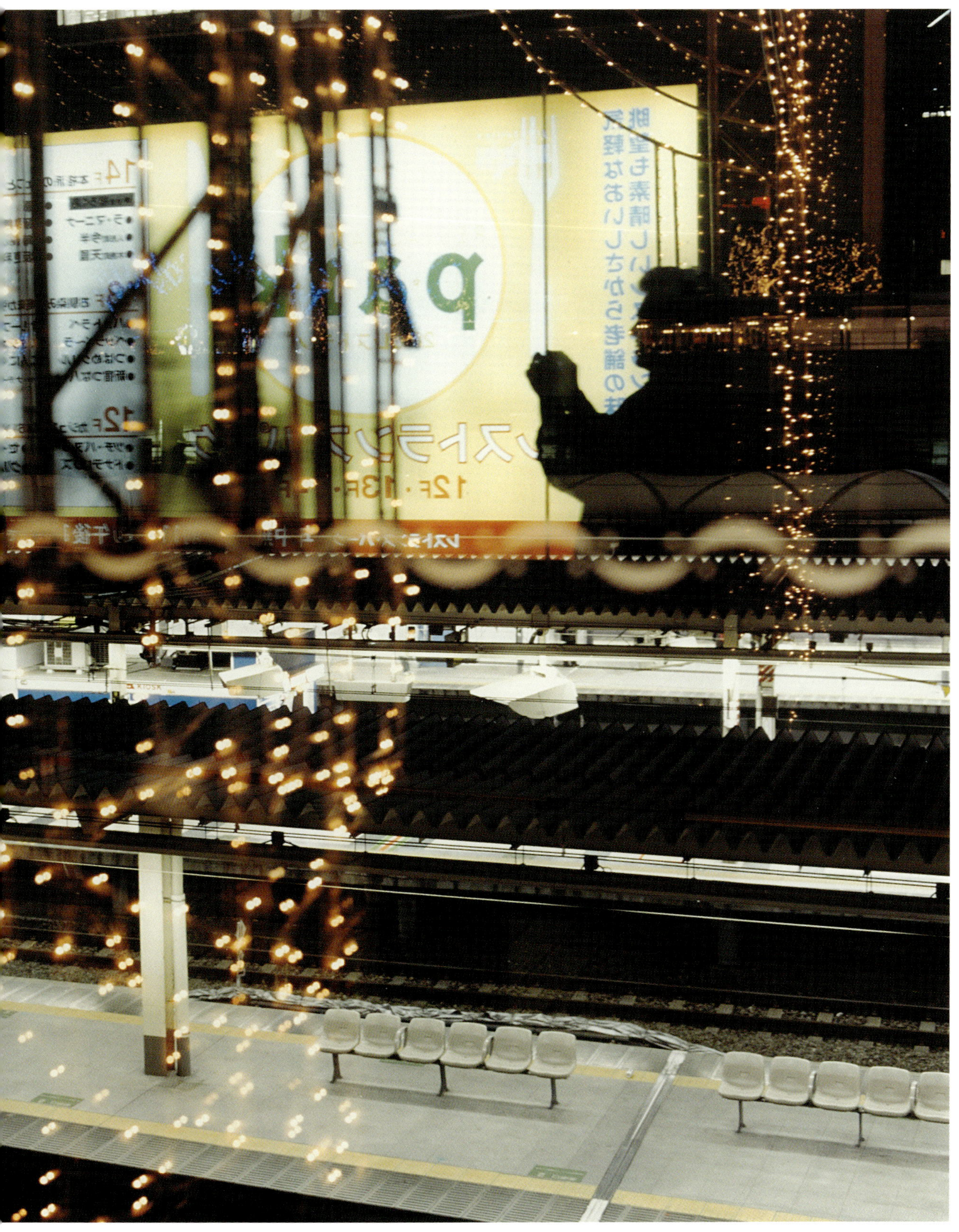

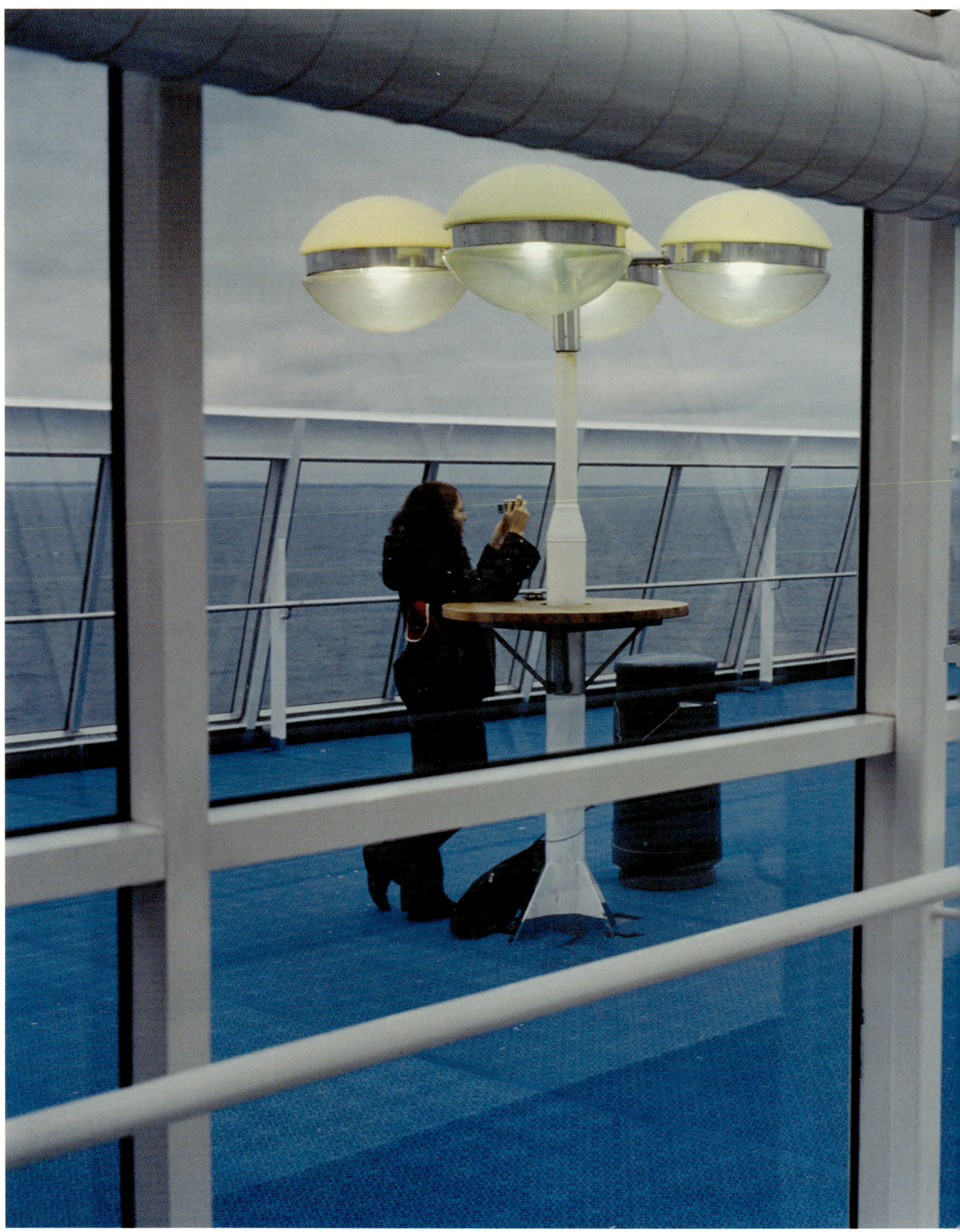

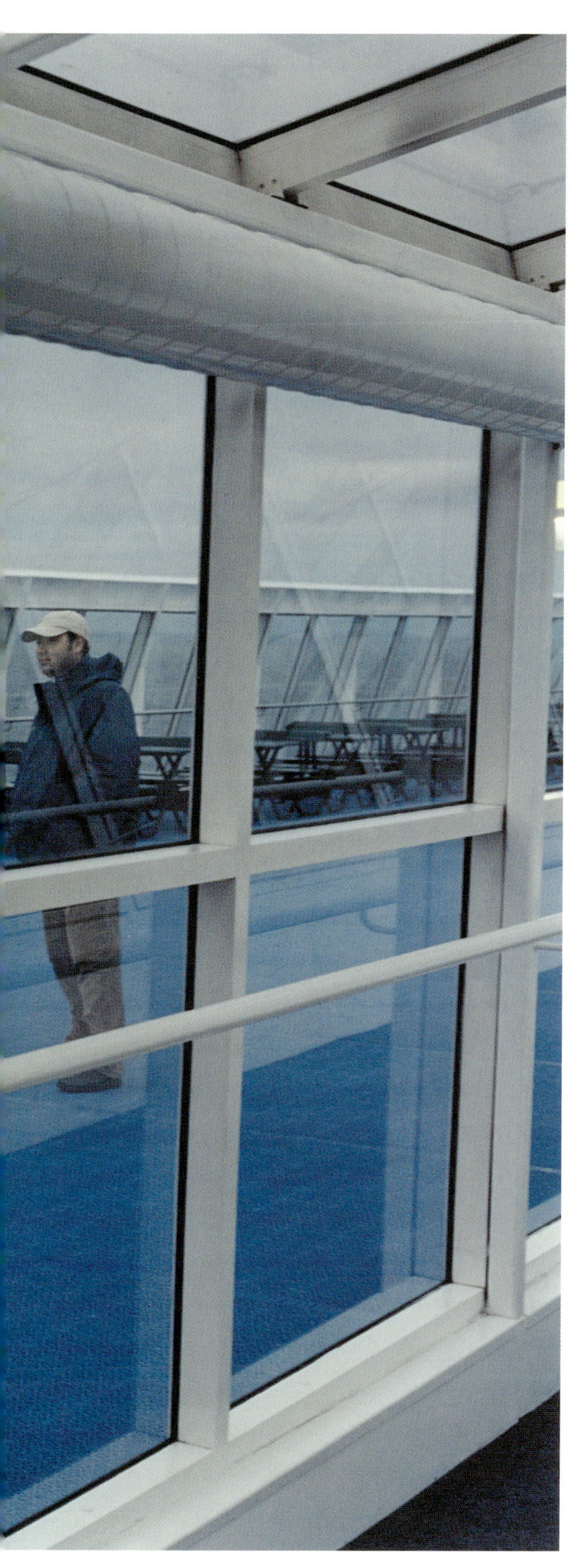

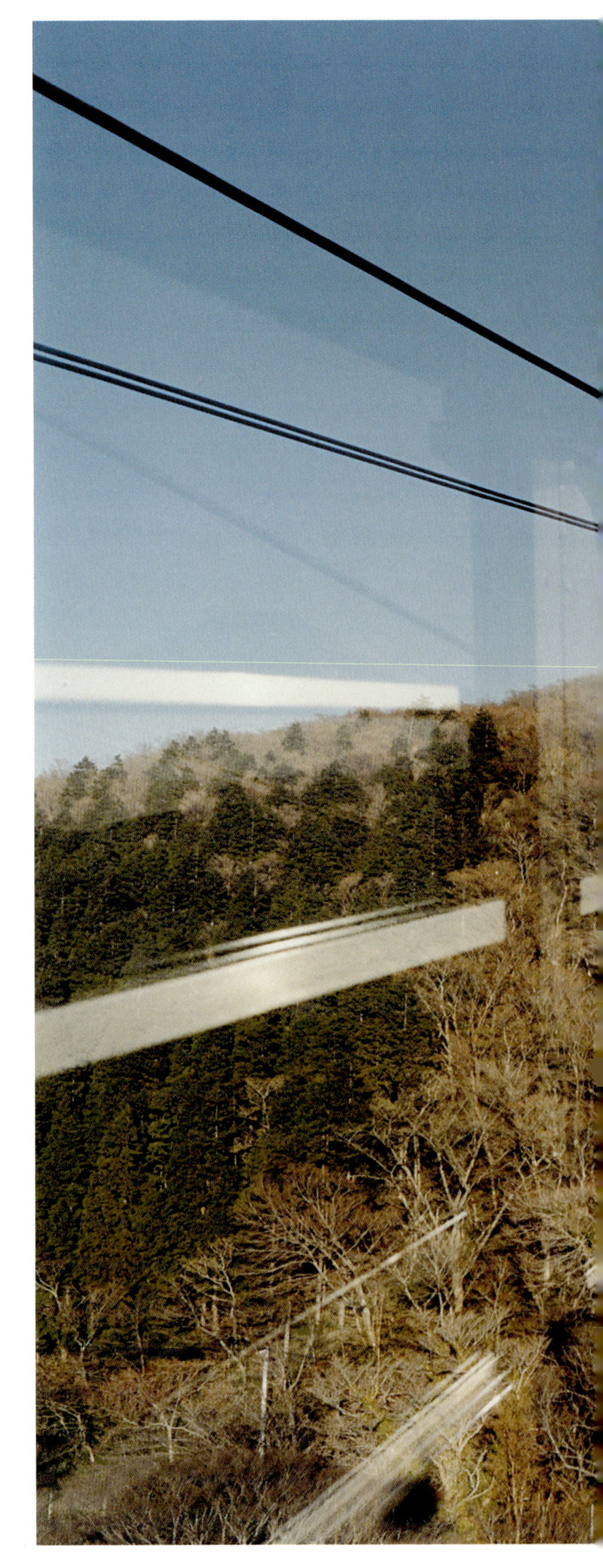

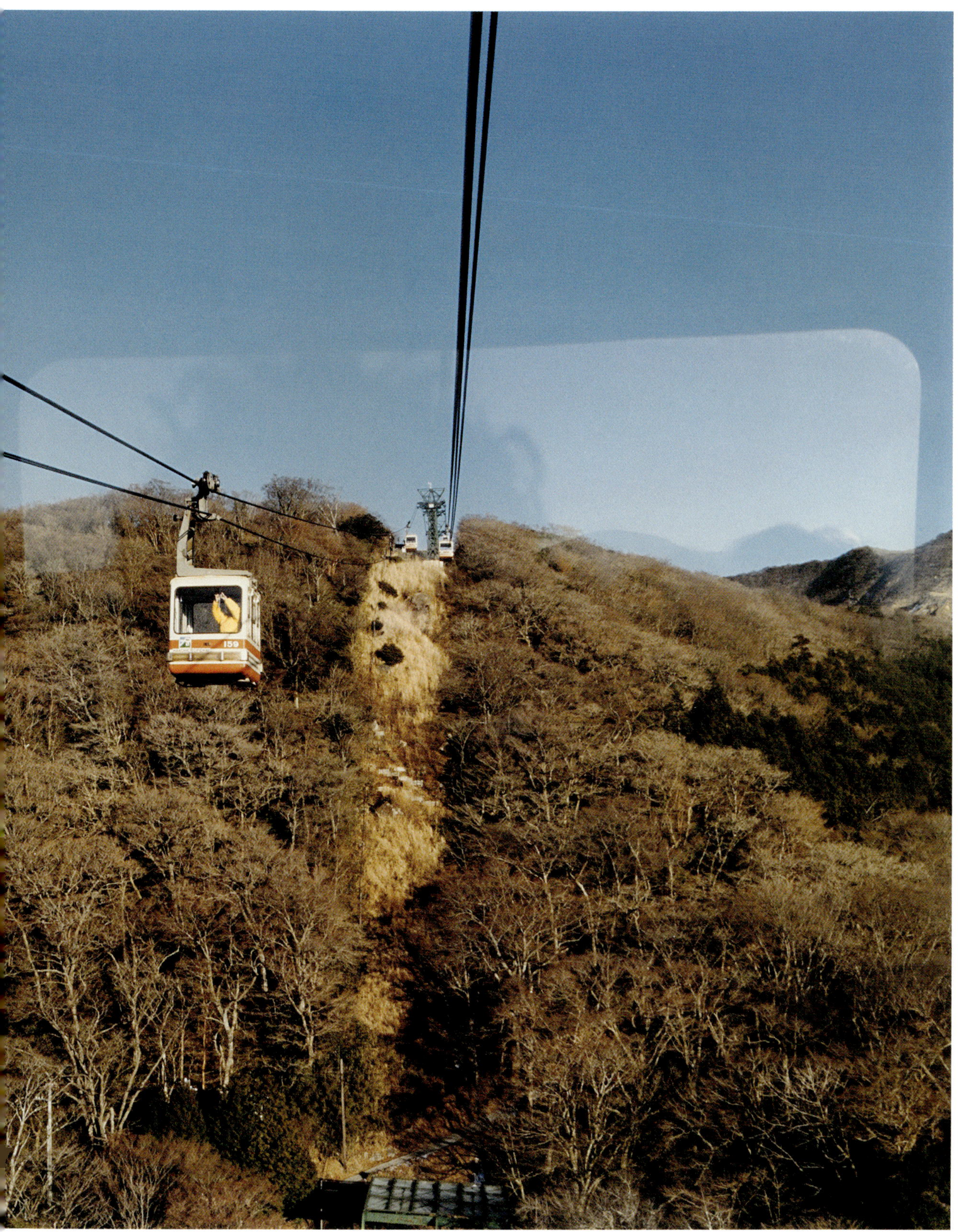
159

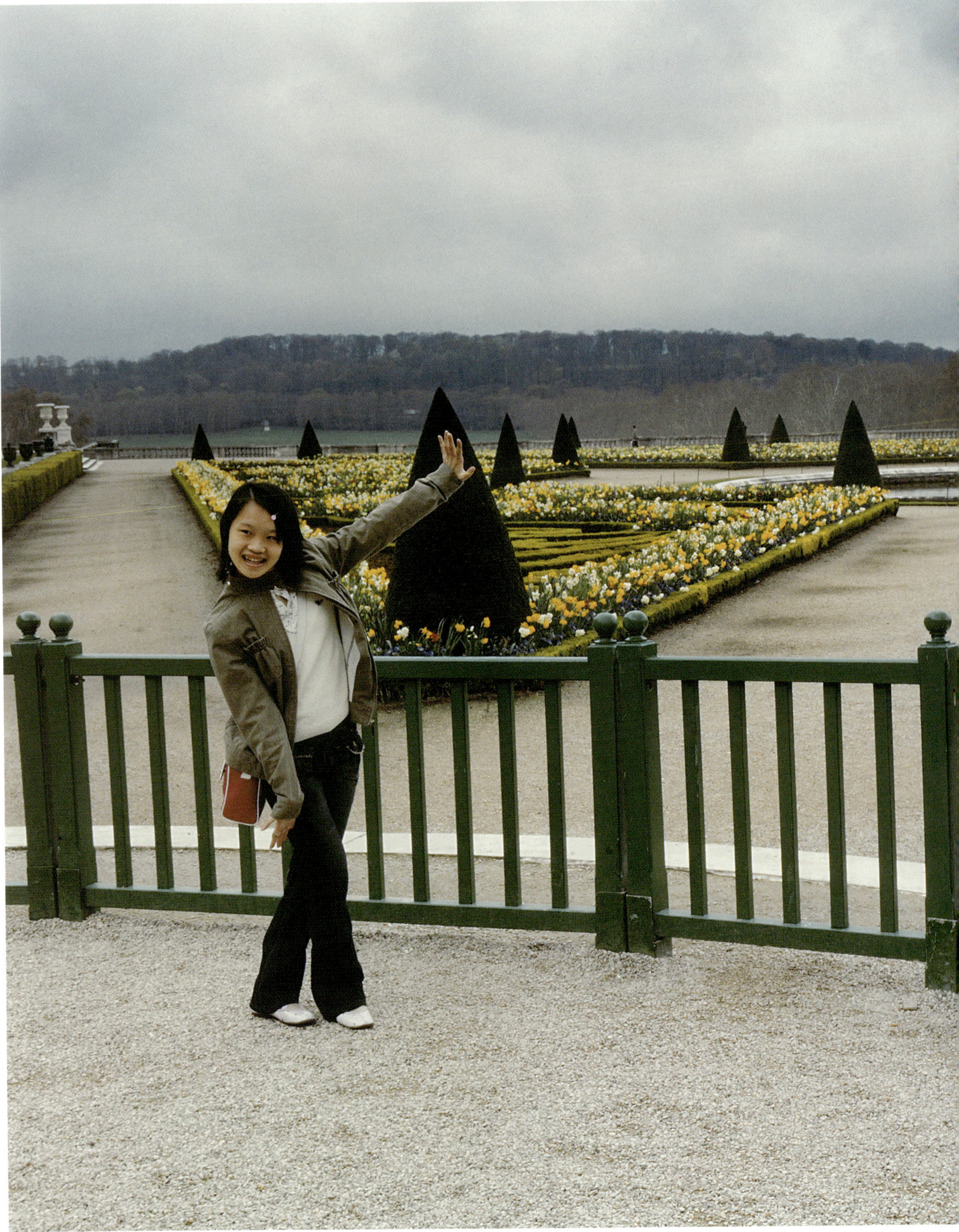

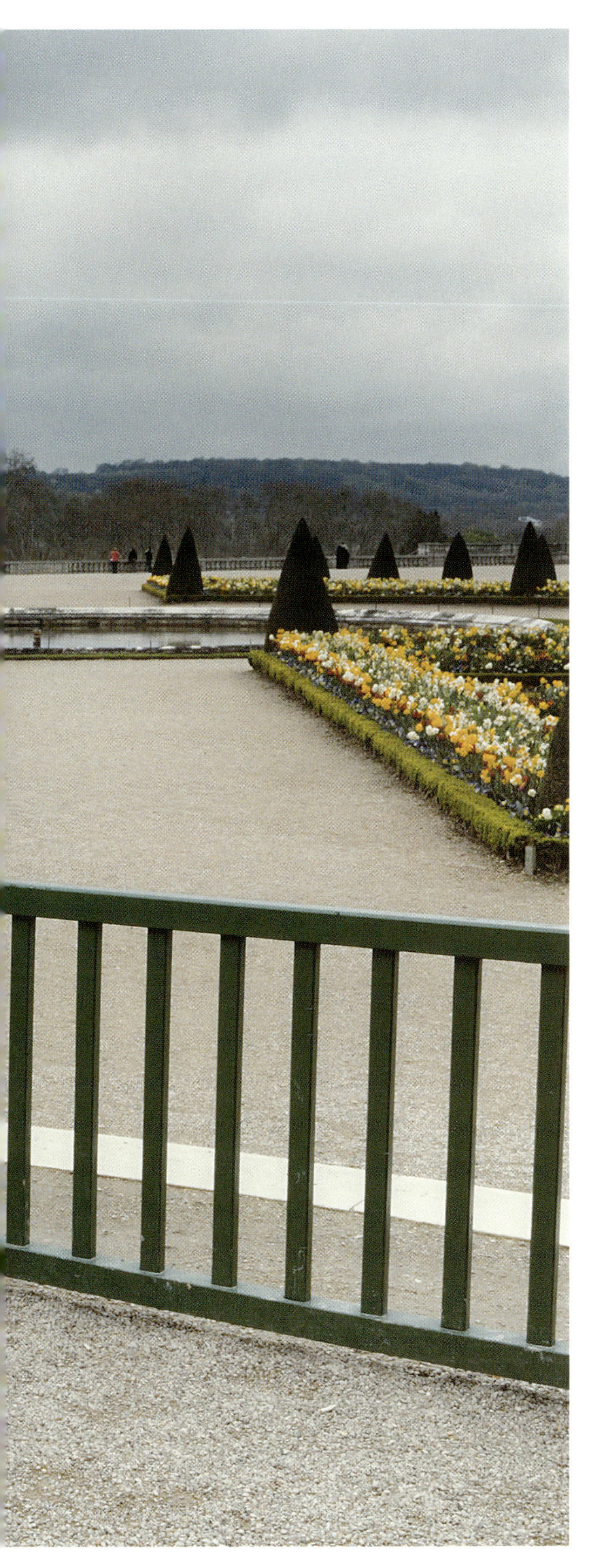

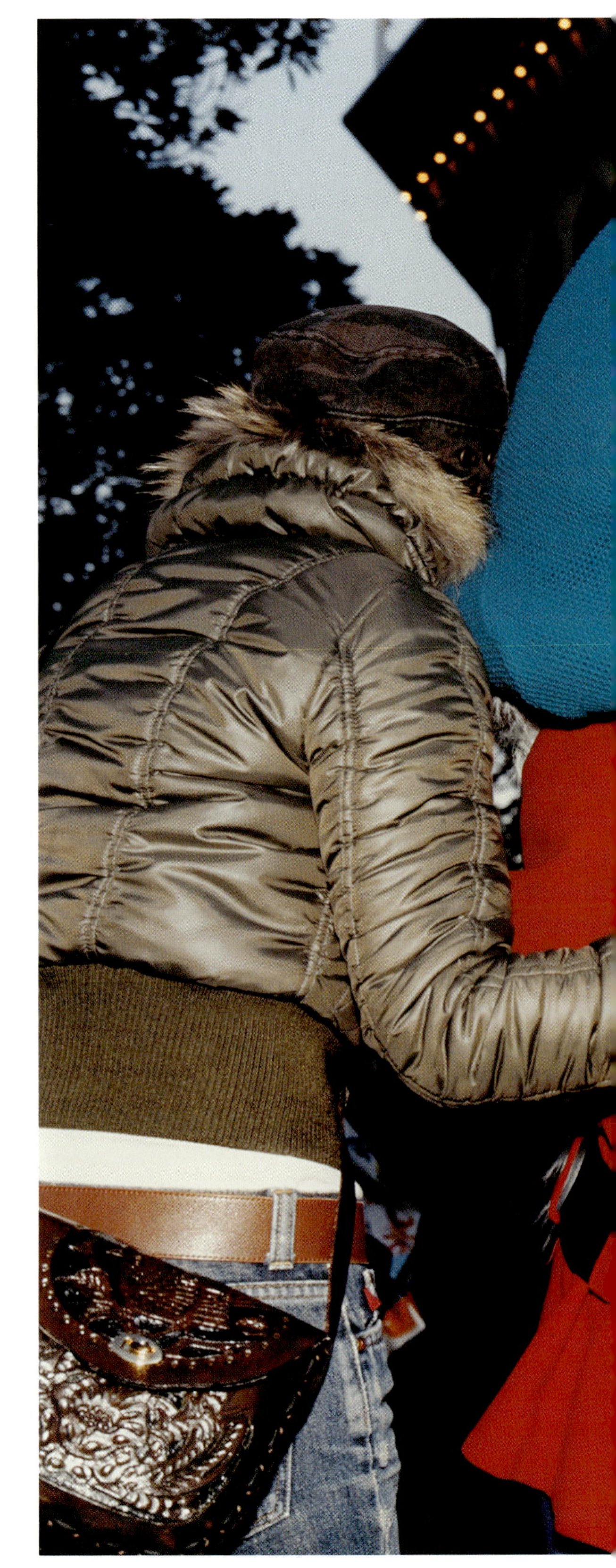

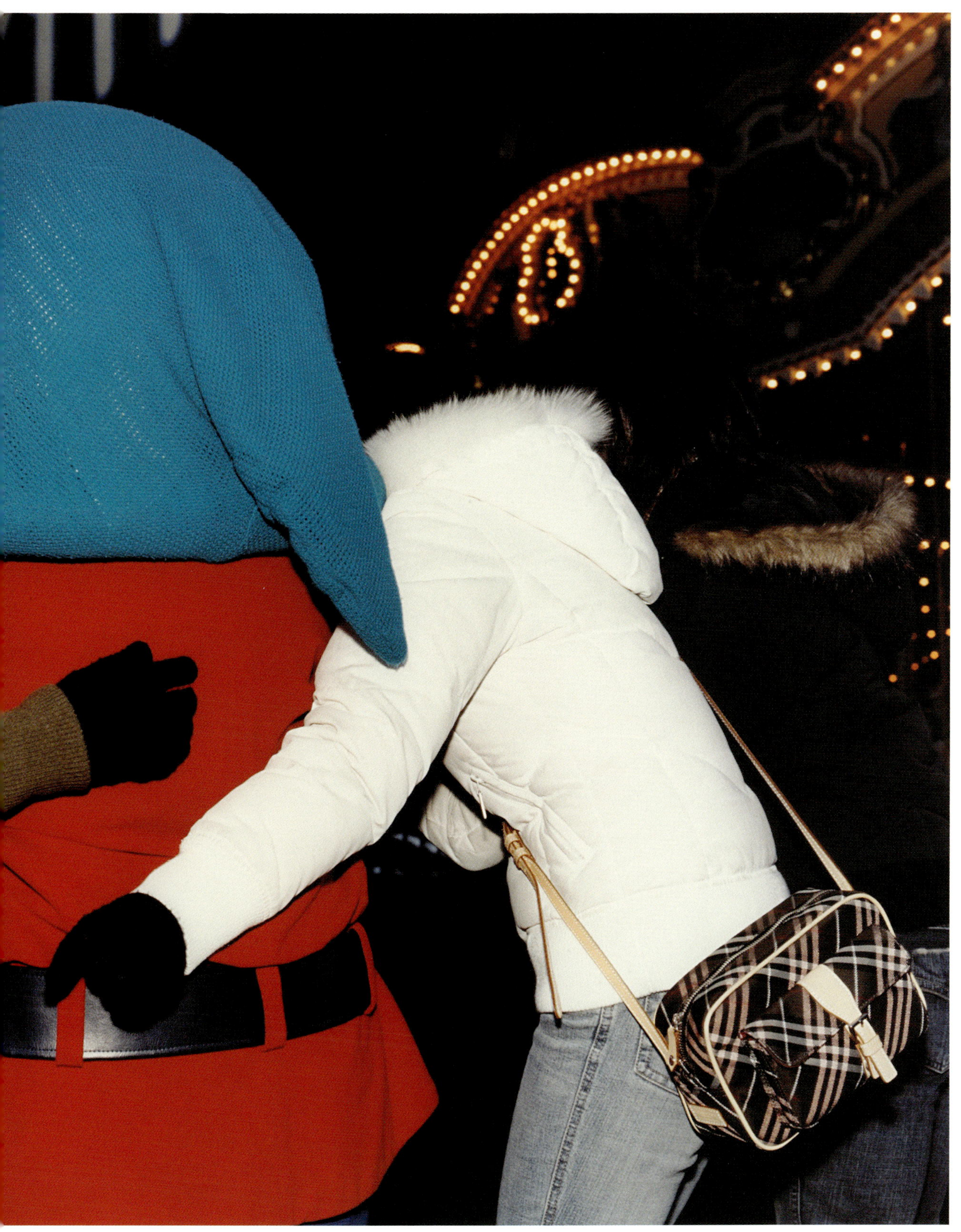

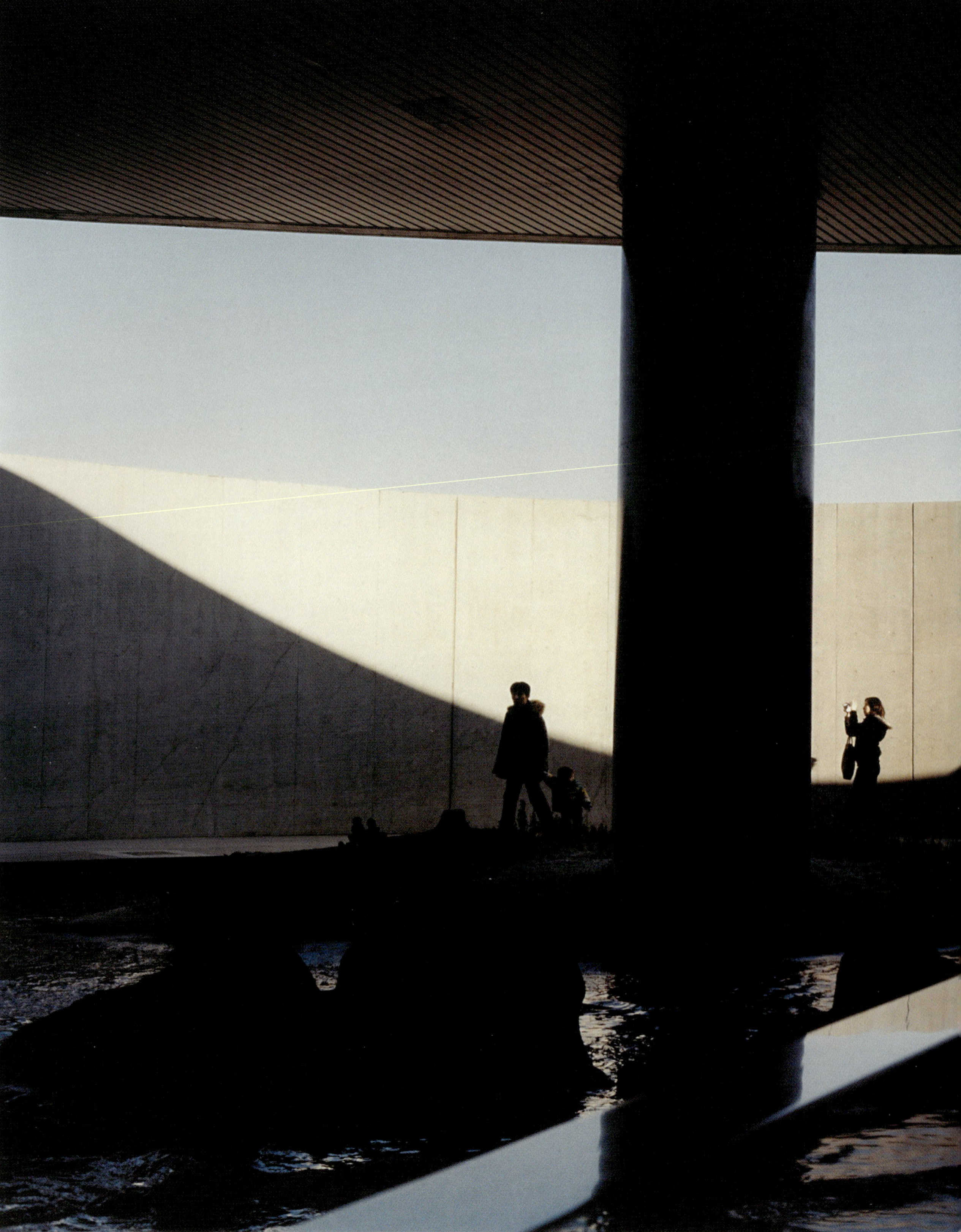

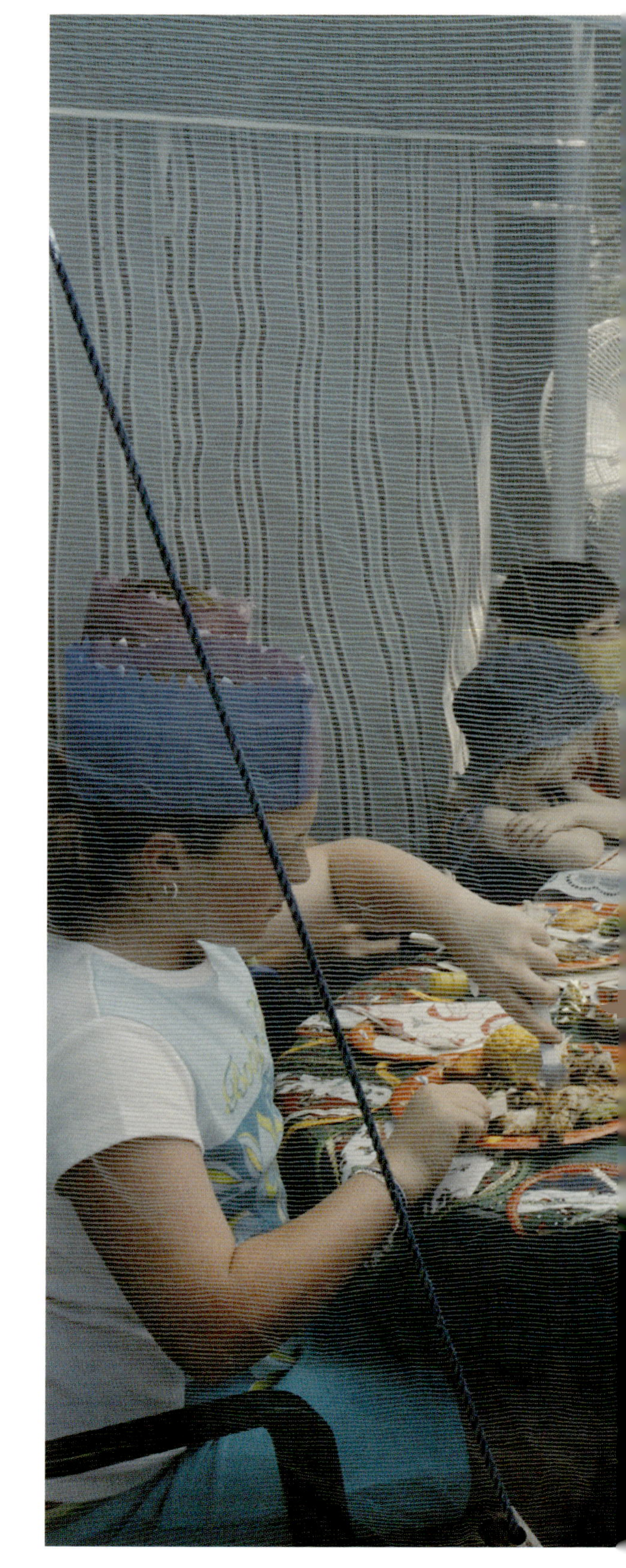

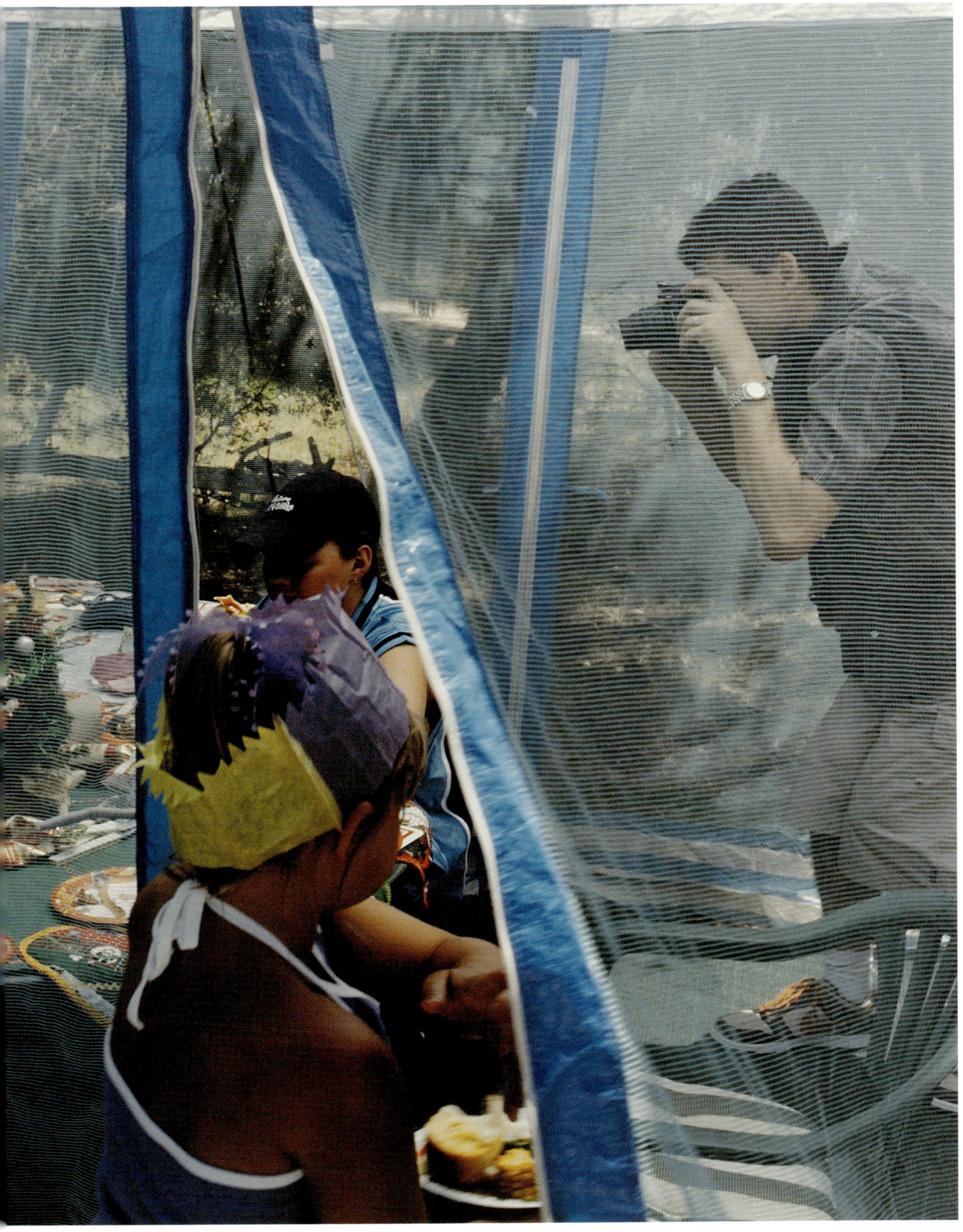

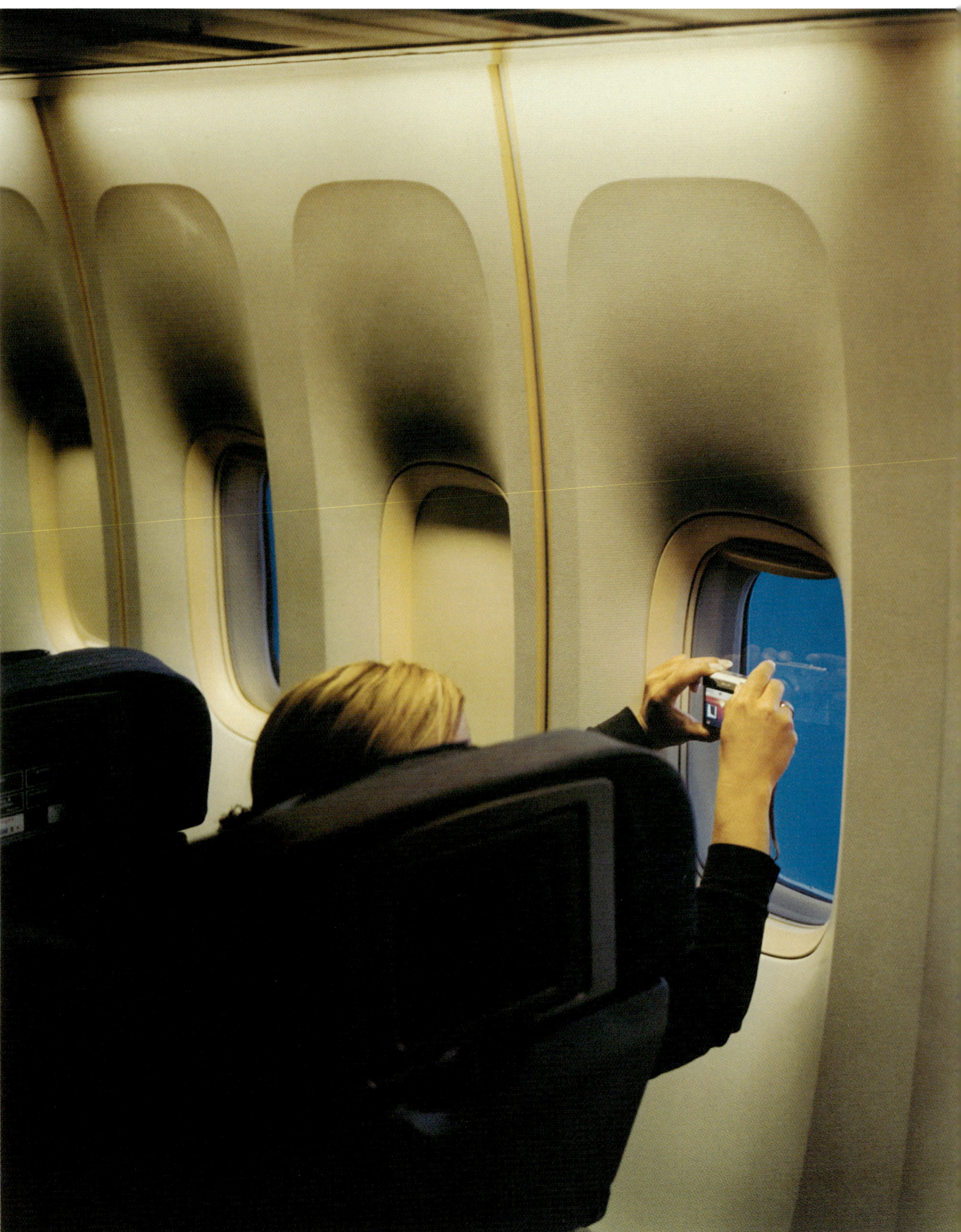

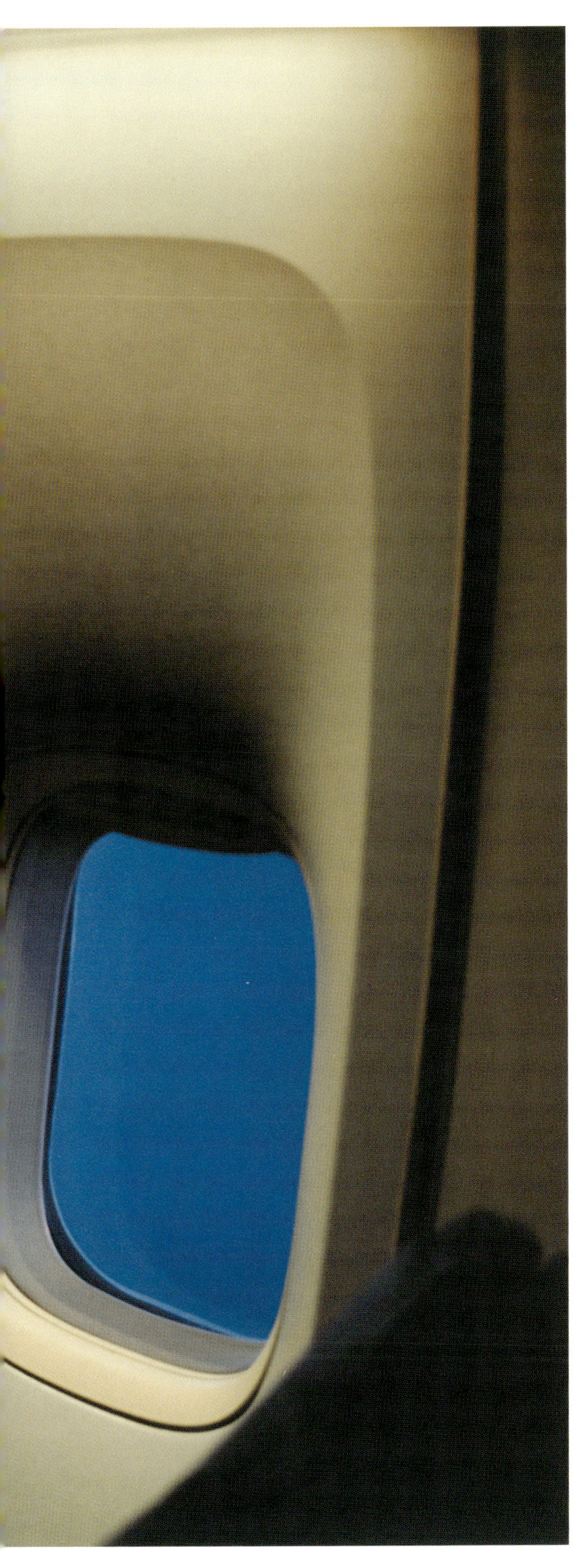

07

10 FIRE EXTINGUISHERS & 13 HOUSEPLANTS 2004–07

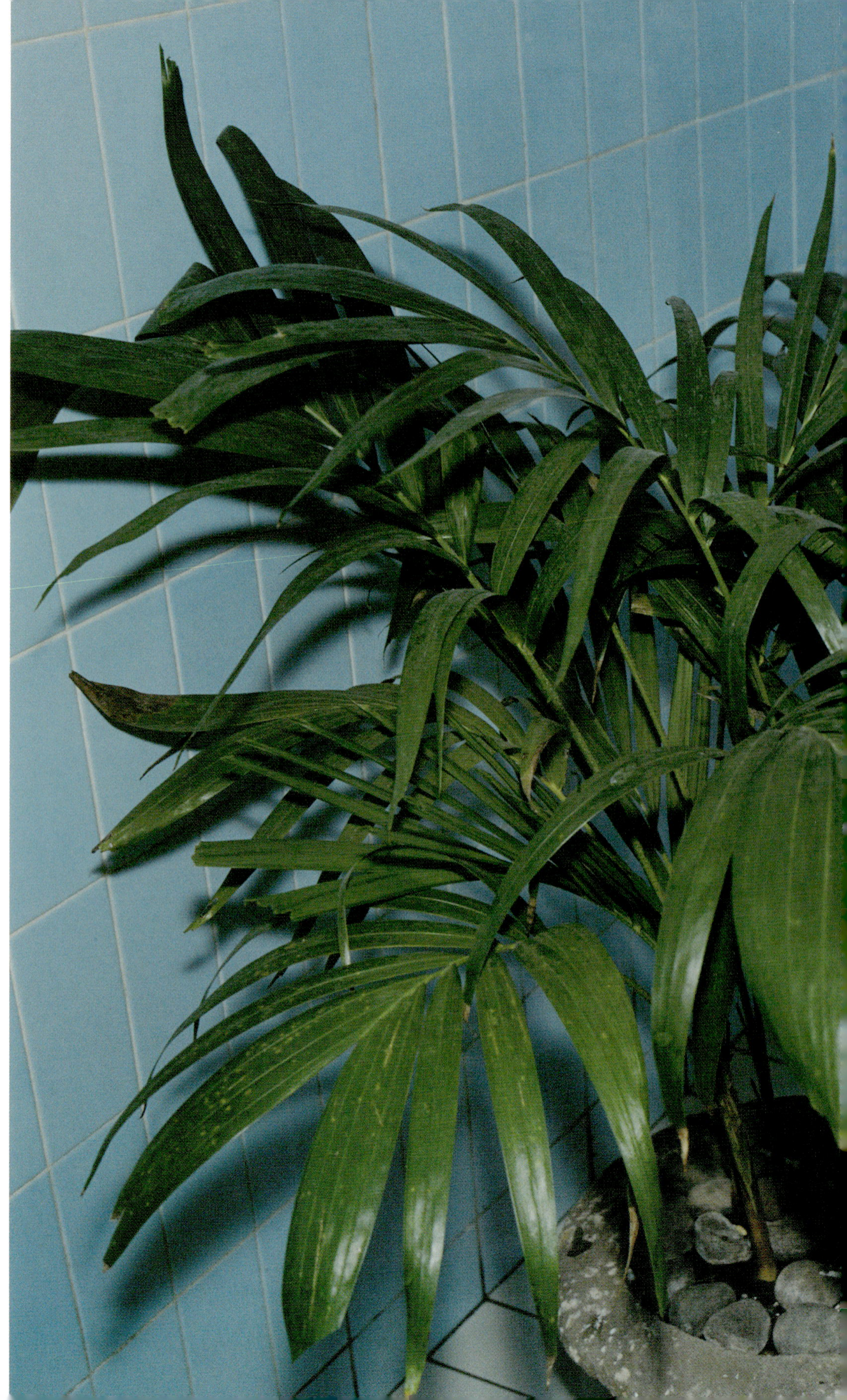

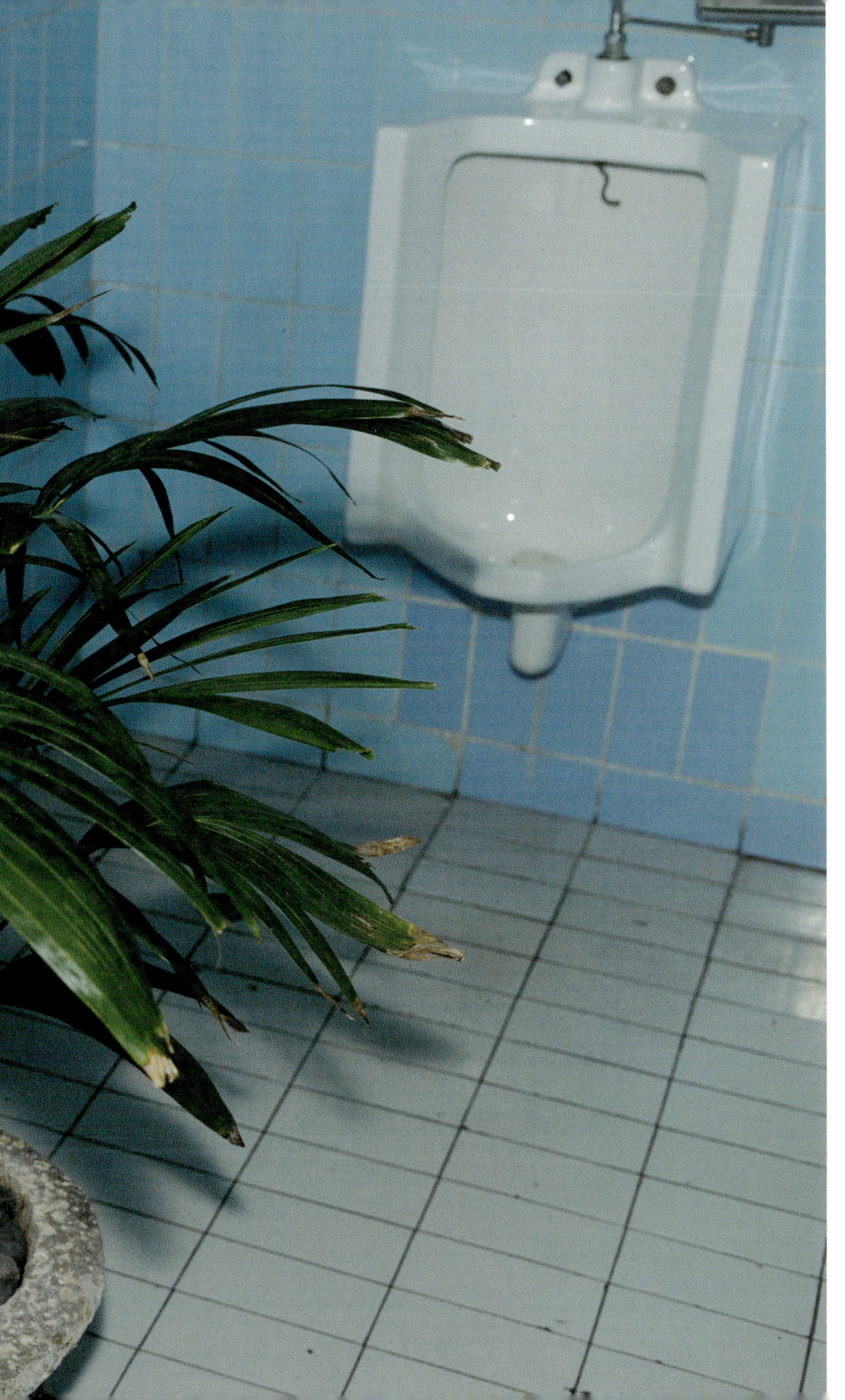

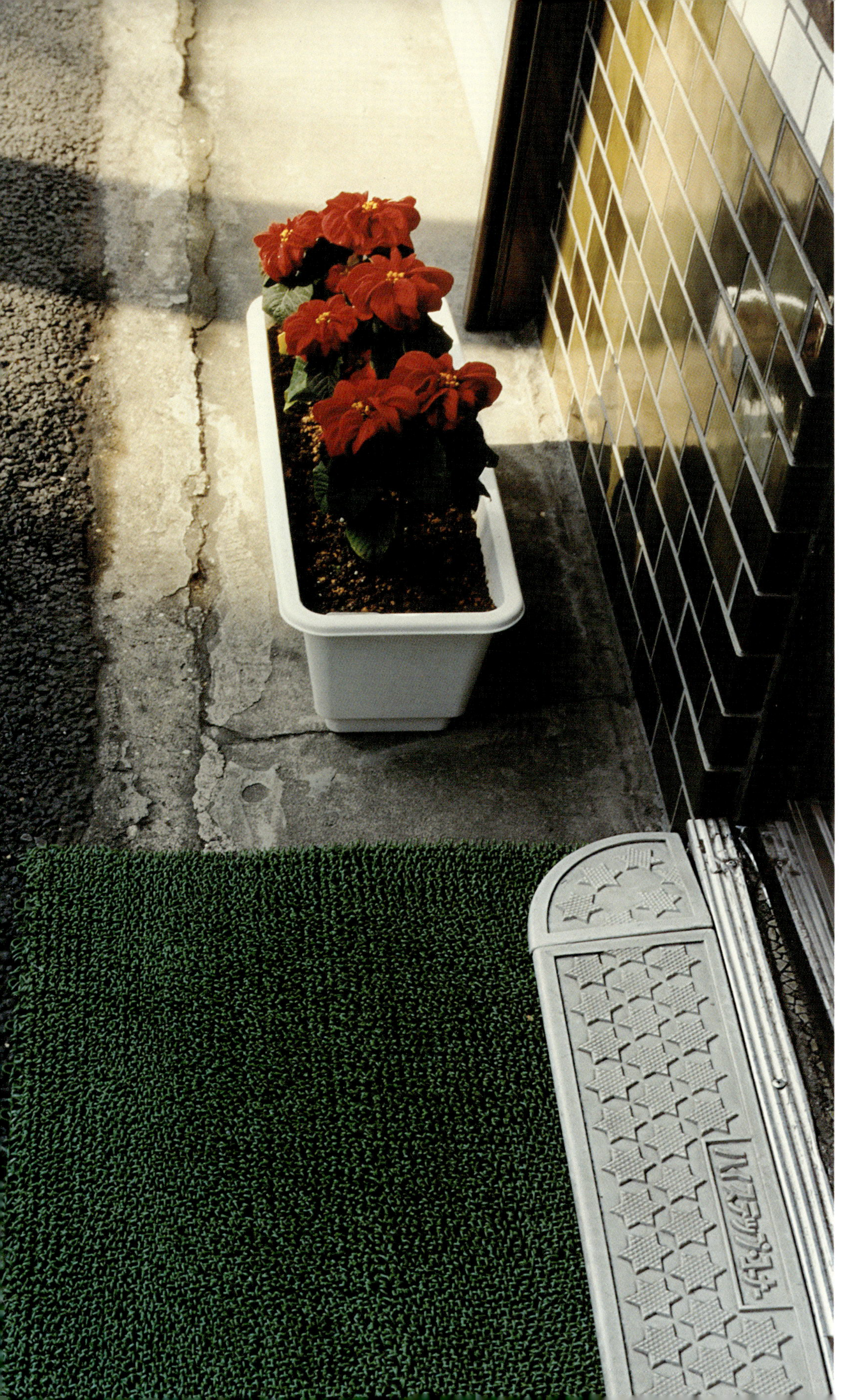

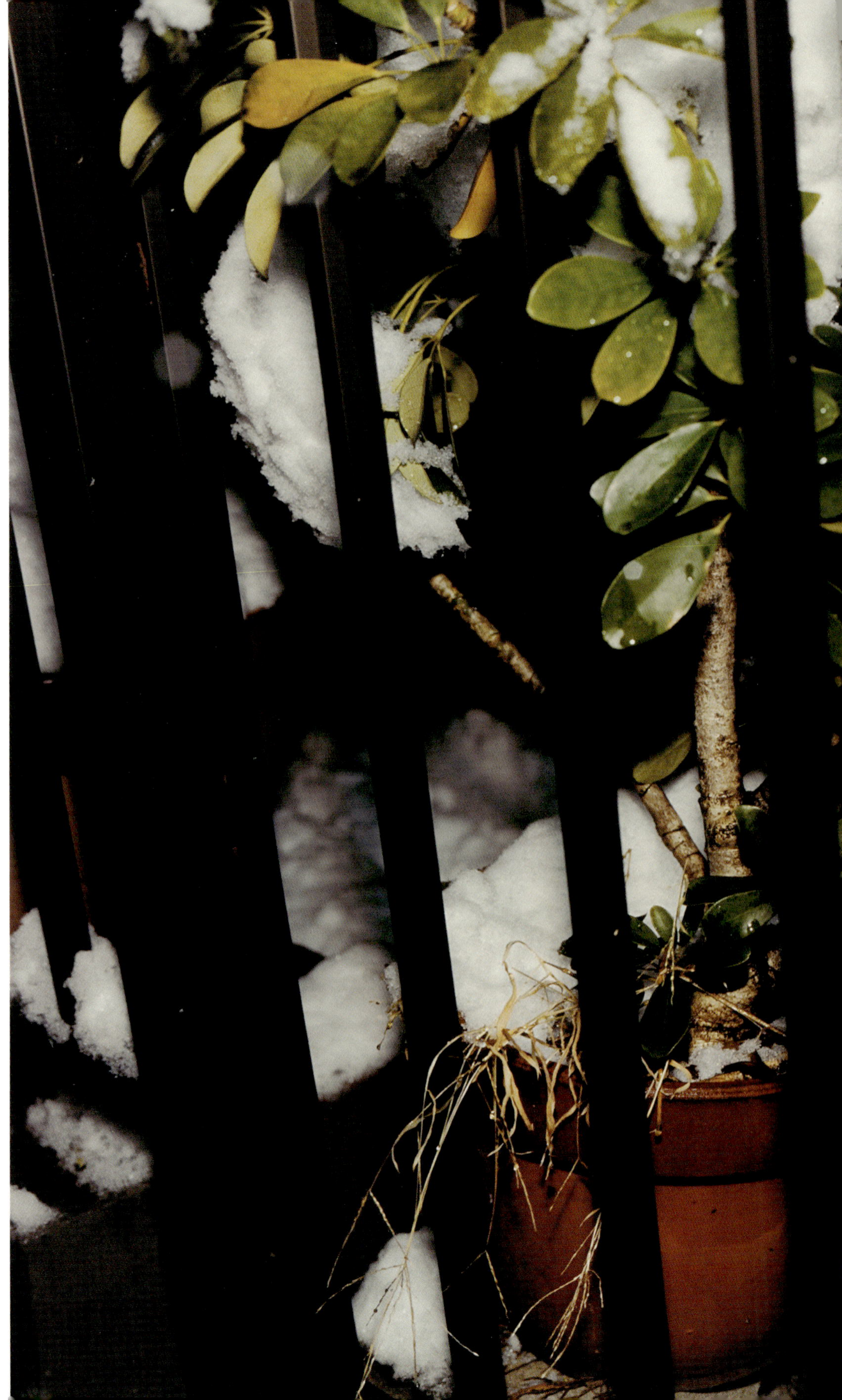

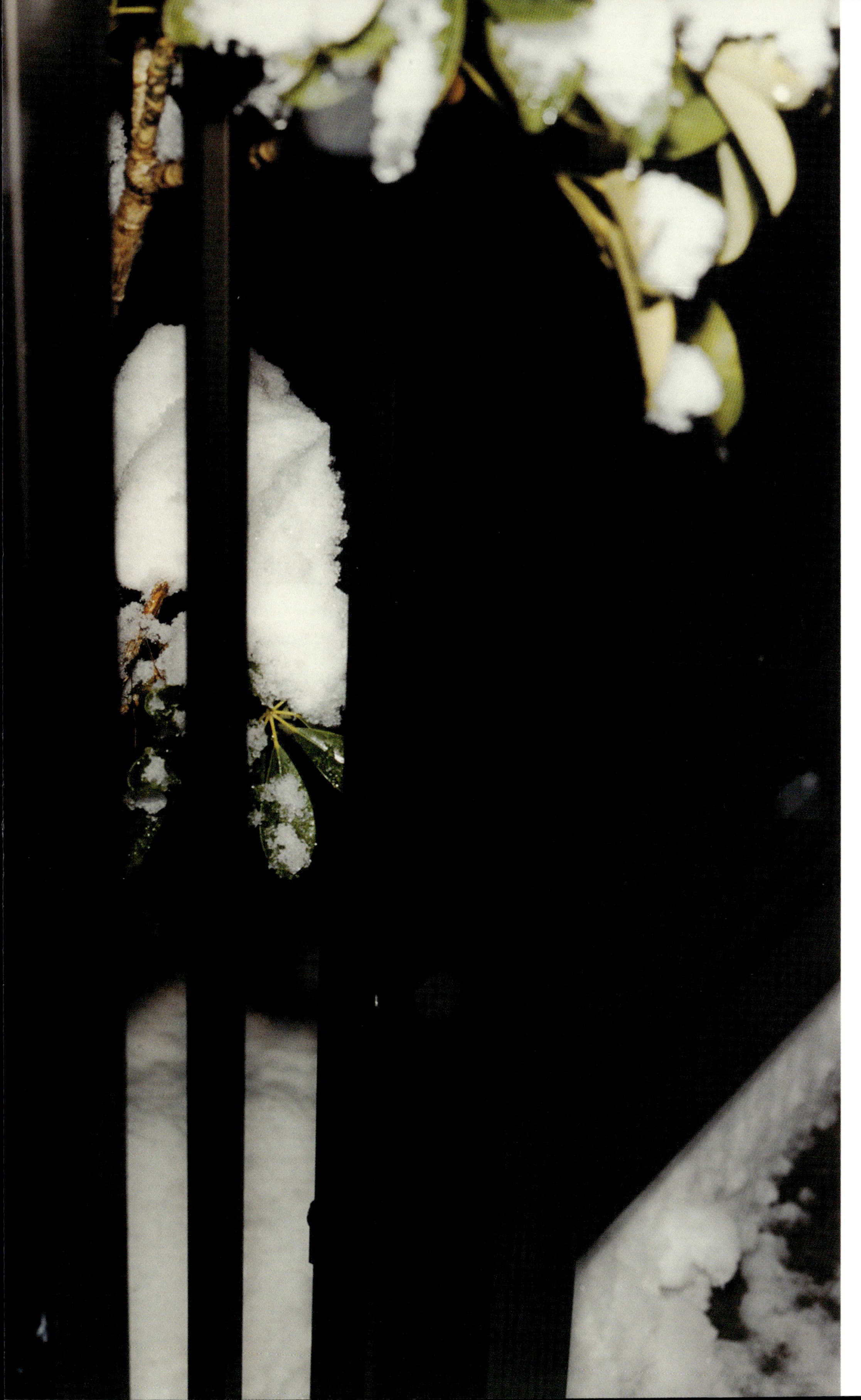

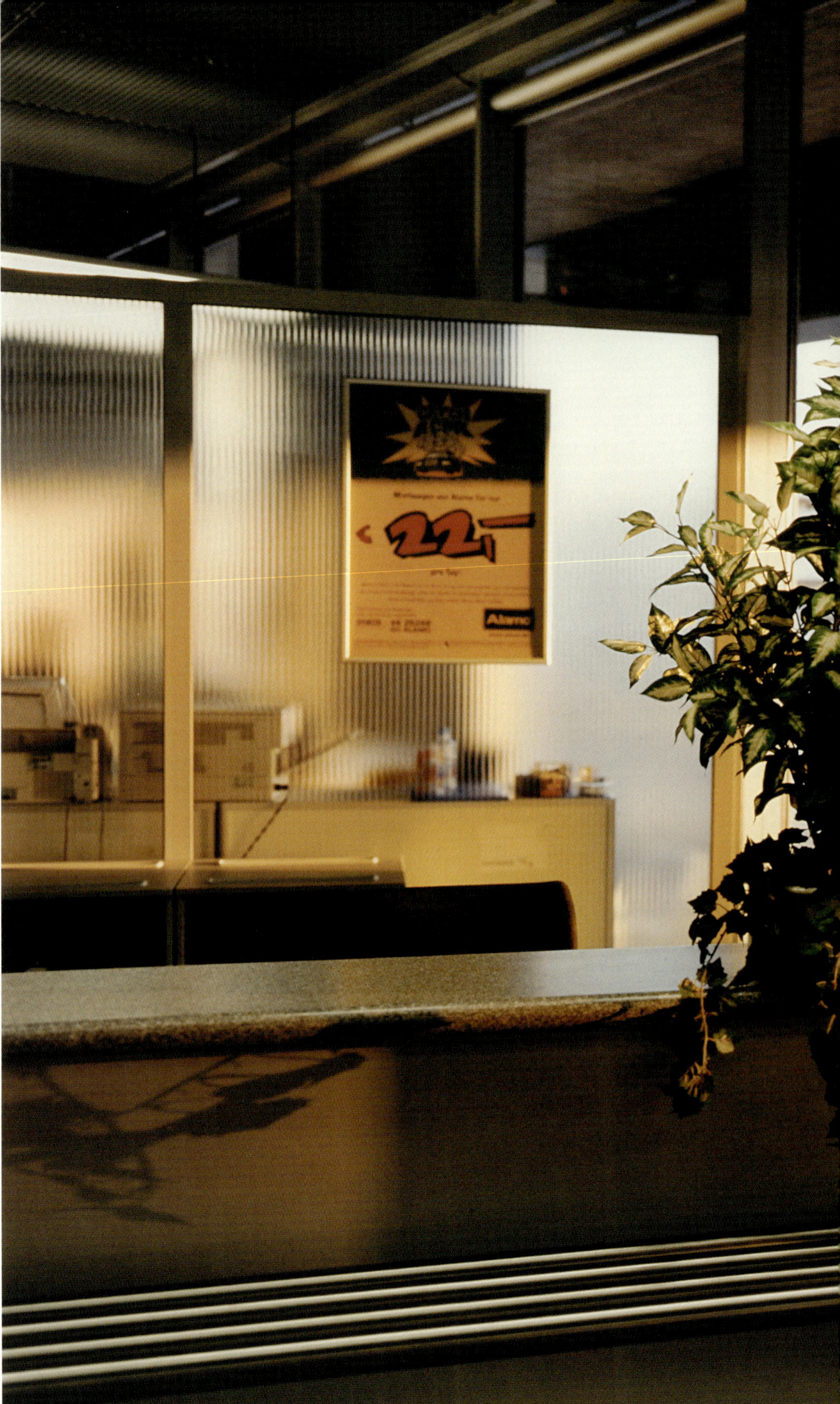
22,–

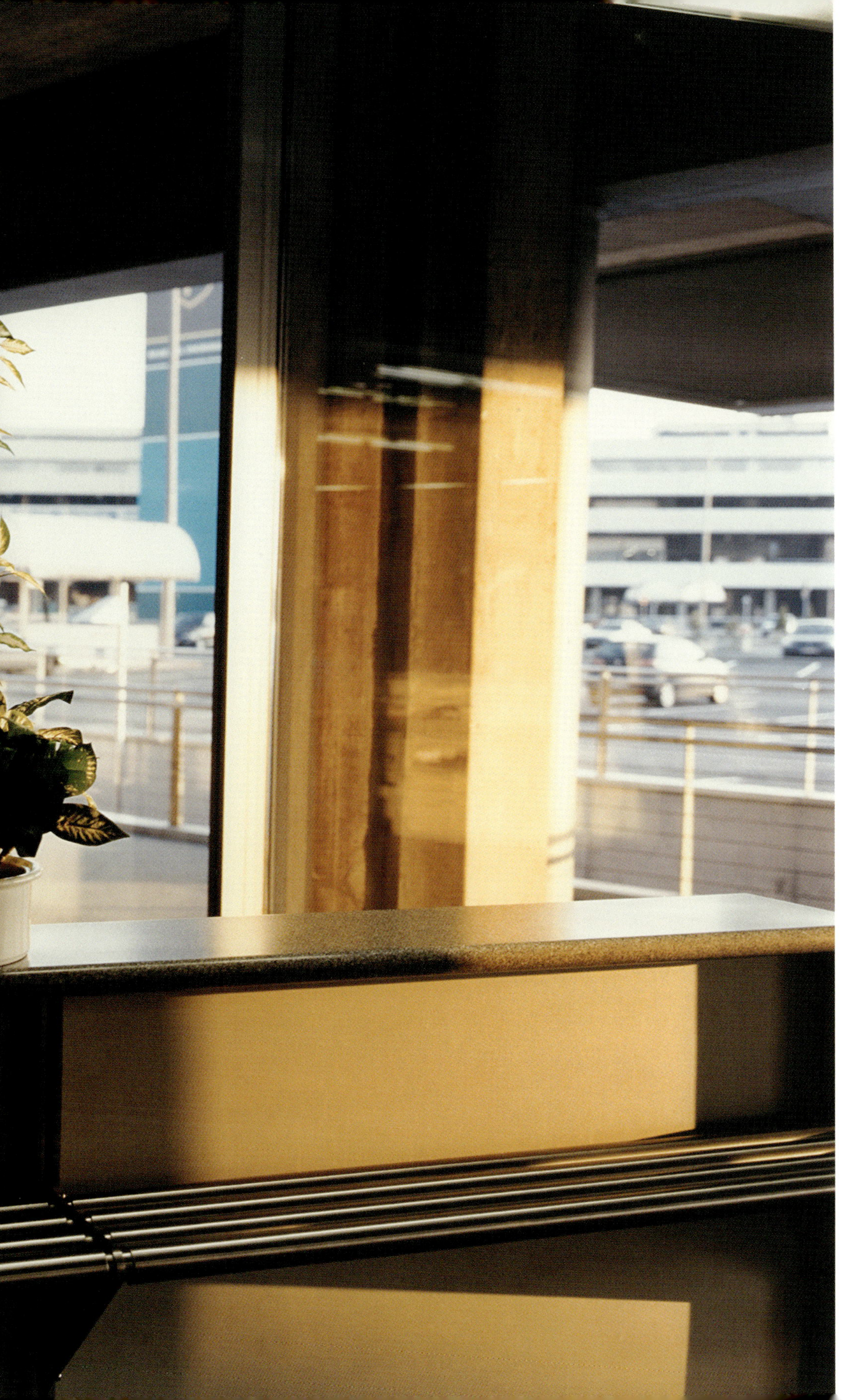

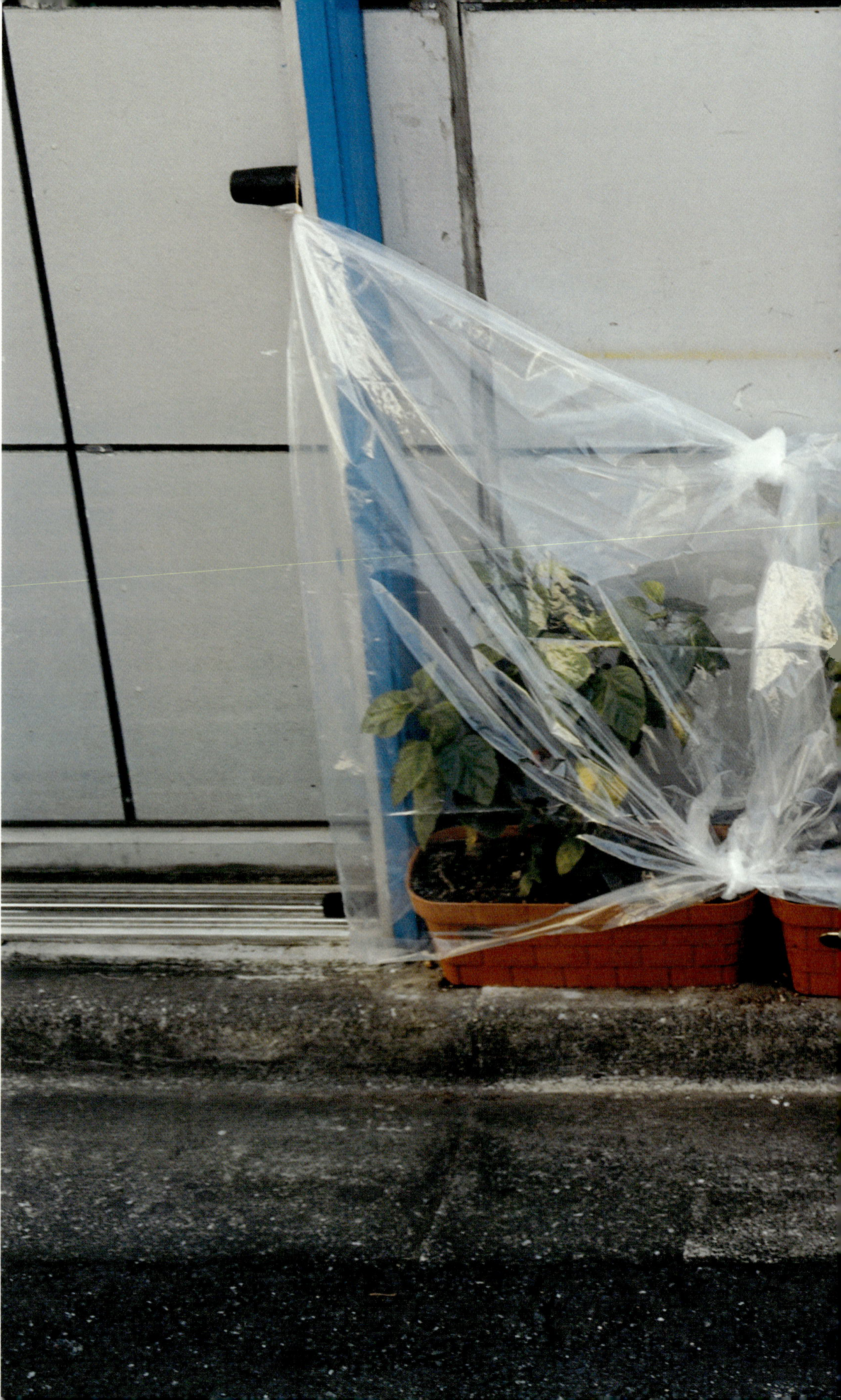

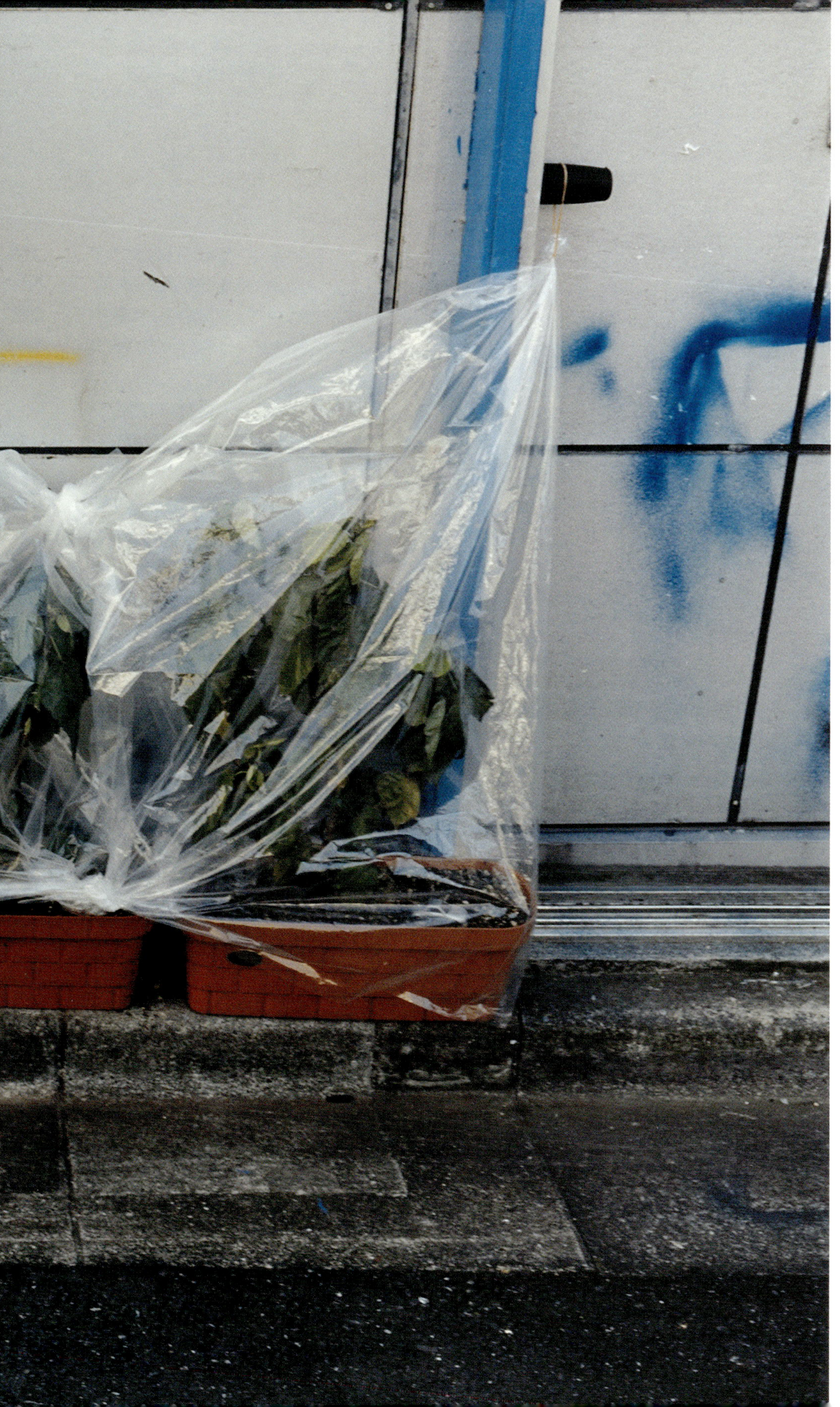

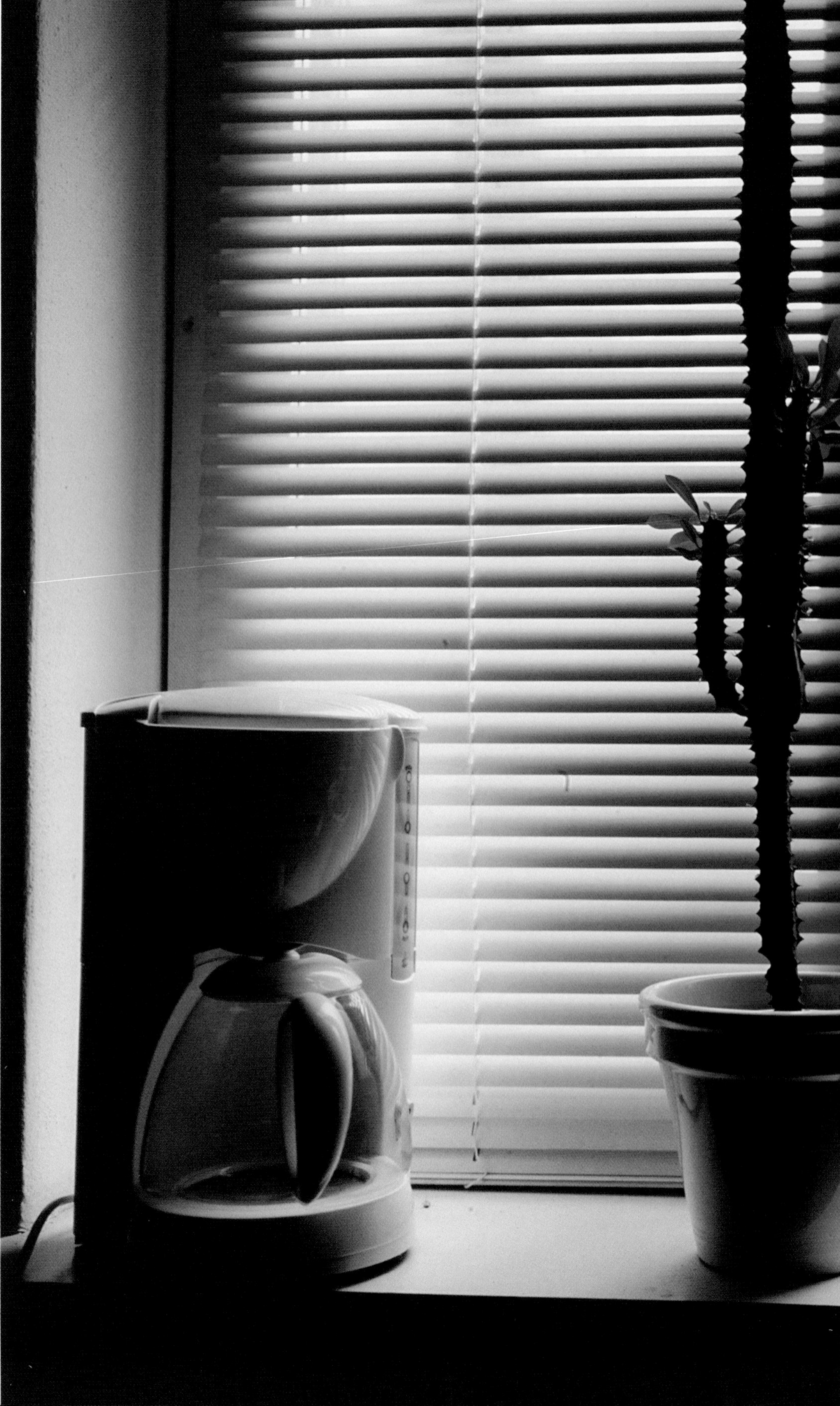

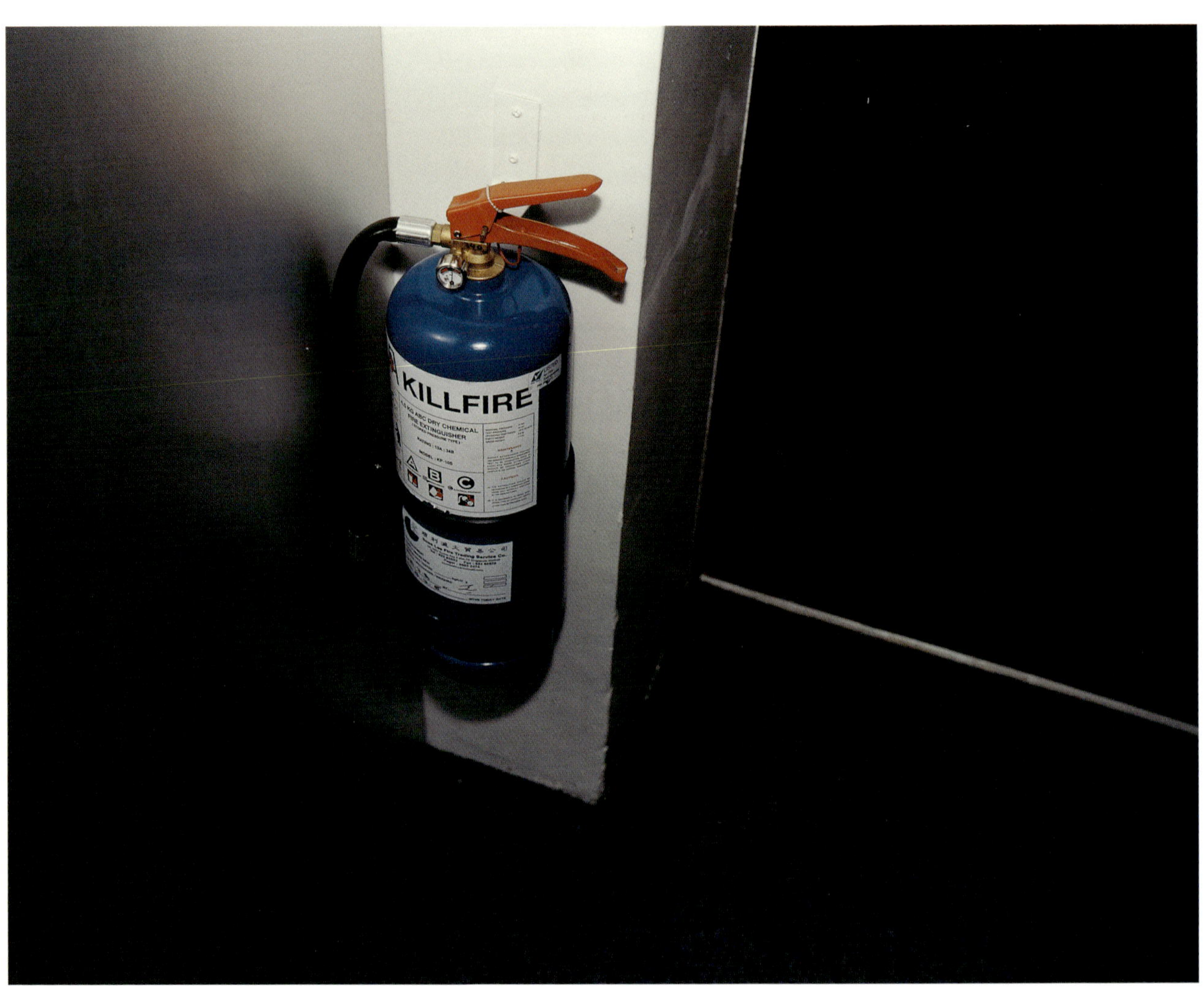
KILLFIRE
ABC DRY CHEMICAL
FIRE EXTINGUISHER
A
B
C

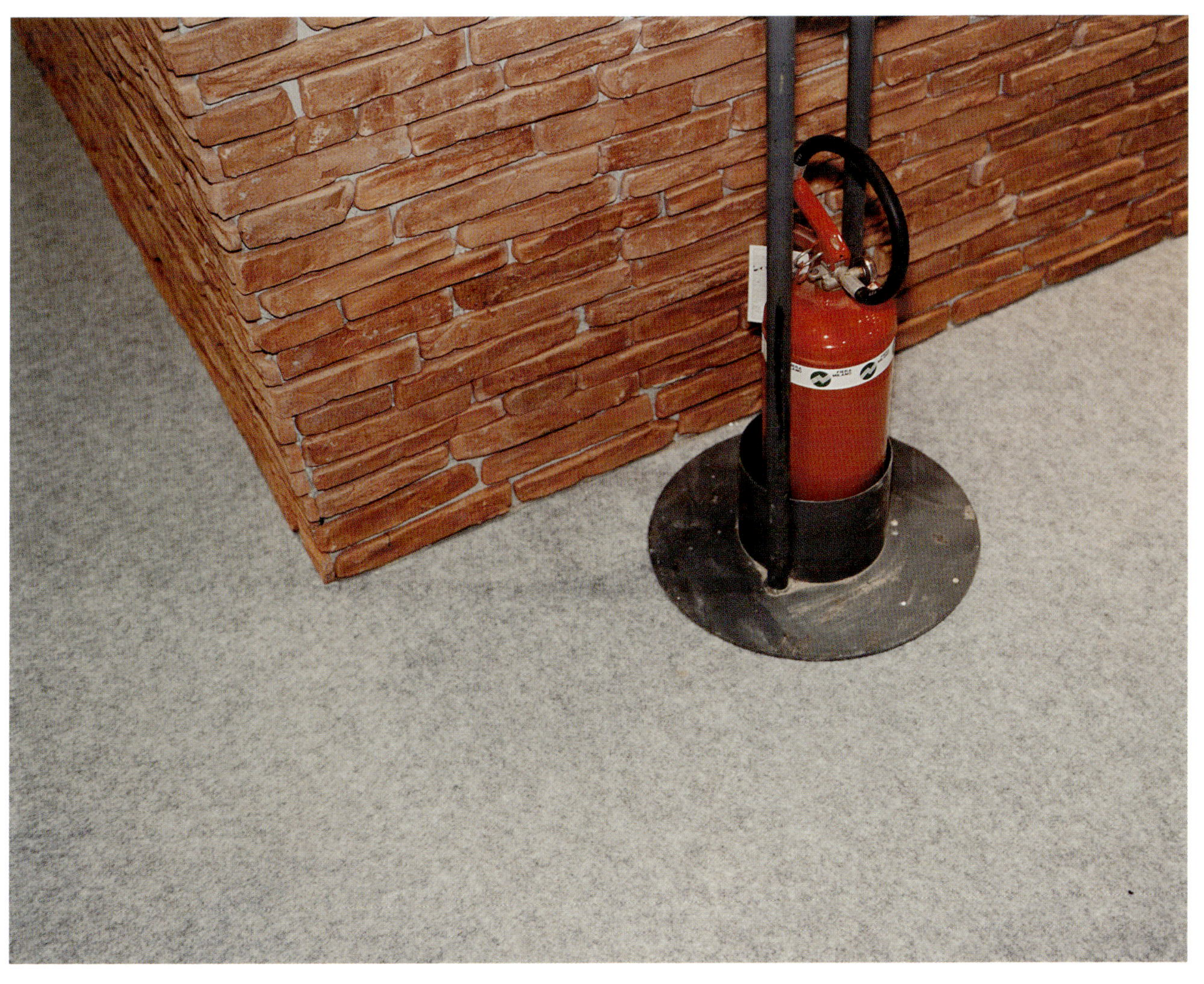

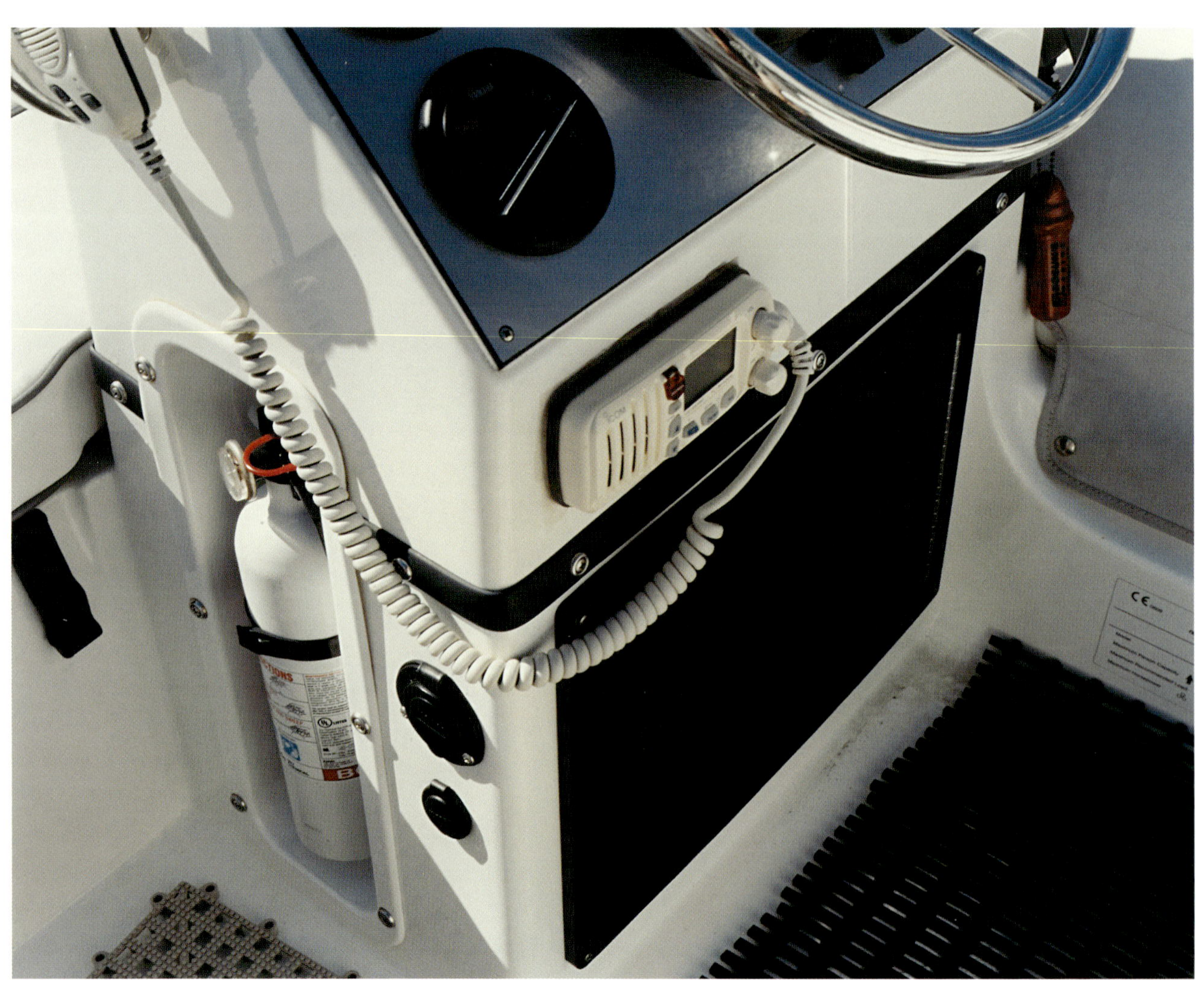

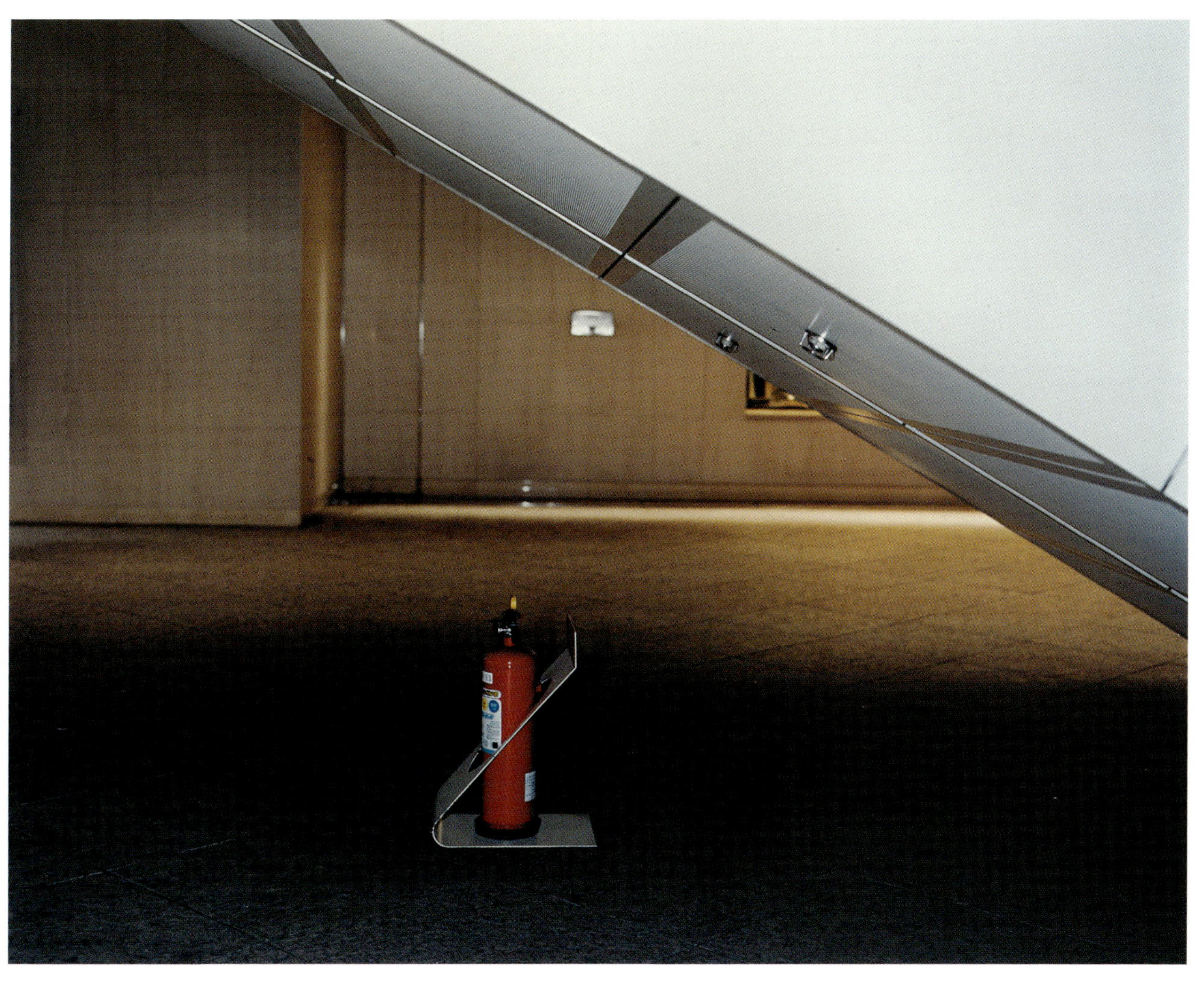

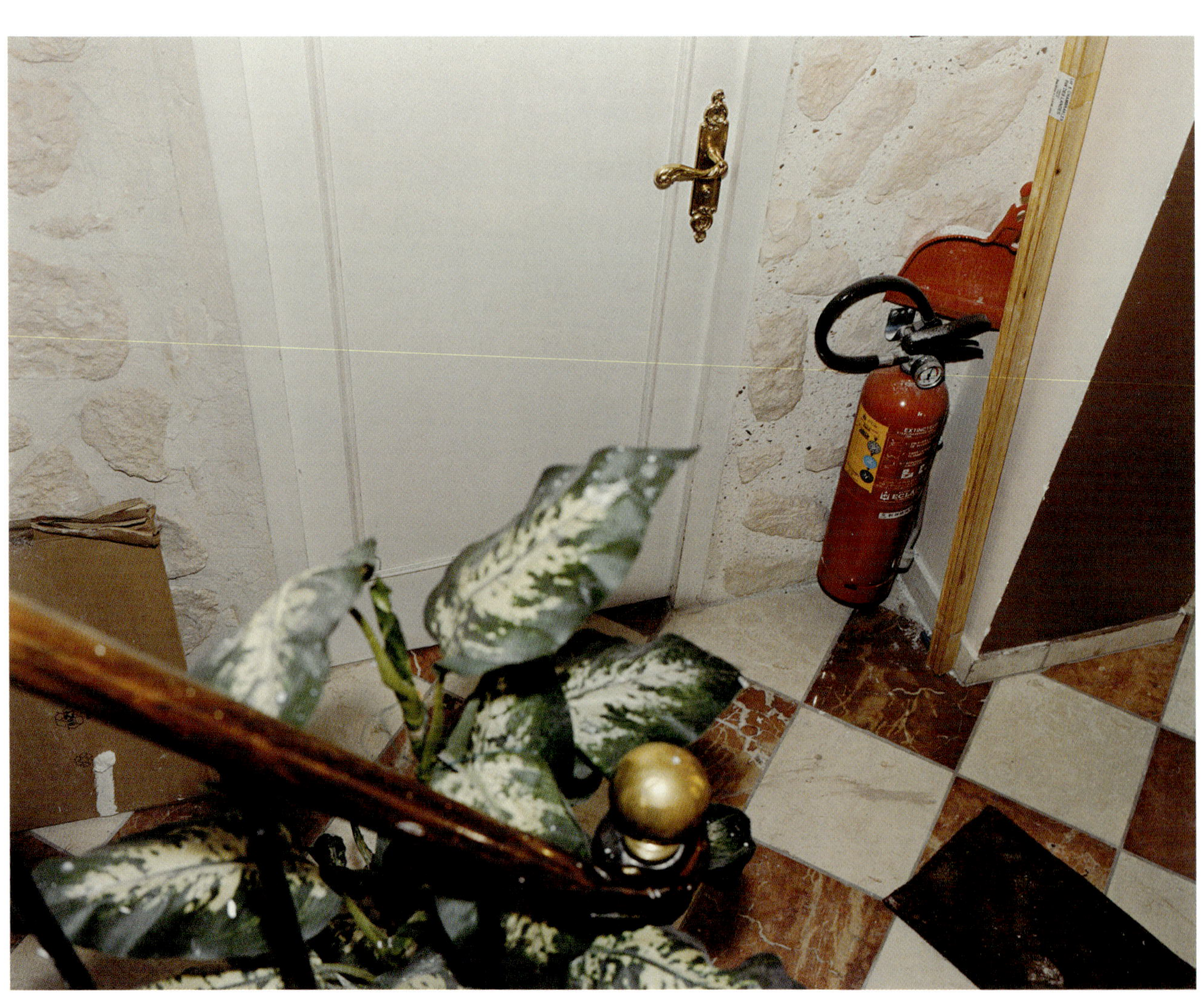

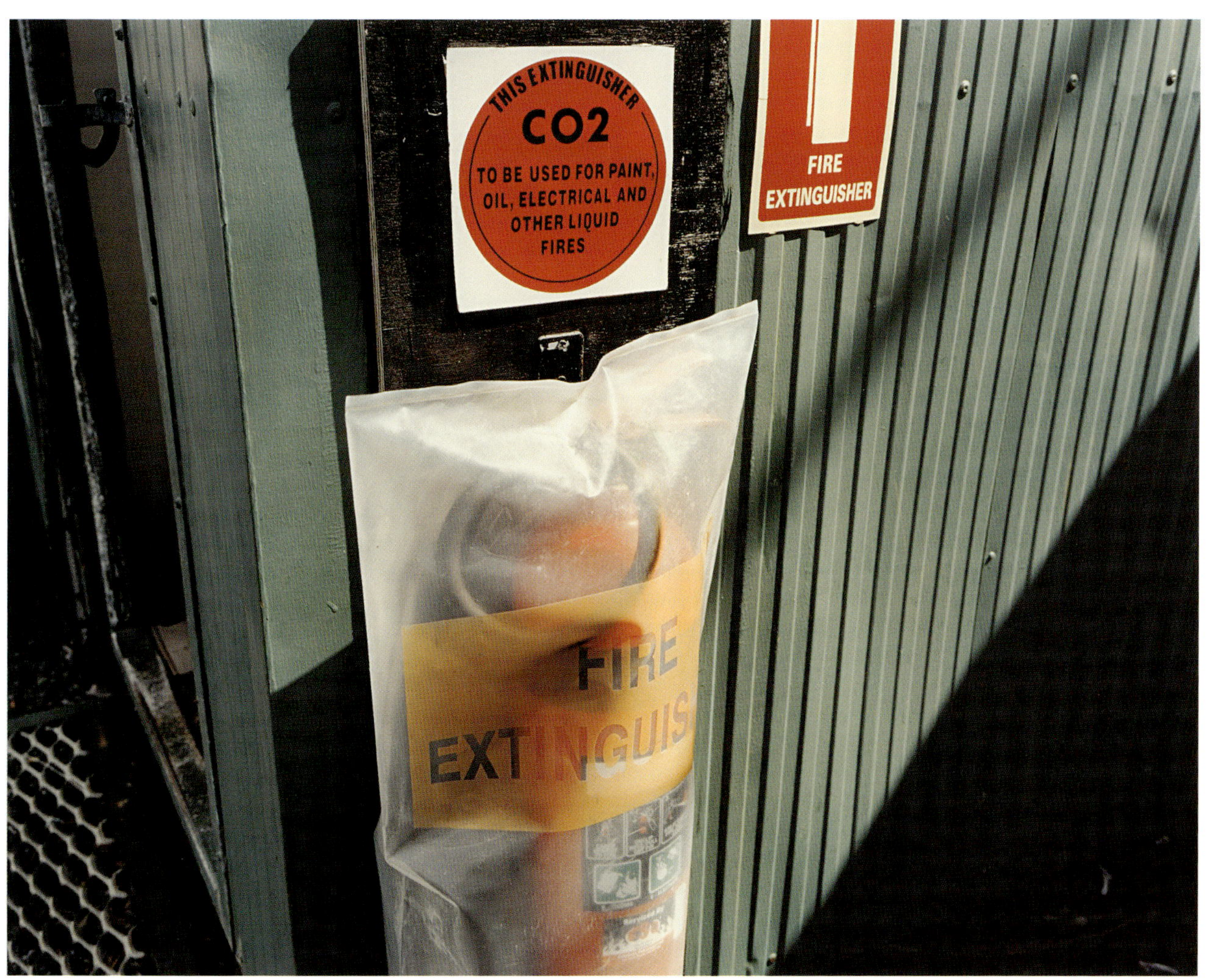
THIS EXTINGUISHER
CO2
TO BE USED FOR PAINT, OIL, ELECTRICAL AND OTHER LIQUID FIRES
FIRE EXTINGUISHER
FIRE
EXTINGUIS

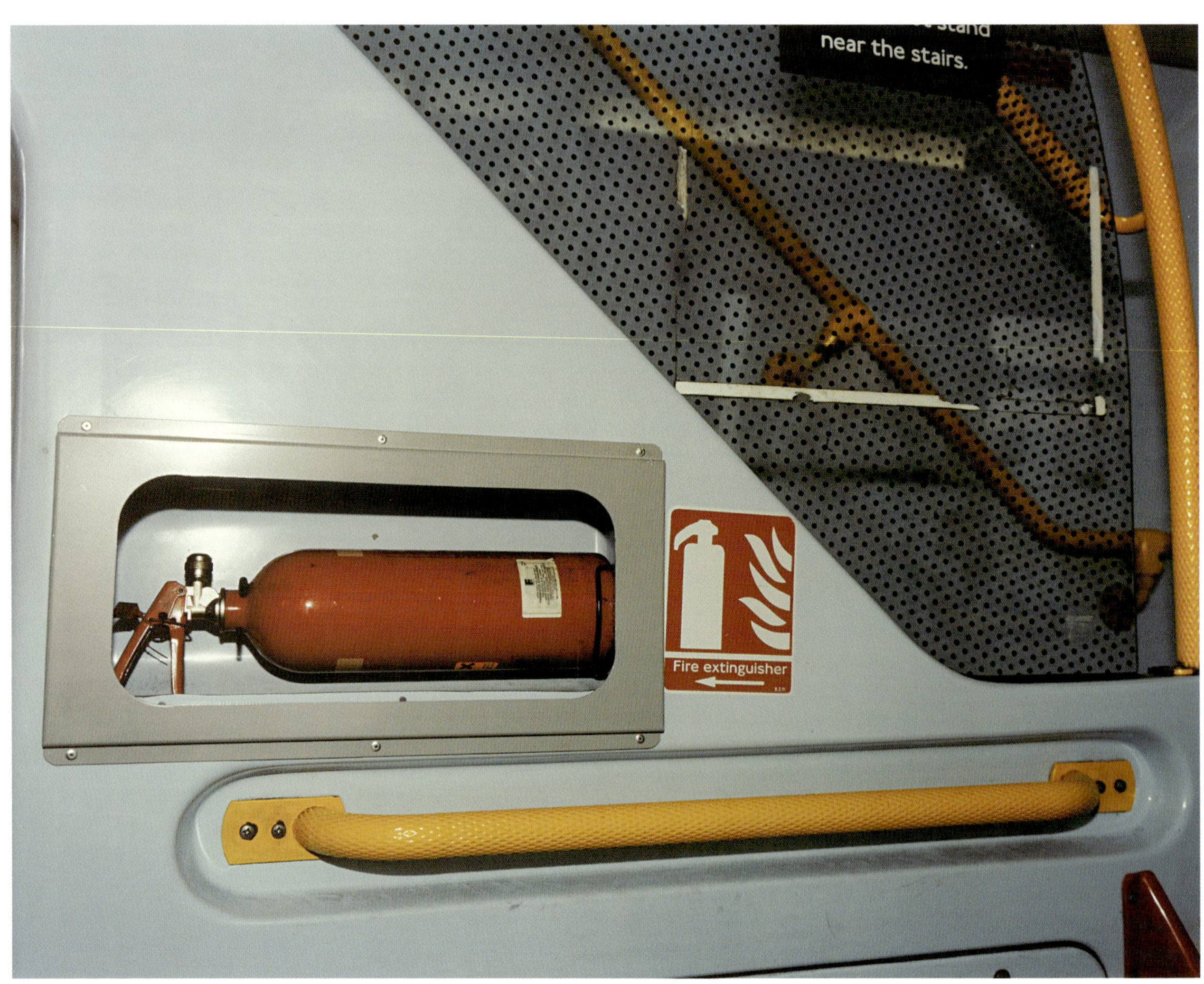
near the stairs.
Fire extinguisher

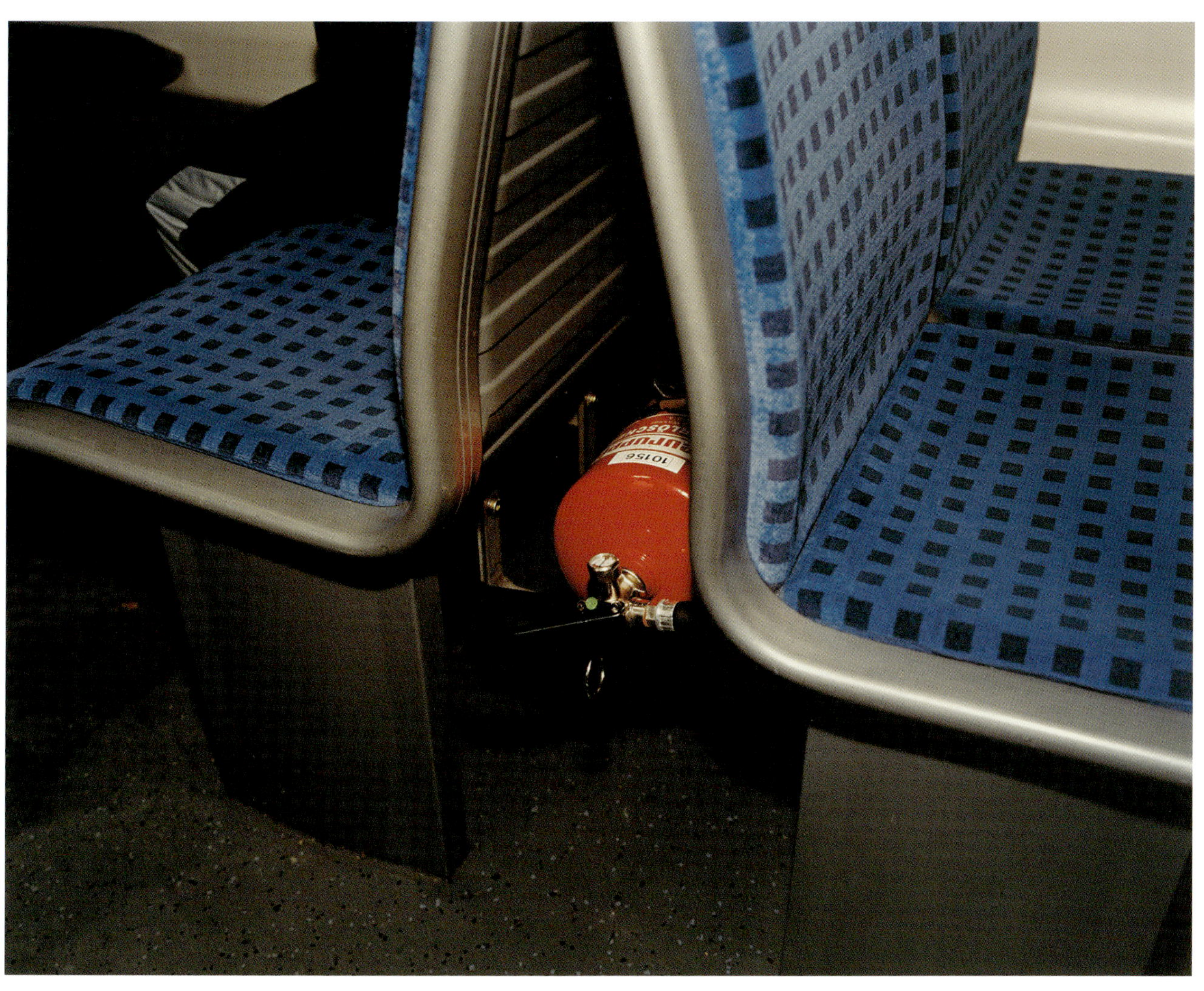
10156

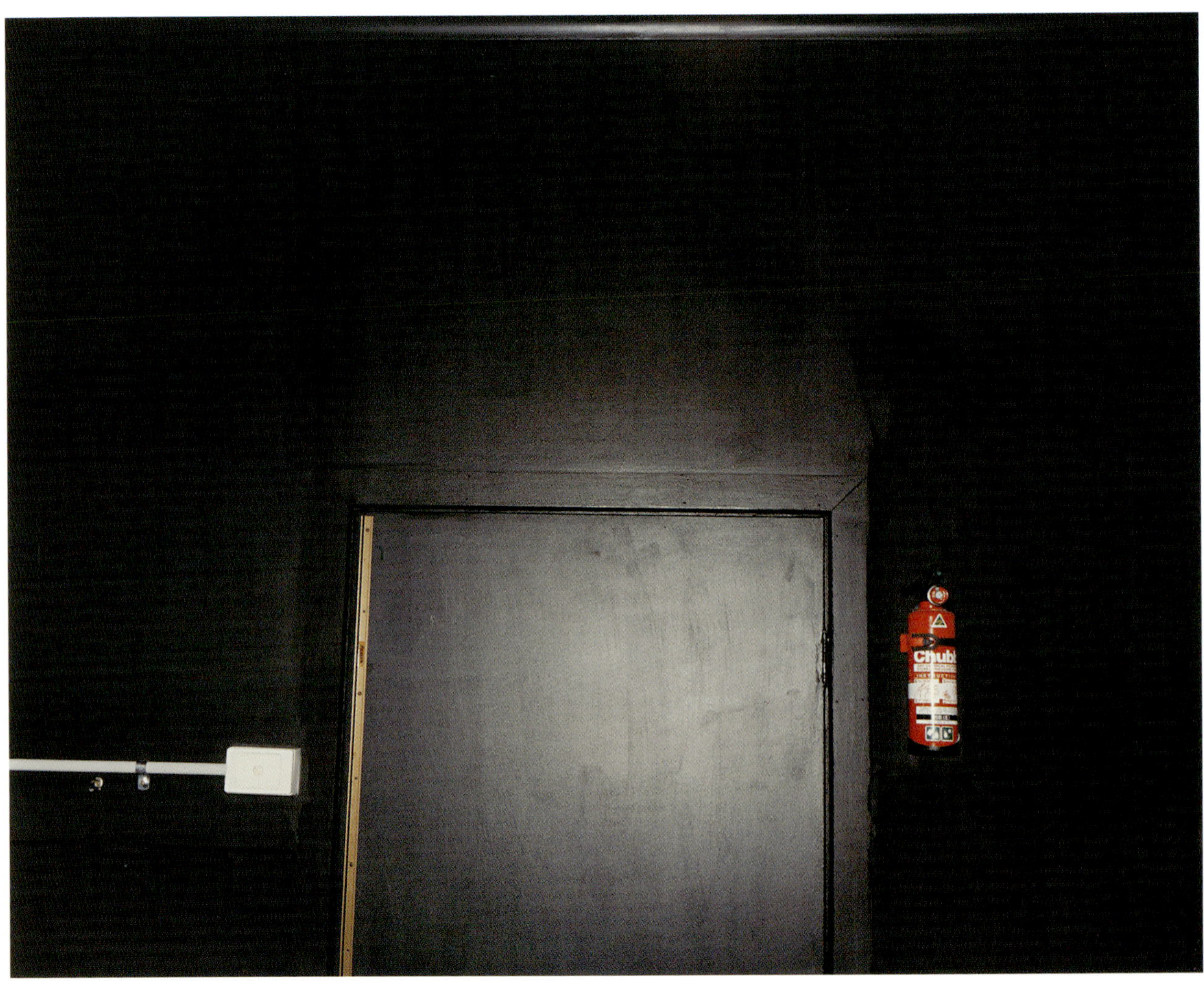

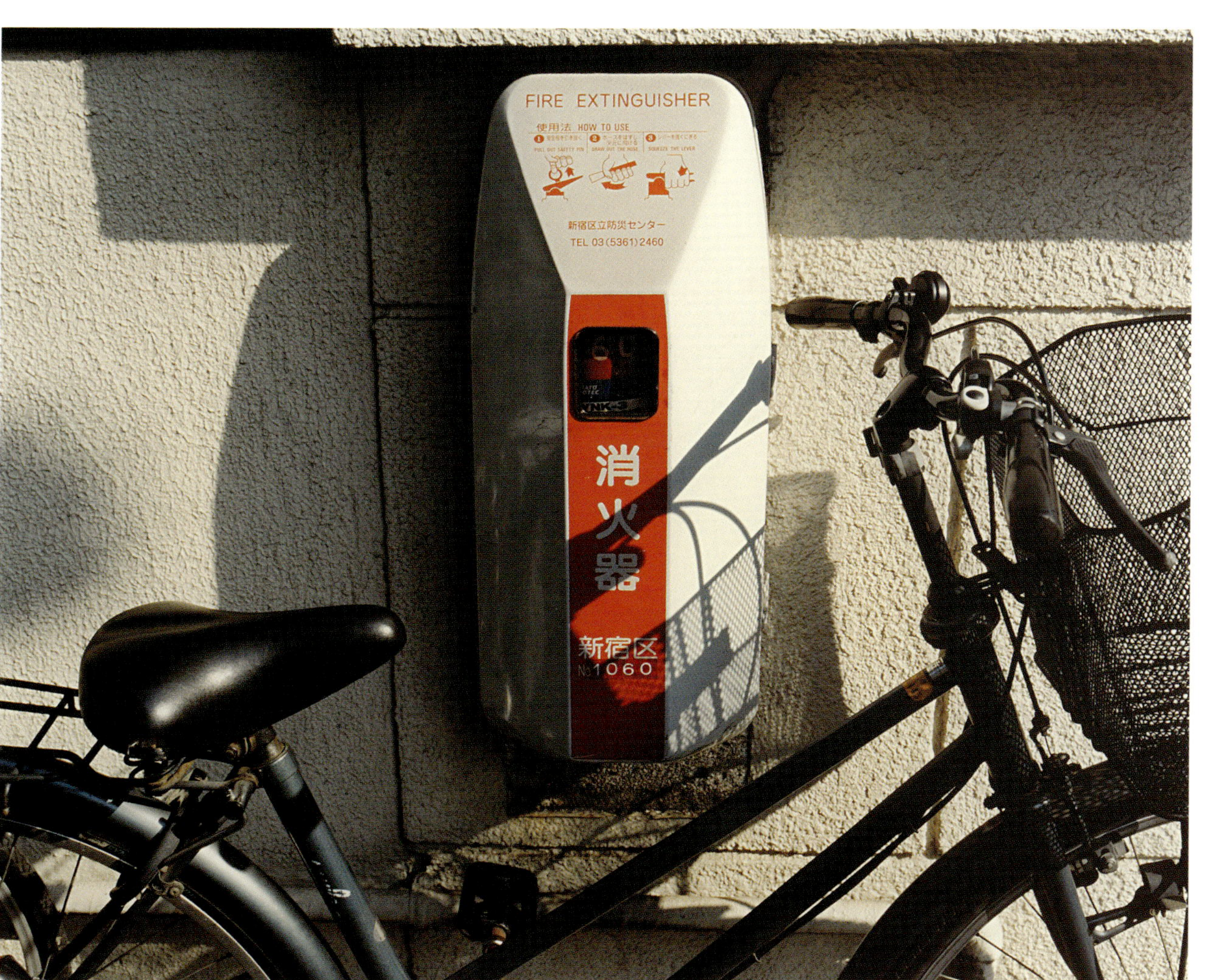
FIRE EXTINGUISHER
使用法 HOW TO USE
新宿区立防災センター
TEL 03(5361)2460
消火器
新宿区
№1060

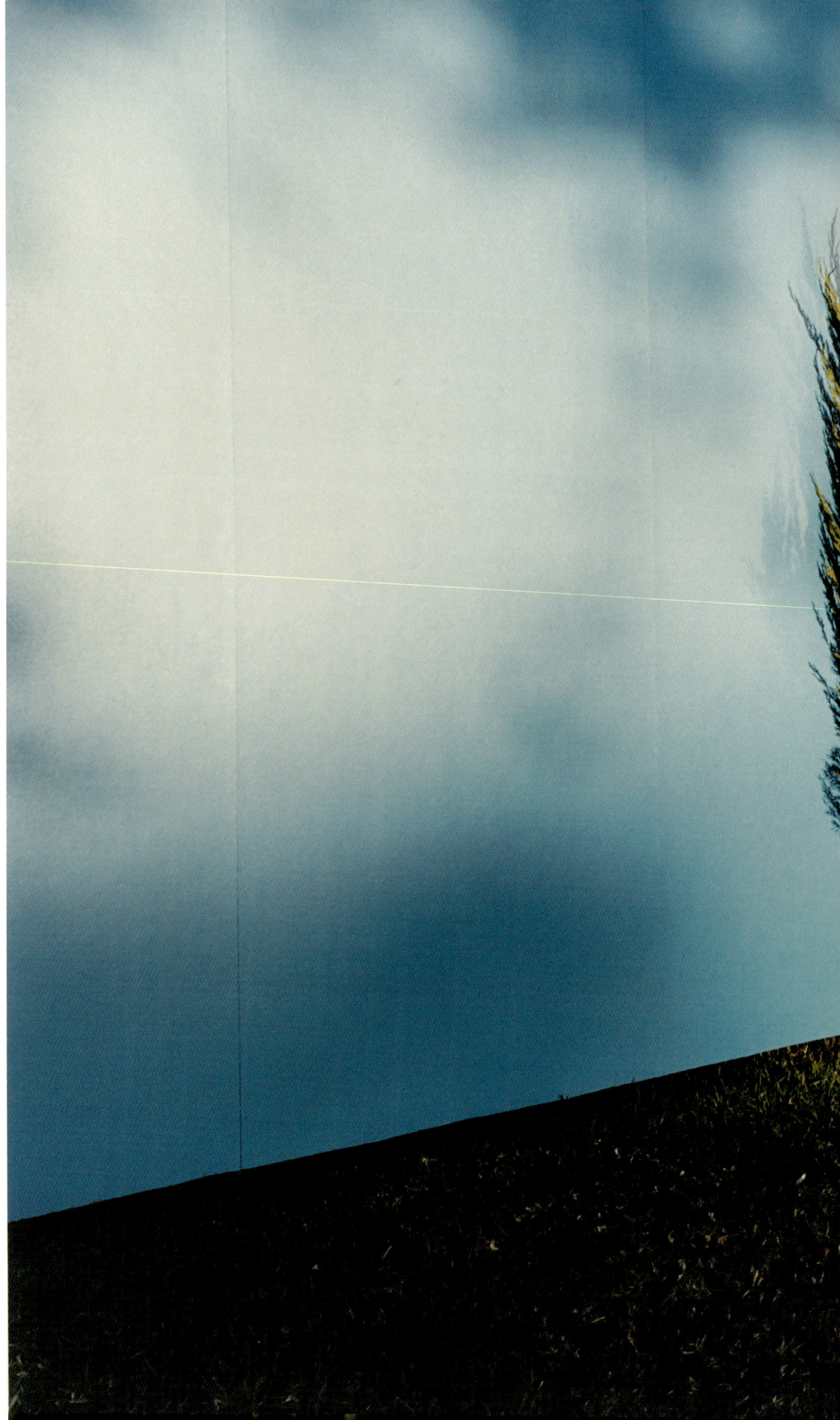

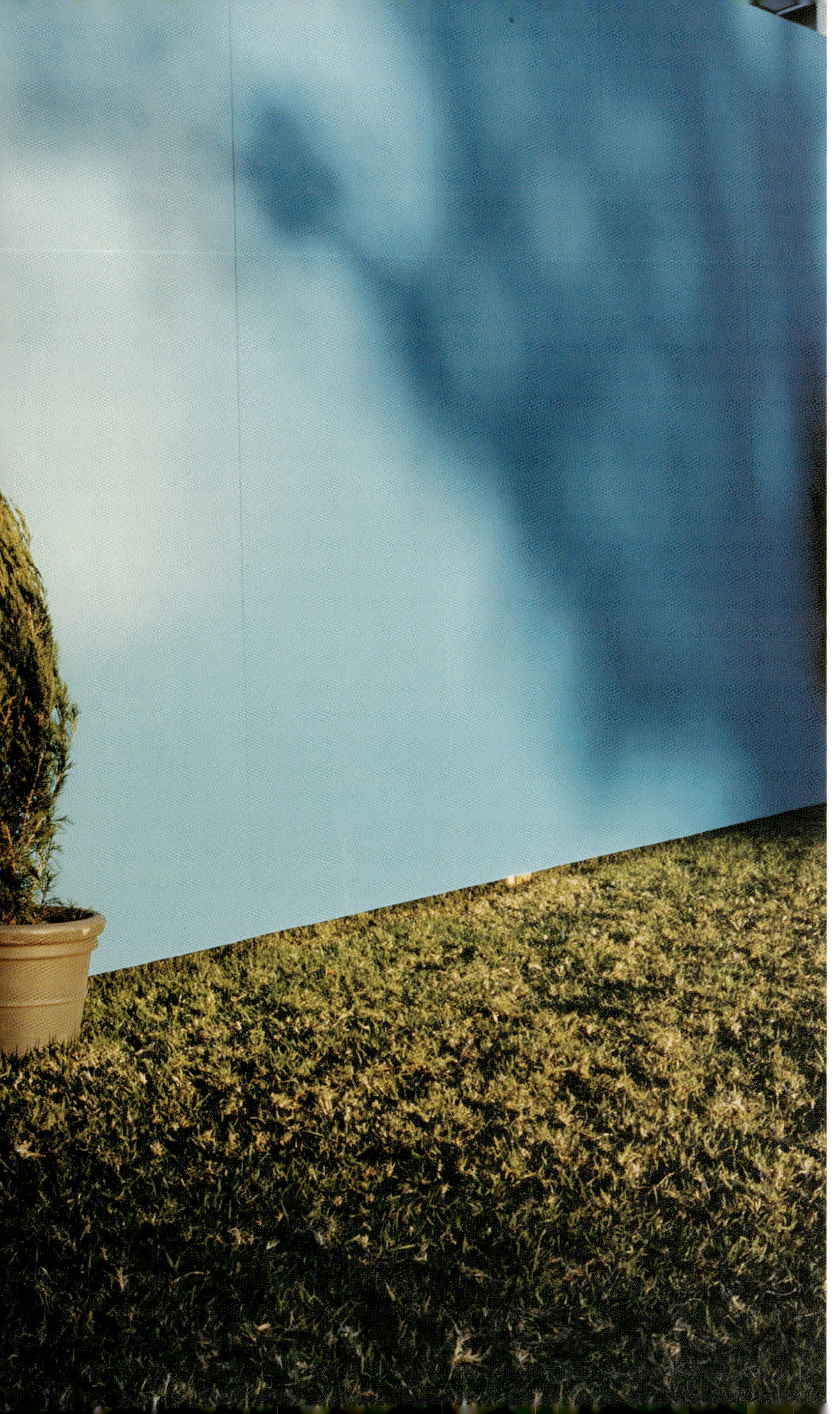

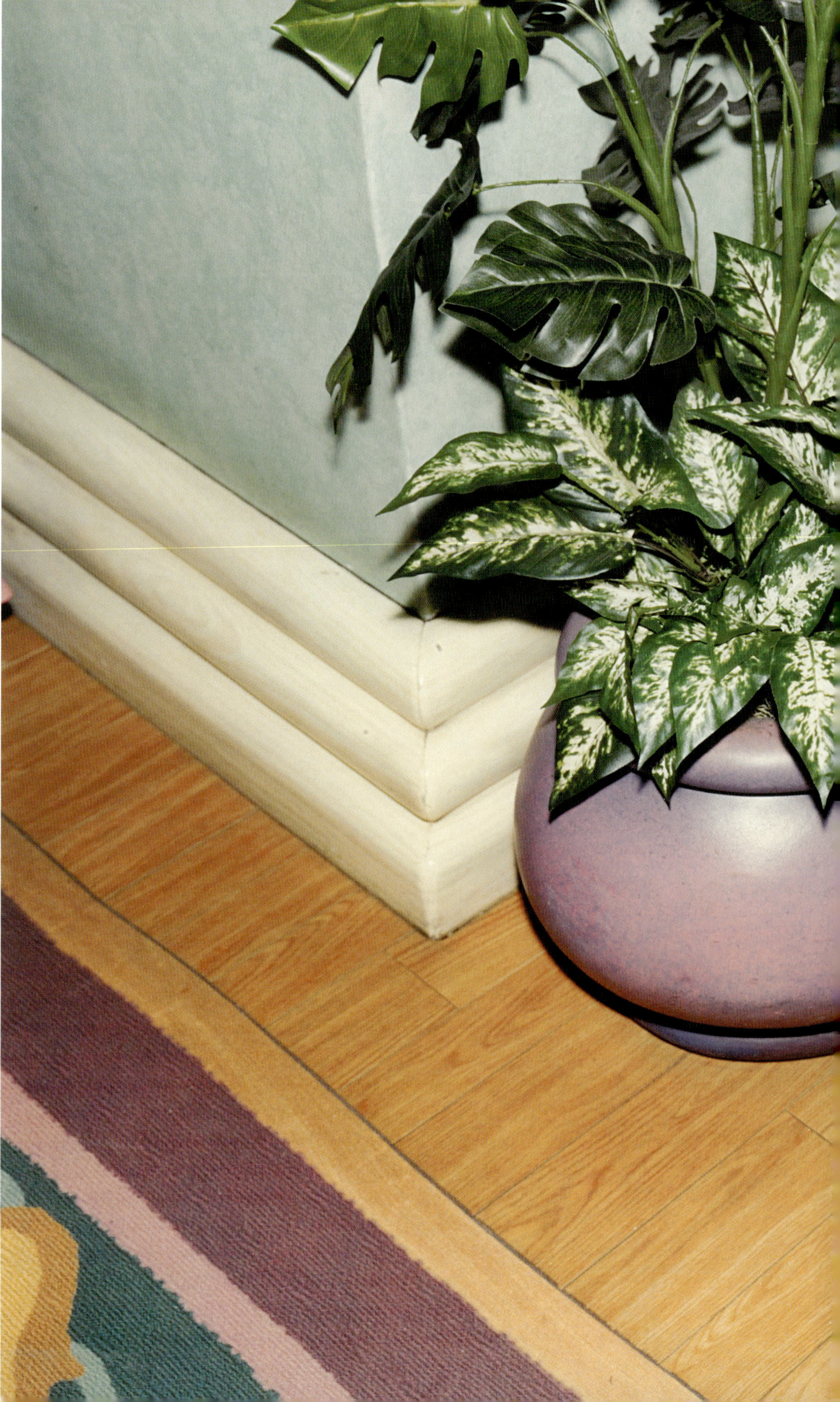

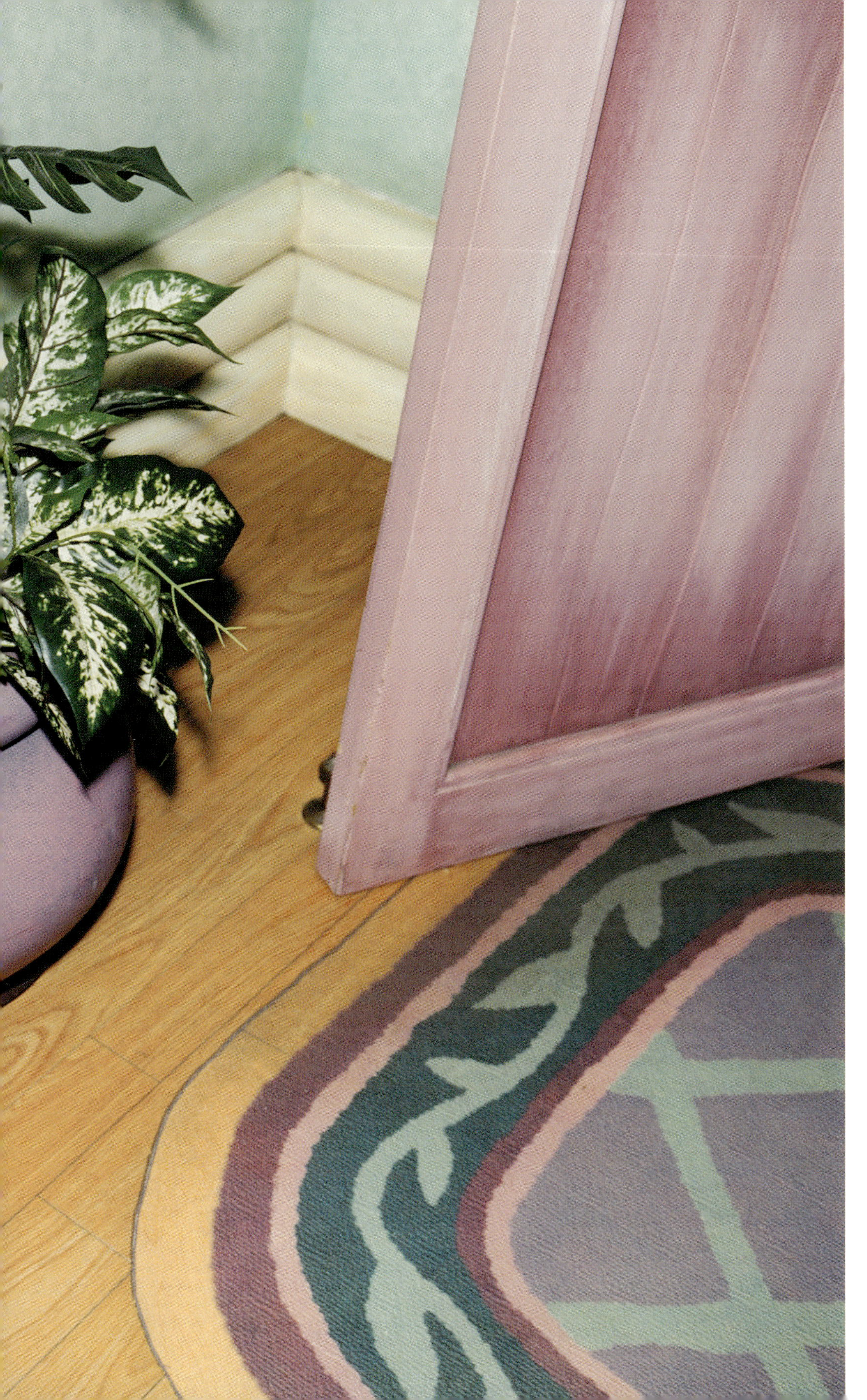

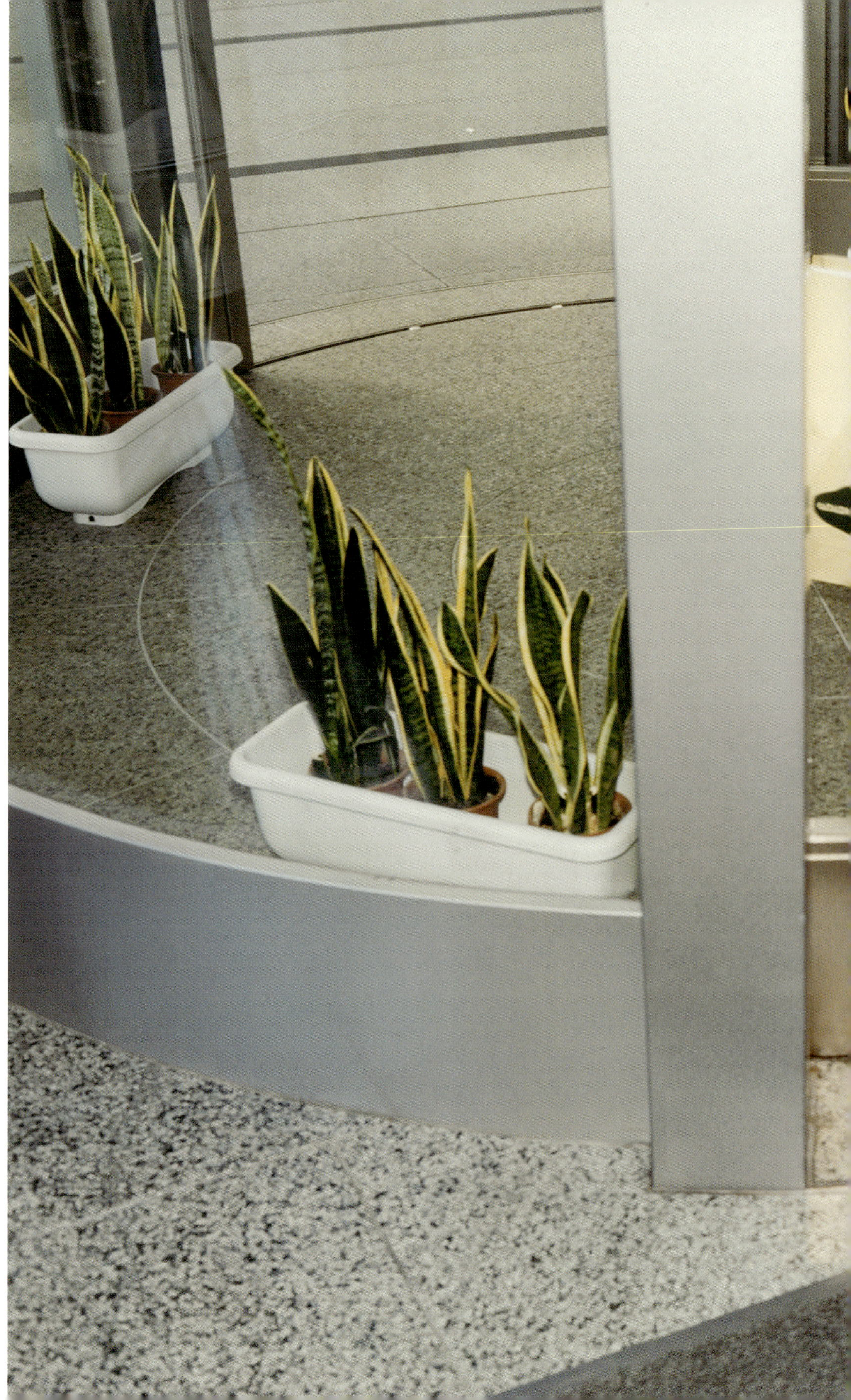

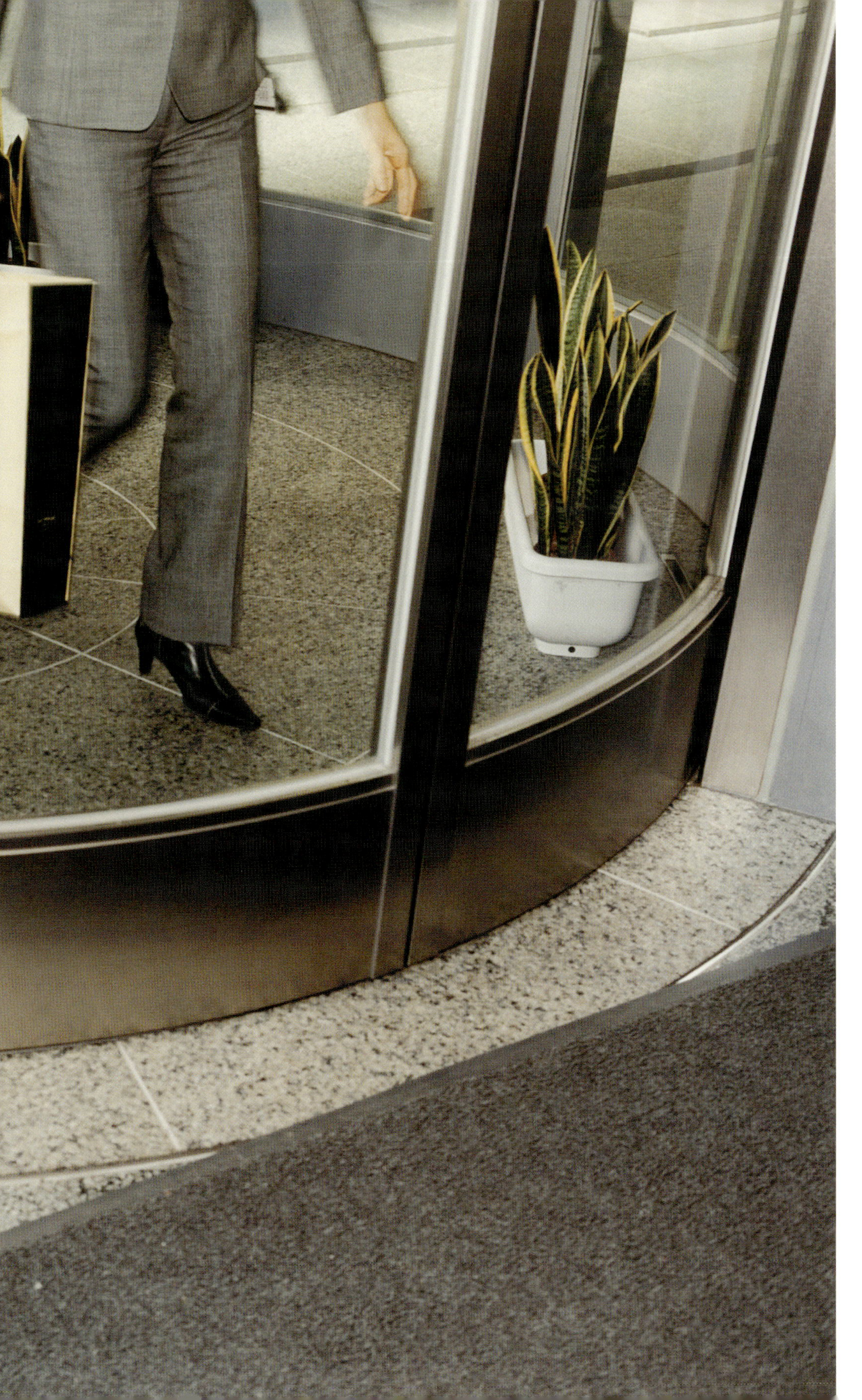

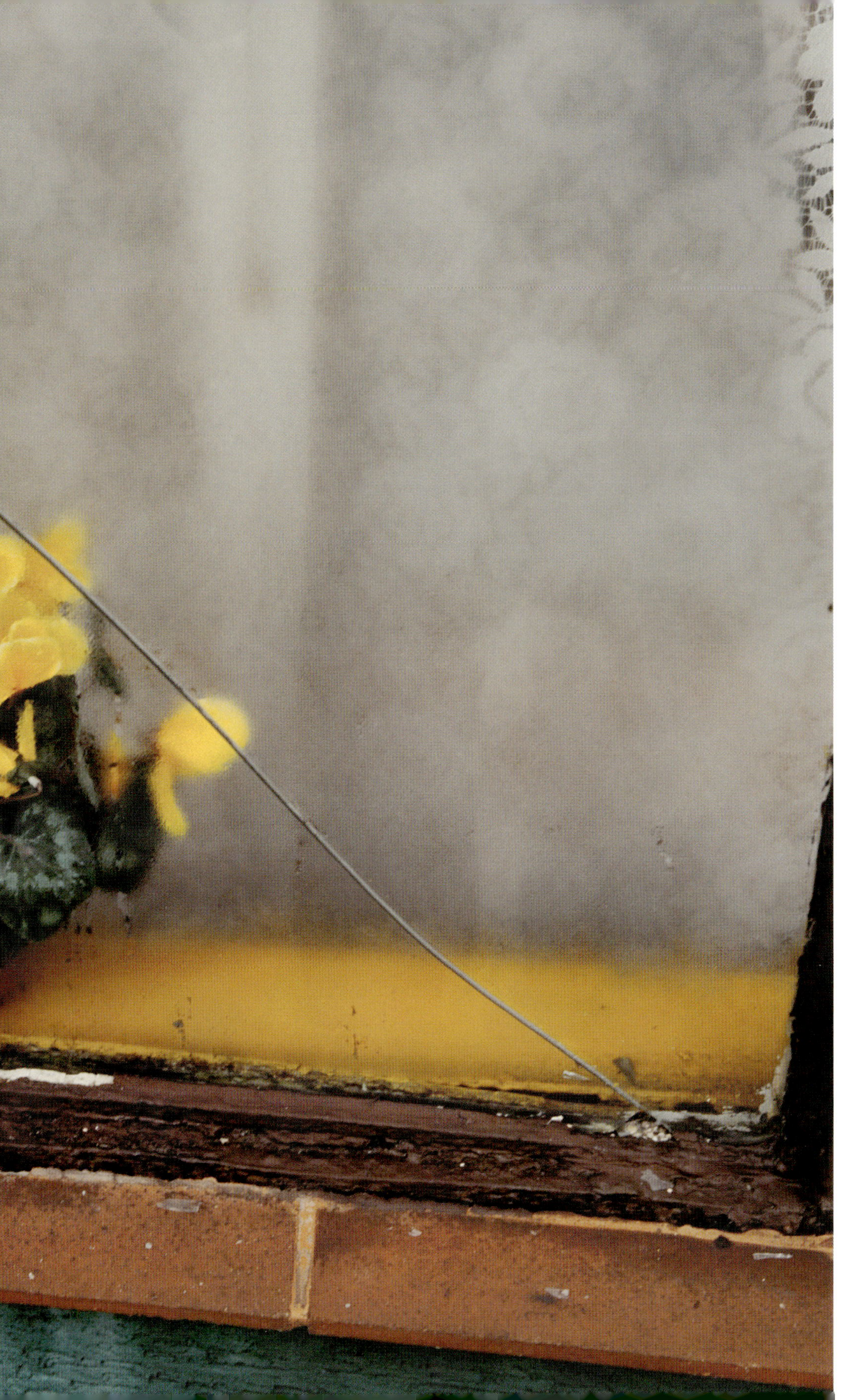

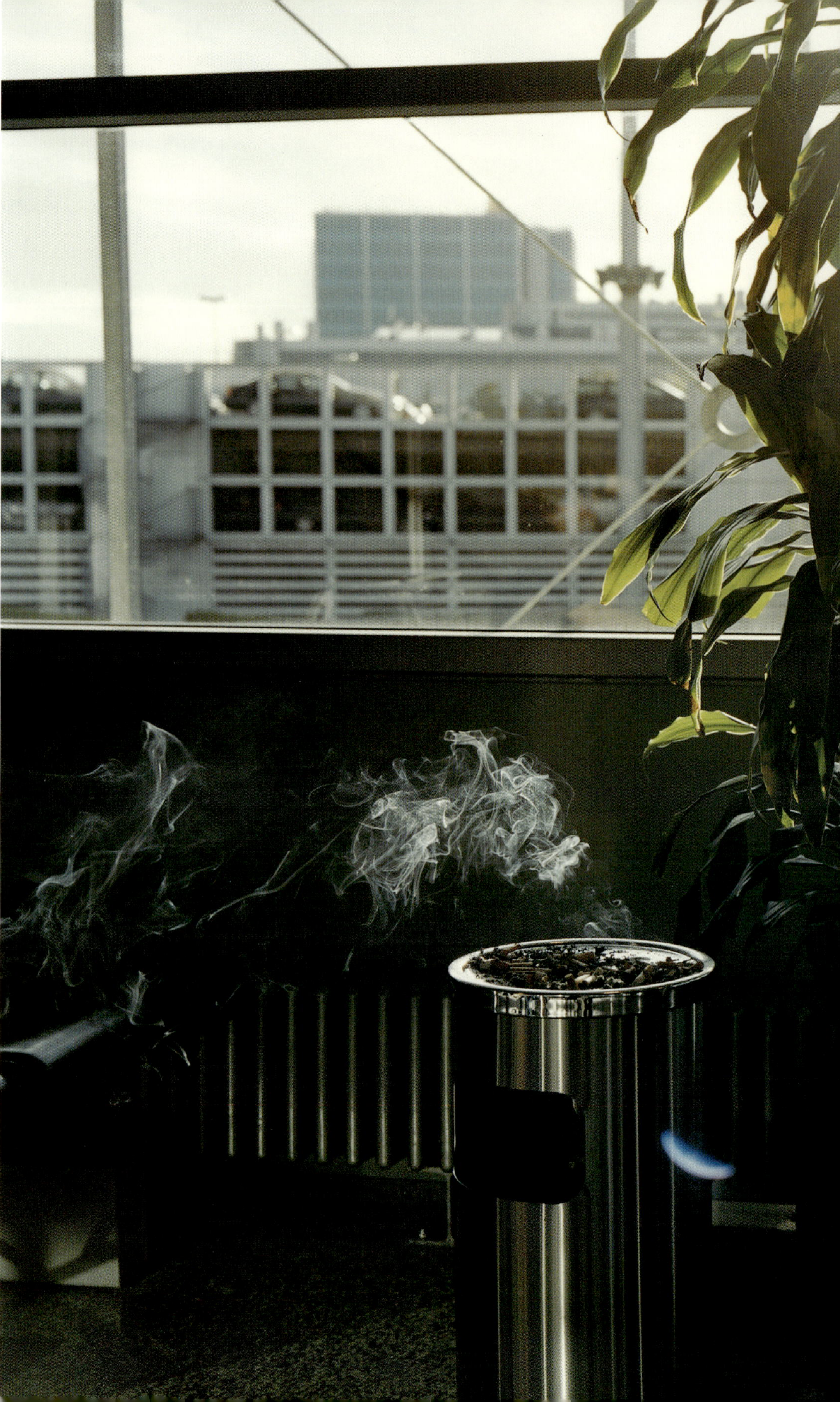

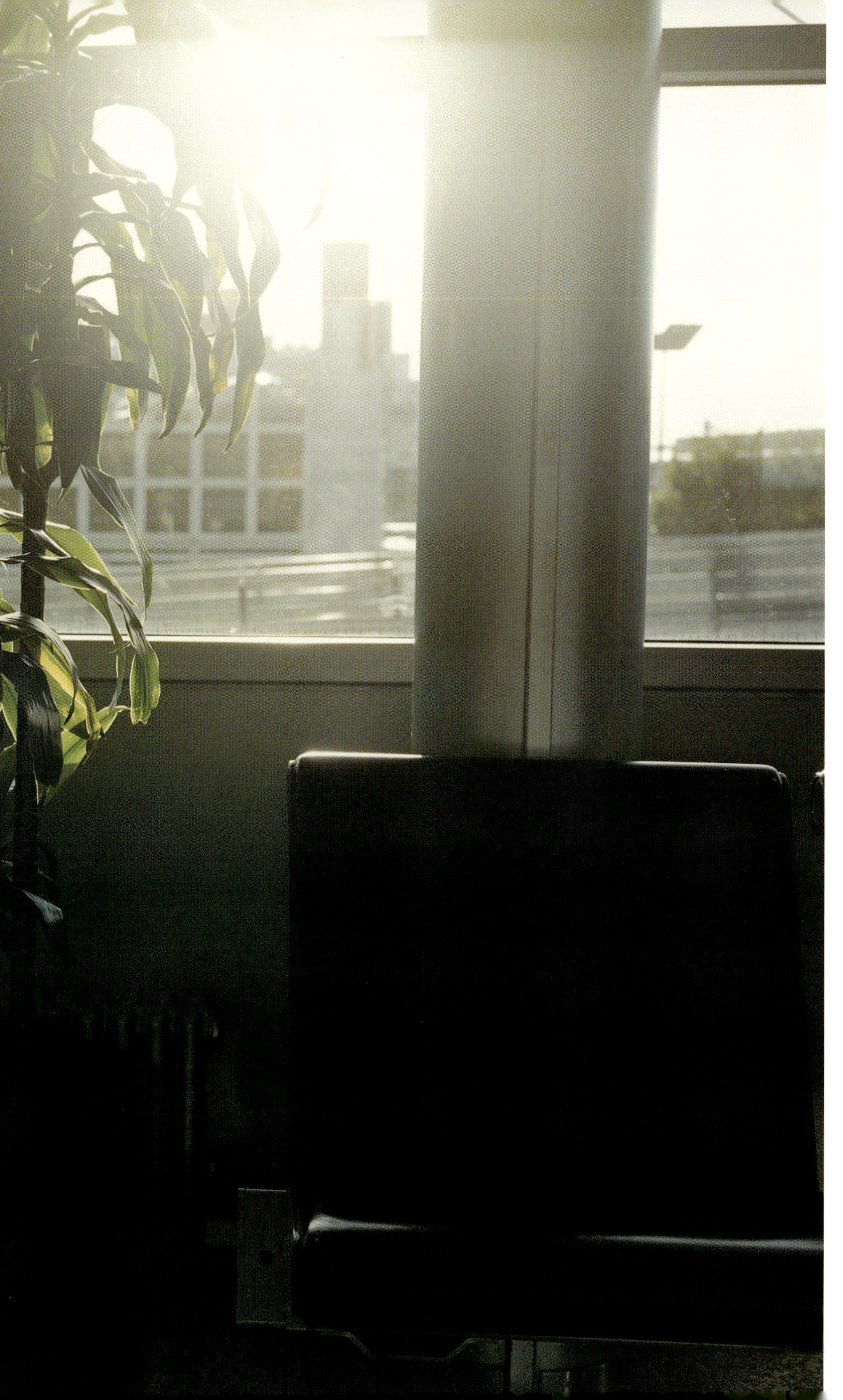

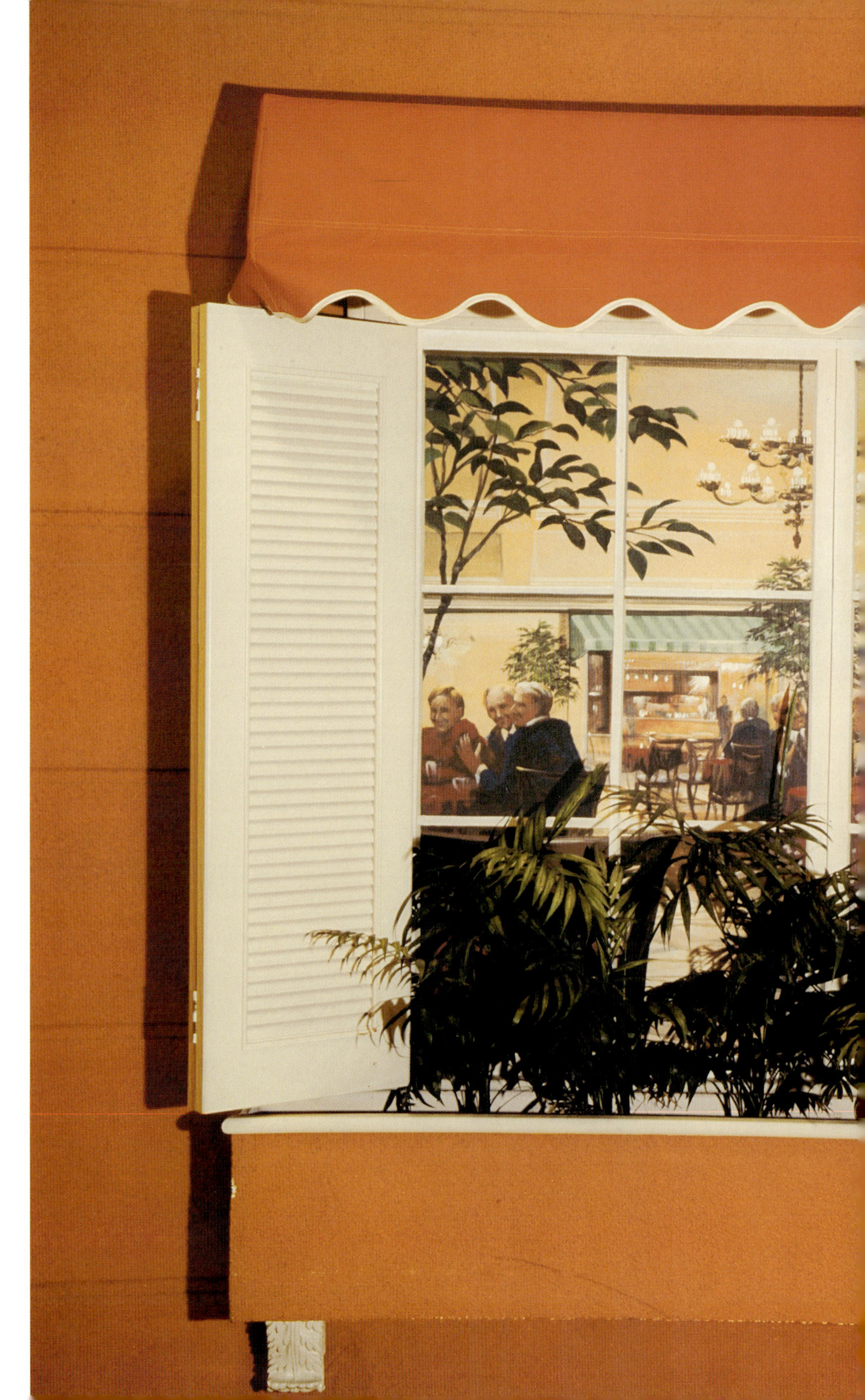

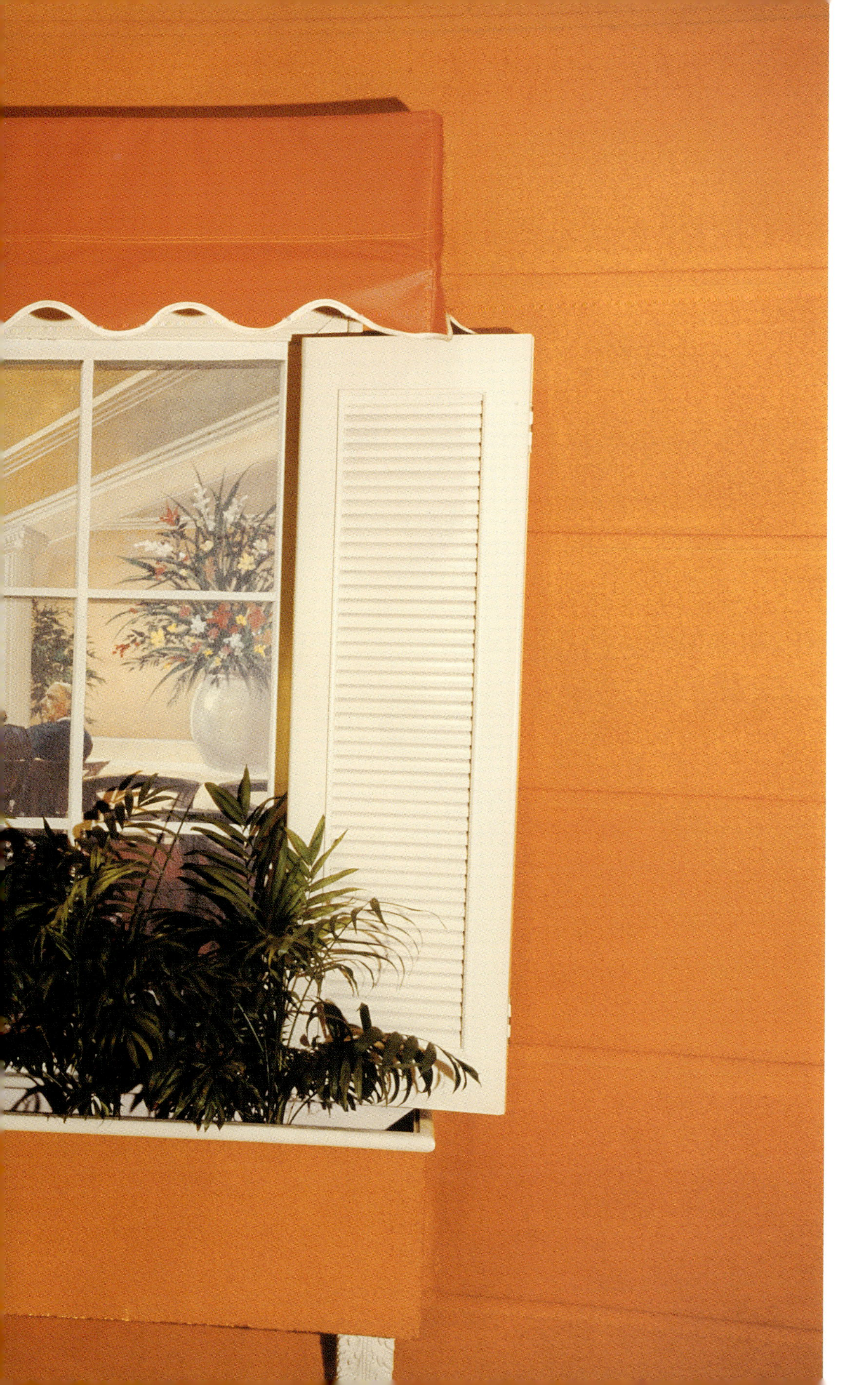

KAWAII BABY
Japan, 2005–06

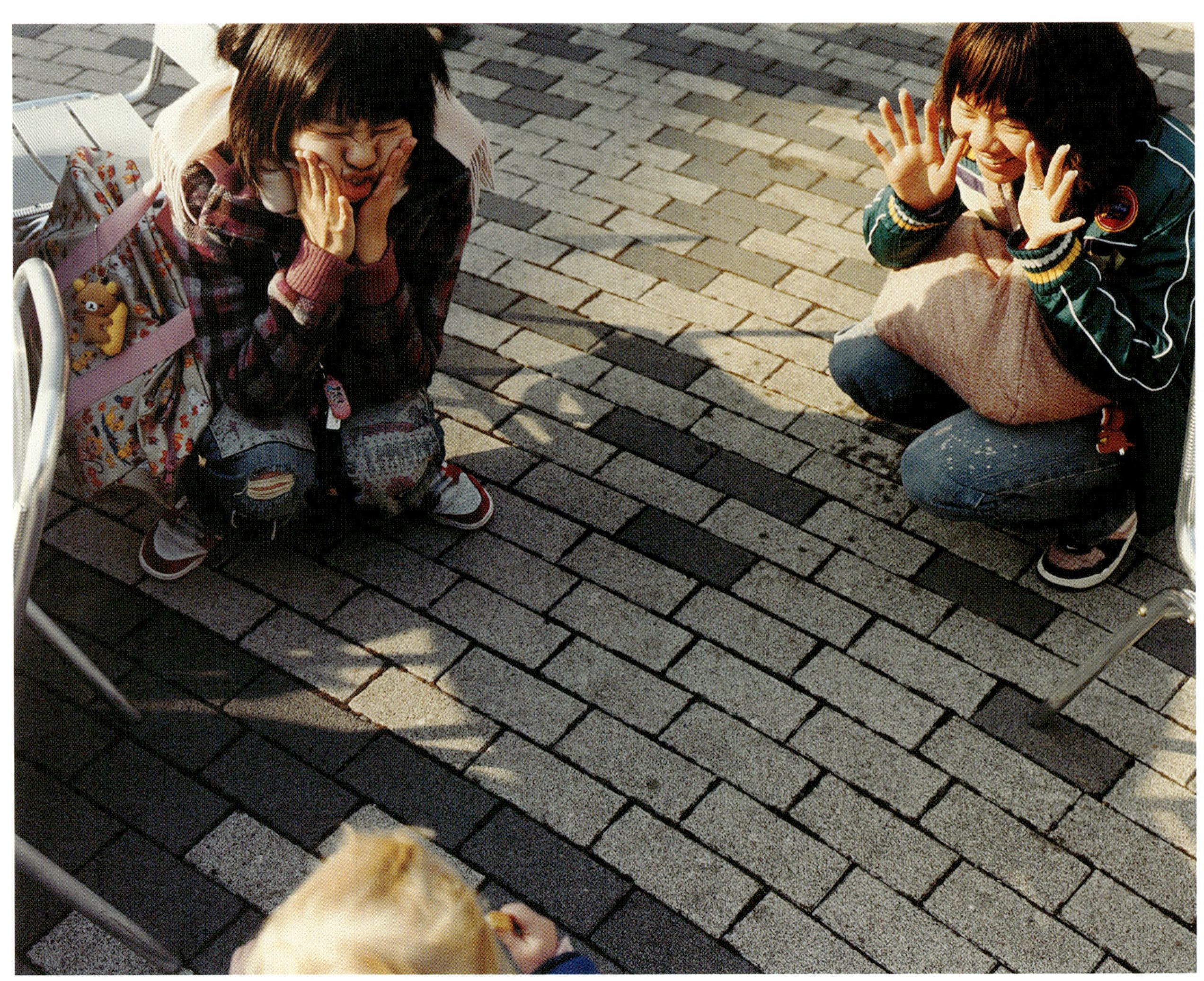

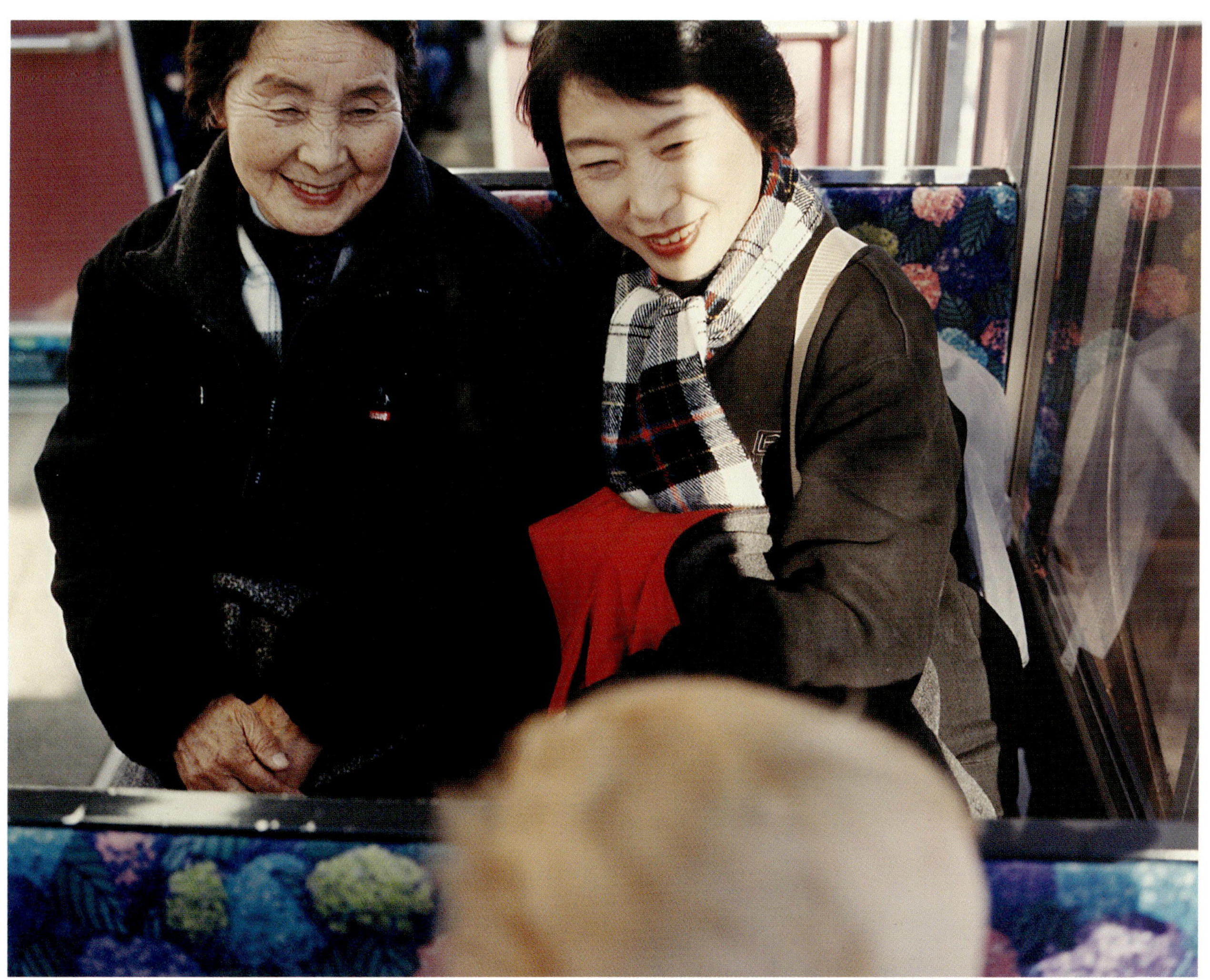

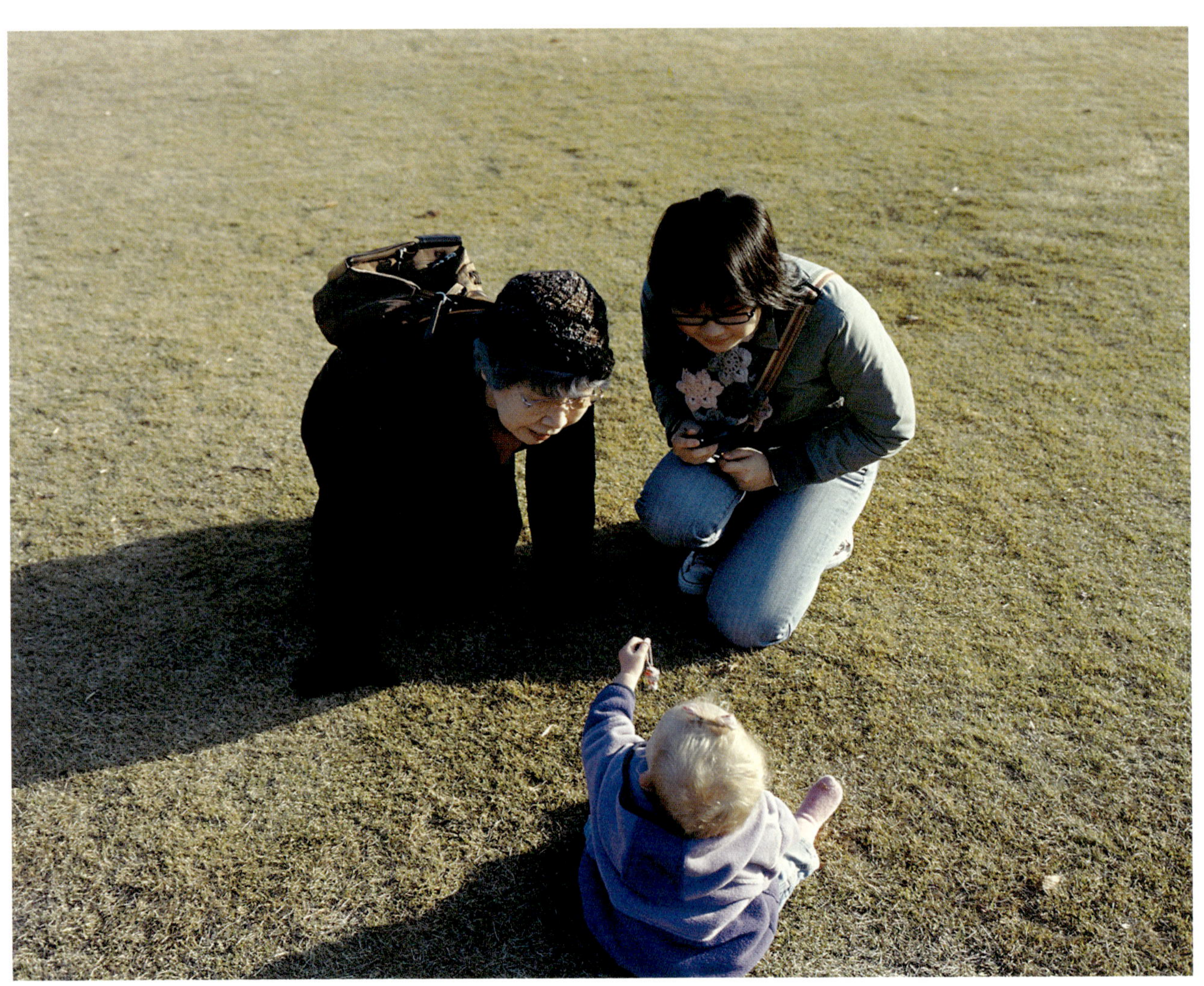

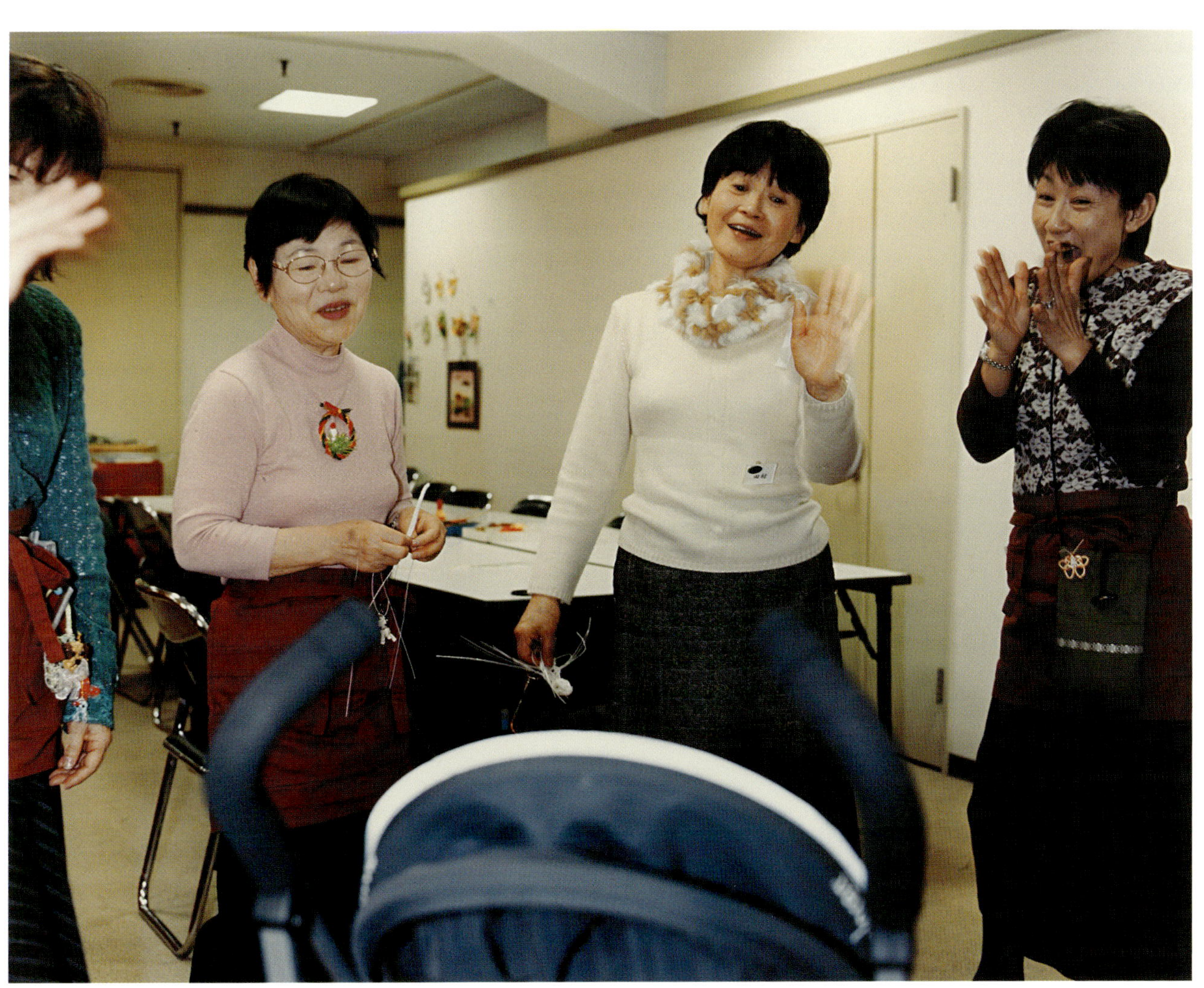

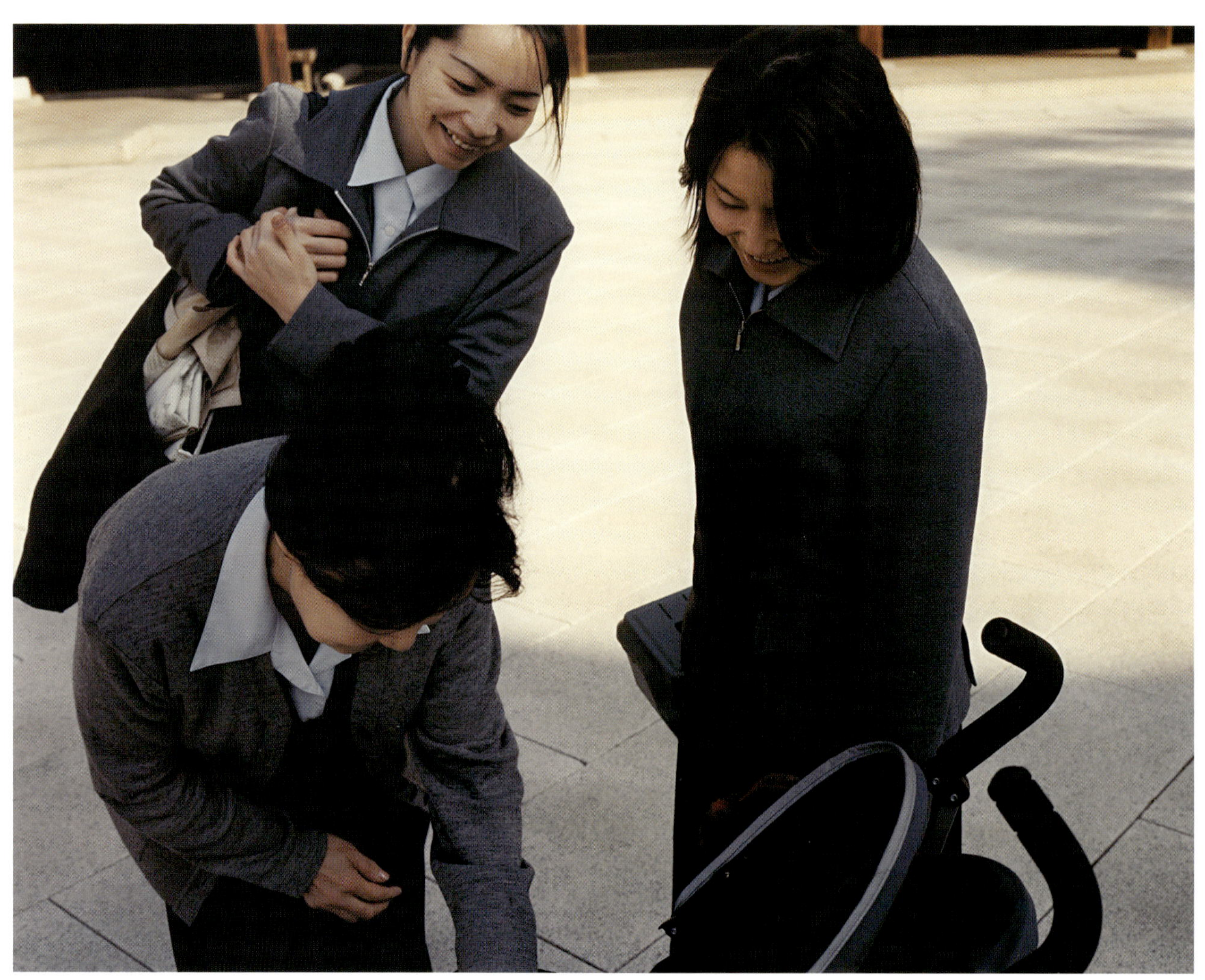

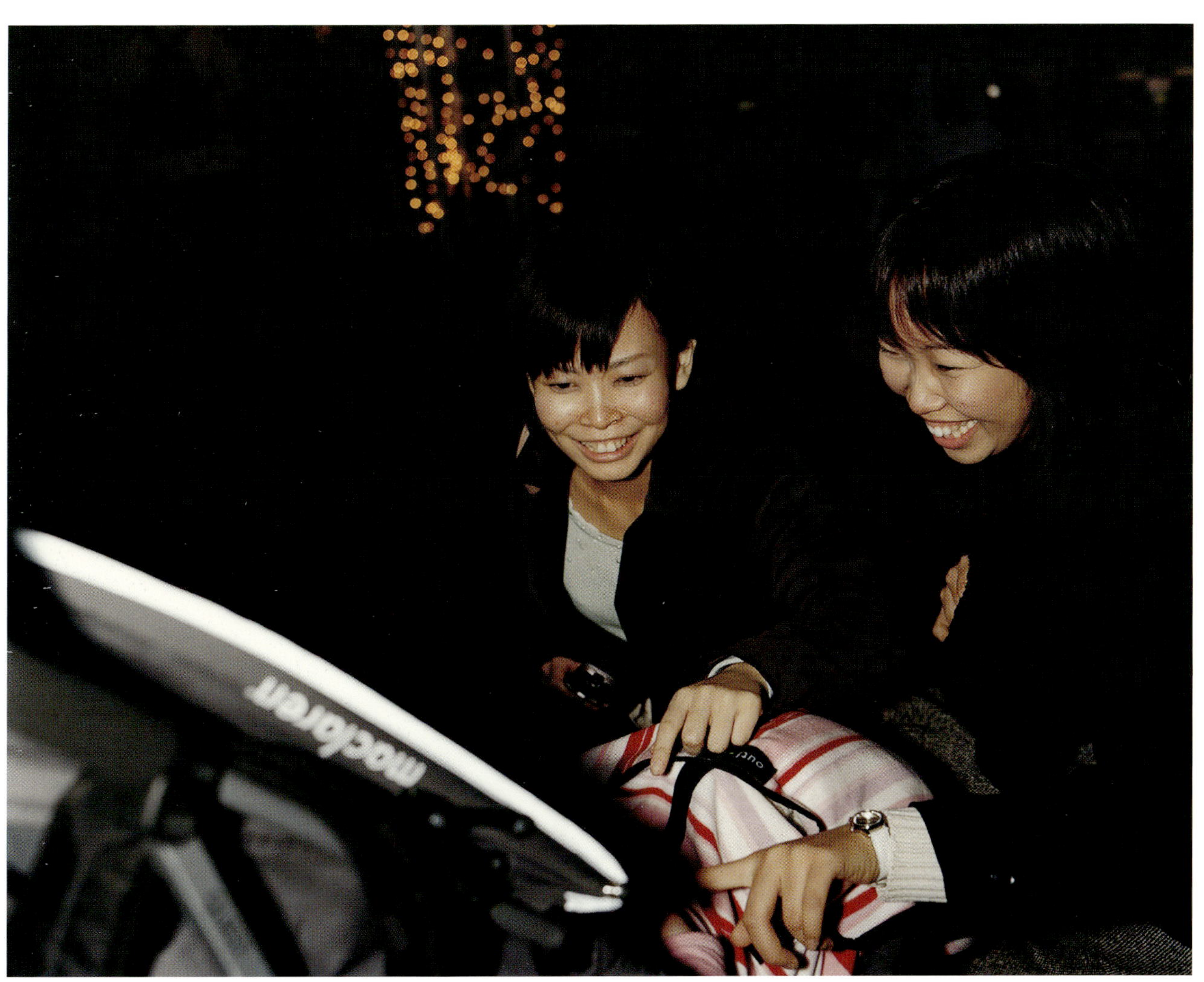
maclaren

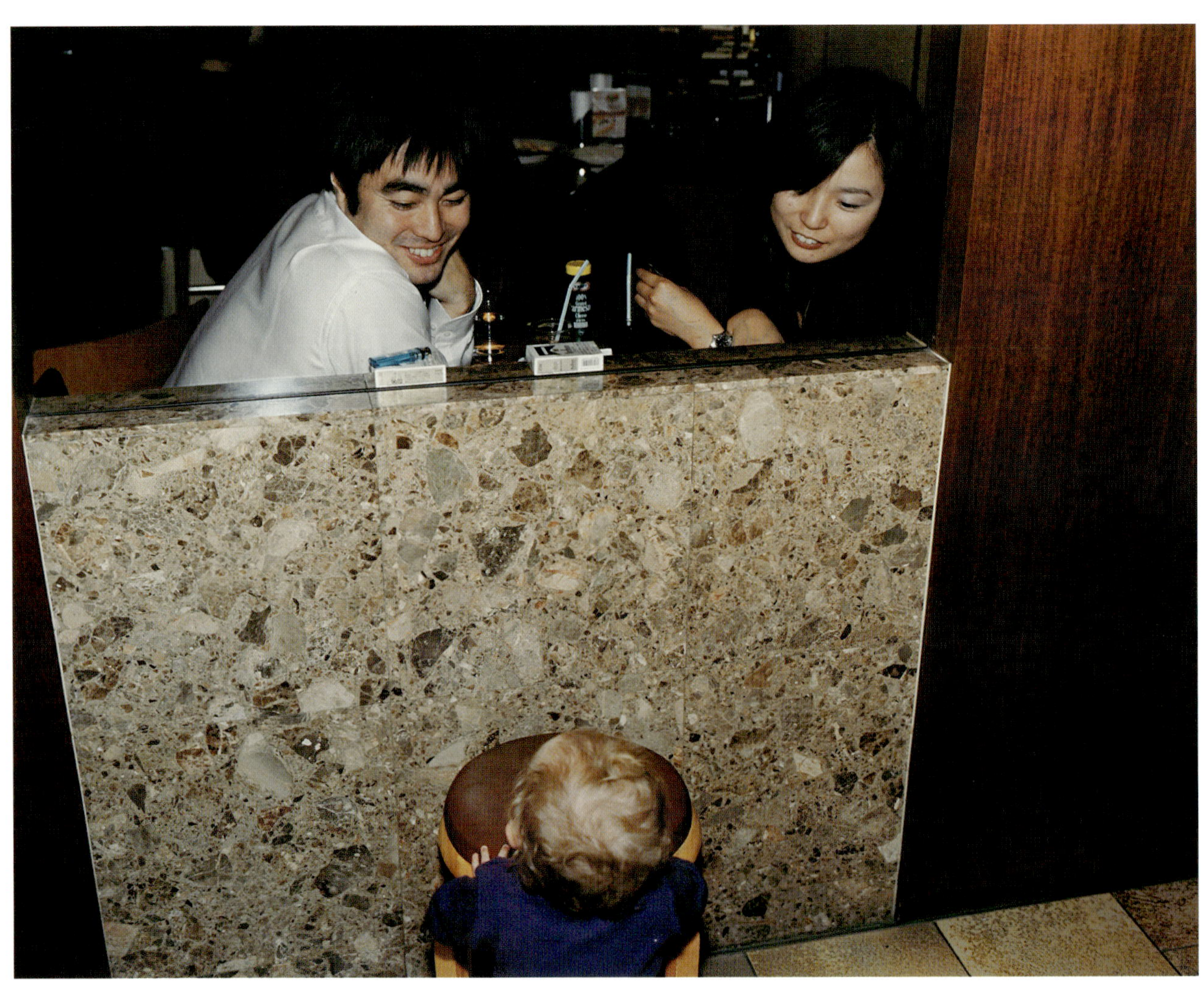

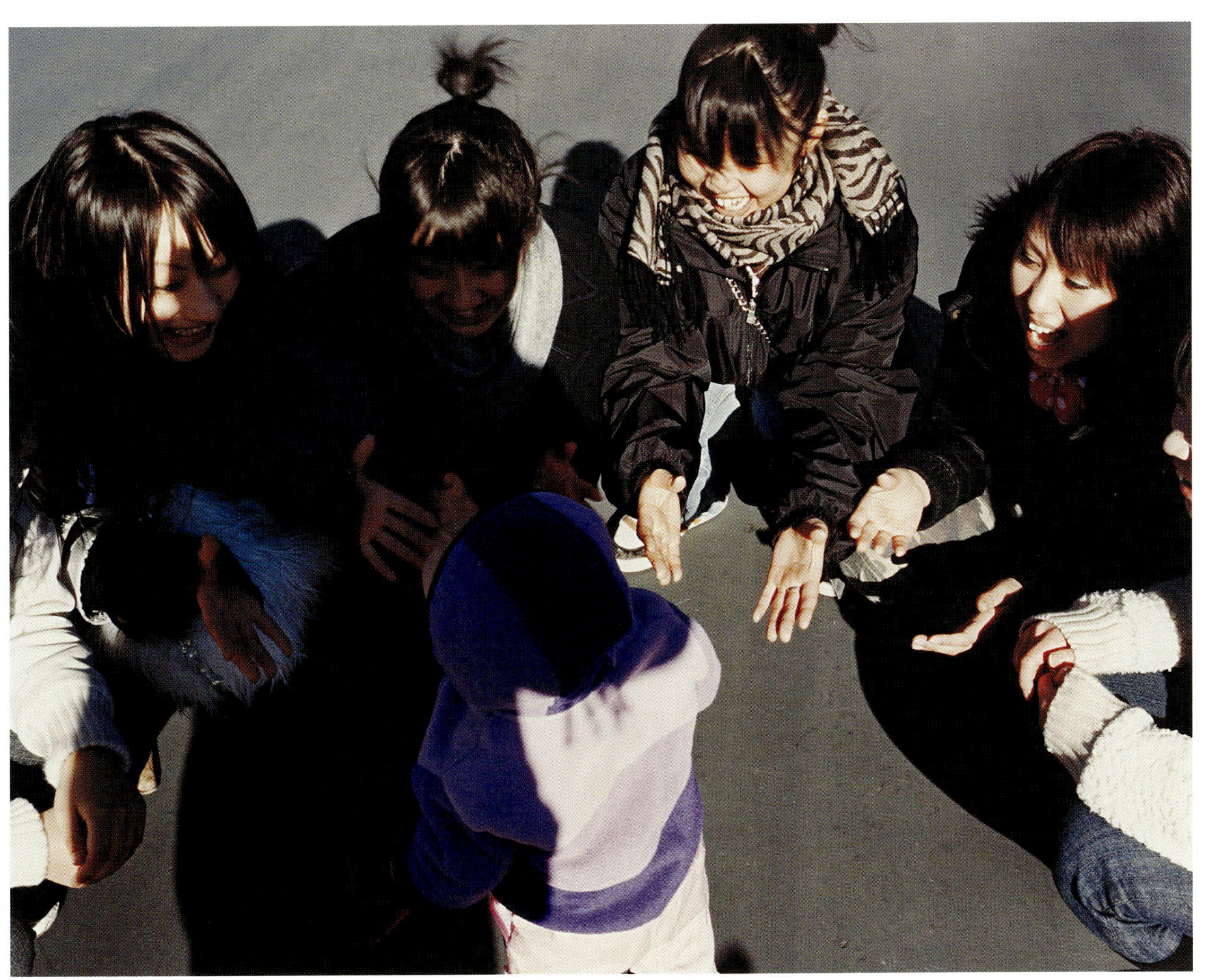

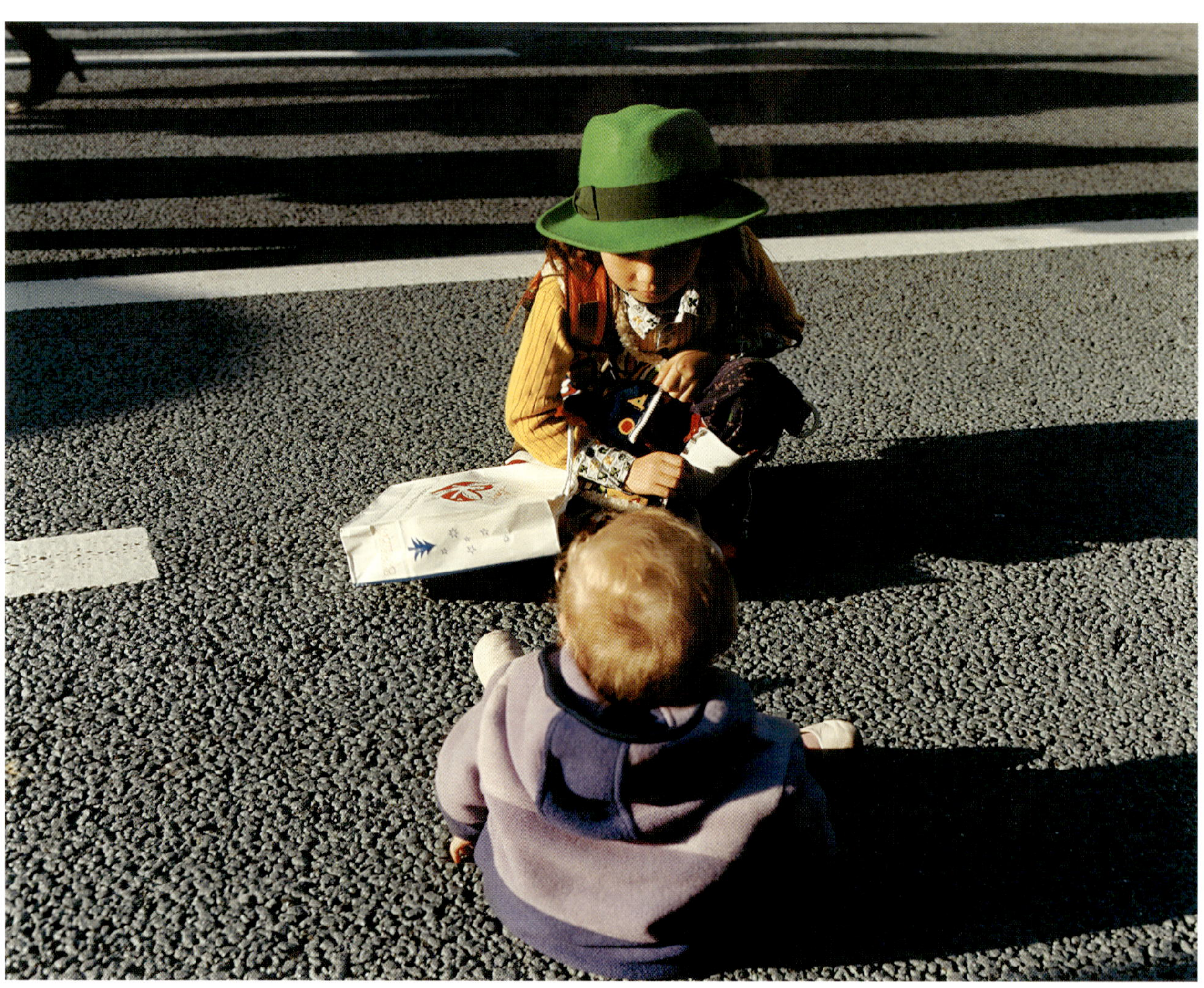

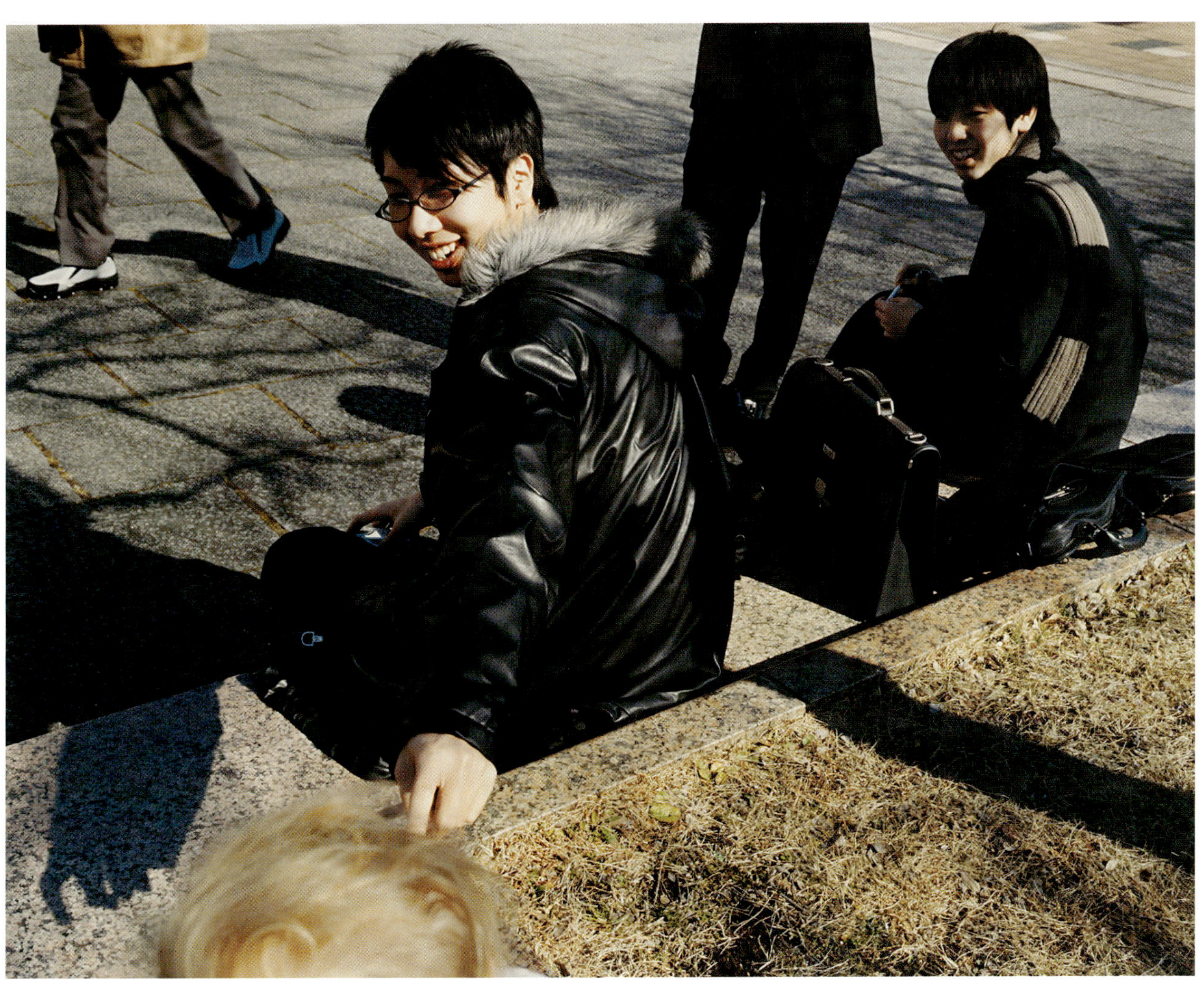

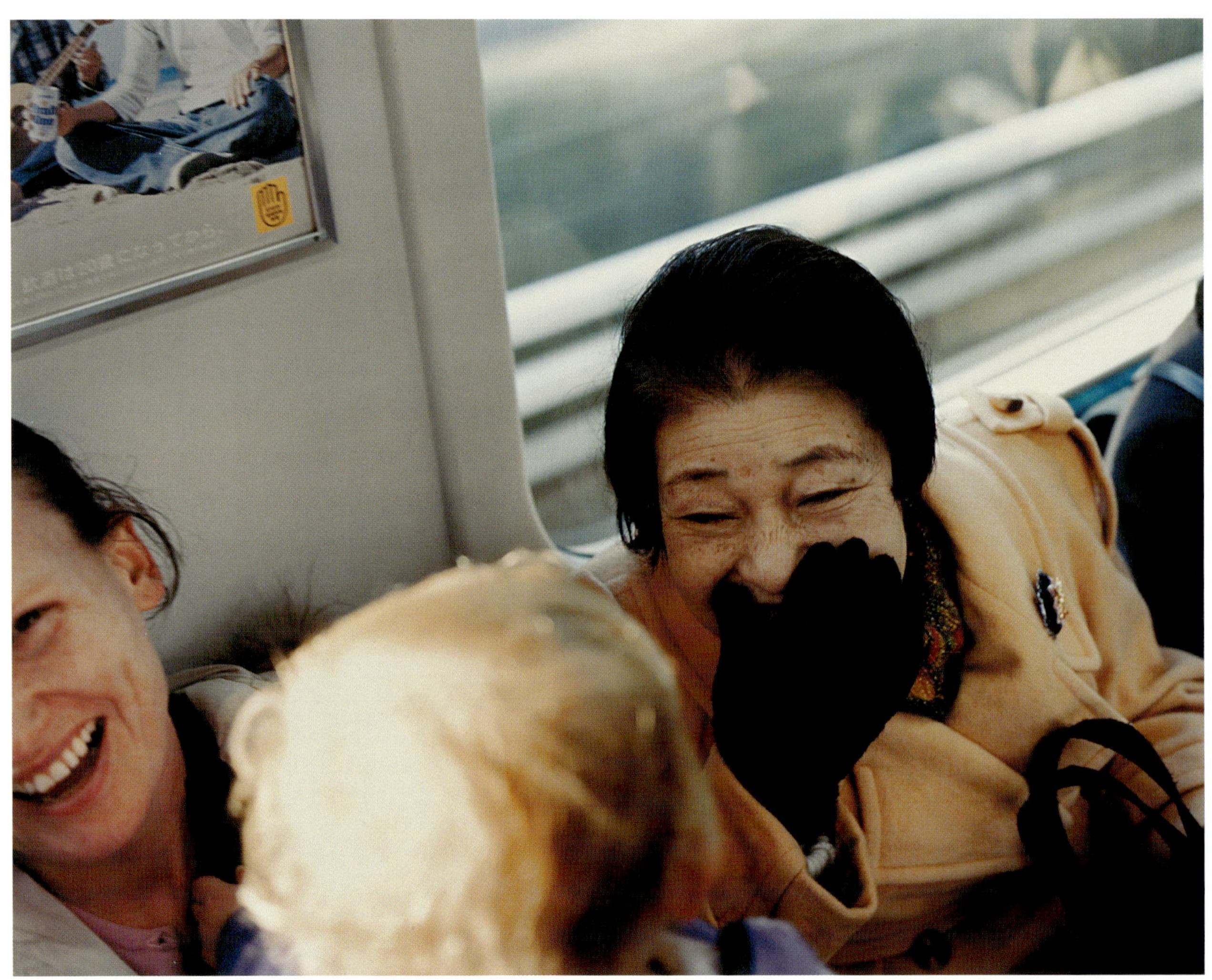

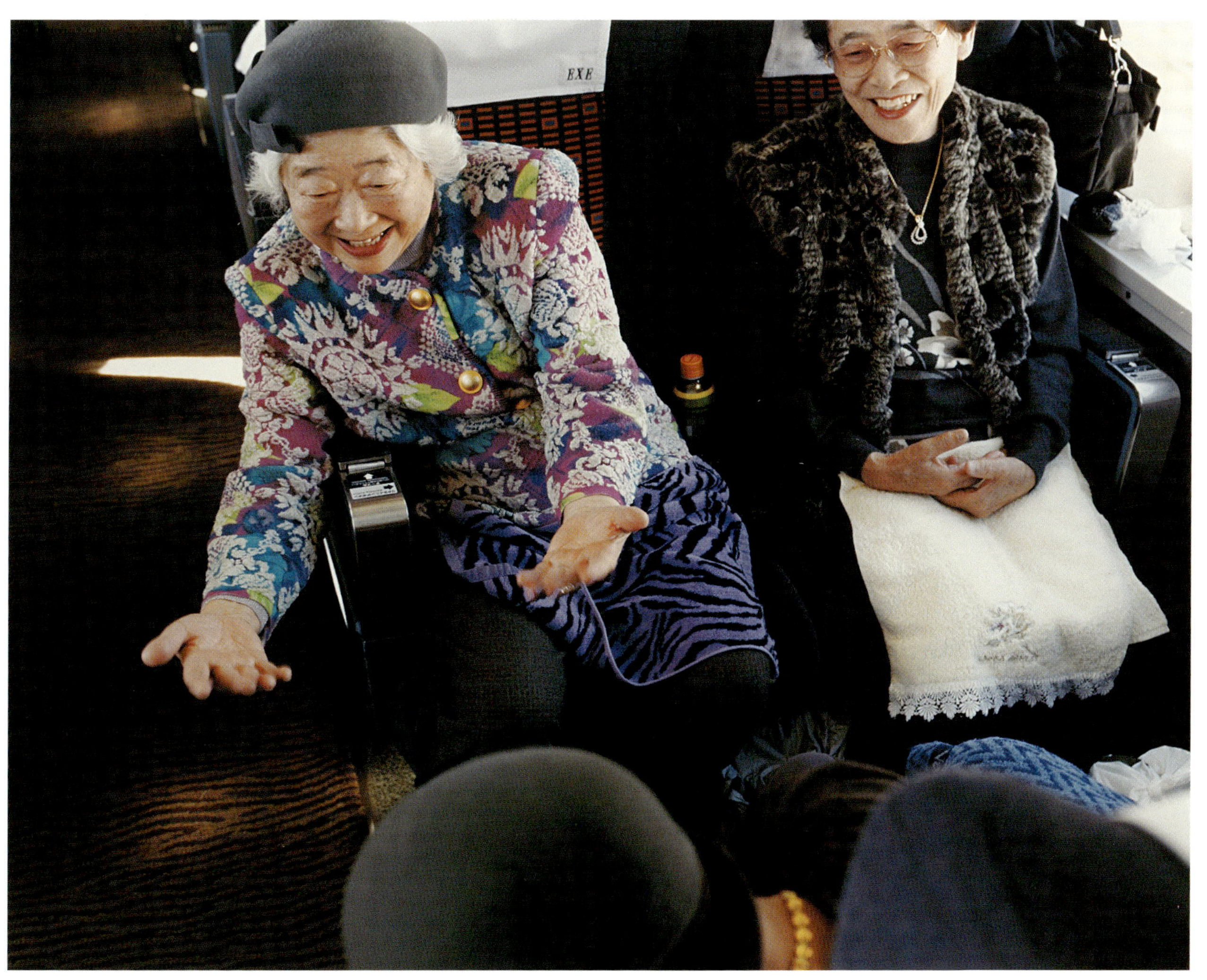
EXE

60

TAGGED
Copenhagen, 2004

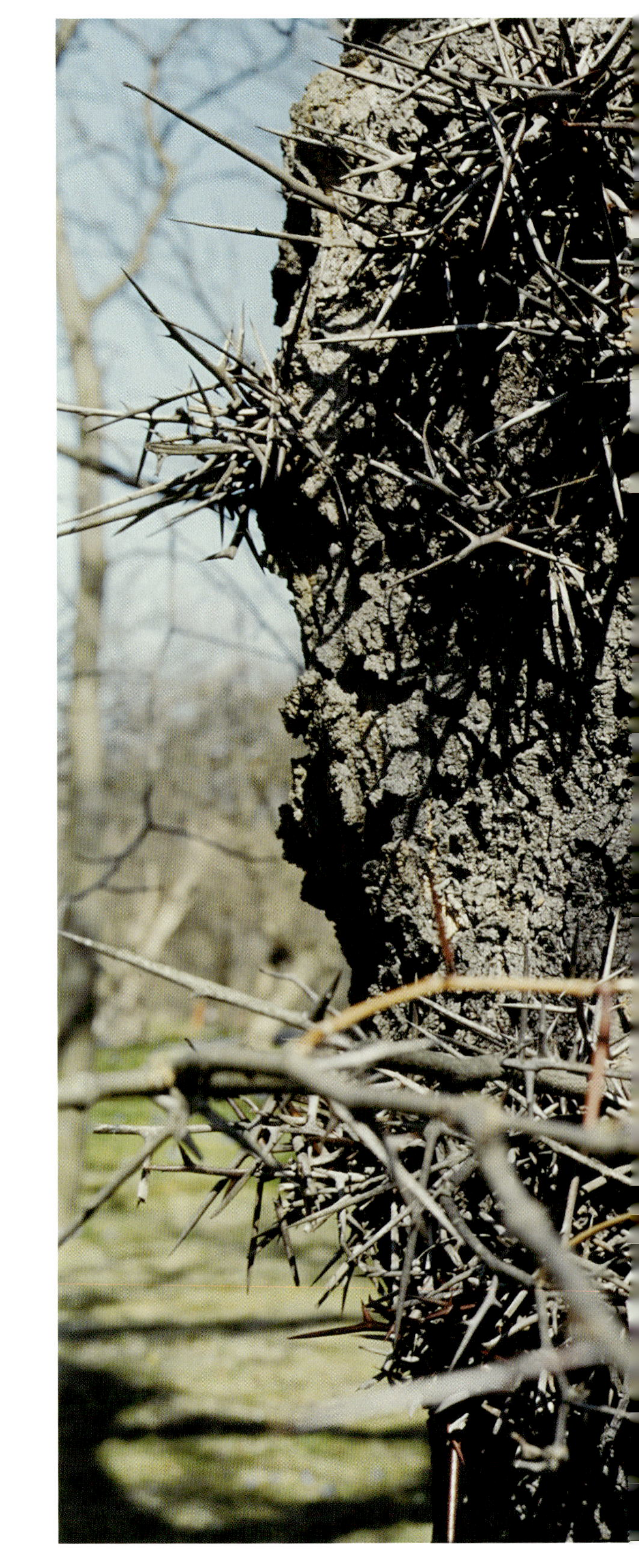

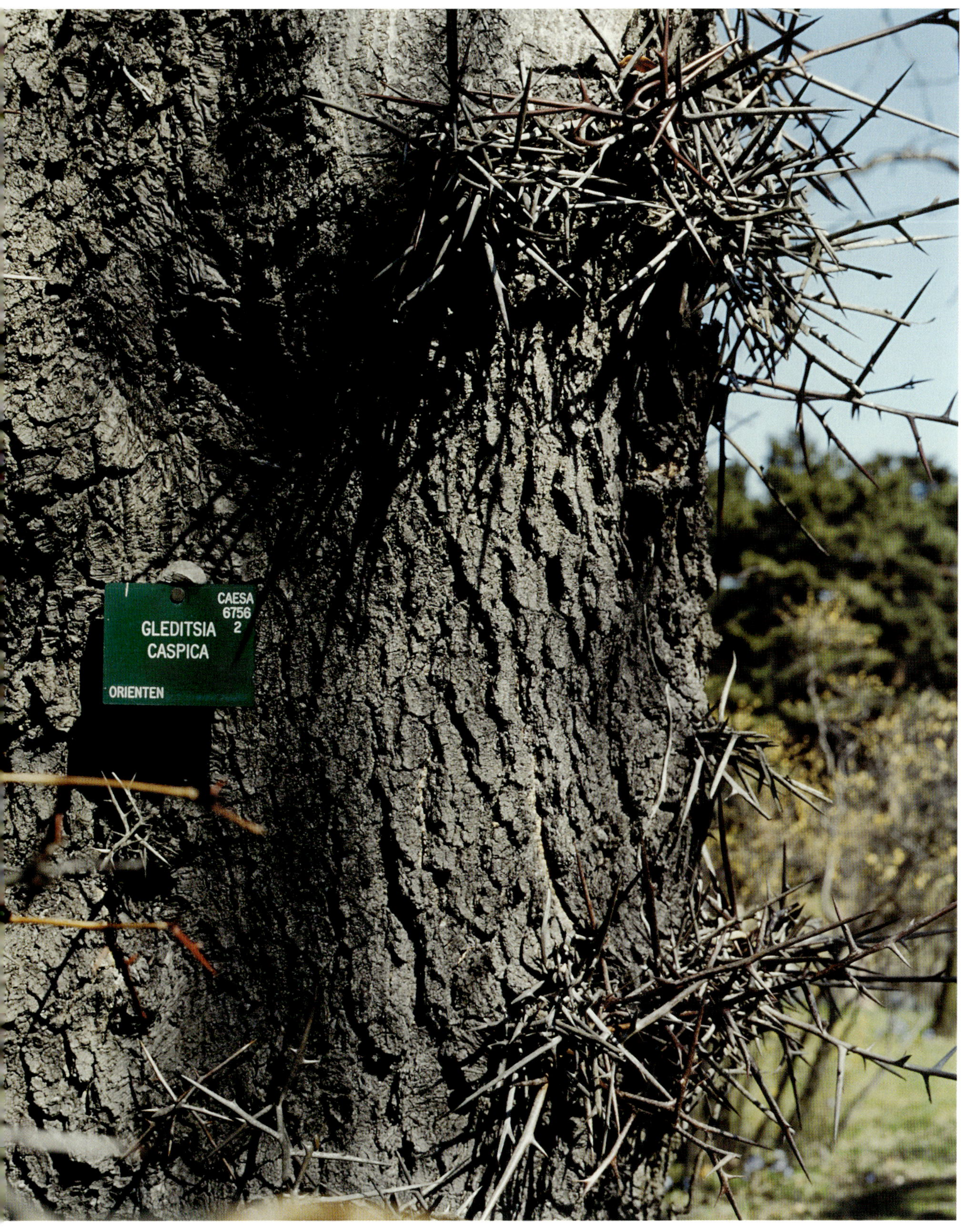
CAESA
6756
2
GLEDITSIA
CASPICA
ORIENTEN

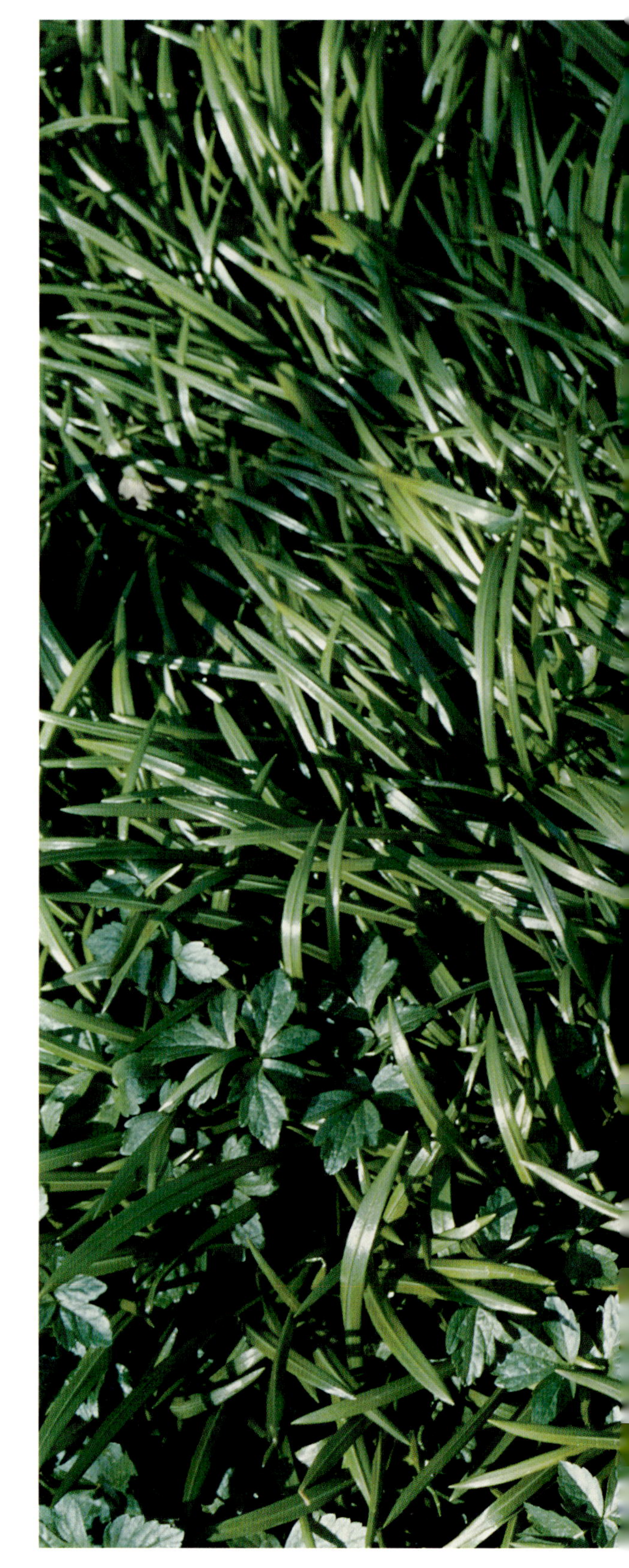

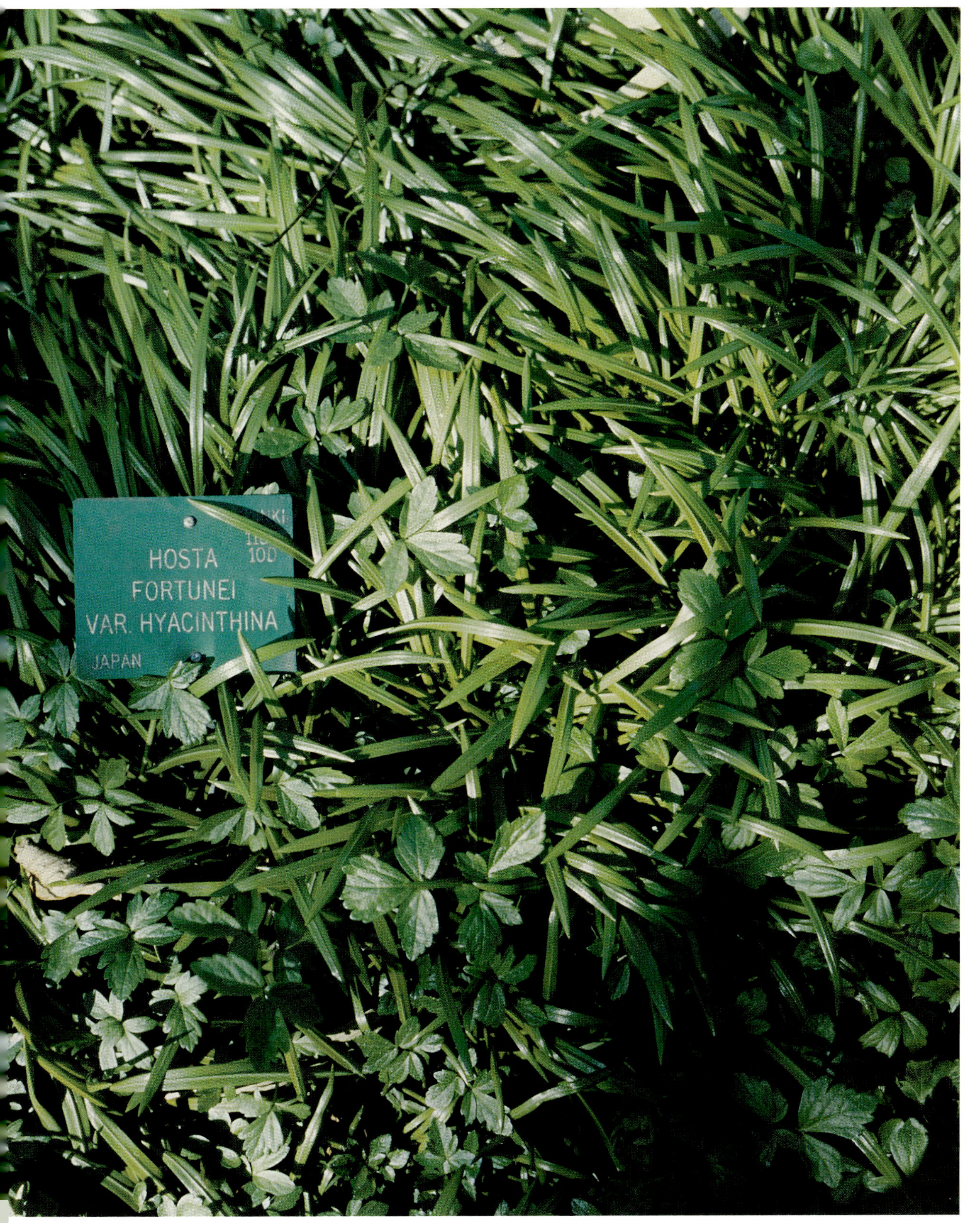
HOSTA
10D
FORTUNEI
VAR. HYACINTHINA
JAPAN

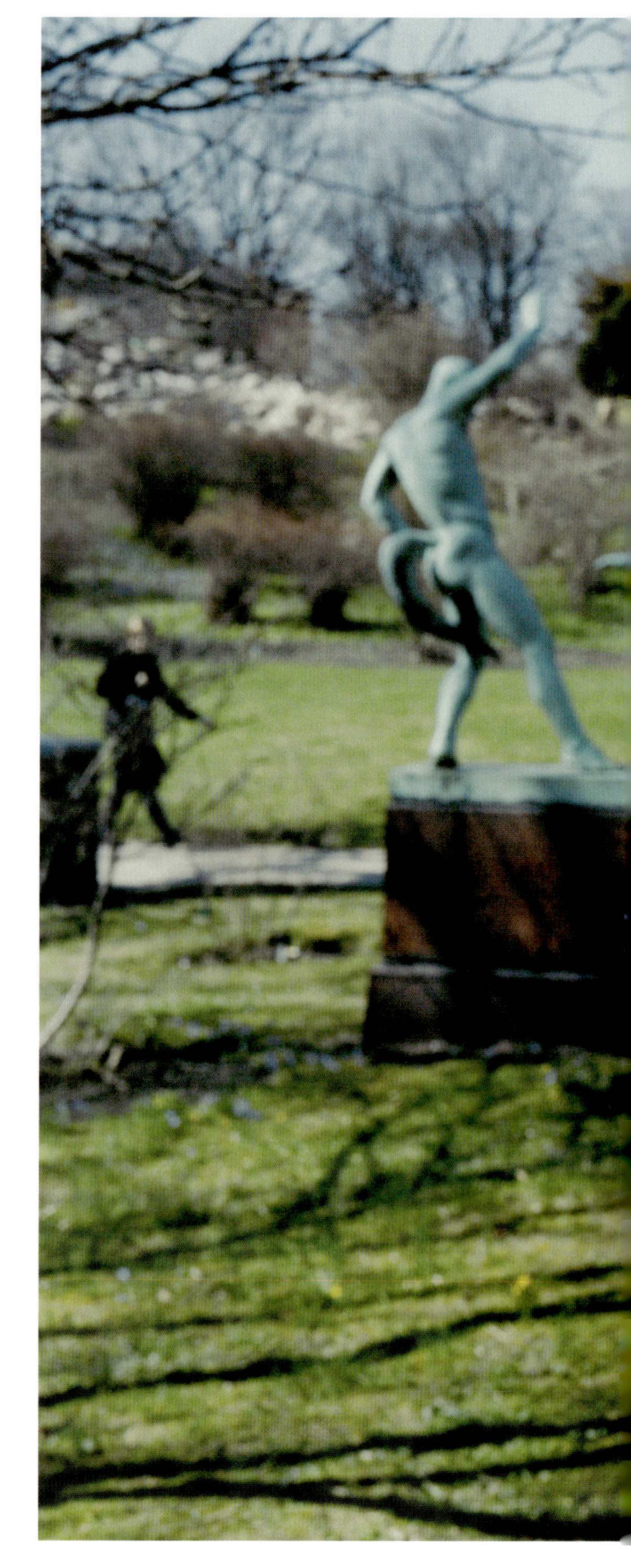

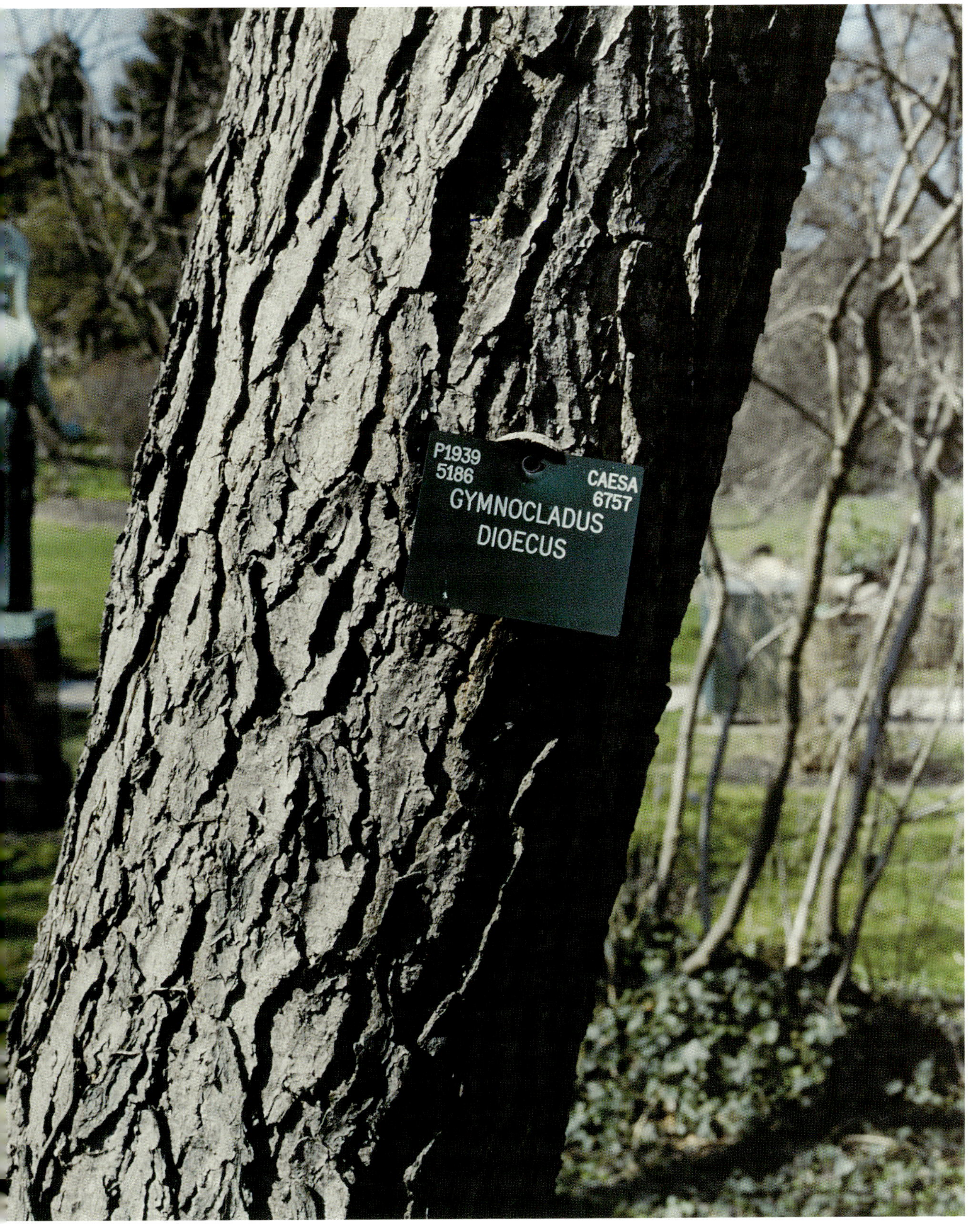
P1939
5186
CAESA
6757
GYMNOCLADUS
DIOECUS

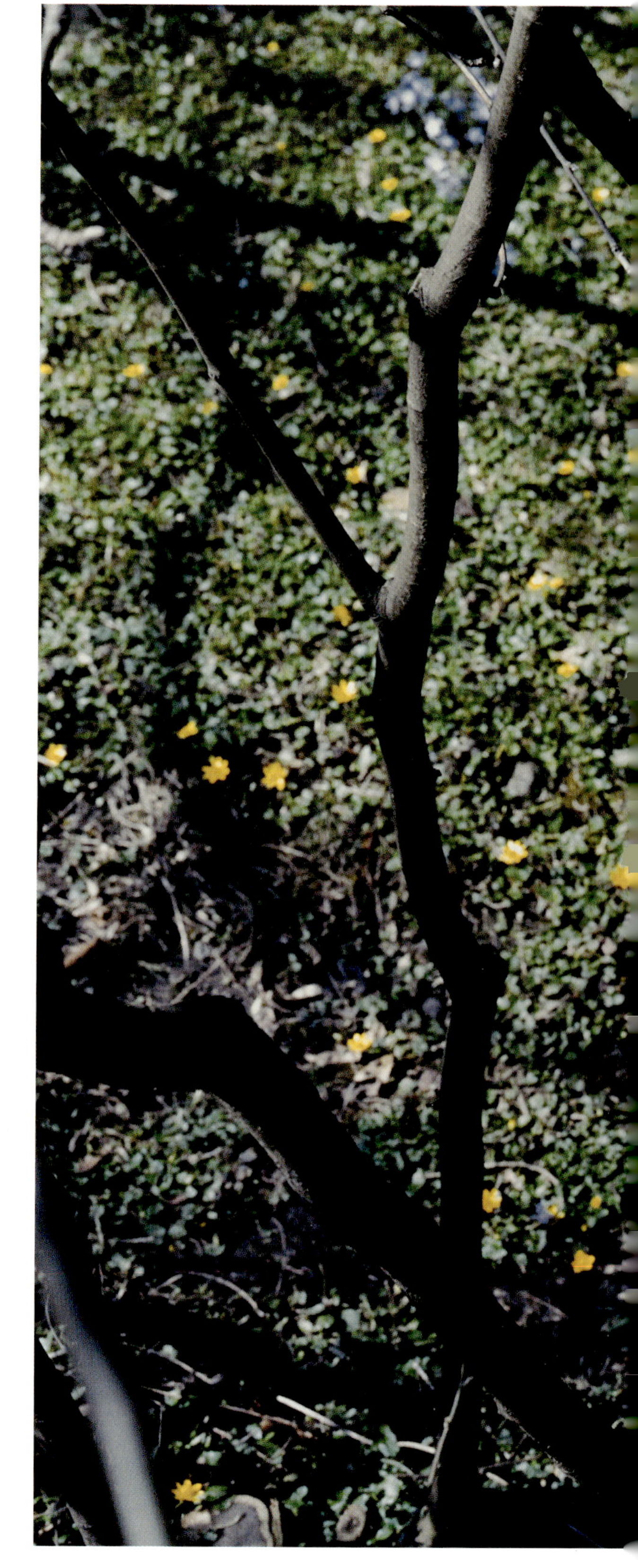

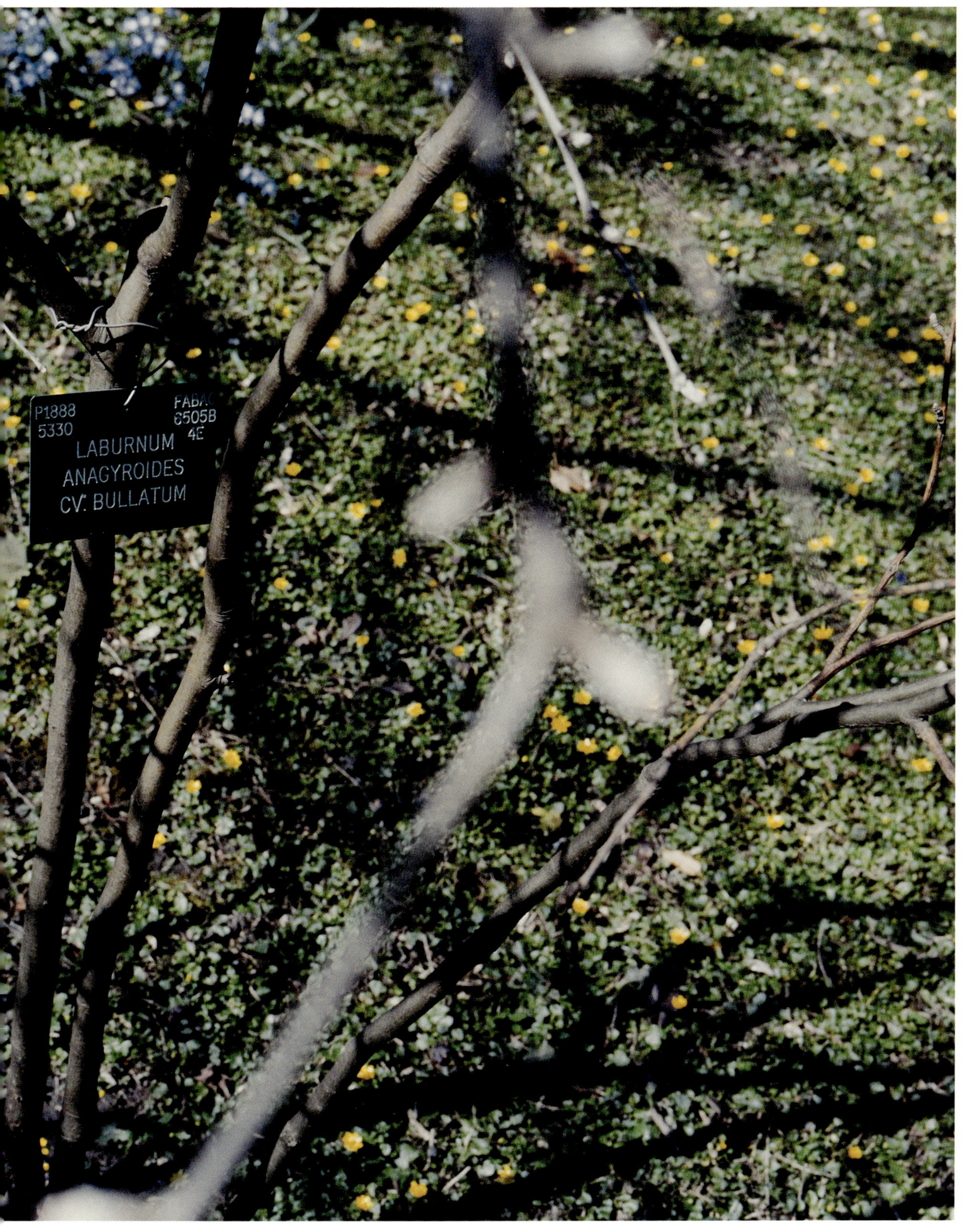
P1888
5330
FABAC
6505B
4E
LABURNUM
ANAGYROIDES
CV. BULLATUM

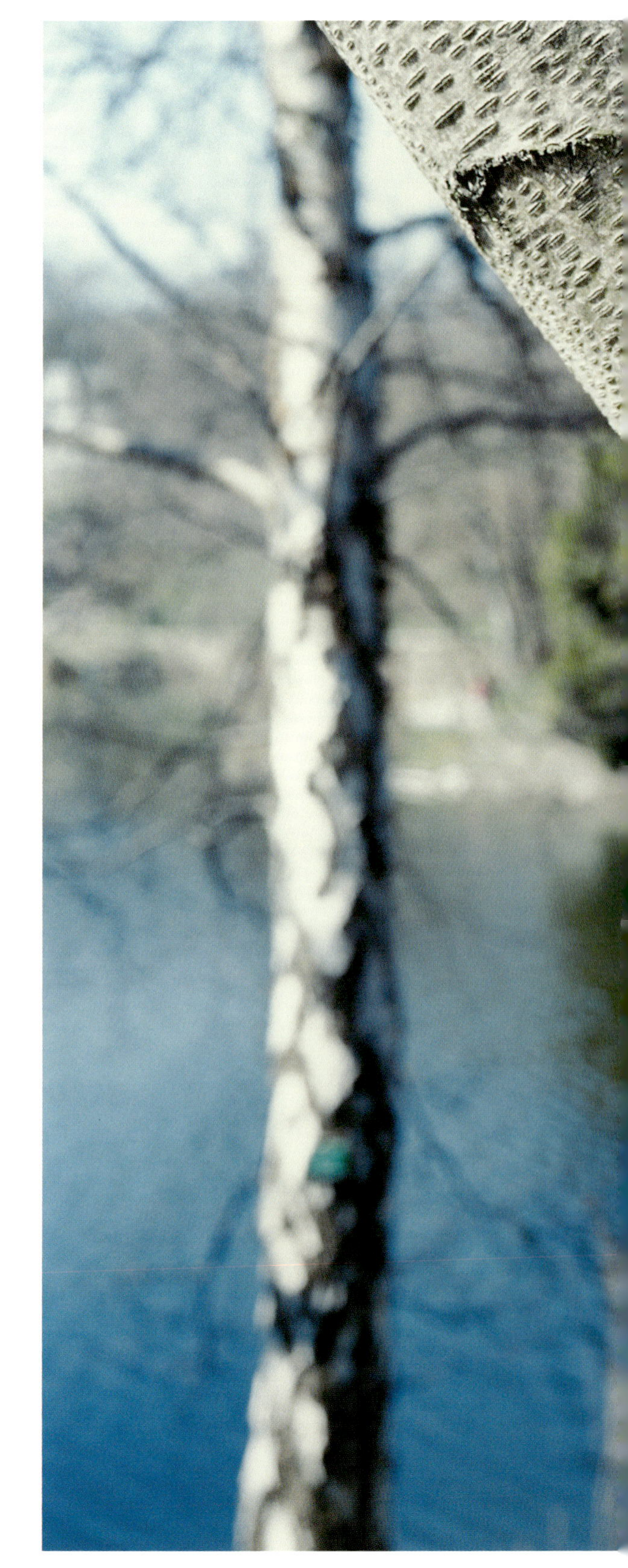

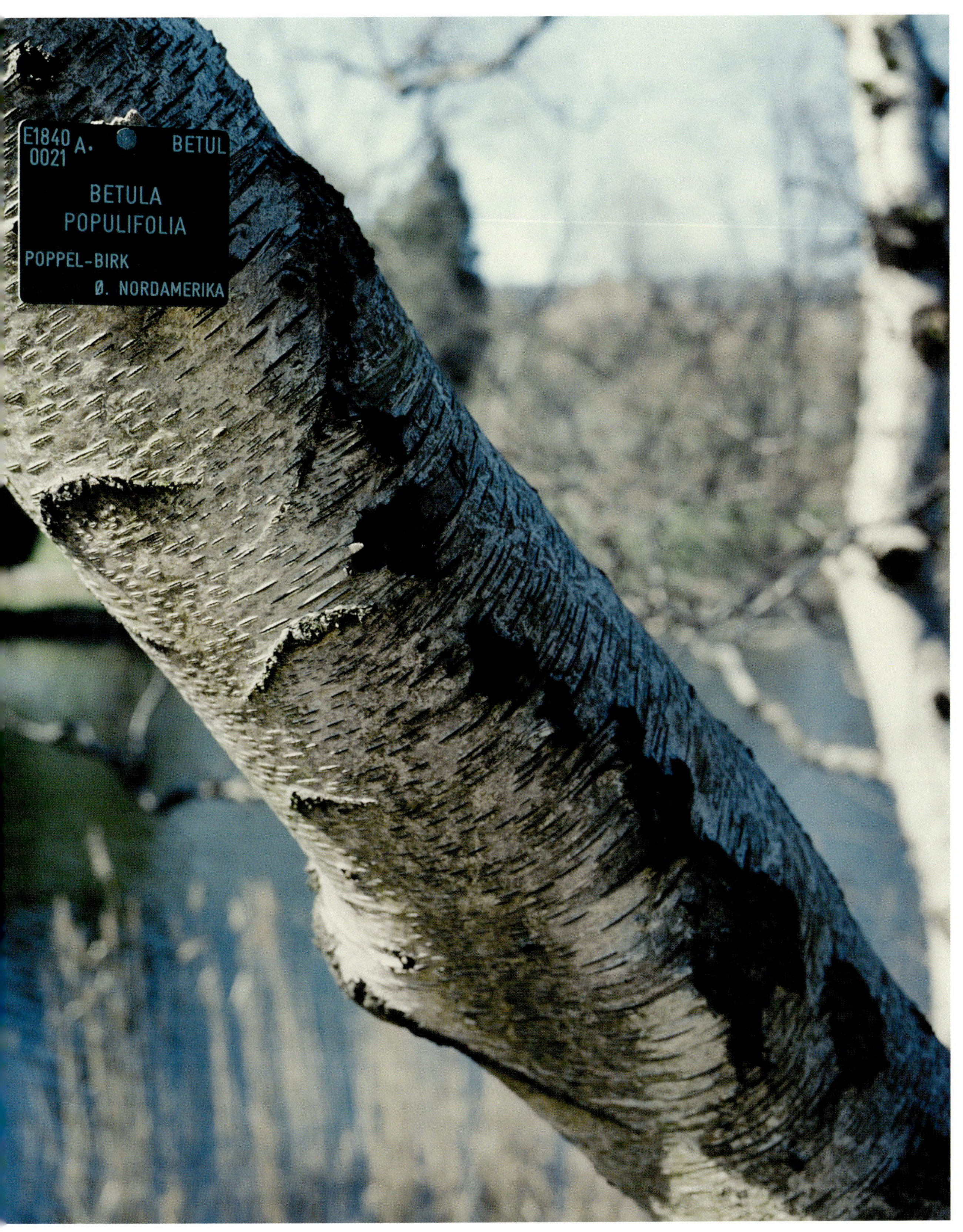
E1840 0021 A. BETUL
BETULA POPULIFOLIA
POPPEL-BIRK
Ø. NORDAMERIKA

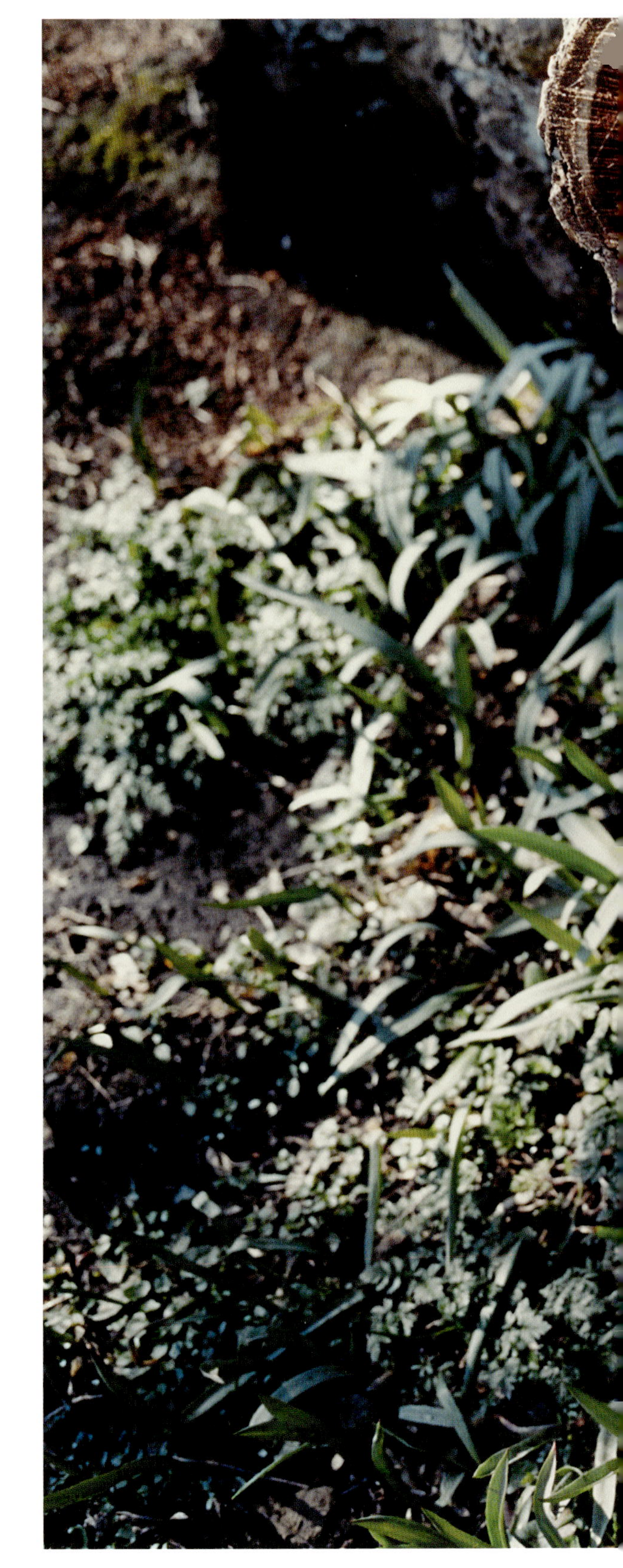

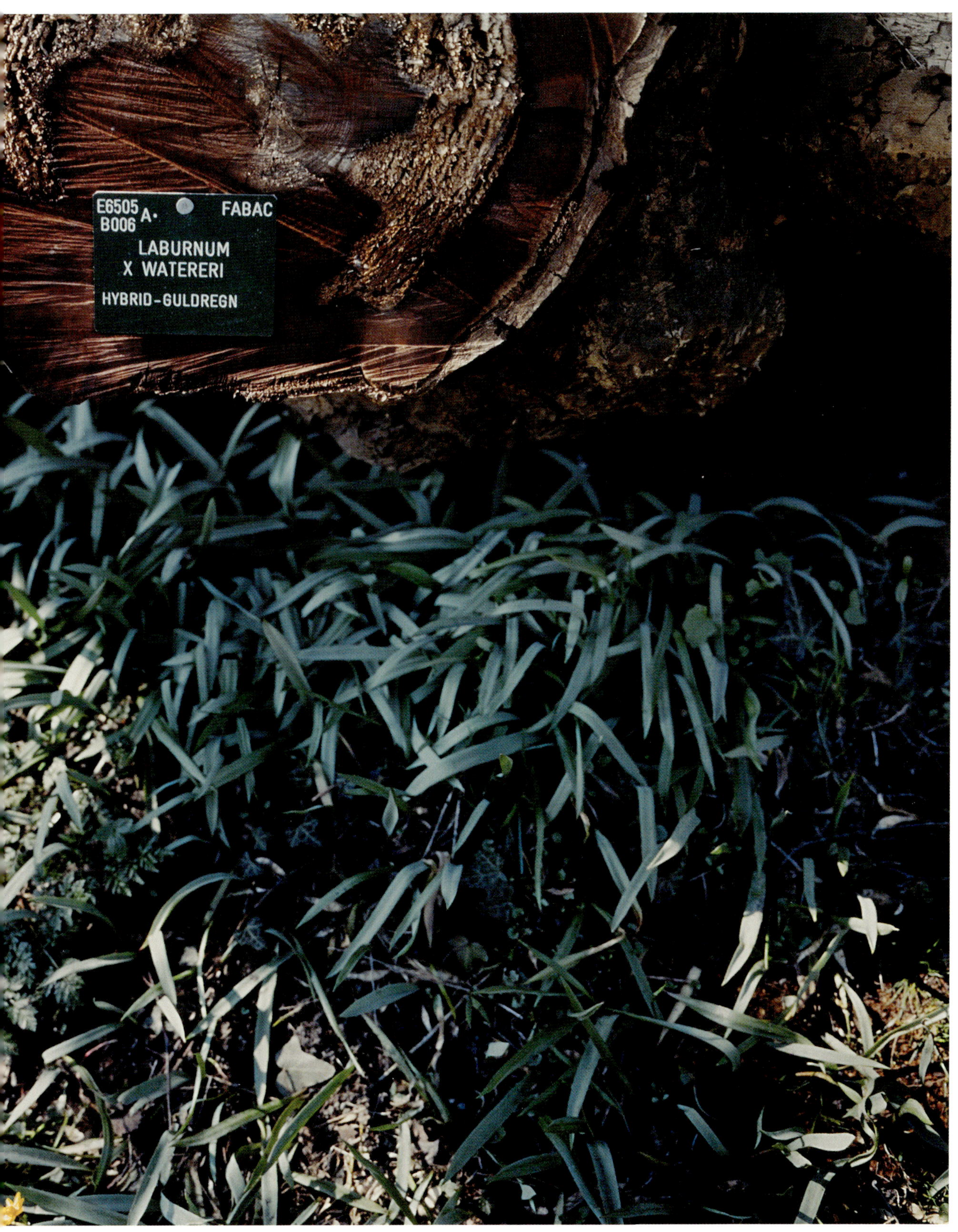
E6505
B006
A.
FABAC
LABURNUM
X WATERERI
HYBRID-GULDREGN

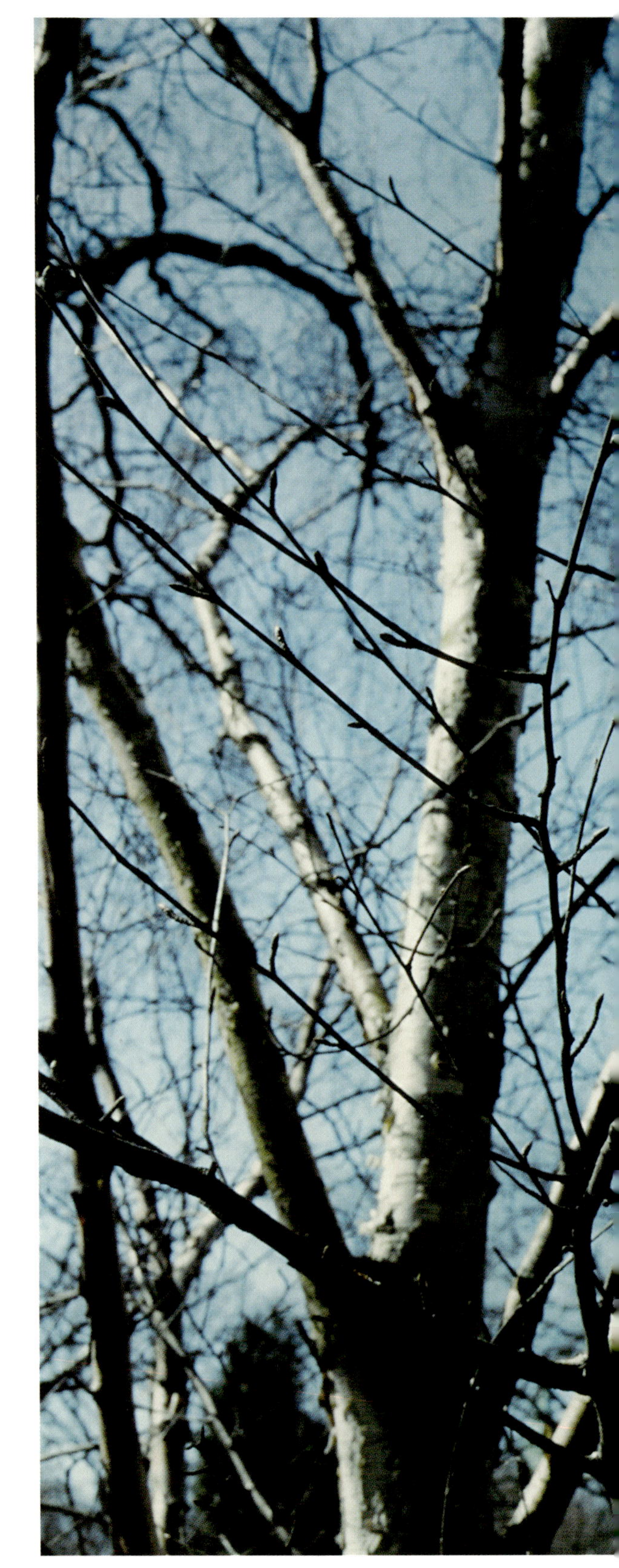

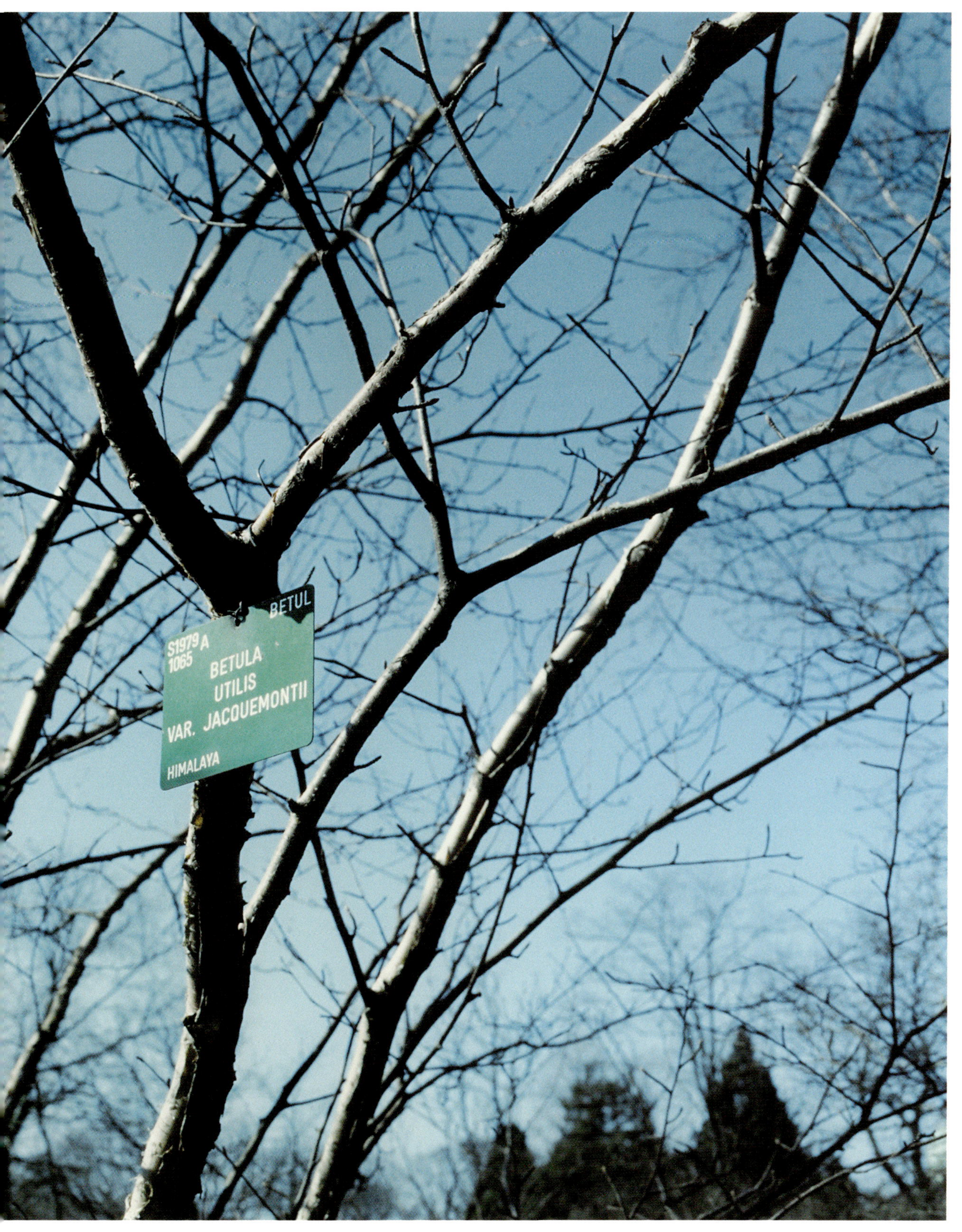
BETUL
S1979 A
1065
BETULA
UTILIS
VAR. JACQUEMONTII
HIMALAYA

10

FEET
Tokyo, 2002

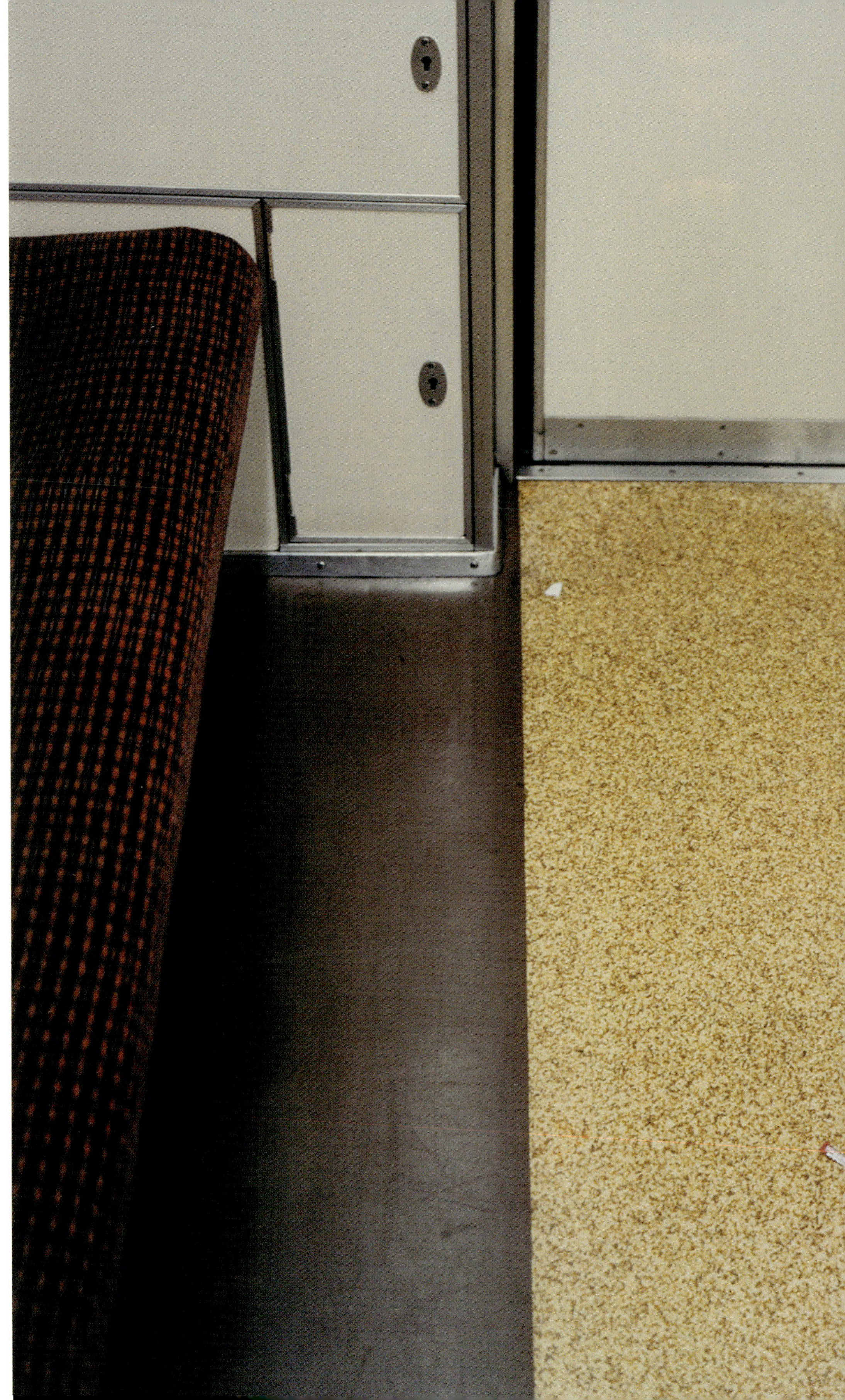

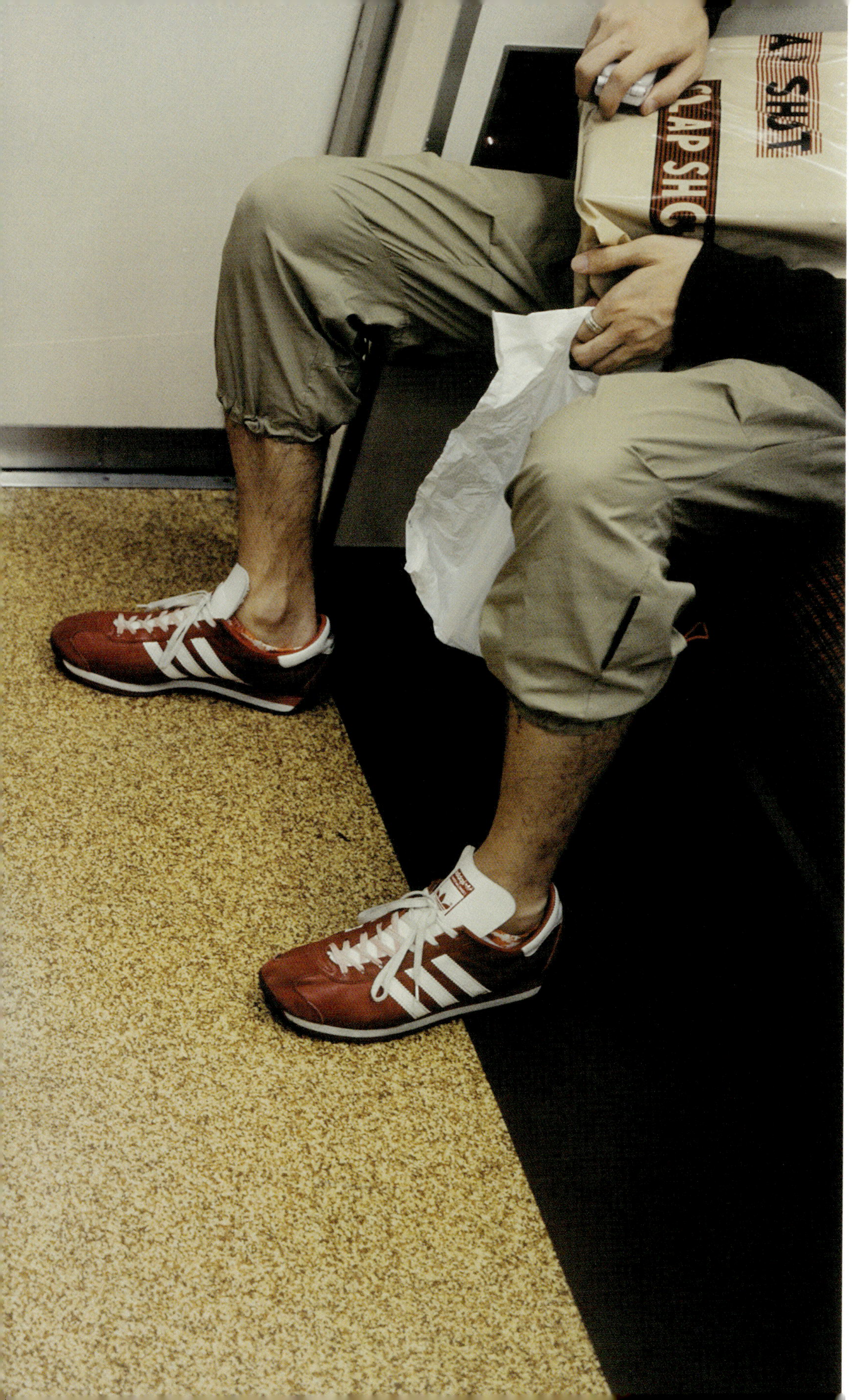

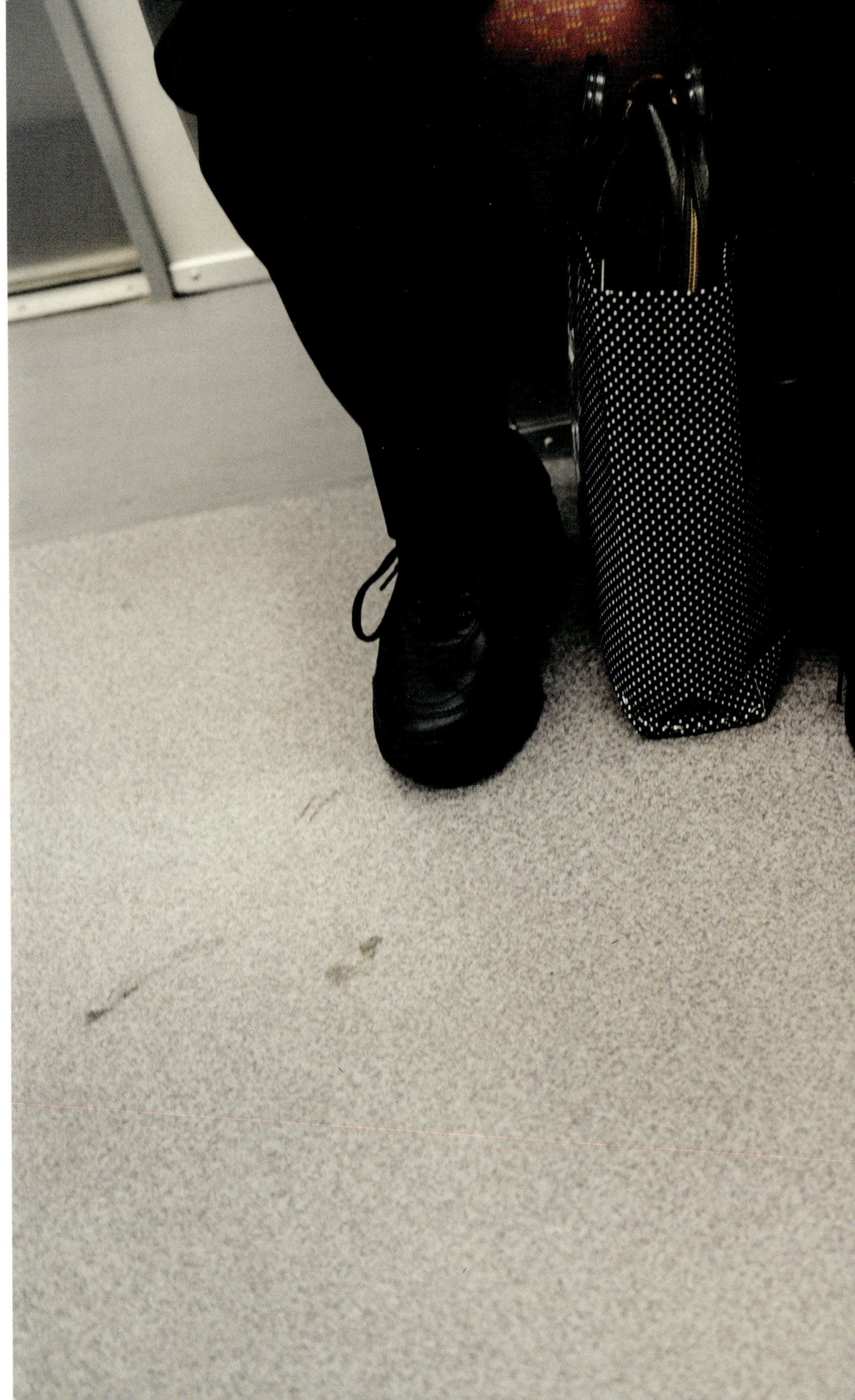

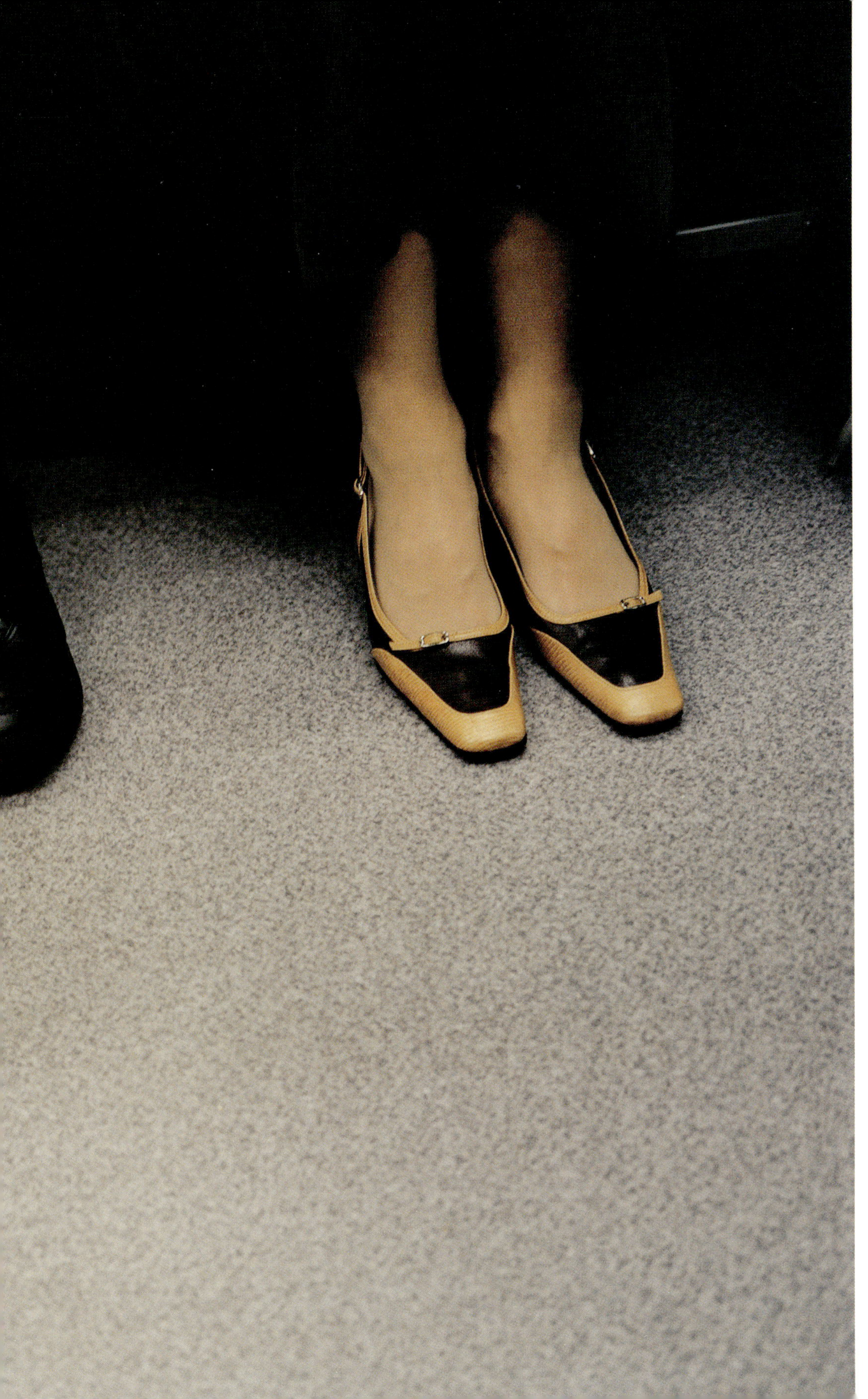

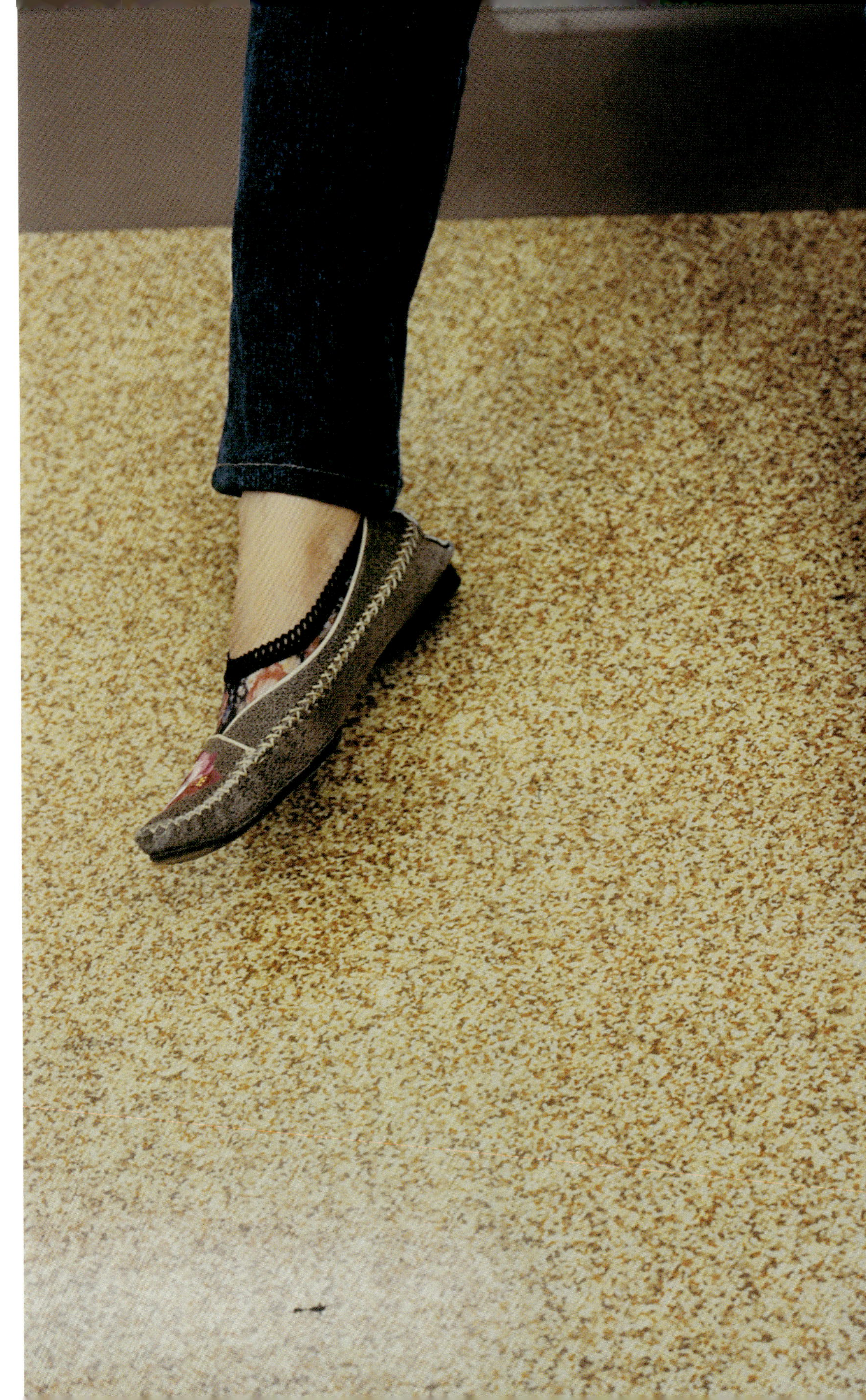

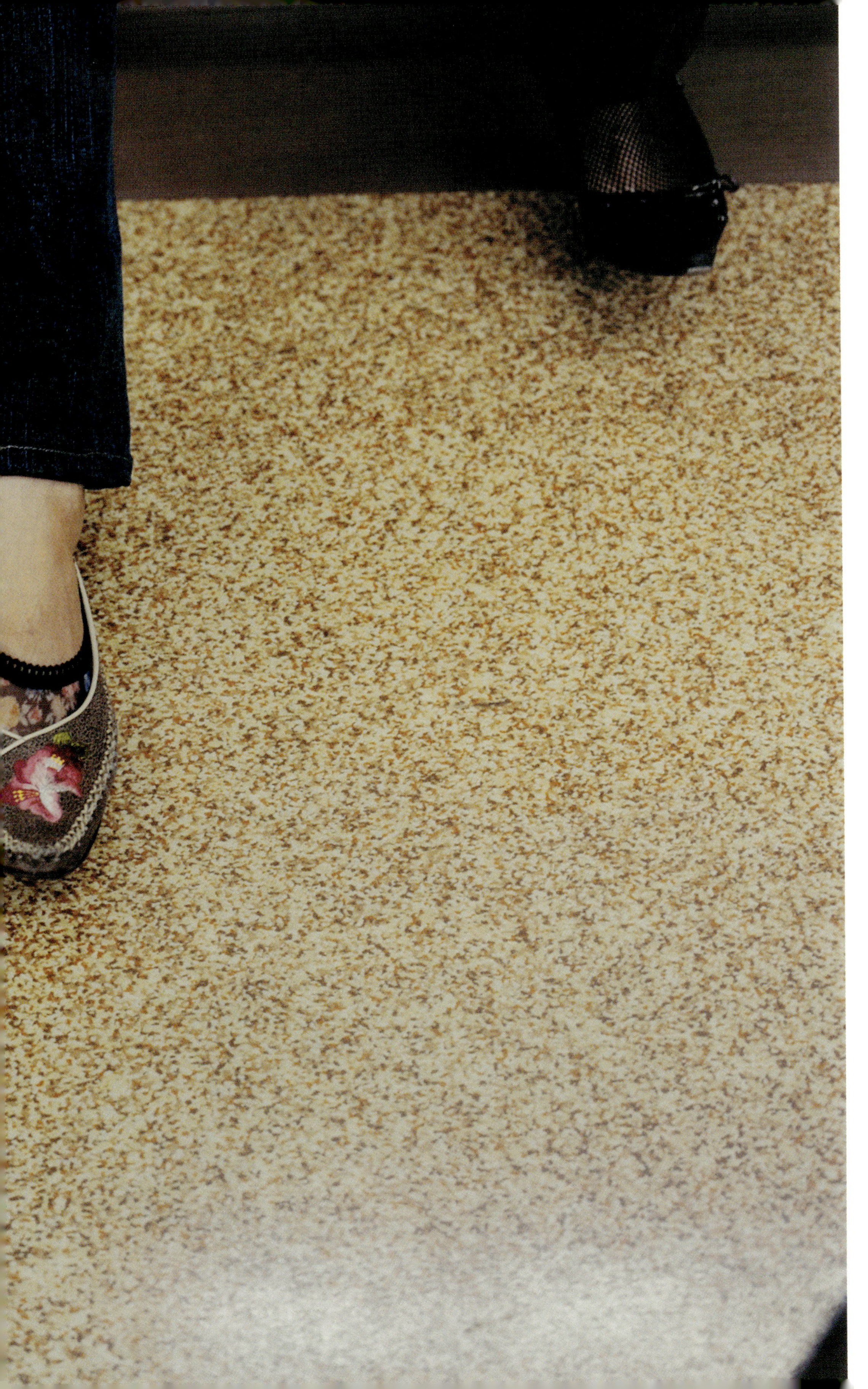

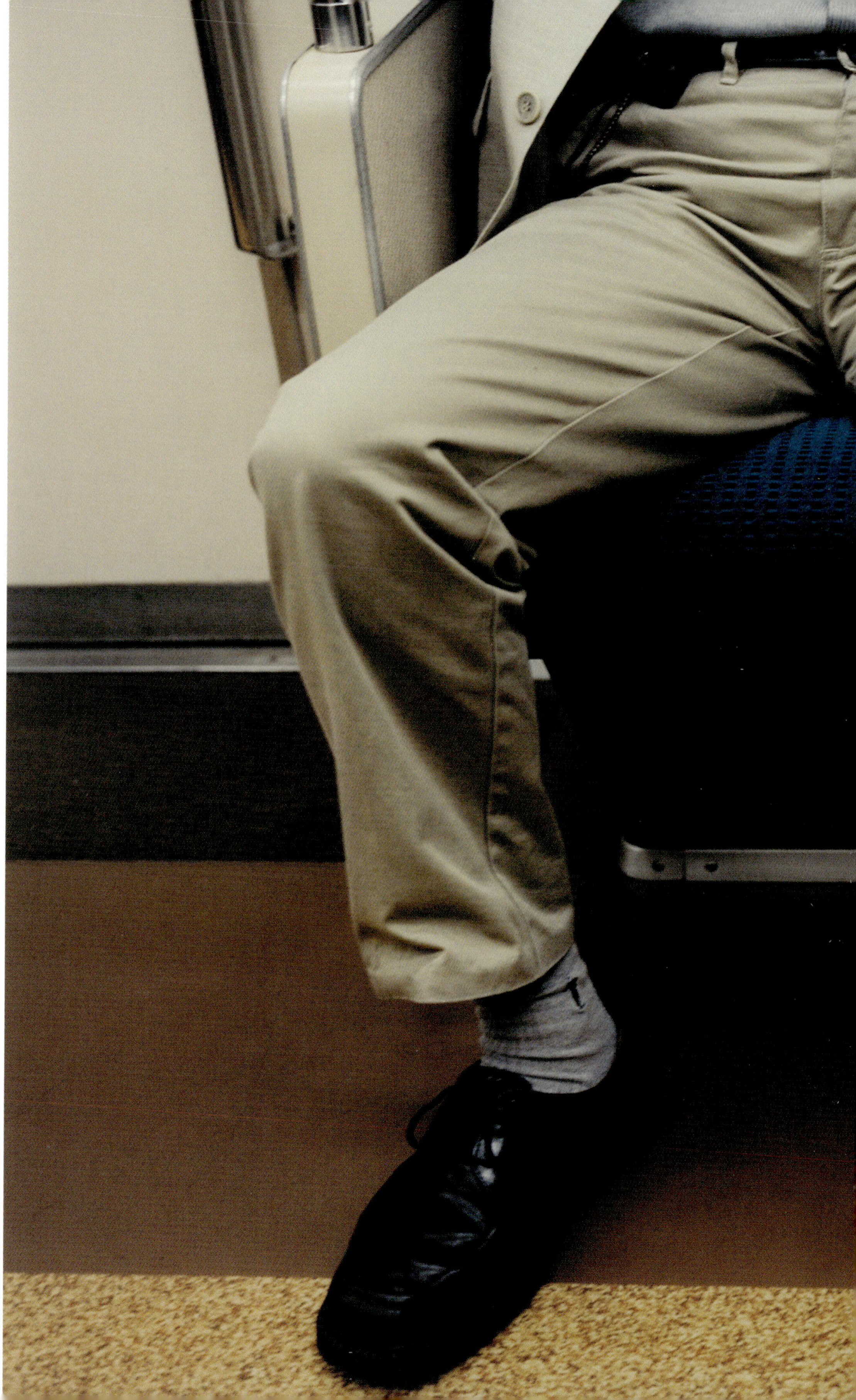

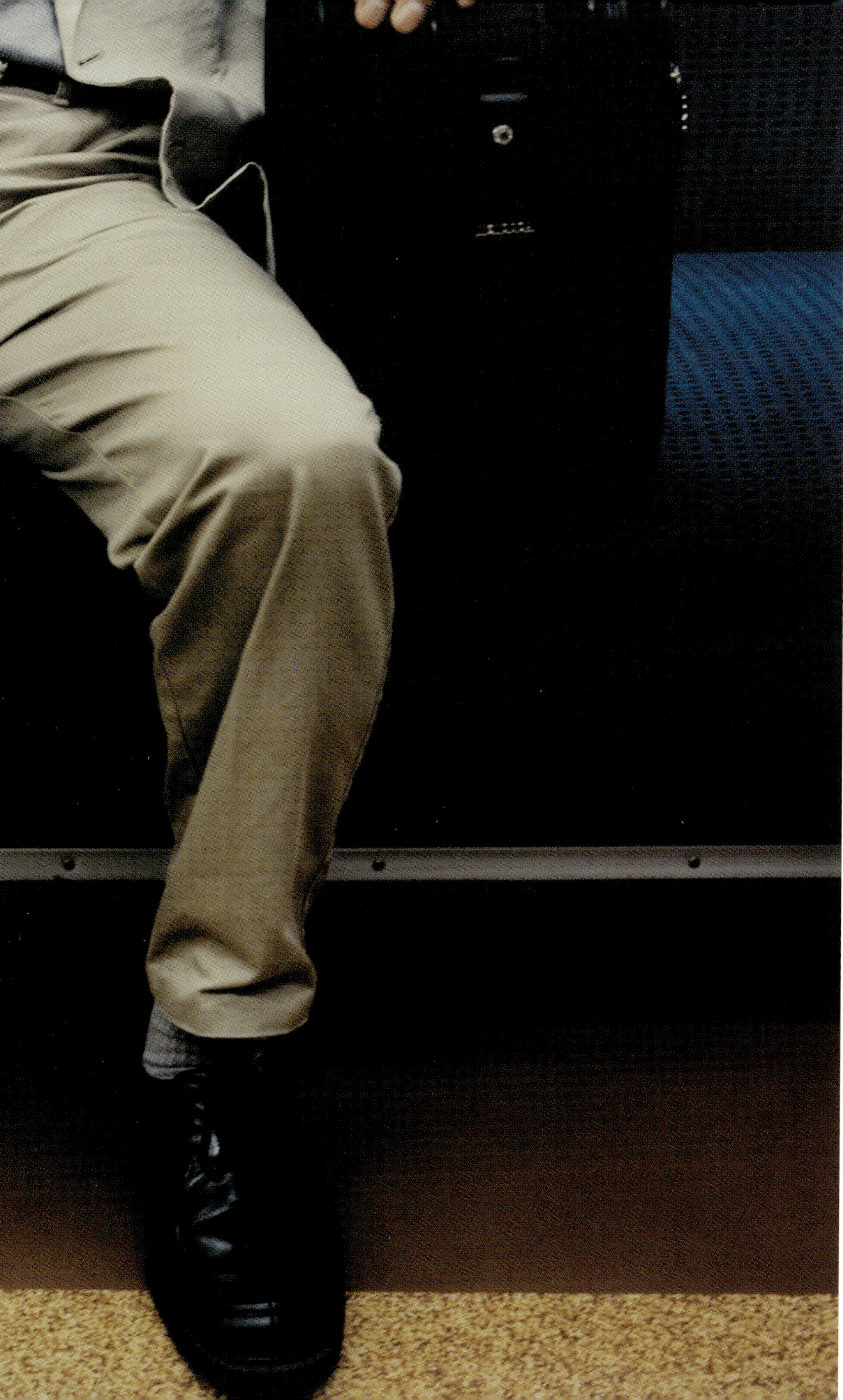

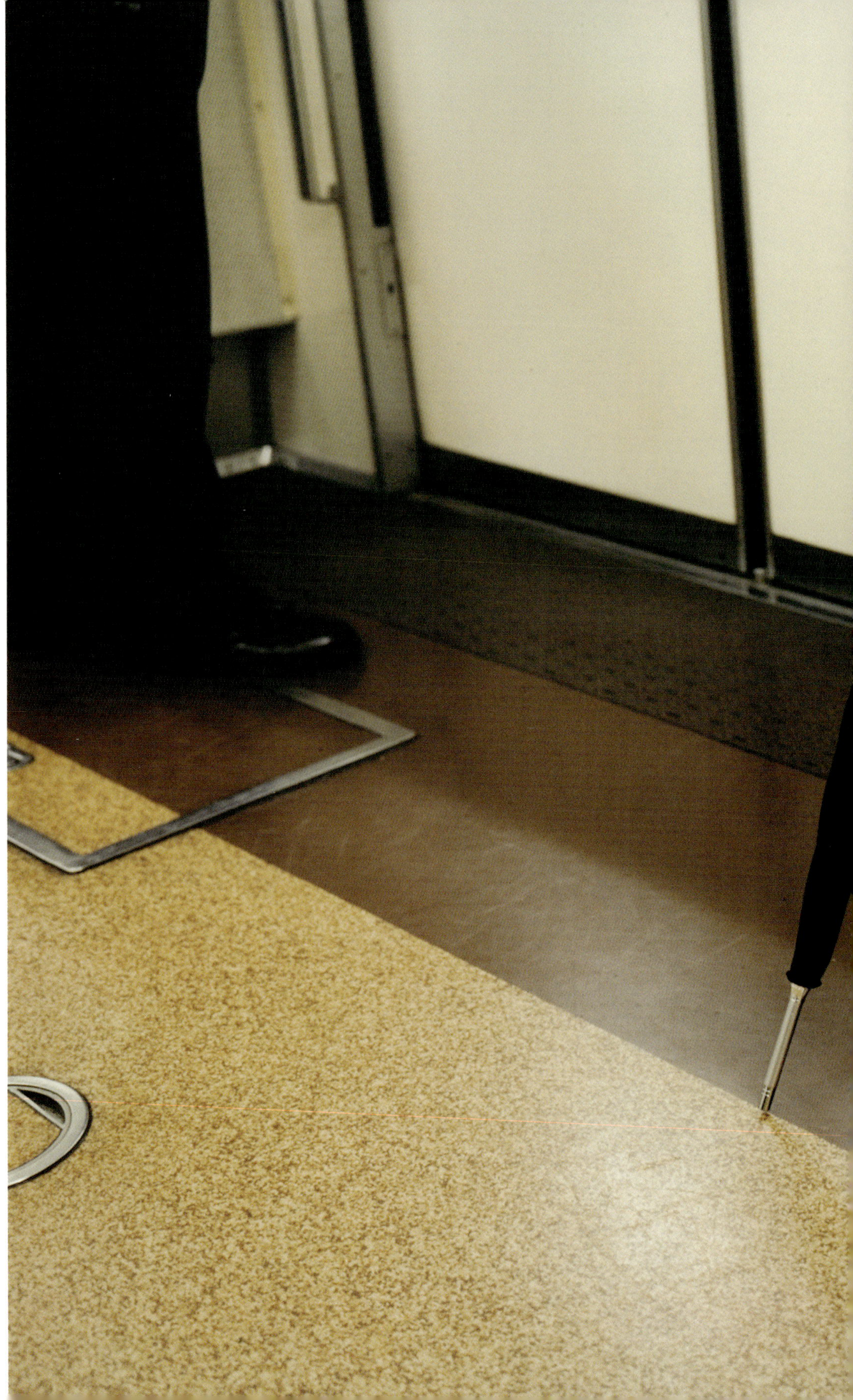

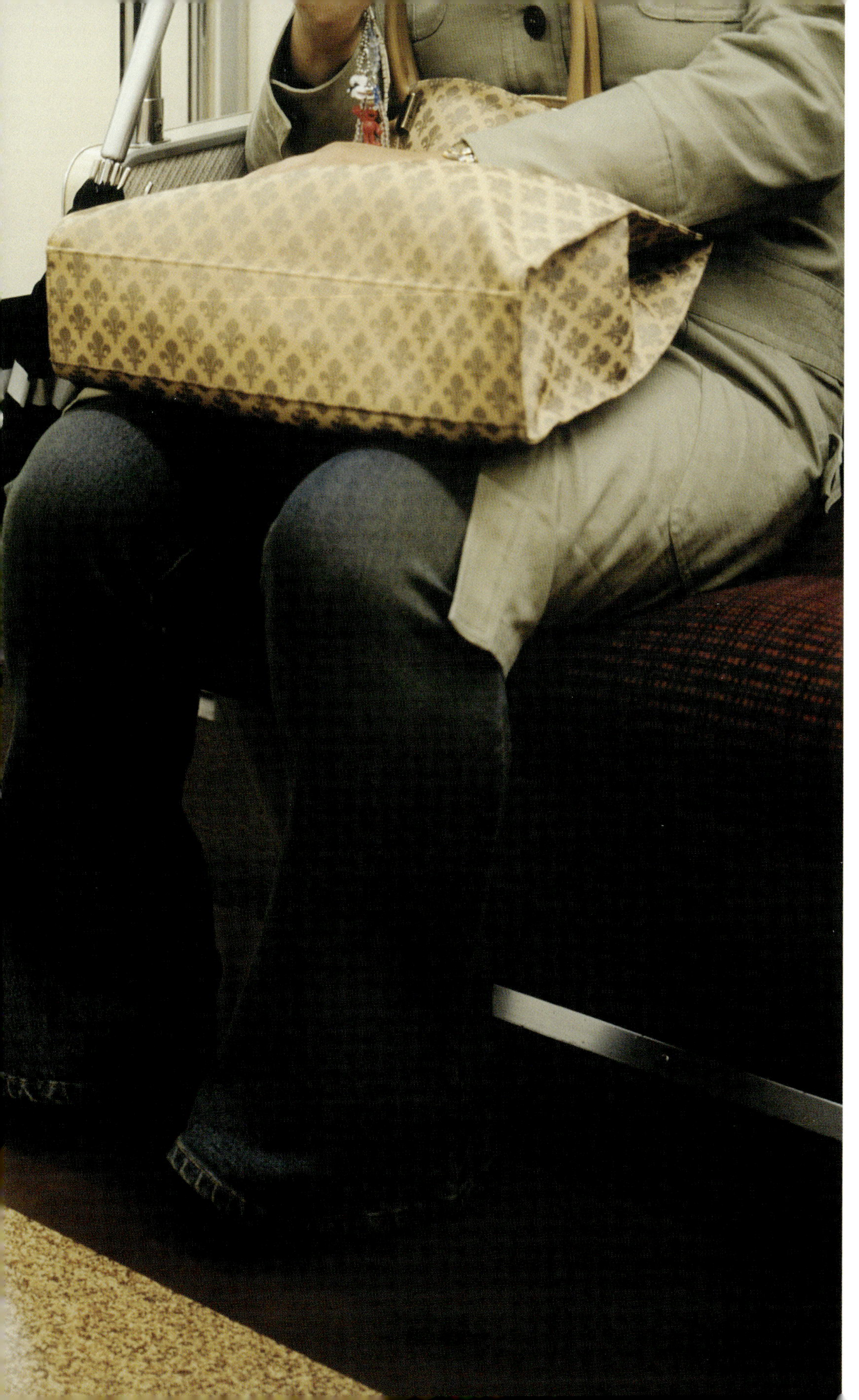

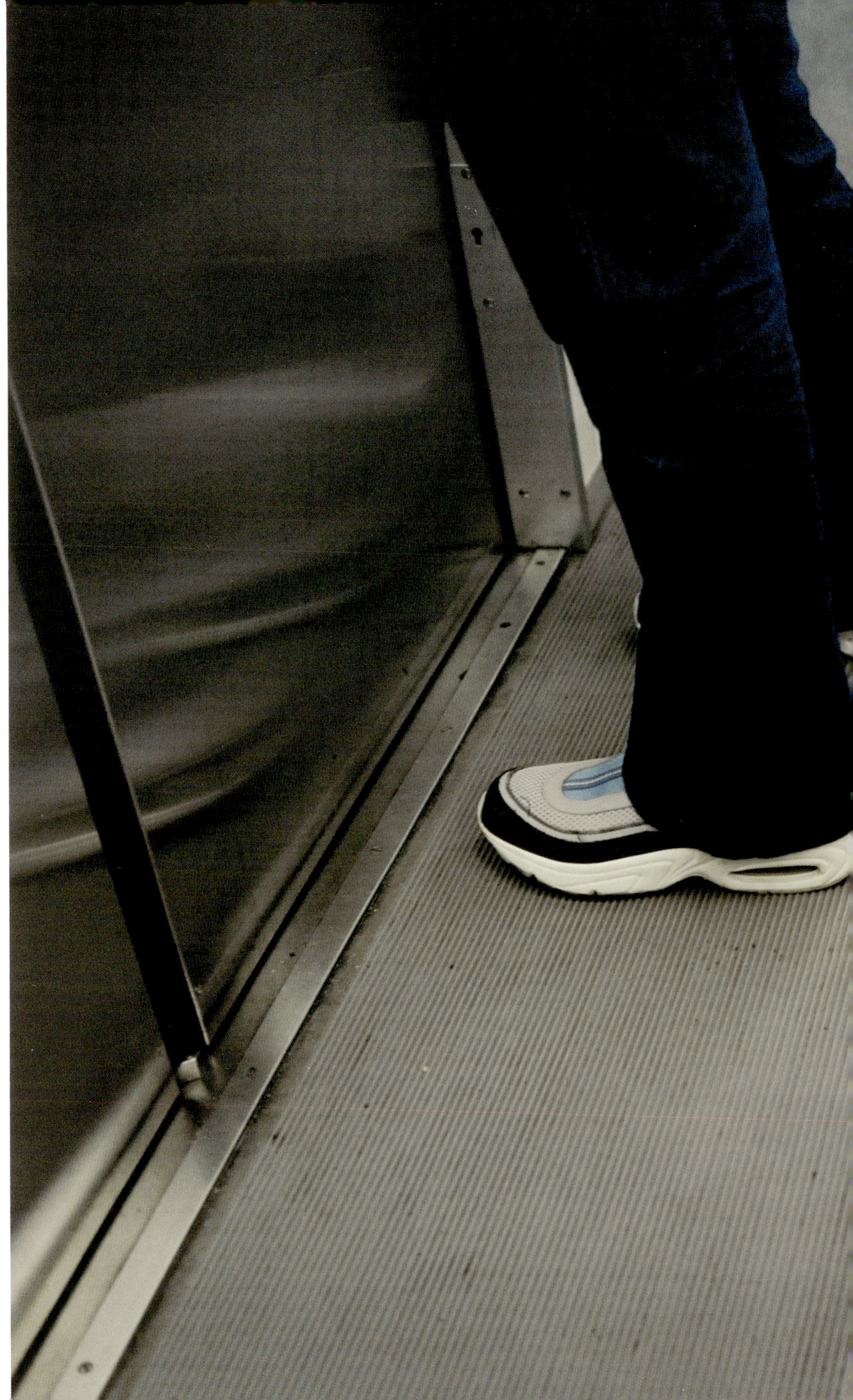

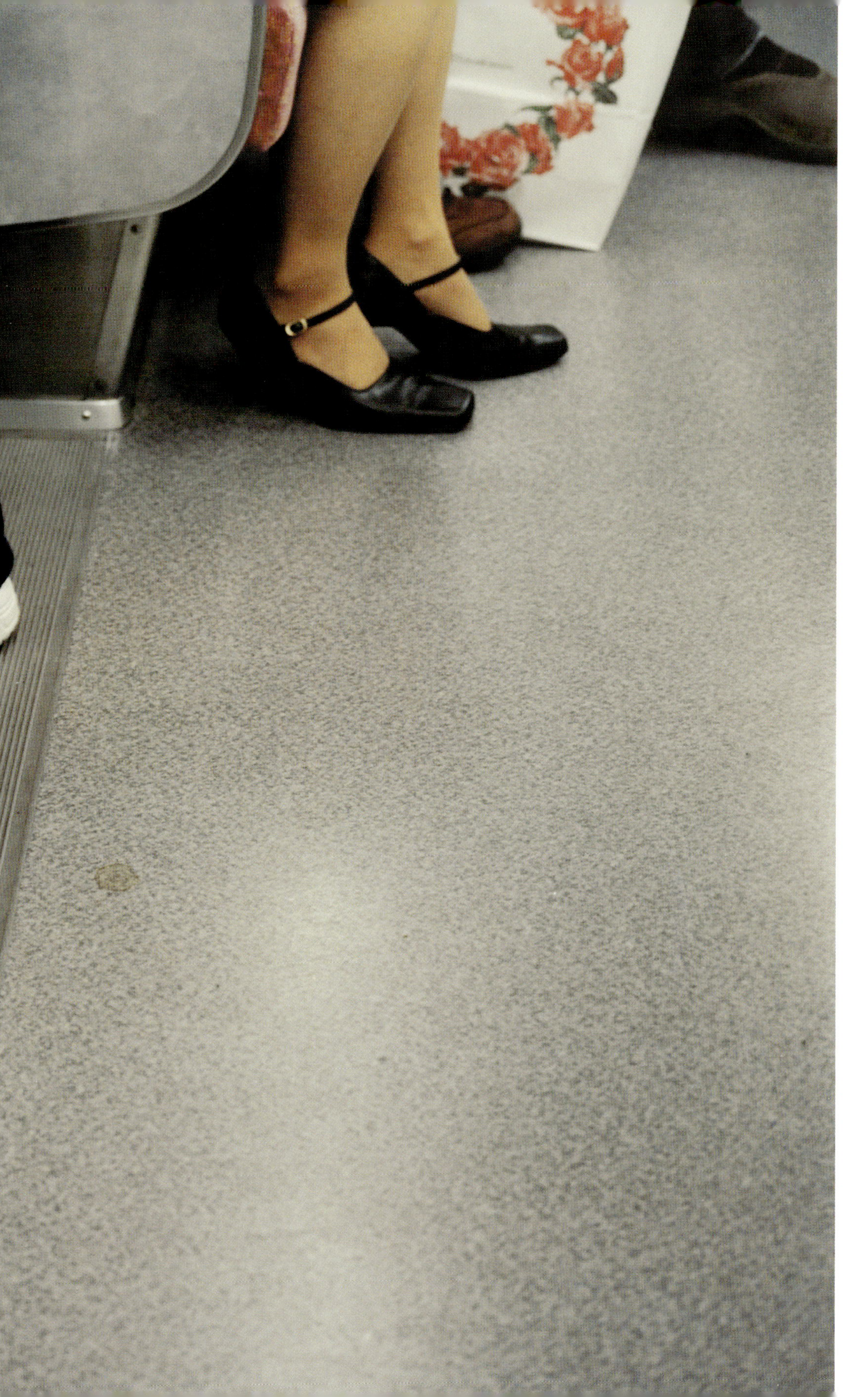

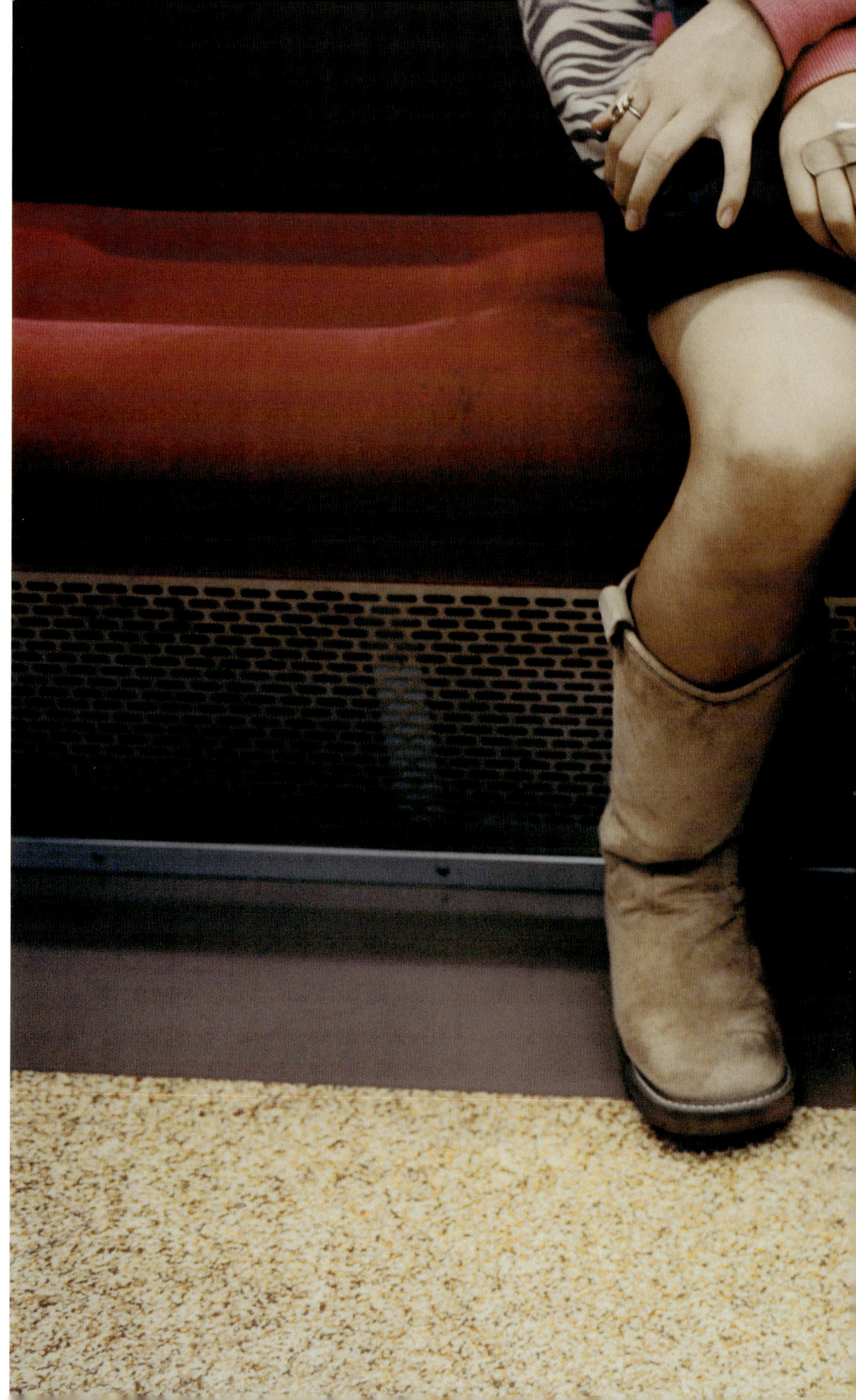

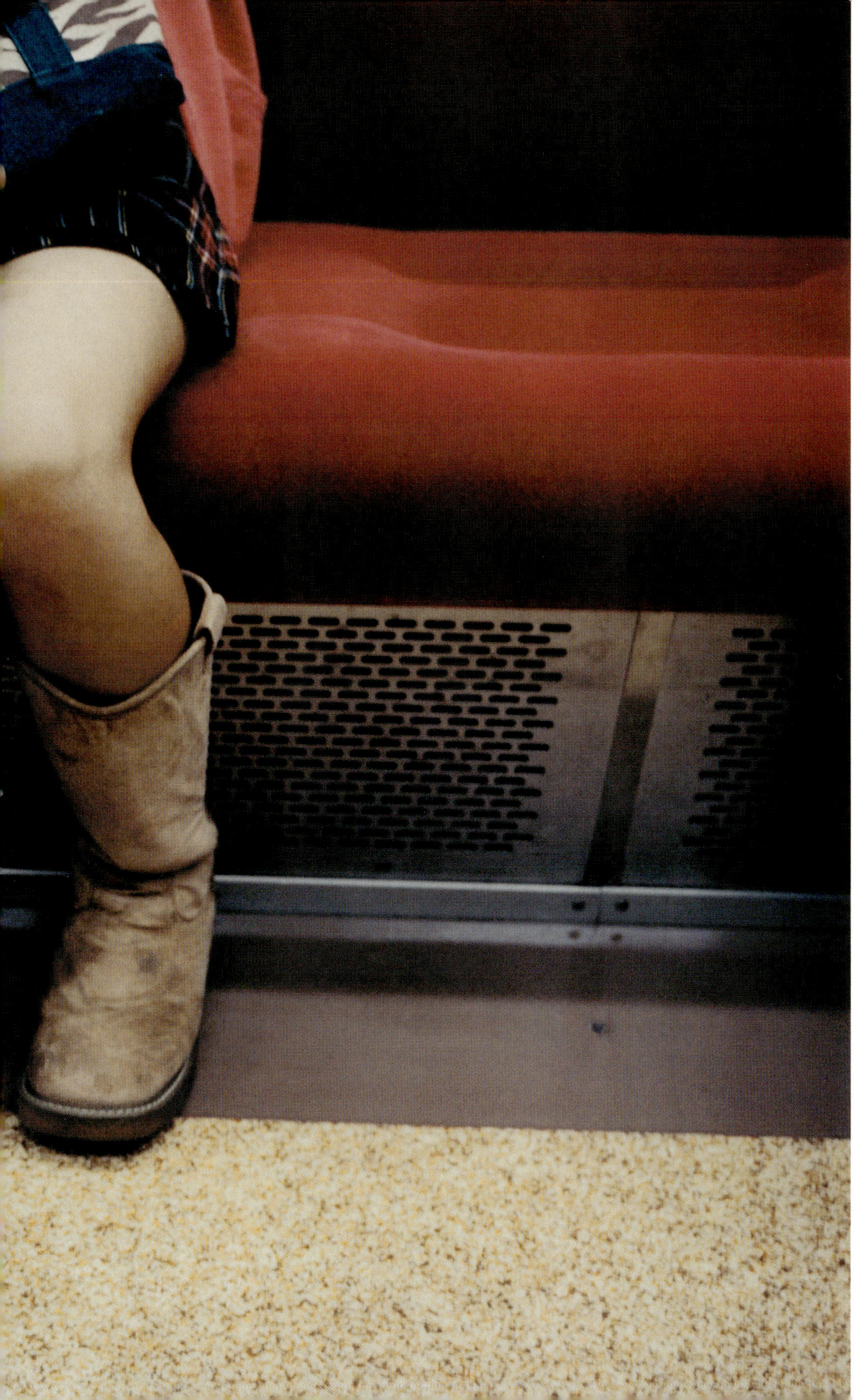

PATTERN RECOGNITION

Bec Dean

Ten Series/106 Photographs is a direct but oblique title for a book, allowing potential readers a measure of what they will encounter, at least in terms of quantity, if not subject matter. As a title it is attuned to our contemporary preoccupation with value. By placing five years of varied photographic practice under this austere rubric, Australian artist Matthew Sleeth, in effect, transforms the identity of each series into anonymous, cold information. Through this gesture Sleeth knowingly nods to the influential photographic books of the American multidisciplinary artist Ed Ruscha. With titles like *Twentysix Gasoline Stations* (1962) and *Thirtyfour Parking Lots* (1967), Ruscha's snapshot series were intentionally prosaic, a collection of "facts" informing an expanded visual enquiry. As a photographer Sleeth shares an interest in the quotidian, and specifically how subjects, objects, and structures from the everyday can be categorized, numbered, decontextualized, or recontextualized. Sleeth, however, extends this formal enquiry into a more personal, and often humorous realm, by seeking out patterns in fleeting moments, the material world, and human behavior.

Unlike Ruscha's "no-style"[1] approach or the rigorous typologies of Bernd and Hilla Becher, Sleeth casually moves between subjects, adopting a fluid approach to photographing ordinary objects, extraordinary landscapes, everyday phenomena, and people. As a result of this approach, which slips effortlessly from micro to macro, Sleeth reveals not only his inveterate curiosity and a desire to drift between the phenomenological and material facets of contemporary life, but also something about his own attitudes toward social mores, propriety and privacy, power and personal limitations.

When viewed as autonomous series, Sleeth's photographs can be regarded variously as witty object studies, graphically sharp street photographs, subtly nuanced landscapes, or ironical portraits. What becomes clear in this book, however, is an overarching imperative that underscores the project as a whole; for the artist to observe and record without provocation; to tread quietly through the world. In some ways this book is a psychogeographical travelogue that reveals as much about Sleeth as it does about the places he has visited. Most of the 106 images were shot overseas, in countries as geographically and culturally remote as Denmark and Japan, and of subjects as distinct from one another as classification labels nailed to tree trunks to women in uniform.

Global travel is critical to Sleeth's practice, but he does not seek to chronicle his journeys or document various locales in the traditional mode of a photojournalist, but rather to engage with unfamiliar terrain and experiences through playfully conceptual frameworks. The images that comprise Red China (2003) are connected to one another through the color red (and its symbolic relationship to communism), and displaced compositions that convey a sense of fragmented temporality and spatiality. The series is suffused with both Sleeth's sense of isolation as a traveler and the psychologically charged nature of his urban encounters.

In her often quoted book *On Photography* (1977), Susan Sontag writes, "Travel becomes a strategy for accumulating photographs. The very activity of taking pictures is soothing, and assuages feelings of disorientation that are likely to be exacerbated by travel."[2] In Pictured (2004–06) Sleeth assumes the position of a traveler taking pictures of other travelers taking pictures, but not through the cool lens usually associated with conceptual photography. He shows us moments of quiet and solitary contemplation: in the extended arm of a woman photographing the sky from the window seat of an airplane; of humor in the bulky yellow form of a tourist floating through space in the capsule of a cable car; and joy in the hilarious attitude of seated friends recording each other's smiling faces on their mobile phones.

While we may look at the images from this series and snicker at the repetition of poses and gestures of individual tourists and groups of friends as they photograph one another, they remind us of the photographer's solitary state. Sleeth would appear to be alone in each foreign place, repeating this observation of other people on holiday and in the company of others. Whether this lone-man-with-a-camera is a fiction or not, as viewers we become part of a photographic doubling that engages with this loneliness. We view the documented instant of a staged pose for another camera, in front of landmarks that are deliberately excluded from the frame, so that we can only guess at their location. The remnants of the Berlin Wall? The steps of the Sydney Opera House? Somewhere in Tokyo? On the fenced perimeter of the sculpted gardens of Versailles, a Japanese girl performs the curtsey of a magician's assistant revealing the finale of a trick. Through Sleeth's perspective, the moment, *her* moment, is distanced from our interpretation.

In an essay written for Sleeth's book *Tour of Duty* (2002), which documented the public-relations exercise that constituted the Australian Defense Force's involvement in East Timorese independence, the writer Paul James observed that Sleeth's photographic "distancing" from the rest of the media cavalcade was deliberate, that it acted as "an ironical comment on the mainstream history of the moment."[3] While Sleeth employed a one-step-removed position in order to challenge the genuineness of Australia's goodwill and the function of photojournalists in East Timor, it is used in several of the more personal series included here in a manner that is more empathetic than ironic.

The series Feet (2002), shot on the Tokyo subway, demonstrates a kind of self-imposed deference to local etiquette. With his lens pointed downward Sleeth records the slightly uncomfortable choreography of disembodied legs and feet in confined spaces. In the final image, a girl wearing suede boots knocks her knees together below crossed hands, while in another, a man wearing chinos spreads his legs wide. There is a dance of contraction and expansion in this series. Feet are aligned toward doors and in neat arrangements from others, establishing territory and personal space. While formally, the photographs create a dynamic sequence of composition and color, they eschew direct human interaction, reflecting the polite circumstances in which they were taken.

In Women in Uniform (2004), Sleeth's most direct series, he photographs women representing a cross-section of service industries (one in the service of God) in a standard three-quarter-length portrait style. Here, uniforms signify social approachability, not a fetish, as the playful title might suggest. These are women accustomed to being asked questions by strangers, used to acquiescing to requests for information. Even the slightly scruffy schoolgirl who closes this sequence stands open and compliant.

The Canadian photographer William Eakin makes images of kitschy, everyday objects as a way of evoking warm feelings and nostalgia for decades past;[4] on the contrary, Sleeth's photographs of ordinary objects are anything but nostalgic. Instead, they are charged with a sense of humor about the present and anxiety toward the future. In Abandoned Umbrellas (2004) a multitude of translucent, spindly forms are shown discarded in the street like broken insects after a storm. Whether crumpled against black and glistening tarmac or comically overstuffed into rubbish bins, these scenes of umbrella wreckage represent a kind of mass-produced failure—disposable objects that don't ever degrade. Conversely, his focus on the aesthetic and colorful placement of fire extinguishers and potted plants in urban and office environments explores the notion of a collective consciousness with a routine awareness of the possibility of disaster and a well-contained longing for communion with nature.

Collective and popular desire is investigated further in his series La Joconde (2005), taken in the Louvre, in which all ten signs giving directions to the *Mona Lisa* are documented, with full flash, in a seemingly hurried fashion. Again Sleeth presents a doubling of imagery in these works, as they are photographs of photocopies of photographs of the original—which is frustratingly never pictured. In Tagged (2004) another potential encounter with a traditional form of beauty—in nature rather than the institution this time—is challenged by signage. Species classification information, hammered into trees—despite a subtle attempt toward camouflage in uniform green—draws focal attention away from the plants themselves, and in Sleeth's images, they are denied elevation to the picturesque. Behind the tree *Gymnocladus Dioecus*, a blurred bronze scene from Greek mythology assumes the role of a peripheral folly, when held up against the veracity of scientific knowledge.

Sleeth's most recent and consciously beautiful images, 12 Views of Mount Fuji (2004–06), also avoid simply celebrating the natural world. The series was conceived as a photographic homage to the pre-photographic perspective of woodblock artist Katsushika Hokusai's *Thirty-six Views of Mount Fuji*; these prints, made in the Ukiyo-e style, influenced early Japanese photography, as well as Japanese tourist photography produced for foreign markets.[5] Hokusai's prints were completed from different vantage points, distances, and terrain from the mountain, but the same vibrantly hued, impassable peak appears in each representation.

Likewise, Sleeth's images address similar questions of viewpoint and distance, while placing them in a contemporary context. In his photographs, the mountain is captured from various modern perspectives: emerging from diaphanous clouds between the seductive folds of a white hotel curtain, as the backdrop to an amusement park ride, as a mere blip in Tokyo's twinkling electric skyline and wedged between apartment blocks. Unlike Hokusai's bold, red mountain, Sleeth's representations of Mount Fuji are always taken from his particular, contemporary vantage point, rather than from within a natural-world context. As such, in Sleeth's images, Mount Fuji stands as a pale, almost ethereal monument, an entity that rests away from the visual noise of a constantly changing urban environment.

The conceptual photographic exercises in Matthew Sleeth's *Ten Series/106 Photographs* reveal patterns and repetition in everyday contemporary experience. While the subject matter here necessarily connects to a wider discourse around the flattening and homogenizing tendencies of globalization (to the detriment of tradition and cultural specificity), Sleeth's practice is infused with emotional agency. This is demonstrated no more effectively than in Kawaii Baby (2005–06) in which Sleeth has recorded the vicarious joy of watching Japanese responses to his toddler daughter in public places. She appears in the frame from behind as a fragment of pink jacket or a soft fuzz of blonde hair, while the delighted faces of strangers—from smoking teenagers to office workers—beam down at her. In one image, a brightly clad Japanese grandmother holds her arms out for an embrace toward the bottom edge of the frame—offering the possibility and hope of intercultural, intergenerational affection and human connection in a cold, fast world.

Bec Dean is curatorial manager at the Australian Centre for Photography, Sydney.

Notes

1. Margit Rowell, *Ed Ruscha, Photographer* (New York: Whitney Museum of American Art; Göttingen: Steidl, 2006), p. 11.
2. Susan Sontag, *On Photography* (New York: Penguin Books, 1977), pp. 9–10.
3. Paul James, "Reintroducing East Timor," in *Tour of Duty* (Melbourne, Australia: Hardie Grant Books, 2002), p. 2.
4. Anne Brydon, "Memorywork," in *Monument* (Winnipeg, Canada: Plug In, Inc., 1997), p. 6.
5. David Odo, "Constructing the Self as 'Other': Early Japanese Tourist Images," in *The Oxford Companion to the Photograph*, Robin Lenman, ed. (Oxford, England: Oxford University Press, 2005), p. 333.

Women in Uniform
50 x 60 in.
(127 x 152 cm)
Type C photographs

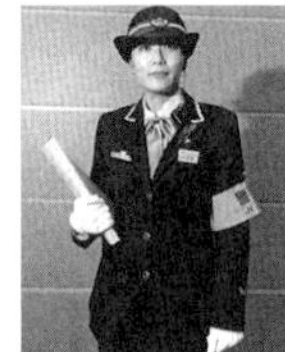
Women in Uniform #3
[Tokyo], 2004

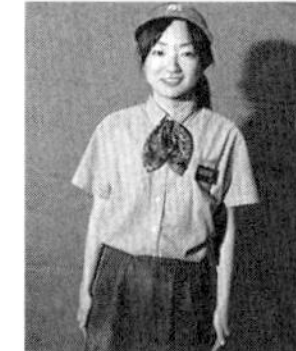
Women in Uniform #6
[Tokyo], 2004

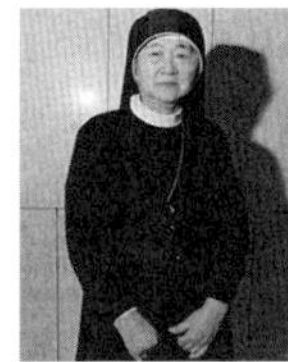
Women in Uniform #5
[Tokyo], 2004

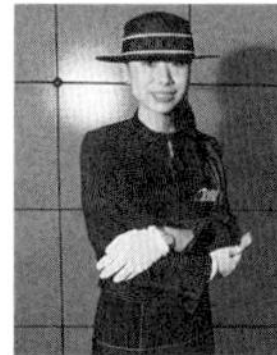
Women in Uniform #4
[Tokyo], 2004

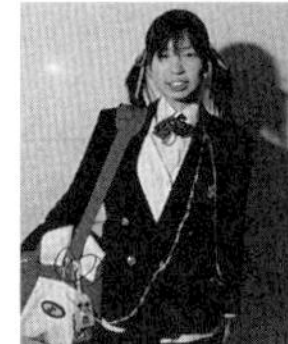
Women in Uniform #1
[Tokyo], 2004

Red China
50 x 60 in.
(127 x 152 cm)
Type C photographs

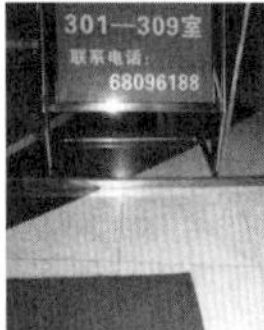

Red China #28
[Beijing], 2003

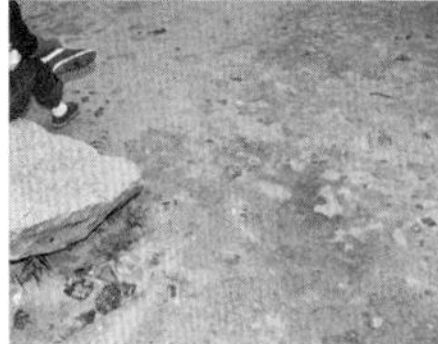
Red China #7
[Beijing], 2003

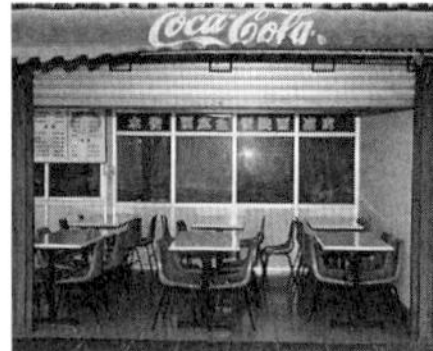

Red China #2
[Beijing], 2003

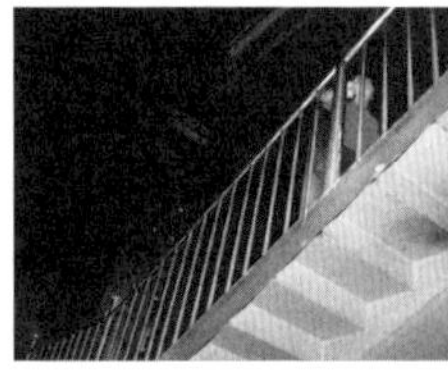
Red China #10
[Beijing], 2003

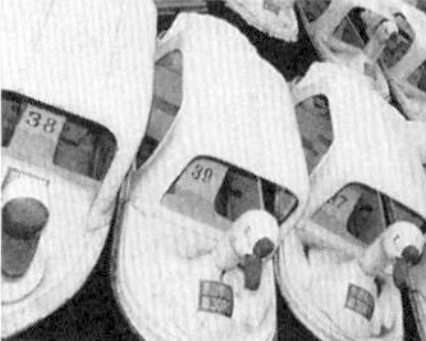
Red China #35
[Beijing], 2003

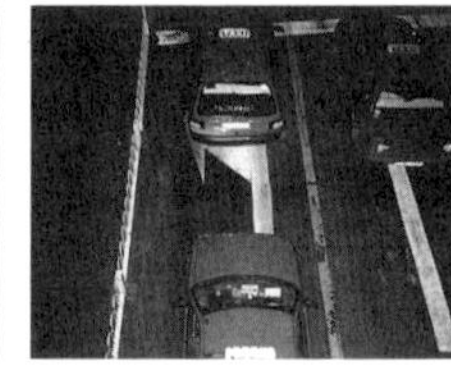
Red China #9
[Beijing], 2003

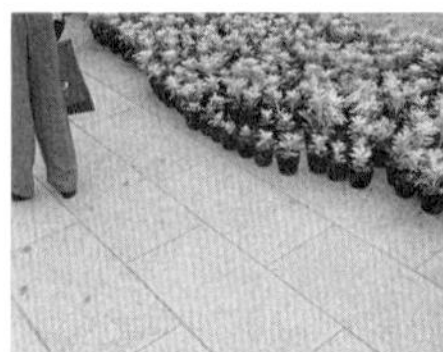
Red China #8
[Beijing], 2003

Abandoned Umbrellas
20 x 24 in.
(50 x 61 cm)
Type C photographs

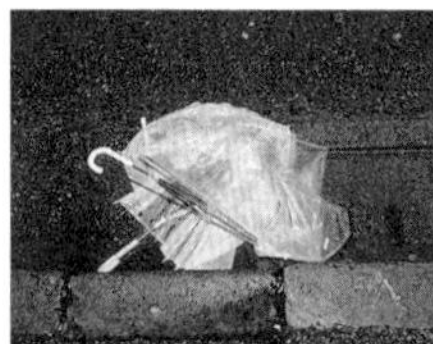
Abandoned Umbrellas #10
[Tokyo], 2004

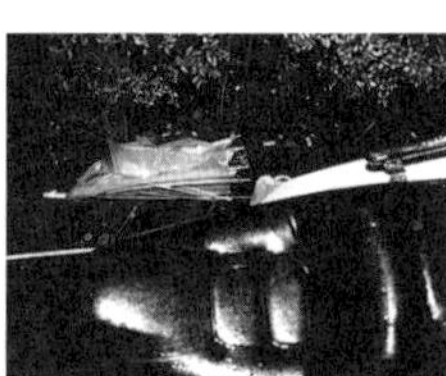
Abandoned Umbrellas #15
[Tokyo], 2004

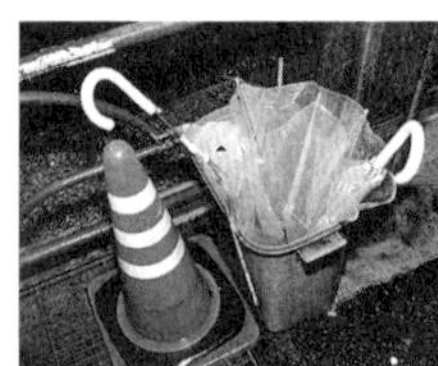
Abandoned Umbrellas #24
[Tokyo], 2004

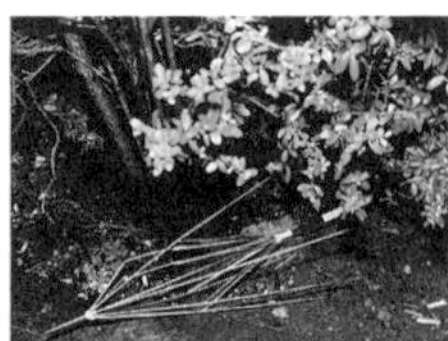
Abandoned Umbrellas #12
[Tokyo], 2004

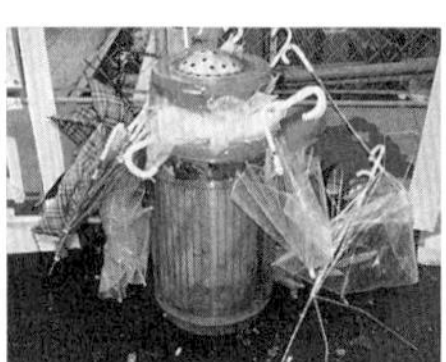
Abandoned Umbrellas #3
[Tokyo], 2004

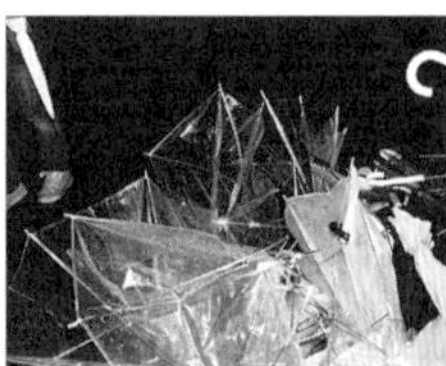
Abandoned Umbrellas #20
[Tokyo], 2004

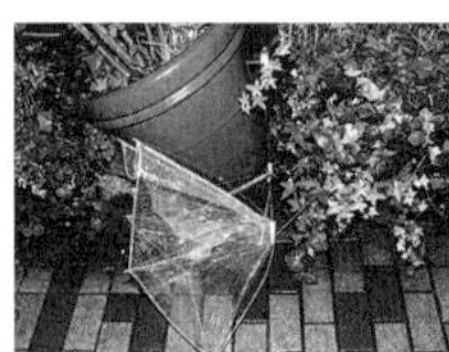
Abandoned Umbrellas #7
[Tokyo], 2004

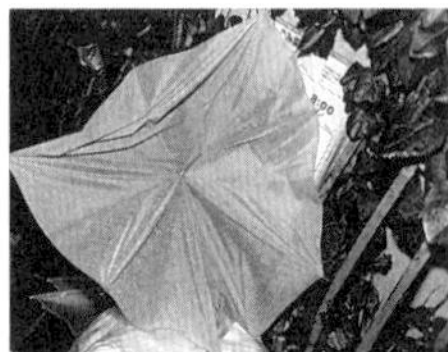
Abandoned Umbrellas #13
[Tokyo], 2004

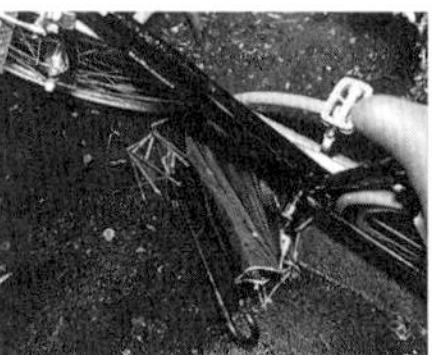
Abandoned Umbrellas #18
[Tokyo], 2004

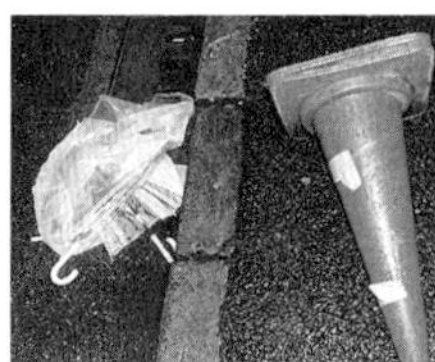
Abandoned Umbrellas #11
[Tokyo], 2004

12 Views of Mount Fuji
50 x 60 in.
(127 x 152 cm)
Type C photographs

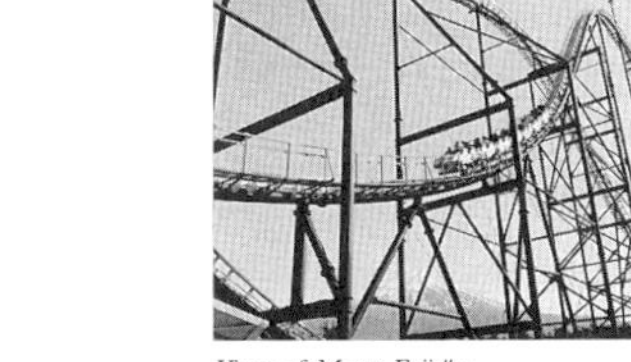
Views of Mount Fuji #4
[Fujikyu Highland Park], 2004

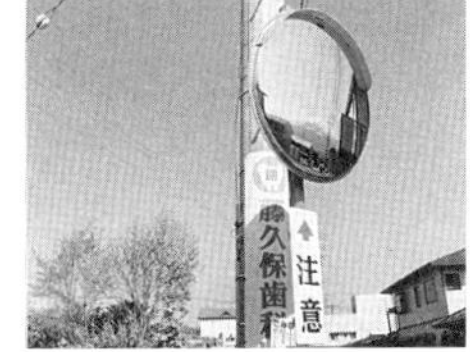

Views of Mount Fuji #22
[Kawaguchiko], 2004

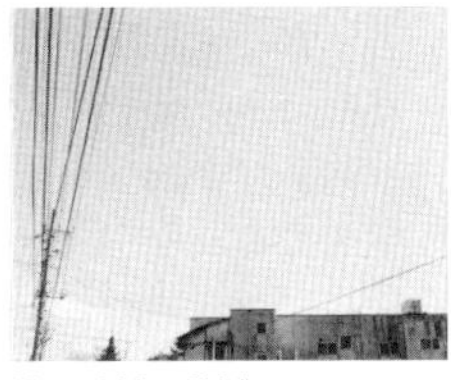
Views of Mount Fuji #19
[Kawaguchiko], 2004

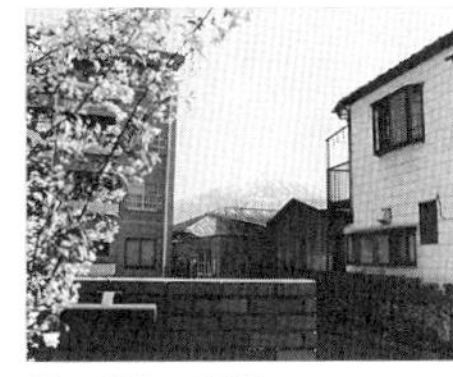
Views of Mount Fuji #27
[Kawaguchiko], 2004

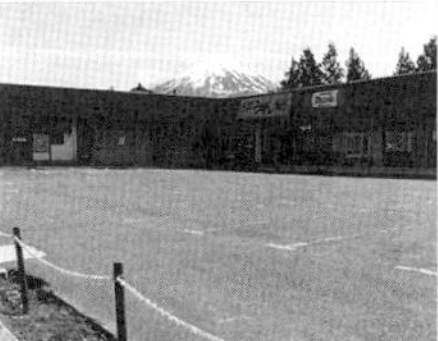
Views of Mount Fuji #16
[Kawaguchiko], 2004

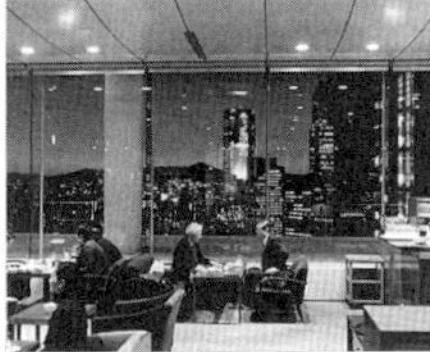
Views of Mount Fuji #43
[Shinjuku Southern Tower], 2005

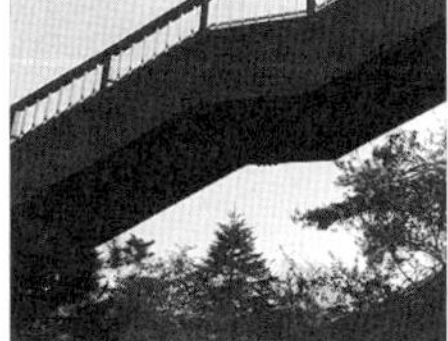
Views of Mount Fuji #7
[Kawaguchiko], 2004

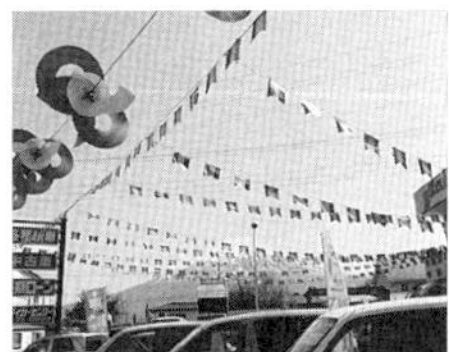
Views of Mount Fuji #24
[Kawaguchiko], 2004

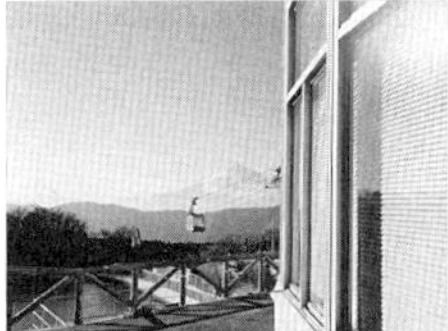
Views of Mount Fuji #50
[Hakone], 2006

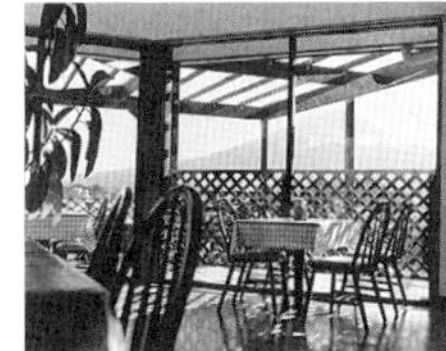
Views of Mount Fuji #35
[Lake Kawaguchiko], 2005

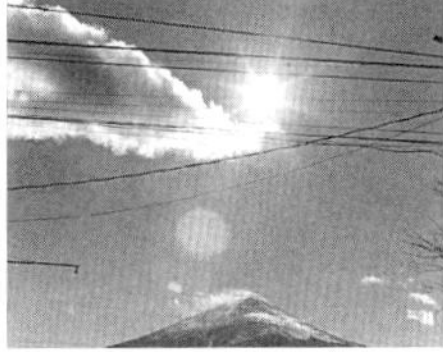
Views of Mount Fuji #40
[Kawaguchiko], 2005

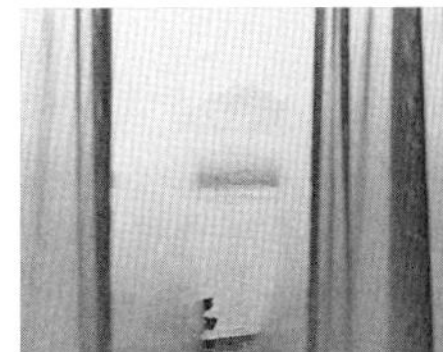
Views of Mount Fuji #44
[Lake Kawaguchiko], 2006

La Joconde
20 x 24 in.
(50 x 61 cm)
Type C photographs

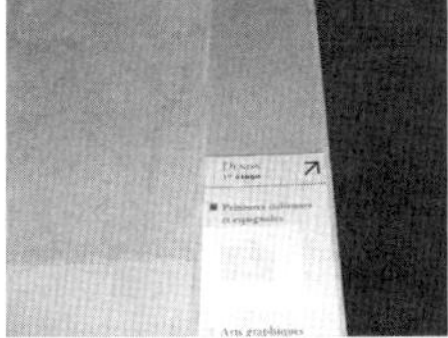
La Joconde #27
[Paris], 2005

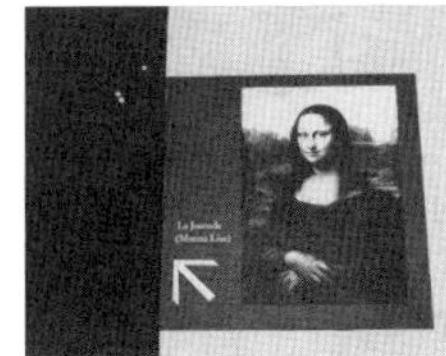
La Joconde #2
[Paris], 2005

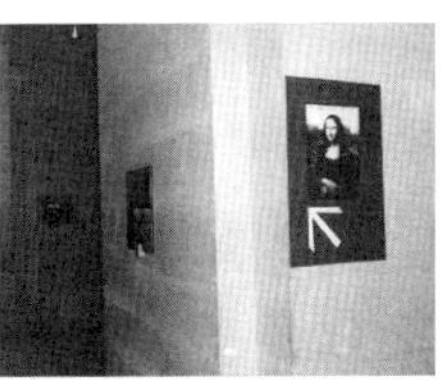
La Joconde #4
[Paris], 2005

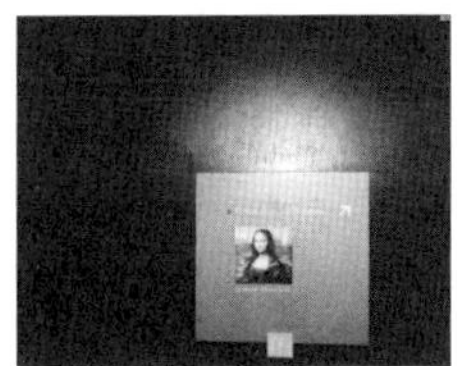
La Joconde #22
[Paris], 2005

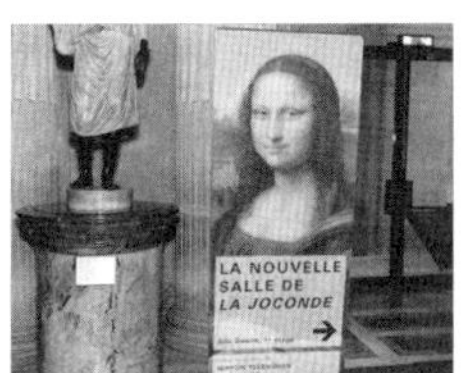

La Joconde #29
[Paris], 2005

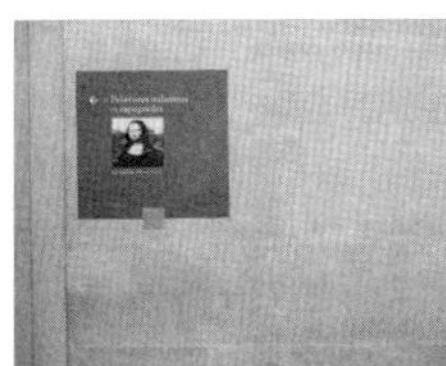
La Joconde #5
[Paris], 2005

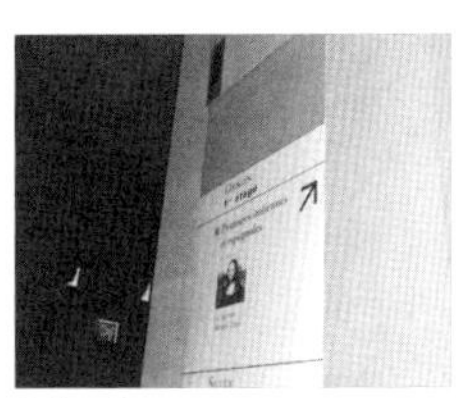
La Joconde #10
[Paris], 2005

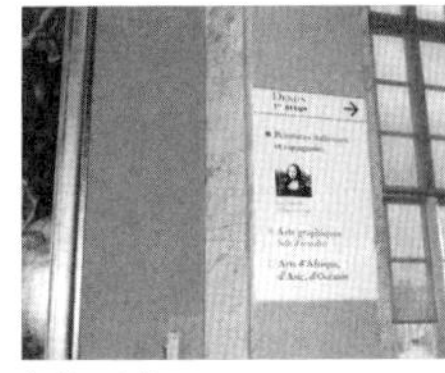
La Joconde #14
[Paris], 2005

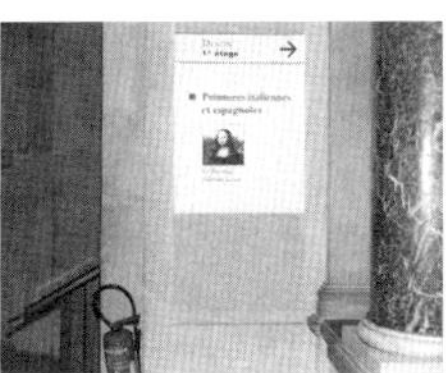
La Joconde #13
[Paris], 2005

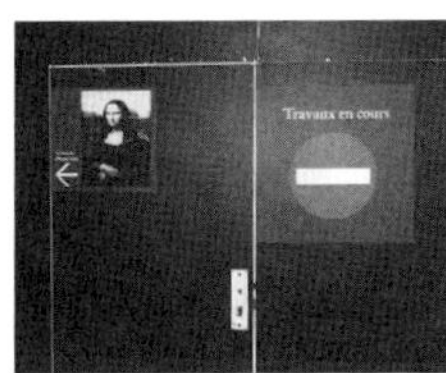
La Joconde #24
[Paris], 2005

Pictured
50 x 60 in.
(127 x 152 cm)
Type C photographs

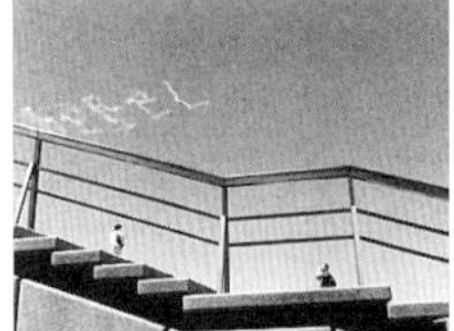
Pictured #13
[Sydney], 2004

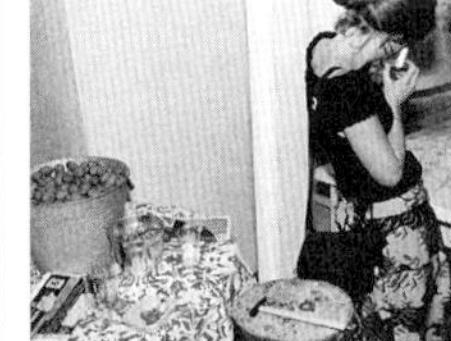
Pictured #3
[Milan], 2004

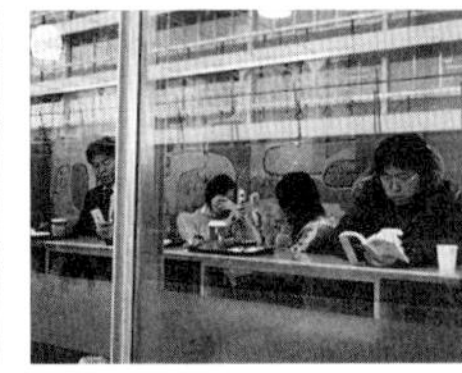
Pictured #29
[Tokyo], 2005

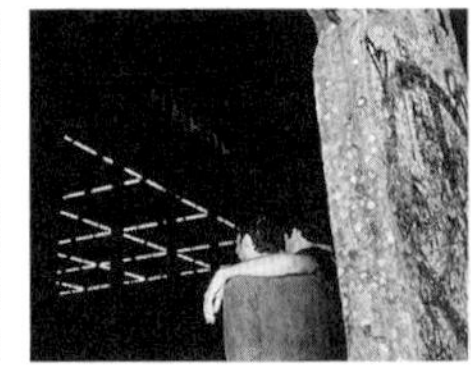
Pictured #28
[Berlin], 2005

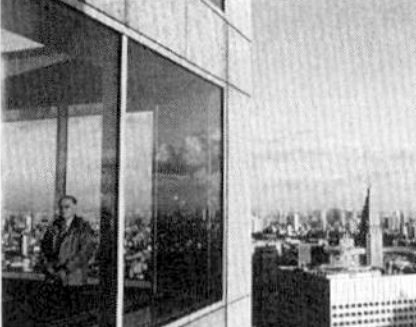
Pictured #31
[Tokyo], 2005

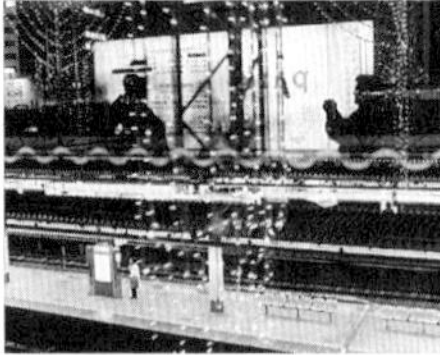
Pictured #36
[Tokyo], 2005

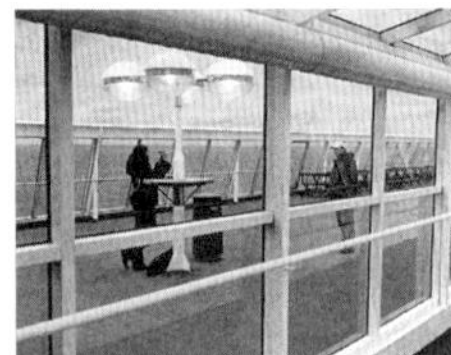
Pictured #37
[Stockholm], 2005

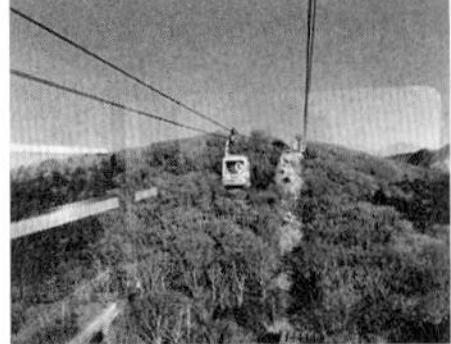
Pictured #34
[Hakone], 2006

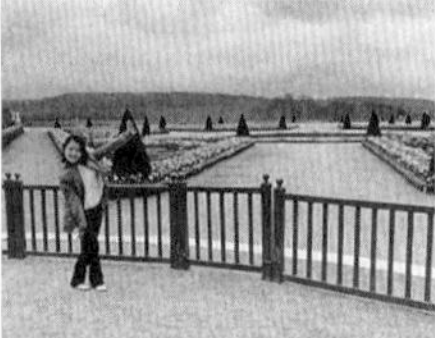
Pictured #6
[Versailles], 2004

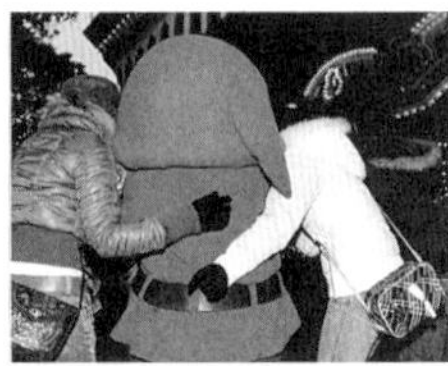
Pictured #33
[Tokyo], 2006

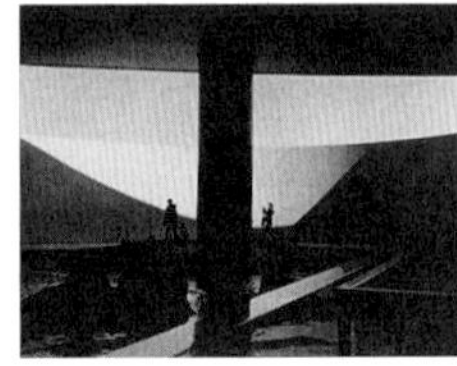
Pictured #40
[Tokyo], 2006

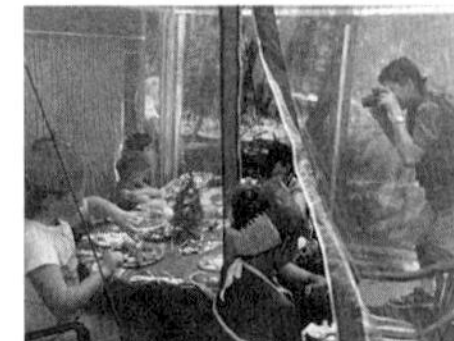
Pictured #23
[Rosebud], 2004

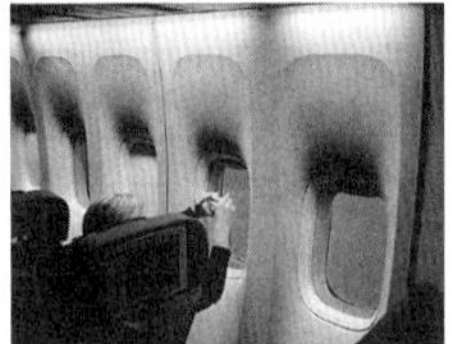
Pictured #15
[plane], 2005

13 Houseplants
20 x 24 in.
(50 x 61 cm)
Type C photographs

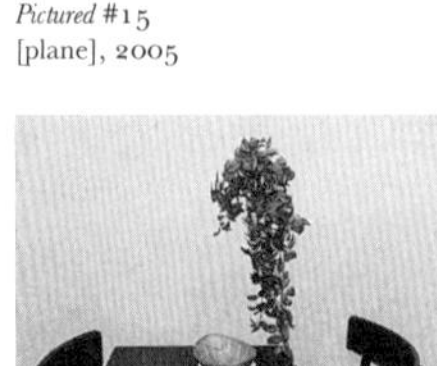
Houseplants #26
[Paris], 2005

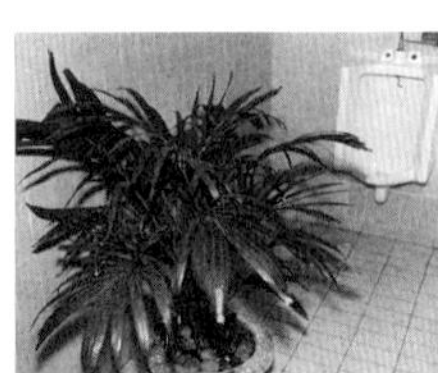
Houseplants #30
[Denpasar], 2005

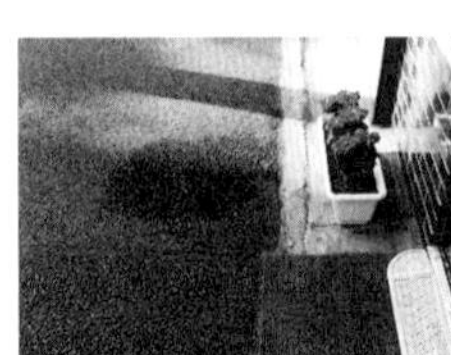
Houseplants #38
[Tokyo], 2005

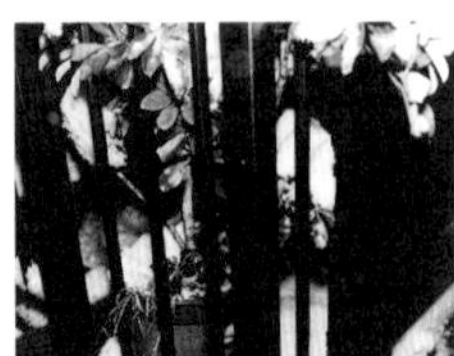
Houseplants #51
[Tokyo], 2006

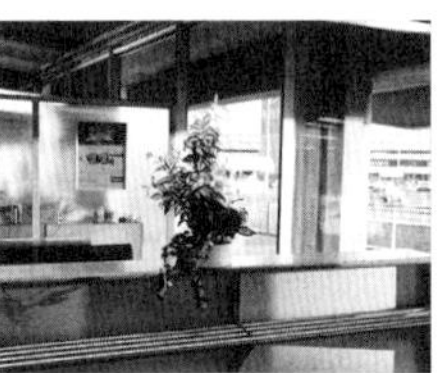
Houseplants #58
[Berlin], 2005

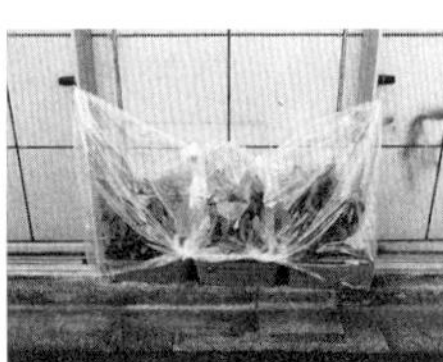
Houseplants #45
[Tokyo], 2005

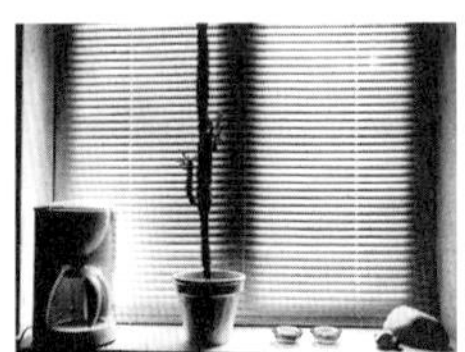
Houseplants #66
[Odense], 2006

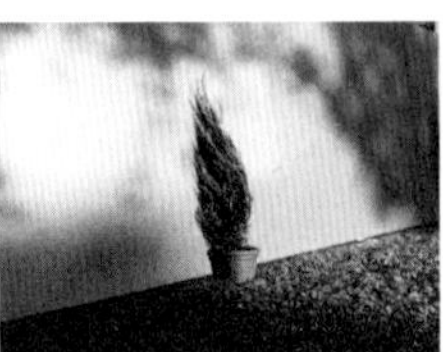
Houseplants #34
[Melbourne], 2006

13 Houseplants (continued)
20 x 24 in.
(50 x 61 cm)
Type C photographs

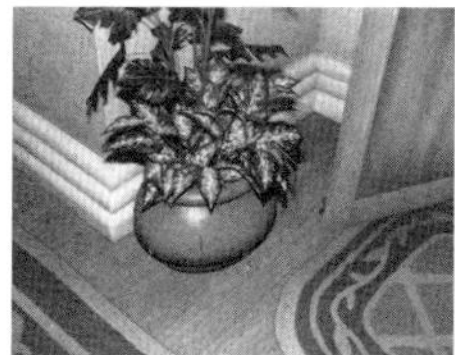
Houseplants #52
[Tokyo], 2006

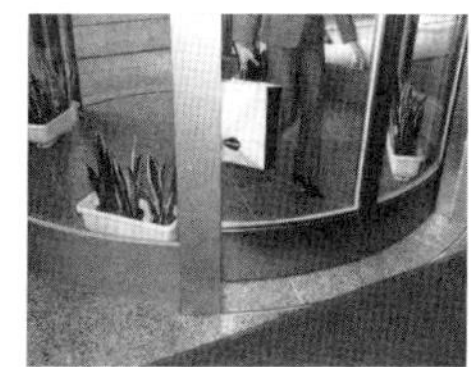
Houseplants #44
[Tokyo], 2005

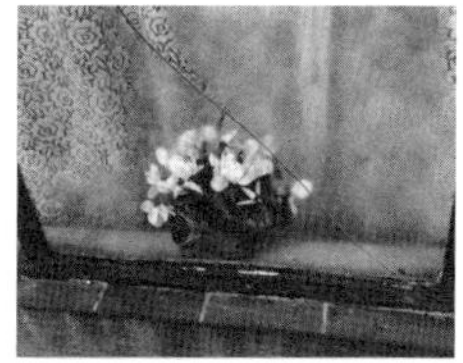
Houseplants #56
[Warsaw], 2006

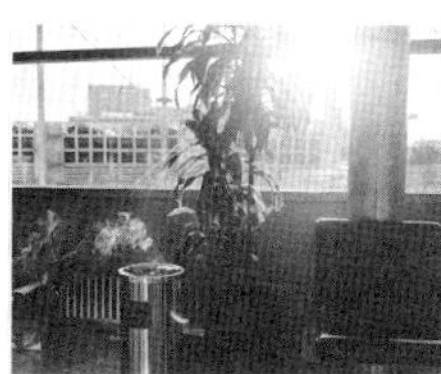
Houseplants #71
[Helsinki], 2006

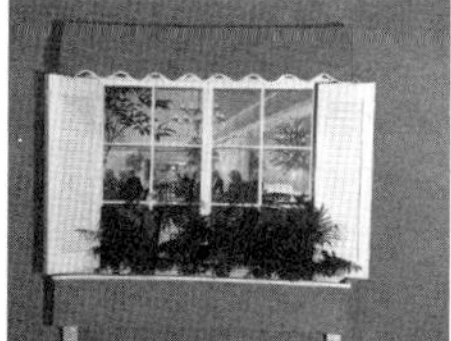
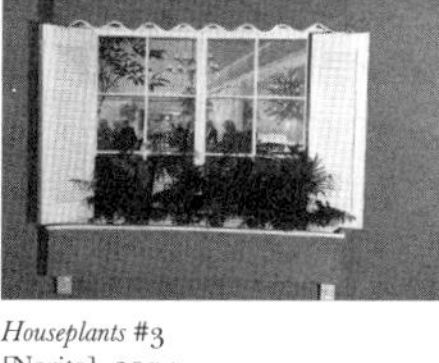
Houseplants #3
[Narita], 2004

10 Fire Extinguishers
20 x 24 in.
(50 x 61 cm)
Type C photographs

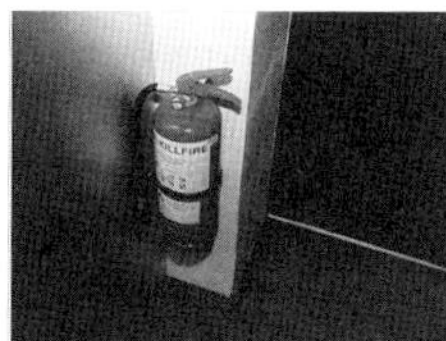
Fire Extinguishers #33
[Munich], 2005

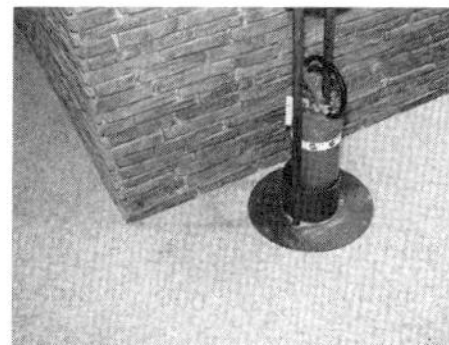
Fire Extinguishers #3
[Milan], 2004

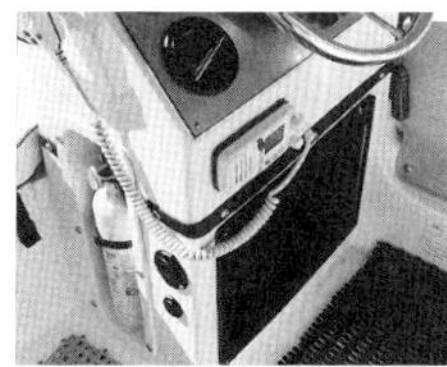
Fire Extinguishers #16
[Sydney], 2005

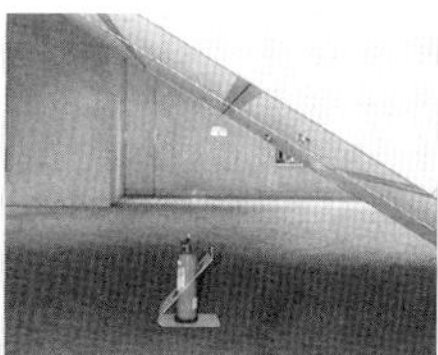
Fire Extinguishers #39
[Yokohama], 2005

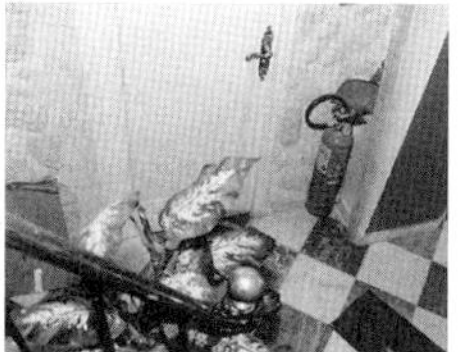
Fire Extinguishers #27
[Paris], 2005

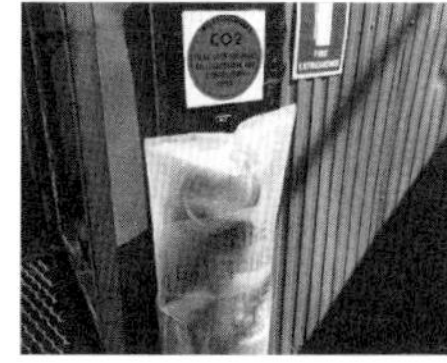
Fire Extinguishers #51
[Hamilton Island], 2007

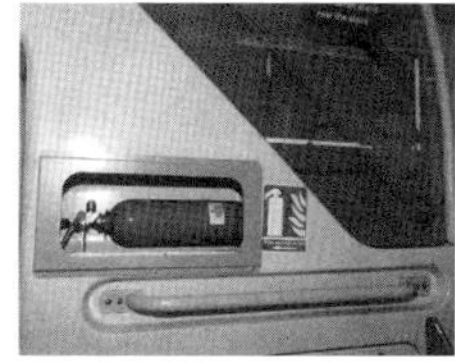
Fire Extinguishers #48
[London], 2006

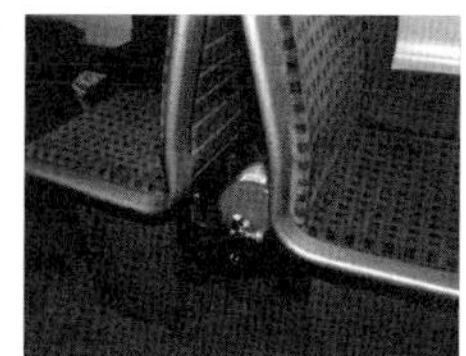
Fire Extinguishers #42
[Cologne], 2006

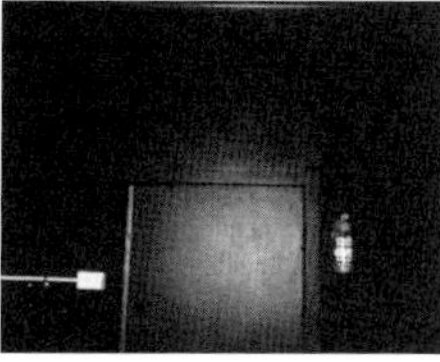
Fire Extinguishers #7
[Melbourne], 2004

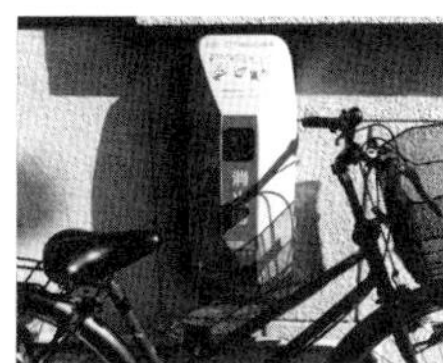
Fire Extinguishers #36
[Tokyo], 2005

Kawaii Baby
20 x 24 in.
(50 x 61 cm)
Type C photographs

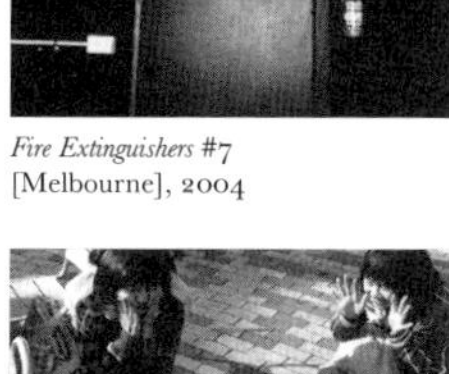
Kawaii Baby #15
[Tokyo], 2006

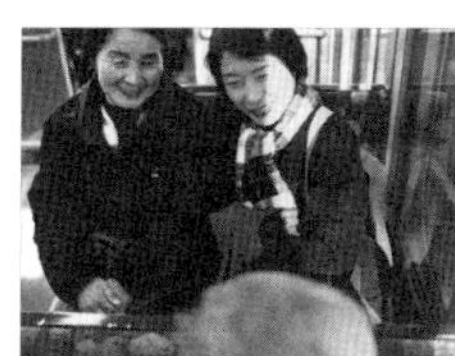
Kawaii Baby #20
[Hakone], 2006

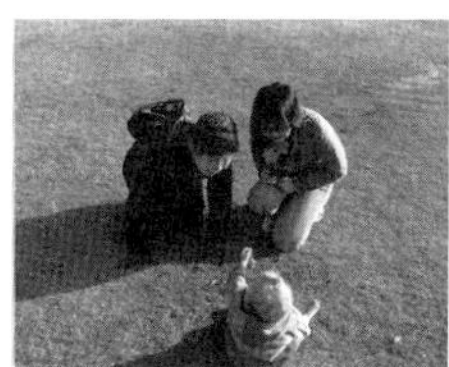
Kawaii Baby #2
[Tokyo], 2005

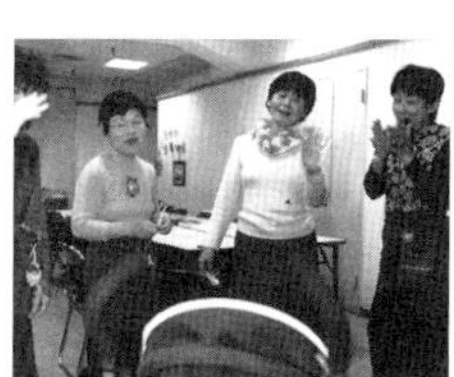
Kawaii Baby #6
[Tokyo], 2005

Kawaii Baby (continued)
20 x 24 in.
(50 x 61 cm)
Type C photographs

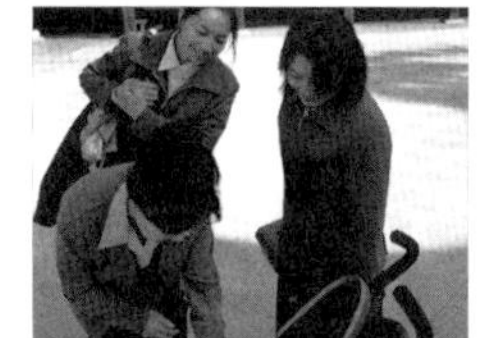
Kawaii Baby #14
[Tokyo], 2006

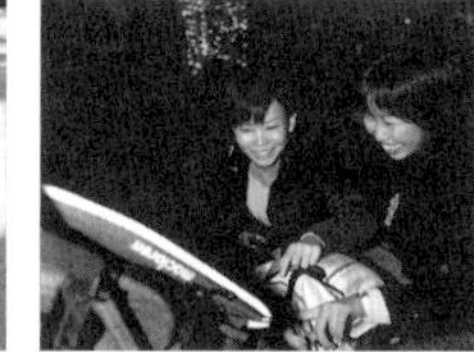
Kawaii Baby #1
[Tokyo], 2005

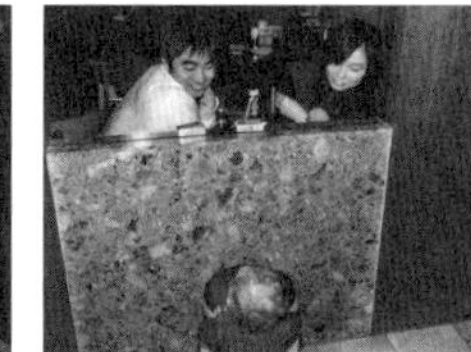
Kawaii Baby #4
[Tokyo], 2005

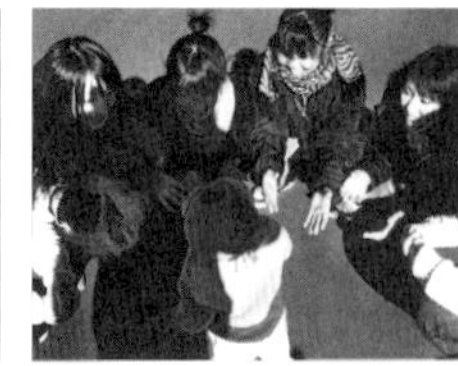
Kawaii Baby #11
[Tokyo], 2006

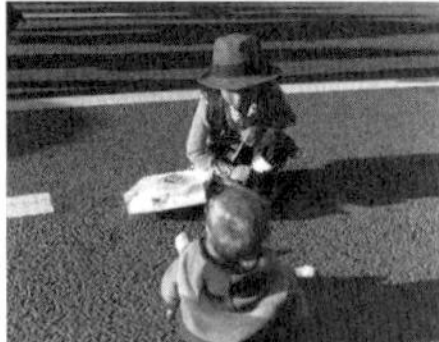
Kawaii Baby #3
[Tokyo], 2005

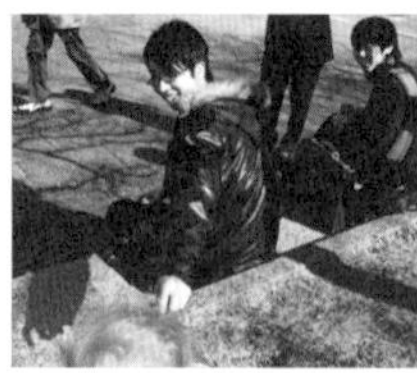
Kawaii Baby #12
[Tokyo], 2006

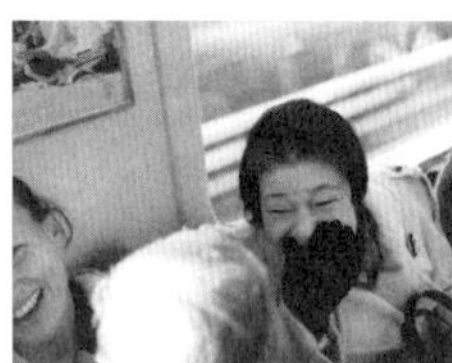
Kawaii Baby #16
[Tokyo], 2006

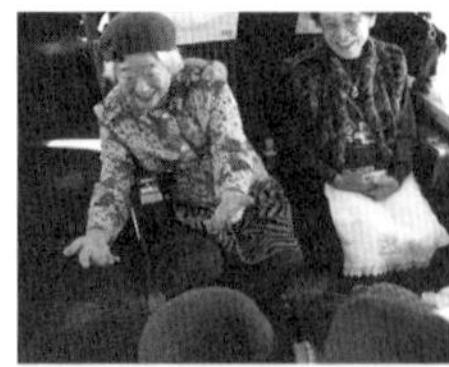
Kawaii Baby #18
[Shinkansen], 2006

Tagged
20 x 24 in.
(50 x 61 cm)
Type C photographs

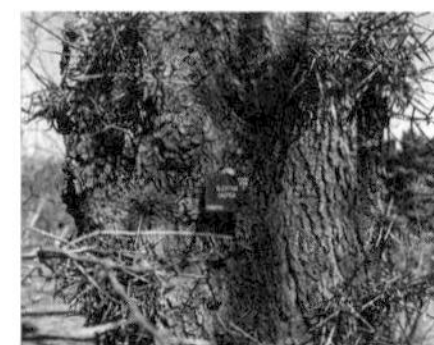
Tagged #12
[Copenhagen], 2004

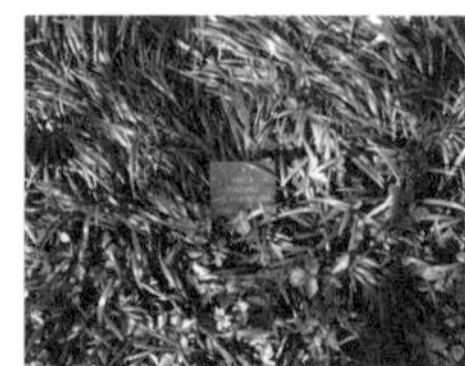
Tagged #14
[Copenhagen], 2004

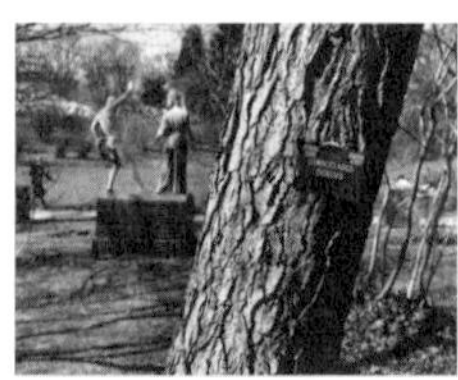
Tagged #8
[Copenhagen], 2004

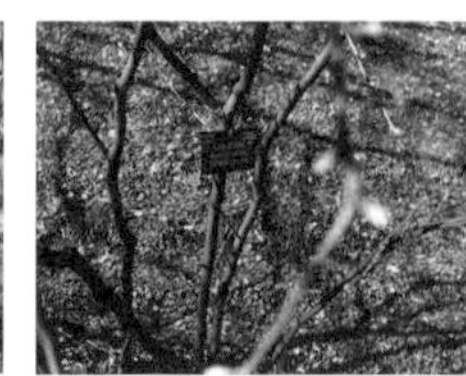
Tagged #7
[Copenhagen], 2004

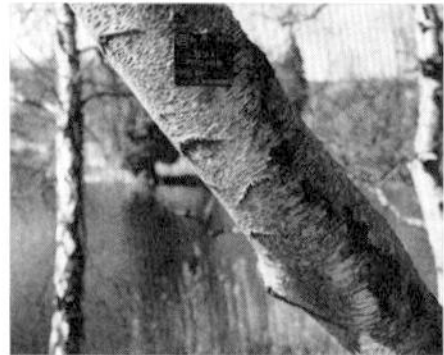
Tagged #15
[Copenhagen], 2004

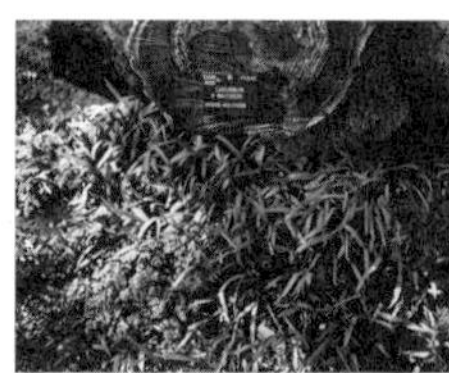
Tagged #6
[Copenhagen], 2004

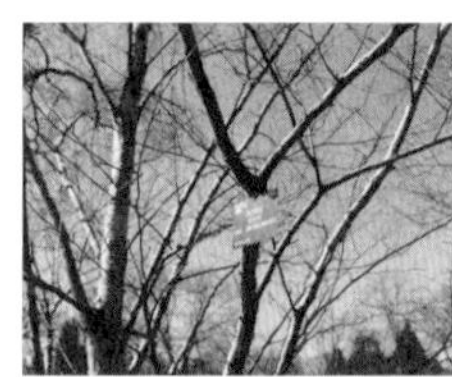
Tagged #16
[Copenhagen], 2004

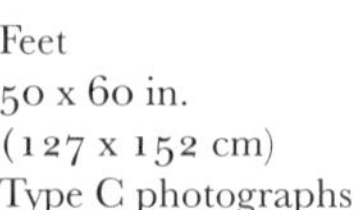
Feet
50 x 60 in.
(127 x 152 cm)
Type C photographs

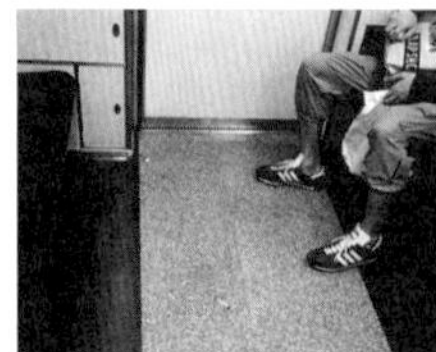
Feet #17
[Tokyo], 2002

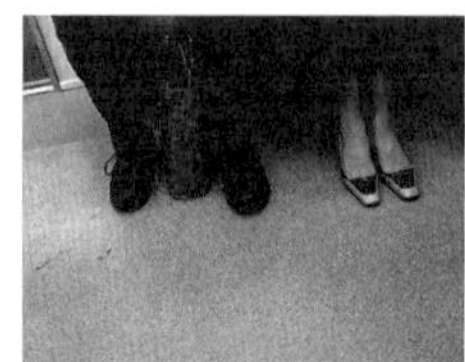
Feet #2
[Tokyo], 2002

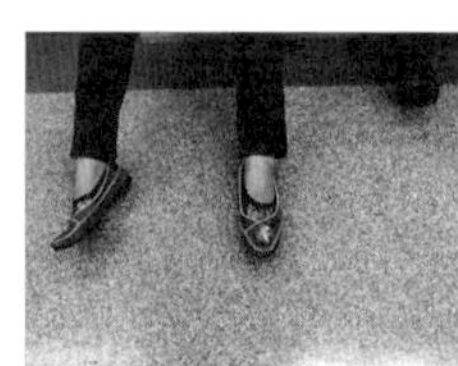
Feet #6
[Tokyo], 2002

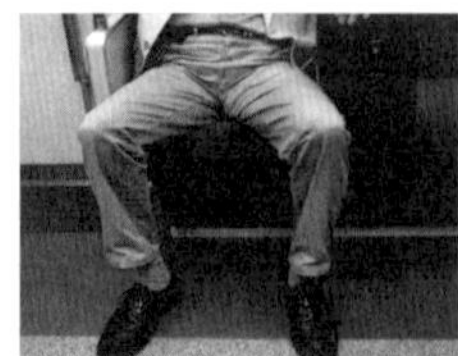
Feet #1
[Tokyo], 2002

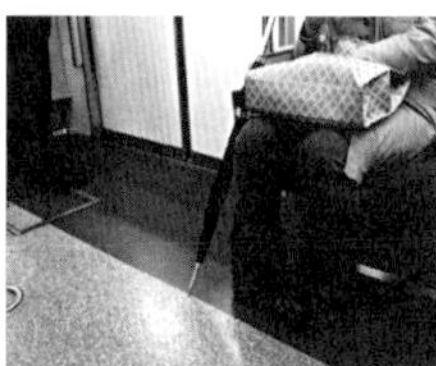
Feet #21
[Tokyo], 2002

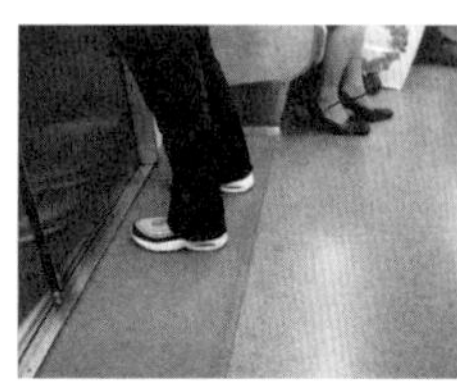
Feet #3
[Tokyo], 2002

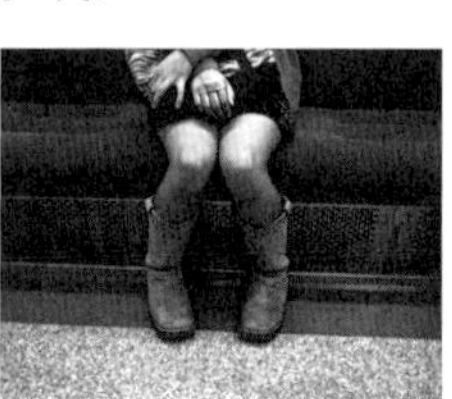
Feet #5
[Tokyo], 2002

MATTHEW SLEETH
born 1972, Melbourne, Australia

EDUCATION

2007 Master of Fine Arts, Royal Melbourne Institute of Technology
1995 Diploma of Photography, Photography Studies College, Melbourne
1993 Bachelor of Arts, Cinema, La Trobe University, Melbourne

SELECTED SOLO EXHIBITIONS

2007
Magnificent Obsessions, Josef Lebovic Gallery at The Depot Gallery, Sydney
Ten Series, Australian Centre for Photography, Sydney
Mixed Tape, Sophie Gannon Gallery, Melbourne
Rosebud, Mornington Penninsula Regional Gallery, Mornington
Silver's, Victorian Arts Centre, Melbourne
Mixed Tape, Daylesford Convent, Daylesford Foto Biennale, Daylesford
12 Views of Mount Fuji, Jan Manton Art, Brisbane

2006
Call of the Wild, Odense Photo Triennale, Fyrtøjet, Odense, Denmark
Rosebud, Josef Lebovic Gallery, Sydney
Pictured, Monash Gallery of Art, Melbourne
Rosebud, Fremantle Prison, Fotofreo Festival, Fremantle

2005
Roaring Days, Horsham Regional Art Gallery, Horsham
Red China, Centre for Contemporary Photography, Melbourne

2004
Tour of Duty, Galerie Lichtblick, Cologne, Germany
Roaring Days, National Trust, Melbourne
Survey, Josef Lebovic Gallery at The Depot Gallery, Sydney

2003
Feet, Citylights, Melbourne

2002
Tour of Duty, Centre for Contemporary Photography, Melbourne

2001
Roaring Days, Leica Gallery, Tokyo
Tour of Duty, Boccalero Gallery, Los Angeles

2000
Roaring Days, Saba Gallery, New York

1998
Roaring Days, Photographers' Gallery, Melbourne
Roaring Days, Stills Gallery, Sydney
Silvers Circus, Leica Gallery, Solms, Germany

1997
Short Stories, Ararat Art Gallery, Ararat
Boys, Warrnambool Art Gallery, Warrnambool
Boys, Prostitutes Collective of Victoria, Melbourne

1996
Short Stories, Stills Gallery, Sydney
Short Stories, Horsham Regional Art Gallery, Horsham
Short Stories, Centre for Contemporary Photography, Melbourne

SELECTED GROUP EXHIBITIONS

2007

Victorians on Vacation, State Library of Victoria, Melbourne
Blast!, Redcliffe City Art Gallery, Redcliffe
Lessons in History, Vol. 1, Grahame Galleries, Brisbane

2006

On the Beach, City Museum, Melbourne
Genuis Loci, 8th International Festival of Photography, Athens
City of Perth Photomedia Prize, Perth Institute of Contemporary Arts, Perth
Another Asia, Noorderlicht Photo Festival, Fries Museum, Leeuwarden, the Netherlands
Bookish: An Exhibition of Artists' Books, Australian Galleries, Melbourne
Light Sensitive: Contemporary Australian Photography, National Gallery of Victoria, Melbourne
Micro Macro City, 10th International Architecture Biennale, Australian Pavilion, Venice
Ulrick and Schubert Award, Gold Coast Arts Centre, Gold Coast

2005

After the Fact, Berlin Photography Festival, Martin-Gropius-Bau, Berlin
Space Between Words, Queensland Centre for Photography, Brisbane
Ulrick and Schubert Award, Gold Coast Arts Centre, Gold Coast
Eye for Photography, State Library of New South Wales, Sydney

2004

In a New Light, National Library of Australia, Canberra
City of Perth Photomedia Prize, Perth Institute of Contemporary Art, Perth
Written with Darkness: From the Patrick Corrigan Collection, UTS Gallery, Sydney
Ulrick and Schubert Award, Gold Coast Arts Centre, Gold Coast
Citibank Portrait Prize, Art Gallery of New South Wales, Sydney
The Bottom Line, Span Galleries, Melbourne

2003

Leica/CCP Documentary Photography Award, Centre for Contemporary Photography, Melbourne
New Portraiture, Exhibition Buildings, (CCP satellite exhibition), Melbourne
Images Against War, Gallery Lichtblick, Cologne, Germany

2002

Images of Australian Men, Monash Gallery of Art, Melbourne

2001

Family, State Library of New South Wales, Sydney
Leica/CCP Documentary Photography Award, Centre for Contemporary Photography, Melbourne

2000

Magic Moments II, Leica Gallery, New York

1997

Endangered Species, Horsham Regional Art Gallery, Horsham
Leica/CCP Documentary Photography Award, Centre for Contemporary Photography, Melbourne

1996

Rage to See, Opera House, Sydney

1993

Felix H. Man Memorial Prize, National Gallery of Victoria, Melbourne

MONOGRAPHS

Rosebud. Melbourne: 3 Deep Publishing, 2007.
Opfikon. Melbourne: M.33, 2004.
Survey. Sydney: Josef Lebovic Gallery, 2004.
home + away. Melbourne: M.33, 2003.
Tour of Duty. Melbourne: Hardie Grant Books, 2002.
Roaring Days. Melbourne: M.33, 1998.

LIMITED-EDITION ARTIST BOOKS

News + Weather. Sydney: Josef Lebovic Gallery, 2007 (edition of seven).
Red China. Sydney: Josef Lebovic Gallery, 2005 (edition of fifteen).
Call of the Wild. Sydney: Josef Lebovic Gallery, 2004 (edition of fifteen).

SELECTED BOOKS AND EXHIBITION CATALOGS

Alan, Susan and Emily McCulloch. *Encyclopedia of Australian Art.* Melbourne: Aus Art Editions, 2006.
Badger, Gerry and Martin Parr. *The Photobook: A History, volume 2.* London/New York: Phaidon, 2006.
Bertram, Nigel and Shane Murray. *Micro Macro City, 10th International Architecture Biennale, Venice.* Canberra: RAIA, 2006.
Crombie, Isobel. *Light Sensitive.* Melbourne: National Gallery of Victoria, 2006.
Foster, Alasdair. *Fotofreo* 2006. Fremantle: City Of Fremantle, 2006.
Melis, Wim. *Noorderlicht: Another Asia.* Groningen: Noorderlicht Photofestival, 2006.
Milne, Peter. *Pictured.* Melbourne: Monash Gallery of Art, 2006.
Thrane, Finn. *Odense Foto Triennale.* Odense, Denmark: Museet for Fotokunst, Brandts, 2006.
Lundström, Jan-Erik. *1st Berlin Photography Festival.* Berlin: Berlin Photography Festival, 2005.
Palmer, Daniel, ed. *Photogenic: CCP* 2000—2004. Melbourne: Centre for Contemporary Photography, 2005.
Davies, Alan. *An Eye for Photography.* Melbourne: Miegunyah Press, 2004.
Dwyer, Tessa. *Bottom Line.* Melbourne: M.33, 2004.
Ennis, Helen. *Intersections.* Canberra: National Library of Australia, 2004.
Foster, Alasdair. *Survey.* Sydney: Josef Lebovic Gallery, 2004.
Gibson, Ross. *Written With Darkness*. Sydney: University of Technology Sydney, 2004.
Maynard, Margaret. *Dress and Globalisation.* Manchester, England: Manchester University Press, 2004.
Papastergiadis, Nikos. *Leica/CCP Documentary Award.* Melbourne: Centre for Contemporary Photography, 2003.
Scott, Jane. *Images of Australian Men*. Melbourne: Monash Gallery of Art, 2002.
Davies, Allan. *Family*. Sydney: State Library of New South Wales, 2001.
Dwyer, Tessa. *Leica/CCP Documentary Award.* Melbourne: Centre for Contemporary Photography, 2001.
McArdle, James. *Phicton*. Horsham: Horsham Art Gallery, 2001.
Palmer, Daniel. *The Bank Book.* Melbourne: M.33, 2001.
Lowenstein, Wendy. *Under the Hook.* Melbourne: Bookworkers Press, 1998.
Ennis, Helen. *Leica/CCP Documentary Award.* Melbourne: Centre for Contemporary Photography, 1997.
Luck, Jason. *Boys.* Melbourne: M.33/Prostitutes Collective of Victoria, 1996.
Thomas, Michael. *Short Stories.* Melbourne: M.33, 1996.
Van Wyk, Susan. *Felix H. Man Memorial Prize*. Melbourne: National Gallery of Victoria, 1993.

SELECTED ARTICLES AND REVIEWS

"World Vision," Ted Colless, *Art Collector,* July/September 2007.
"Matthew Sleeth: Pictured," Melissa Miles, *Eyeline,* Spring 2006.
"Matthew Sleeth," Zolton Zavos, *Riot,* August 2006.
"A Lens Aimed at Undermining the Idea of Truth," Chris Boyd, *Australian Financial Review,* July 2006.
"Matthew Sleeth: Rosebud," Mark Mordue, *Art Collector,* July/September 2006.
"In the Frame," Melissa Hart, *Monash Gallery Art Magazine,* Winter 2006.
"Northern Exposure," Barbara Messer, *Australian Creative,* April/May 2006.
"Carry on Camping," Andrew Rule, *Good Weekend Magazine,* January 7, 2006.
"Repositioning Photography," Tim Morrell, *Artlink,* Summer 2006.
"Matthew Sleeth, 50 Most Collectable Artists," Andrew Frost, *Art Collector,* January/March 2006.
"Tour of Duty/Opfikon," Irina Tchmyreva, *Foto,* issue 103, 2005.
"Post Factum," Irina Tchmyreva, *Foto,* issue 103, 2005.
"Politisches Pladoyer: das erste Berlin Photography Festival," Ralf Hanselle, *Zitty,* September 29, 2005.
"Auf Dem Weg Zur Metropole," Horst-Peter Zeinert, *LW Photography,* February 2005.
"Red China," Kyla McFarlane, *Photofile,* Winter 2005.
"Show Not Tell—Matthew Sleeth," Gillian Bartlett, *Desktop,* June 2005.
"Red China," Ashley Crawford, *The Age,* May 8, 2005.
"Fine Frame," Andrew Frost, *The Age,* May 8, 2005.
"Snap Happy," Alex McDonald, *State of the Arts,* April/June 2005.
"The Moment," Melissa Hart, *Monash Gallery Art,* Autumn 2005.
"home + away," Max Pam, *Photofile,* Winter 2004.
"Survey," Robert McFarlane, *Sydney Morning Herald,* July 27, 2004.
"Matthew Sleeth Censored," Megan Backhouse, *The Age,* March 31, 2004.
"Matthew Sleeth—Tour of Duty," Alasdair Foster, *Photofile,* Summer 2004.
"home + away," *Artlink,* Vol. 24, issue 1, 2003.
"There and Back Again," Tanya Fabijanic, *Black & White Magazine,* November 2003.
"Matthew Sleeth," Robin Gower, *Australian Creative,* October/November 2003.
"Feet," *The Age,* August 21, 2003.
"Tour of Duty," Jane Fletcher, *Source,* issue 32, Autumn 2002.
"The Way It Is," Simon Bainbridge, *British Journal of Photography,* August 28, 2002.
"Icons and Other Pictures," Daniel Palmer, *Australian Art Collector,* July/September 2002.
"No Guts, No Glory," B. Manger, *Postwest,* issue 20, July 2002.
"Tour of Duty," *The Sunday Age,* May 5, 2002.
"Tour of Duty," Gillian Bartlett, *Desktop,* May 2002.
"Tour of Duty," *The Age,* March 30, 2002.
"Focus on Propaganda and Nationalism," Gabriella Coslovich, *The Age,* March 27, 2002.
"The Bank Book," Esther Milne, *Real Time,* February 2002.
"CCP/Leica Prize," Robert McFarlane, *Sydney Morning Herald,* December 20, 2001.
"Views from Down Under," Alison Holland, *Black & White Magazine,* October 2001.
"CCP/Leica Prize," *The Age,* August 18, 2001.
"Lost Empire," Meg Mundell, *Big Issue,* July 9, 2001.
"30 Under 30," Claire Sykes, *Photo District News,* March 2001.
"Felix H. Man Memorial Prize," *The Age,* December 15, 1999.
"Rising Star," Anthony LaSala, *Photo District News,* October 1999.
"Roaring Days," *Artlink,* September 1999.
"Marginalia," Peter Milne, *Artlink,* September 1999.
"Roaring Days," Peter Eastway, *Better Photography,* Winter 1999.
"Roaring Days," *The Bulletin,* December 8, 1998.
"Roaring Days," Robert McFarlane, *Sydney Morning Herald,* December 2, 1998.
"Roar Material," Kate Fuller, *Australian Magazine,* November 7, 1998.
"Innercity Living," Meg Ullman, *Fashion Journal,* Spring 1997.
"Matthew Sleeth," Sally Rawlings, *Panorama,* June 1997.
"Average Boys," A. Bunn, *Warrnambool Standard,* March 6, 1997.
"Hot Shots," Kirsten Galliot, *Who Weekly,* December 16, 1996.
"Short Stories," Robert McFarlane, *Sydney Morning Herald,* December 9, 1996.
"Wrought Images," Sebastian Smee, *Sydney Morning Herald,* December 6, 1996.
"Short Stories," Anne Marsh, *Herald Sun,* August 14, 1996.
"Short Stories," *The Age,* July 31, 1996.
"Short Stories," Paul Burrows, *Professional Photography,* January 1996.
"Artist Hits Out at Censorship," S. Edlich, *Mail Times,* October 14, 1996.
"Stories of the Street," Belinda Parsons, *The Age,* July 23, 1996.
"History as It Happens," Jane Sullivan, *The Age,* April 15, 1995.

COLLECTIONS

Australian War Memorial, Canberra
Brandts Museet for Fotokunst, Odense, Denmark
City of Boroondara Collection, Melbourne
Patrick Corrigan Collection, Sydney/Brisbane
Daryl Hewson Collection, Brisbane
Deutsche Bank Collection, Sydney
Gadens Collection, Sydney/Brisbane
Horsham Regional Art Gallery, Horsham
Ipswich Regional Gallery, Ipswich
Monash Gallery of Art, Melbourne
Monash University Museum of Art, Melbourne
National Gallery of Victoria, Melbourne
National Library of Australia, Melbourne
National Portrait Gallery, Canberra
Queensland University Technology, Brisbane
State Library of Victoria, Melbourne
State Library of New South Wales, Sydney
State Library of Queensland, Brisbane
Tweed Heads Regional Gallery, Tweed Heads
Westmeade Children's Hospital, Sydney

For Sal & Lola

Front cover: *Houseplants* #26 [Paris], 2005

Some of the images in this book were created with the assistance of the Australian Government through the Australia Council, its arts funding and advisory body.

Matthew Sleeth's work is supported by Kodak Professional.

Editor: Michael Famighetti
Photo Editor: Helen Frajman
Designer: Fabio Ongarato
Production Director: Matthew Pimm

The staff for this book at Aperture Foundation includes:
Ellen S. Harris, *Chief Executive Officer*; Michael Culoso, *Director of Finance and Administration*; Lesley A. Martin, *Executive Editor, Books*; Nancy Grubb, *Executive Managing Editor, Books*; Susan Ciccotti, *Production Editor*; Sarah Henry, *Production Manager*; Andrea Smith, *Director of Communications*; Kristian Orozco, *Director of Sales and Foreign Rights*; Diana Edkins, *Director of Exhibitions and Limited-Edition Photographs*; Laura Cooke, Yass Etemadi, Daisy Lumley, *Work Scholars*

First edition
Printed and bound in Singapore
10 9 8 7 6 5 4 3 2 1

Library of Congress Control Number: 2007922978
ISBN 978-1-59711-054-9

Aperture Foundation books are available in North America through:
D.A.P./Distributed Art Publishers
155 Sixth Avenue, 2nd Floor
New York, N.Y. 10013
Phone: (212) 627-1999
Fax: (212) 627-9484

Aperture Foundation books are distributed outside North America by:
Thames & Hudson
181A High Holborn
London WC1V 7QX
United Kingdom
Phone: + 44 20 7845 5000
Fax: + 44 20 7845 5055
Email: sales@thameshudson.co.uk

aperturefoundation

547 West 27th Street
New York, N.Y. 10001
www.aperture.org

The purpose of Aperture Foundation, a non-profit organization, is to advance photography in all its forms and to foster the exchange of ideas among audiences worldwide.